EGYPTIAN OBELISKS

BY

HENRY H. GORRINGE
LIEUTENANT-COMMANDER UNITED STATES NAVY

FIFTY-ONE FULL-PAGE ILLUSTRATIONS

THIRTY-TWO ARTOTYPES, EIGHTEEN ENGRAVINGS, AND ONE CHROMO-LITHOGRAPH

ISBN: 978-1-63923-639-8

All Rights reserved. No part of this book maybe reproduced without written permission from the publishers, except by a reviewer who may quote brief passages in a review to be printed in a newspaper or magazine.

Printed: January 2023

Published and Distributed By:
Lushena Books
607 Country Club Drive, Unit E
Bensenville, IL 60106
www.lushenabks.com

ISBN: 978-1-63923-639-8

TO

WILLIAM H. VANDERBILT

IN RECOGNITION OF THE ENLIGHTENED MUNIFICENCE TO WHICH
NEW YORK IS INDEBTED FOR THE POSSESSION OF ONE OF
THE MOST INTERESTING MONUMENTS OF THE OLD
WORLD, AND OF THE MOST ANCIENT RECORD
OF MAN NOW KNOWN TO EXIST ON
THE AMERICAN CONTINENT.

very truly yours,
W. H. Vanderbilt

PREFACE.

AT the request of Lieut.-Commander Gorringe I long ago promised to prepare for him an account of the transactions which led to his undertaking the important operation so clearly and so fully described by him in this book. From that promise I may hold myself released. He has embodied all the essential features of these transactions in the admirable narrative which has grown under his hands, as I hoped that it would, into a full and interesting history of the Egyptian obelisks.

The pains and skill with which this history has been constructed out of the few and fragmentary records which remain to us of these august monuments, illustrate the spirit in which Lieut.-Commander Gorringe accepted and executed the trust confided to him by Mr. Vanderbilt in the interest and for the benefit of the people of New York.

It is easy, and of course it is becoming, to applaud the success of such an enterprise.

But no man knows so well as I do the discouragements and difficulties through which success was won, and it appears to me to be my duty, therefore, to bear witness here once for all to the absolute simplicity of purpose and single-minded public spirit to which New York is indebted for the possession of the great obelisk of Alexandria. No arguments were needed to commend the project either to Mr. Vanderbilt, whose liberality made it practicable, or to Mr. Evarts, who put and kept all the machinery of the State Department at work to accomplish it. But from the day in August, 1879, on which Lieut.-Commander Gorringe sailed for Europe on his mission, to the day in January, 1881, on which, in the presence of assembled thousands, the majestic monolith swung at a motion of his lifted finger into its final resting-place in the Central Park, his indomitable energy was confronted at every step, not only with that wholesome and bracing public indifference to such undertakings which success always startles into enthusiasm, but with all the obstacles which private greed and the eternal quarantine of official imbecility could put in his way. He has repeatedly acknowledged his obligations to his able and well-selected assistants, Lieutenant Seaton Schroeder of the United States Navy, and Mr. Frank Price, of New York. But his best coadjutors were his own purpose and his own patience, of which he cannot speak, and which I put on record here.

W. H. H.

CONTENTS.

CHAPTER I.
Removal of the Alexandrian Obelisk, "Cleopatra's Needle," to New York. . . . PAGE 1

CHAPTER II.
The Archæology of the New York Obelisk. 59

CHAPTER III.
Removal of the Luxor Obelisk to Paris. 77

CHAPTER IV.
Removal of the Fallen Obelisk of Alexandria to London. 96

CHAPTER V.
Re-erection of the Vatican Obelisk. 110

CHAPTER VI.
Record of all Egyptian Obelisks. 119

CHAPTER VII.
Notes on the Ancient Methods of Quarrying, Transporting, and Erecting Obelisks. . . 146

CHAPTER VIII.
Analysis of the Materials and Metals Found with the Obelisk at Alexandria. . . . 161

Index. 177

LIST OF ILLUSTRATIONS.

PLATE.		FACING.
	WILLIAM H. VANDERBILT. . . . . *Artotype.*	Dedication.
I.—	The Alexandrian obelisk, "Cleopatra's Needle." Alexandria, Egypt, October, 1879. . . . . *Artotype.*	PAGE. 1
II.—	Elevation of the obelisk, raised from pedestal, with machinery in position for turning. Alexandria. . . . . . *Photo-engraving.*	2
III.—	Side elevation. Preparations for releasing machinery. Alexandria. "	2
IV.—	Excavations at Alexandria, showing pedestal, steps and position of crabs. *Artotype.*	4
V.—	The crabs as found. . . . . "	6
VI.—	The staging. November 5, 1879. . . . . . "	8
VII.—	The obelisk encased and stayed. The hoisting shears with trunnions suspended to them. . . . . *Artotype.*	10
VIII.—	Turning the obelisk. December 6, 1879. . . . "	12
IX.—	The obelisk horizontal. December 6, 1879. . . . . "	14
X.—	City and port of Alexandria. The overland route proposed. The water route followed. . . . . . . *Photo-engraving.*	16
XI.—	Steps and pedestal. Section and plan. . . . "	18
XII.—	Preparations for launching. Section through caisson and Obelisk. Caisson afloat. Alexandria. . . . . . . *Photo-engraving.*	20
A.—	Lowering and launching the caisson. . . . "	20
XIII.—	Embarking the pedestal. . . . . . . *Artotype.*	22
XIV.—	Embarking the obelisk. . . . . . . "	24
XV.—	Embarking the obelisk. Section and plan. . . . *Photo-engraving.*	24
XVI.—	The steamer "Dessoug," with obelisk on board, ready for departure from Alexandria. . . . . *Artotype.*	26
XVII.—	Disembarking the pedestal. New York. . . . "	28
XVIII.—	Trucking the pedestal.	30
B.—	Laying the corner-stone. . . . . . . "	32
XIX.—	Obelisk on pontoons entering landing-stage at 96th Street, New York. Section and plan of disembarking stage. . . . *Photo-engraving.*	34
XX.—	Disembarking the obelisk. . . . . . . *Artotype.*	36
XXI.—	Cross section through obelisk and pontoons. Side elevation of obelisk and pontoons. . . . . . . *Photo-engraving.*	38
XXII.—	Obelisk crossing the Hudson River Railroad. . . . *Artotype.*	40
XXIII.—	Route of the obelisk in New York. . . . *Photo-engraving.*	42
XXIV.—	Land transportation. Turning apparatus. Trestle in Central Park. "	44
C.—	Iron channels and marine railway.	46

List of Illustrations.

PLATE			FACING PAGE
XXV.—Transporting the obelisk.		*Artotype.*	48
XXVI.—Obelisk crossing main drive in Central Park.		"	50
XXVII.—Turning the obelisk. The obelisk horizontal.		..	52
D.—Turning the obelisk. Turned 45°.		..	54
XXVIII.—Placing the obelisk on its pedestal in Central Park, January 22, 1881.		*Photo-engraving.*	56
XXIX.—The New York obelisk.		*Artotype.*	58
XXX.—The four faces of the pyramidion.		"	62
XXXI.—The four sides of the obelisk.			64
XXXII.—Antique model of the temple of On (Heliopolis).			70
E.—Portrait of Cleopatra, photographed from her coins.		"	72
XXXIII.—French apparatus for lowering and erecting the Luxor obelisk.		*Photo-engraving.*	84
XXXIV.—Embarkation of the French obelisk.		"	86
XXXV.—The English method of erecting the London obelisk.			104
XXXVI.—The English cylinder for sea transport.		"	106
XXXVII.—The London obelisk.		*Artotype.*	108
XXXVIII.—Apparatus for transporting and erecting the Vatican obelisk.		*Photo-engraving.*	112
XXXIX.—The remaining obelisk and ruins of temple at Luxor.		*Artotype.*	120
XL.—The obelisks at Karnak.		"	122
XLI.—The obelisk at Heliopolis and Pompey's Pillar at Alexandria.			124
XLII.—The Constantinople and Paris obelisks.		..	126
XLIII.—The twelve Roman obelisks.			128
Re-erecting the Constantinople obelisk in the fourth century A. D.			159
XLIV.—Thin sections of the New York obelisk in polarized light.		*Chromo-lithograph.*	162
XLV.—The Khedives Ismaïl and Tewfik.		*Artotype.*	175

THE ALEXANDRIAN OBELISK. (CLEOPATRA'S NEEDLE.)

CHAPTER I.

REMOVAL OF THE NEW YORK OBELISK.

SITUATION AND SURROUNDINGS OF THE OBELISK IN ALEXANDRIA.

THE standing obelisk of Alexandria was generally the first and the last of Egypt's numerous monuments to be visited by travellers. The accompanying illustration recalls the feeling of disgust aroused by some of its surroundings. Something more than curiosity was needed to induce one to approach near enough and remain long enough to examine and appreciate it. Situated in the outskirts of the city, near the Ramleh railway depot, it was a familiar object to the foreign element, many of whom live at Ramleh and passed it twice, often four times a day; and yet no one deemed it worthy of protection and care, even to the extent of preventing its defacement and the accumulation of offal around it. Two men made a business of breaking pieces from the angle of the shaft and edges of the intaglios for sale to relic hunters. The disagreeable odors and clamors for *backsheesh*[1] hastened the departure of strangers, who rarely devoted more than a few seconds to its examination. It would be impossible for any thing to have been more neglected and less appreciated than was the Alexandrian obelisk by the residents of Alexandria and tourists who passed through the city en route to the Nile.

There is, however, much that is attractive and worthy of attention in its former surroundings. The Arab fort, to the left in the picture, stands on the ruins of one of those magnificent structures that adorned the ancient city and made second only to Rome in the beginning of the Christian era. The shore is strewn with huge blocks of granite, syenite, and marble, many of them covered with Egyptian hieroglyphs and Greek and Roman inscriptions. Fragments of columns and capitals lie scattered about and buried in the débris that has accumulated in the vicinity; the bottom of the sea is so cumbered with the ruins of these structures that the shore is difficult to approach, even in a small boat, nearer than half a mile. The foundation of one very large building is distinctly traceable under water when the sea is smooth; and about one hundred yards from the beach there is a broken column sticking up from the bottom of the sea, nearly equal in diameter to Pompey's pillar. This was the quarter of the royal palaces, which included the gymnasium, the museum, containing the famous library, and the Cæsareum. It was at the entrance to the last-mentioned that the Romans, to commemorate their conquests, re-erected the obelisks that had been removed from the ancient Egyptian temple of On, at Heliopolis. Nothing could have been more out of place and less in keeping with the purposes for which it was designed than was the obelisk as it stood at Alexandria.

The gradual subsidence of the land in this part of North Africa has caused the sea to approach nearer to the site of the obelisk, until it was about eighty feet from the base, and its level about the same as that of the lower step. The constant washings of the surf had begun to affect the foundation, and for the last fifteen years the obelisk has been gradually inclining more and more toward the sea. In a few years it must have fallen, and almost certainly have been broken by the fall. But a more ignoble fate threatened it, in the proposition of some of the foreign residents of Alexandria to erect an apartment-house on the adjacent ground around the obelisk, which was to adorn the court-yard.

Originally designed to symbolize the highest attribute of nature, the re-creative power; forming an

---

[1] Arabic for gift.

2   *Removal of the New York Obelisk.*

essential feature of one of the most famous temples ever erected by man, in which Moses was educated and of which he became a high-priest; the votive offering of one of the most celebrated Pharaohs, and bearing the records of another equally celebrated, the obelisk had become a Roman trophy to commmemorate the subjugation of Egypt, and was threatened either with destruction by neglect, or preservation as a means of advertising a hotel or apartment-house. His Highness, Ismail, the Khedive, who realized the importance of preserving so valuable and interesting a relic and record of the past, and his own inability to do so, merits the thanks not only of the nation to whom he intrusted its preservation, but of all those of every nation who appreciate the necessity of preserving such monuments as long as they will resist the ravages of time. Some objection has been made to removing it from its "antique surroundings." The most prominent surroundings in Alexandria were a railway depot, a new apartment-house, and an Arab fort.

NEGOTIATIONS THAT LED TO THE GIFT AND ITS REMOVAL.

The first suggestion looking to the removal of an obelisk from Egypt to the United States was made by His Highness, Ismail, the Khedive of Egypt, at the time of the opening of the Suez Canal in 1869, to Mr. William Henry Hurlbert. In September, 1877, after the removal of the prostrate obelisk of Alexandria to England by Mr. John Dixon, Mr. Louis Sterne of London, a friend of Mr. Dixon, being in New York, informed Mr. Hurlbert, then editor of the *New York World*, that Mr. Dixon, through his relations with Egypt, could secure the gift to the United States of the standing obelisk at Alexandria, and that he would be glad to do this, and to undertake to remove it to New York, if the cost of the operation could be defrayed. Mr. Hurlbert requested Mr. Sterne to open a correspondence on the subject with Mr. Dixon, which resulted in an understanding that Mr. Dixon would secure and bring to America the standing obelisk of Alexandria, if the sum of fifteen thousand pounds sterling could be guaranteed to him. After consulting with Mr. Chauncey M. Depew and Judge Ashbel Green, Mr. Hurlbert put himself in communication with Mr. William H. Vanderbilt, and Mr. Vanderbilt, as the result of a single conversation on the subject, liberally agreed to guarantee the payment of the sum named by Mr. Dixon. This was at once cabled to London by Mr. Hurlbert. A congratulatory reply by cable was received from Mr. Sterne in behalf of Mr. Dixon. But a correspondence followed from which it soon appeared that Mr. Dixon relied upon Mr. Hurlbert to secure the gift of the obelisk through the government of the United States. This materially changed the character of the negotiation; but finding Mr. Vanderbilt most willing to stand by his liberal offer as long as might be necessary to secure the desired result, Mr. Hurlbert consulted Mr. Evarts, then Secretary of State, who cordially agreed to instruct the agents of the State Department to undertake the matter. At the instance of Mr. Evarts, a letter was accordingly written to him as Secretary of State by Mr. Henry G. Stebbins, then Commissioner of Public Parks of New York City, requesting him to open negotiations with the Khedive for securing the standing obelisk of Alexandria for New York City. Mr. Evarts, in a letter dated October 19, 1877, wrote to Consul-General E. E. Farman that, "in view of the public object to be subserved, you are instructed to use all proper means of furthering the wishes expressed in Mr. Stebbins' letter," a copy of which was enclosed. In a letter dated November 24, 1877, Mr. Farman wrote to Mr. Evarts as follows: "I fear, however, that there will be serious opposition to the removal of the obelisk from the city of Alexandria, so much, in fact, that although the Khedive might personally desire to gratify the wishes of the citizens of New York, he would not think it best to grant their request."

On March 4, 1878, Mr. Farman reported to Mr. Evarts that he had had an interview with the Khedive, who "made no special objection to the transportation of an obelisk to the city of New York," and that "during the conversation he (the Khedive) had said that he did not think it best to talk about the removal of the one at Alexandria, but he would take into consideration the question of one of those at Ancient Thebes."

From March 4, 1878, to May 17, 1879, Mr. Farman was untiring in his efforts to obtain an obelisk. His negotiations were conducted verbally until the latter date, when the following correspondence ensued.

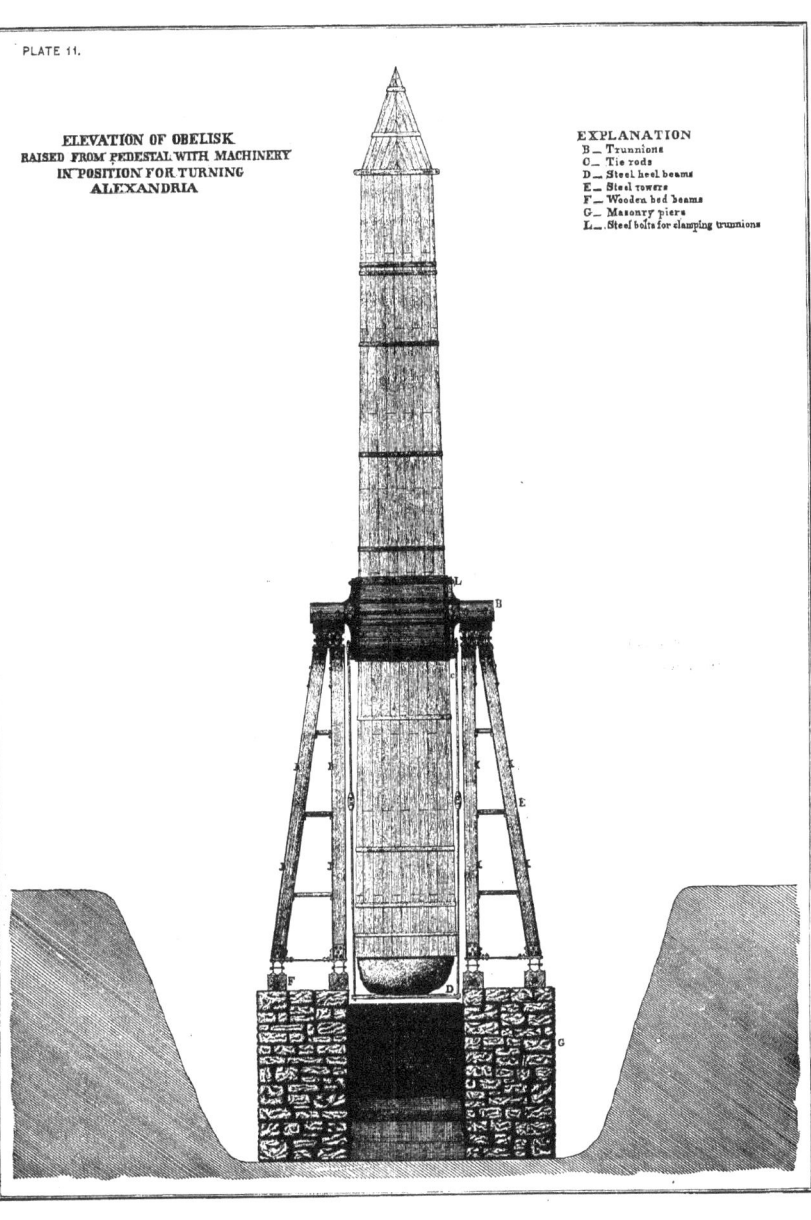

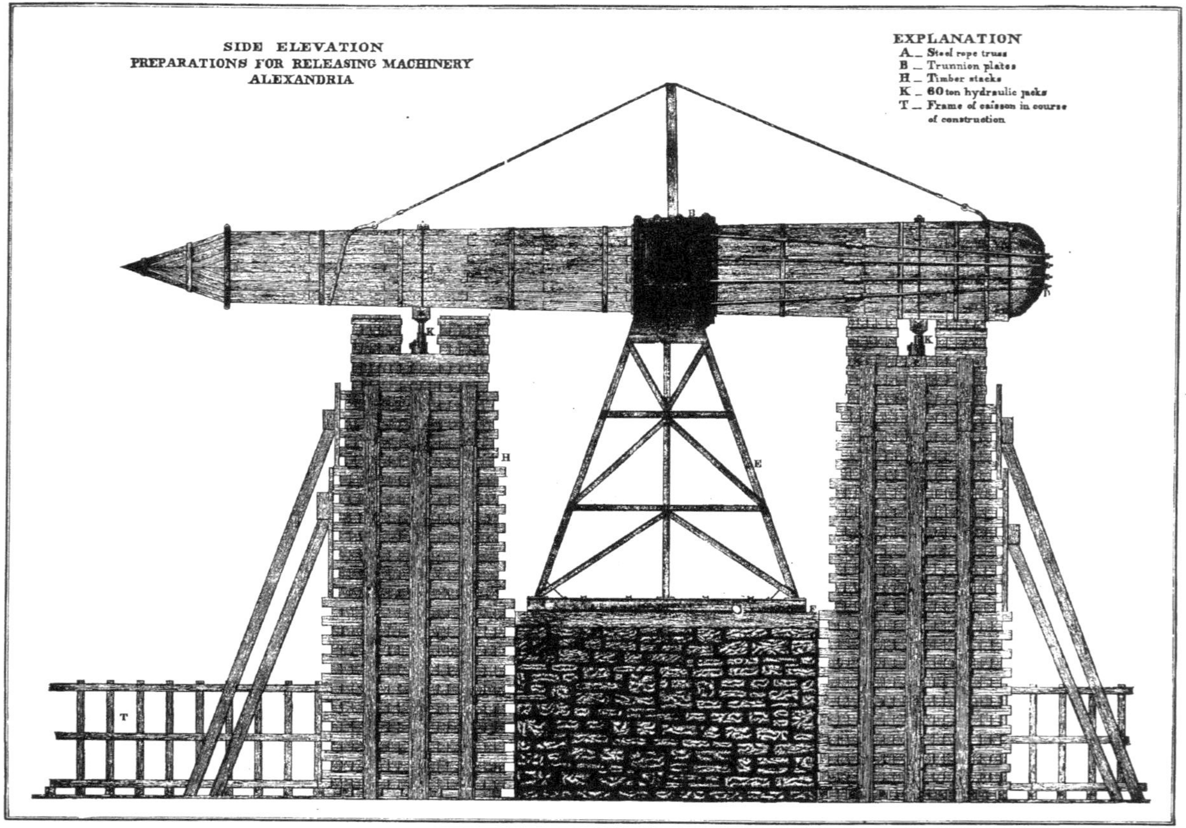
SIDE ELEVATION
PREPARATIONS FOR RELEASING MACHINERY
ALEXANDRIA
EXPLANATION
A _ Steel rope truss
B _ Trunnion plates
H _ Timber stacks
K _ 60 ton hydraulic jacks
T _ Frame of caisson in course of construction
B
K
K
H
E
T

Plate III.

Removal of the New York Obelisk.

MR. FARMAN TO CHÉRIF PACHA, Minister of Foreign Affairs.
(*Translation from the French.*)

CAIRO, *May* 17, 1879.

EXCELLENCY: Referring to the different conversations that I have had the honor to have with your Excellency, in which you have informed me that the government of His Highness the Khedive is disposed to present to the city of New York, to be transported and erected there, the obelisk of Alexandria, I should be pleased if your Excellency would have the kindness to definitely confirm in writing the gift of this monument.

It is understood that its transportation is to be effected at the expense of certain citizens of the said city of New York.

I beg to assure your Excellency, in advance of the warm thanks of my government for having thus favorably responded to the representations I have made to the government of His Highness the Khedive, in accordance with the instructions that I had received on this subject.

I have every reason to hope that the monument, which is thus soon to be transported and set up in the city of New York, will always be a souvenir and a pledge of the friendship that has ever existed between the government of the United States and that of His Highness the Khedive.

I beg your Excellency to accept the renewed assurance of my high consideration.

(Signed)   E. E. FARMAN.

CHÉRIF PACHA, Minister of Foreign Affairs, TO MR. FARMAN.
(*Translation.*)

[MINISTER OF FOREIGN AFFAIRS, NO. 343.]

CAIRO, *May* 18, 1879.

MR. AGENT AND CONSUL-GENERAL: I have taken cognizance of the dispatch which you did me the honor of writing me on the 17th of the current month of May.

In reply, I hasten to transmit you the assurance, Mr. Agent and Consul-General, that the government of the Khedive, having taken into consideration your representations and the desire which you have expressed in the name of the government of the United States of America, consents, in fact, to make a gift to the city of New York of the obelisk known as Cleopatra's Needle, which is at Alexandria on the sea-shore.

The local authorities shall therefore be directed to deliver this obelisk to the representative of the American government, and also to facilitate, in every thing that shall depend upon them, the removal of this monument, which, according to the terms of your dispatch, is to be done at the exclusive cost and expense of the city of New York.

I am happy, Mr. Agent and Consul-General, to have to announce to you this decision, which, while giving to the great city an Egyptian monument, to which is attached, as you know, a real archæological interest, will also be, I am as yourself convinced, another souvenir and another pledge of the friendship that has constantly existed between the government of the United States and that of the Khedive.

Be pleased to accept, Mr. Agent and Consul-General, the expression of my high consideration.

(Signed)   CHÉRIF.

CONSUL-GENERAL FARMAN TO SECRETARY EVARTS.

U. S. AGENCY AND CONSULATE-GENERAL, CAIRO, *May* 22, 1879.

HONORABLE W. M. EVARTS, Secretary of State, Washington, D. C.

SIR: I have the honor to inform you that the negotiations entered into to procure an Egyptian obelisk for the city of New York have been successful.

The government of His Highness the Khedive has generously given to that city the obelisk at Alexandria known as "Cleopatra's Needle."

I enclose a copy of the original notes in French that were exchanged between his Excellency, Chérif Pacha, and myself on this subject, after a verbal understanding had been arrived at, and also their translation into English.

The gift of this ancient and well-known monument cannot be regarded as other than a very great mark of favor on the part of the government of Egypt toward that of the United States, and a proof of its high appreciation of the friendship that has ever existed between these countries.

The two obelisks that have been removed to Europe in modern times were obtained under circumstances entirely different from those now existing, and they were themselves objects which, in consequence of their situation and condition, were much less appreciated than Cleopatra's Needle. They were both presented many years ago by Mohammed Ali, one to the English and the other to the French government. The latter now at Paris was taken nearly half a century since from Luxor, in the vicinity of which are three other obelisks and many colossal ruins, which were at that time seldom visited by Europeans. The one lately taken to London had long been lying on the shore of the sea at Alexandria, nearly or wholly buried in the sand. That, however, which is given to the city of New York is still standing, and is the veritable "Cleopatra's Needle," and the only obelisk properly known by that name. It constitutes, with Pompey's pillar, the only relics of the ancient city of Alexandria that are of any interest. It is known by every school-boy in the United States, and its removal to New York will long remain one of the marked events of history.

From the inscriptions upon it it is supposed to have been first erected at Heliopolis (On of the Scriptures) in the reign of Thothmes III, about 1590 years before the commencement of the Christian era, according to the chronology of Marietta Bey, or about 150 years later according to that of Wilkinson.

The site of Heliopolis, which is about five miles east of Cairo, is now marked by a single monolith, though that ancient city was reputed to have been "full of obelisks." The one, however, which remains is the oldest of all the large Egyptian monuments of this character, having been erected in the reign of Usortesen I, nearly 3,000 years before Christ.

Heliopolis, or, as the word imports, the city of the sun, was known by the ancient Egyptians as the dwelling of Ra (Helios). The Sun Temple of this city was of a very remote origin, and having been destroyed or neglected was restored by Amenhat I, the immediate predecessor of Usortesen I.

The obelisks at Heliopolis were undoubtedly placed in pairs at the entrance of the Sun Temple, perhaps on each of its four sides. They were emblems of the sun's rays, and were therefore frequently dedicated to this god and to his temple. The characters engraven in the granite were originally filled with gold or gilded bronze, and were spoken of as "illuminating the world with their rays."

Heliopolis was also the seat of one of the most famous schools of antiquity, but the city had lost its importance and fallen into decay some time before the commencement of the Christian era.

Cleopatra's Needle was taken to Alexandria previous to or during the reign of Tiberius (A. D. 14–37), and was placed, with its companion now in London, on the shore of the sea in front of the Temple of Cæsar. Why it bears the name of Cleopatra's Needle is not known. She died about sixty years before the completion of this temple, but it may have been commenced by her. The central row of hieroglyphical inscriptions on the obelisk refers to Thothmes III, who is here called the "Child of the Sun," and said to be "endowed with power, life, and stability." Other inscriptions were afterward added by Ramses II, and by another Pharaoh.

I hope to be able to send you hereafter a full translation of all its hieroglyphics.

I have the honor to be, sir, your obedient servant,

(Signed)   E. E. FARMAN.

SECRETARY EVARTS TO CONSUL-GENERAL FARMAN.

DEPARTMENT OF STATE, WASHINGTON, D. C., *June* 13, 1879.

E. E. FARMAN, Esquire.

SIR: I have to acknowledge the reception of your dispatch of the 22d ultimo, with its enclosures, in which you inform the Department that the negotiations entered into to procure an Egyptian obelisk for the city of New York have been successful, and that the government of His Highness the Khedive has generously presented to that city the obelisk known as Cleopatra's Needle.

It is a source of great gratification to this government, that through the generosity of the Khedive this country is soon to come into the possession of such an interesting monument of antiquity as Cleopatra's Needle, and you are therefore instructed to inform His Highness that the great favor he has conferred upon this Republic by making this gift is highly appreciated, and that it is felt that such a rare mark of friendship cannot but tend to still further strengthen the amicable relations which have ever subsisted between the two countries, and will cause the memory of the Khedive to be long and warmly cherished by the American people.

The historical account of the obelisks of Egypt which your dispatch contains has been read with interest.

I am, sir, your obedient servant,

(Signed)   W. M. EVARTS.

The successful issue of the American negotiations having been at once communicated by the Secretary of State to Mr. Hurlbert, that gentleman immediately notified Mr. John Dixon that the standing obelisk of Alexandria had been secured, and that if he was still prepared to undertake to bring it to New York the sum of fifteen thousand pounds originally named by him would be guaranteed to him by Mr. Vanderbilt, who, however, desired that no public mention of his name should be made in connection with the subject. Mr. John Dixon replied at once to Mr. Hurlbert that he would undertake the removal, but that he could not do this unless the sum named could be increased to twenty thousand pounds. Mr. Dixon's experiences with the ship "Cleopatra," in which he conveyed the prostrate obelisk of Alexandria to London doubtless explained this advance in terms. Mr. Hurlbert, without consulting Mr. Vanderbilt on the subject, at once declined to entertain this new proposition, and at his request Mr. Henry G. Stebbins kindly undertook to receive for him propositions for the transportation of the monolith to the United States. Several such propositions were received and submitted to Mr. Hurlbert, but none of them were approved by him.

Removal of the New York Obelisk.

Negotiations were still pending, when my attention was called to the announcement in the *World* of June 17, 1879, that the obelisk had been given to the United States and the money needed for its removal had been provided. Previously, however, I had become interested in the subject through a visit to Alexandria, where the removal of the fallen obelisk to London was frequently discussed. I communicated my intention to undertake the work of removal to no one but Lieutenant Seaton Schroeder, U. S. N., and obtained, under difficulties, the needed information from which to develop my plans. I examined those of the French officer, Lebas, who removed one of the Luxor obelisks to Paris, and those of Mr. Dixon, who removed the fallen obelisk to London, and rejected both as unsuited to the conditions under which the standing obelisk of Alexandria must be removed to New York.

Careful development of original plans and an estimate of the cost of executing them resulted in an offer to Mr. Hurlbert to undertake the work, and, eventually, in the receipt, through Mr. Stebbins, of the following letter.

MR. VANDERBILT TO LT.-COMDR. GORRINGE.

NEW YORK, *Aug.* 4, 1879.

LIEUT. H. H. GORRINGE, U. S. Navy.

DEAR SIR: I have learned that you have or can procure the facilities to remove to the city of New York the obelisk now standing at Alexandria, in Egypt, known as "Cleopatra's Needle."

As I desire that this obelisk may be secured for the city of New York, I make you the following proposition: If you will take down and remove said obelisk from its present position to this city, and place it on such site as may be selected with my approval by the Commissioners of Parks, and furnish and construct at your own expense on said site a foundation of mason work and granite base of such form and dimensions as said Commissioners and myself may approve, I will, on the completion of the whole work, pay to you seventy-five thousand dollars.

It is understood, however, that there is to be no liability on my part until the obelisk shall be so received and placed in position in the city of New York, and the same to be in as good condition as it now is. It is understood, further, that this agreement binds also my executors and administrators; you to accept this proposition in writing on the receipt thereof, and agree to execute the same, and complete the work fully in every respect within one year from the date hereof.

Very truly yours,

(Signed)   W. H. VANDERBILT.

NEW YORK, *Aug.* 6, 1879.

MR. W. H. VANDERBILT.

DEAR SIR: I hereby acknowledge the receipt of your letter of August 4, 1879, relating to the removal of the obelisk from Alexandria, Egypt, to New York, and its erection on a site to be selected with your approval, and I accept the proposition and the conditions named therein.

Very truly yours,

(Signed)   HENRY H. GORRINGE, *Lieut.-Comdr., U. S. N.*

An almost insurmountable difficulty in securing the money to carry on the work ensued; but it was finally overcome by the tender of a sum sufficient to commence operations by a friend of many years' standing, Mr. Louis F. Whitin, of New York, who was unwilling to let such an important work escape me for want of means to undertake it. This essential preliminary having been arranged, a leave of absence was granted to me by the Navy Department at the request of Secretary Evarts, who also handed me the following letters.

Removal of the New York Obelisk.

DEPARTMENT OF STATE, WASHINGTON, *Aug.* 1, 1879.

N. D. COMANOS, Esquire, Vice-Consul-General of the United States at Cairo, Egypt.

SIR: Referring to Mr. Farman's correspondence with the Department in regard to the presentation, by His Highness the late Khedive, of an obelisk to the city of New York, I have now to inform you that, at the request of the citizens of that city interested in securing that munificent gift of His Highness for the adornment of their native city, the Secretary of the Navy has granted to Lieutenant-Commander Gorringe, of the United States Navy, leave of absence for any requisite time for the purpose of superintending the transportation, from Alexandria to New York, of the obelisk known as "Cleopatra's Needle."

This dispatch will be handed to you in person by Lieutenant-Commander Gorringe, who is about to proceed to Egypt in fulfilment of the interesting and responsible task entrusted to him. I desire to bespeak for him all proper official and personal aid you can render him in his undertaking, and especially that you will accredit him to the government of the Khedive as the person authorized on behalf of this government to receive, in the name of the city of New York, and to convey thither, His Highness' generous gift.

I am, sir, your obedient servant,

(Signed)   W. M. EVARTS.

DEPARTMENT OF STATE, WASHINGTON, *Aug.* 21, 1879.

N. D. COMANOS, Esquire, U. S. Vice-Consul-General at Cairo, Egypt.

SIR: I have to inform you that Lieutenant-Commander Gorringe, of the United States Navy, has been detailed and directed by this government to proceed to Alexandria, Egypt, and receive the obelisk now standing in that city and known as Cleopatra's Needle and lately presented by the government of Egypt to the city of New York, and to transport the same to the last-named city.

You are instructed to officially inform the Egyptian government, through its Minister of Foreign Affairs, that Lieutenant-Commander Gorringe is authorized, on the part of the government of the United States and as its representative, to receive and remove the obelisk.

You will also extend to him such aid as you may be able to give and as he shall require in the accomplishment of his work.

He will ship to Alexandria a considerable amount of machinery, lumber, etc., to be employed in removing the obelisk from its present position and placing it on board the steamer that will be sent to receive it, and you will aid him, if you are able to do so, in getting this machinery through the custom-house without payment of duties. As the machinery is only to be used in Egypt in removing and embarking the obelisk, and then is to be immediately re-shipped to the United States, this government does not think it should properly be subjected to duty.

It will, however, be proper to follow such rules as have already been established in similar cases, for instance, in the case of the iron and other material used in the construction of the caisson and in the removal of the obelisk lately taken by Mr. Dixon to London, if the same was shipped to Alexandria expressly for that purpose.

I am, sir, your obedient servant,

(Signed)   W. M. EVARTS.

DEVELOPING THE PLANS.

The Paris and London obelisks were transported in vessels built expressly for the purpose. The "Luxor" was built of wood in Toulon, and sailed to Egypt; the "Cleopatra" was built of iron in London, and shipped in pieces to Alexandria. Neither of these vessels had adequate motive power. As the voyages they had to perform were coasting, and as it was not necessary for them to go out of sight of land or get beyond easy reach of safe harbors, there seemed no objection to their making the voyages in tow. Yet these voyages were made under the greatest difficulties; and the behavior of both vessels in a sea-way was very bad. The captain of the "Cleopatra" reported that she pitched sixteen times a minute. This is inexplicable, for the progressive motion of the waves and the speed of the vessel in an opposite direction would have to be exceptional to produce so many oscillations. The "Luxor" is reported to have rolled so violently that her crew had difficulty in holding on.

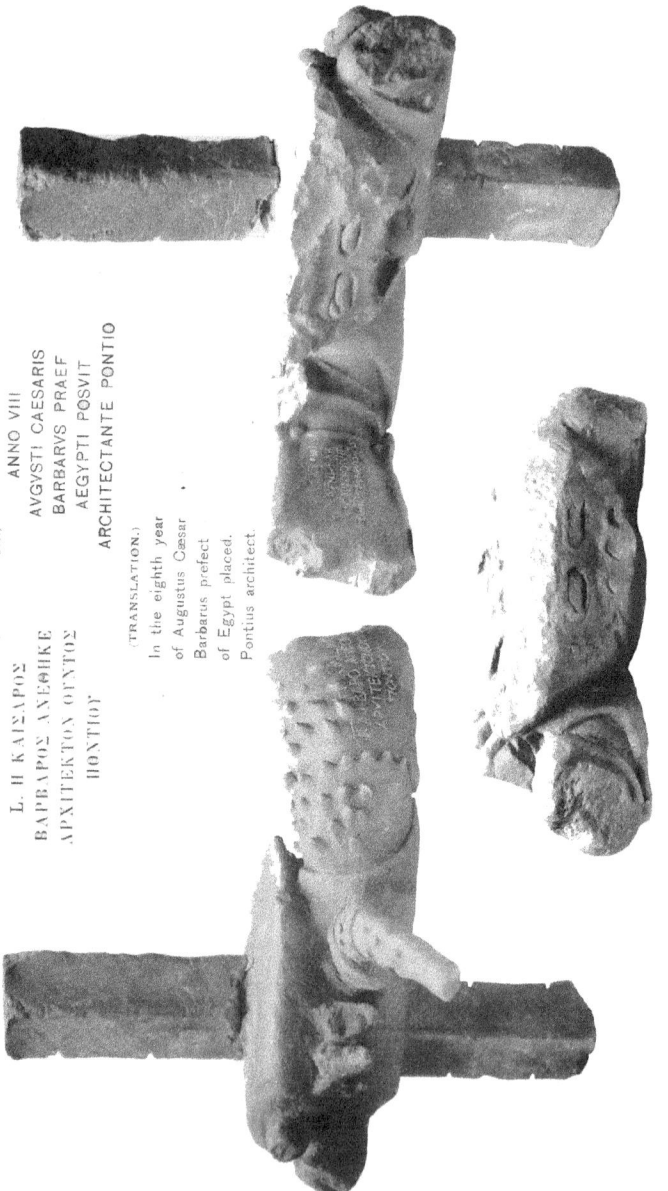

THE CRABS AS FOUND

These experiences were not needed to convince a mariner that the vessel in which the New York obelisk was to be transported must be large enough to take care of herself under all conditions of weather, and must have her own motive power. Such a vessel could not have been built around the obelisk for much less than the whole amount that was to be paid for its removal, and there was no alternative but to embark it on an ordinary vessel. For this there was no precedent. The one-hundred-ton guns made in England and shipped to Italy were the largest and heaviest masses that had ever been placed intact into a ship's hold. To accomplish this and for disembarking them, hydraulic cranes had been constructed in England and at Spezzia at a cost greatly exceeding the sum that was to cover the whole cost of removing the obelisk.

Its size was as embarrassing as its weight. No vessel has hatches that will admit a mass sixty-nine feet in length. It could not have been carried on deck in safety without strengthening the vessel at great expense. In the hold, below the water-line, was the only place where it could be securely stowed and saefly transported, and how to get it there was the one thing on which the whole operation of removing it successfully turned.

The plan devised and successfully executed consisted simply in embarking and disembarking the obelisk while the bow of the vessel was out of water, through an aperture opened expressly for the purpose and subsequently closed for the voyage. The details of execution will be given further on.

Besides my own, three other plans were proposed for transporting the obelisk by sea. The first one was proposed by the owner of a bark that had been engaged in transporting heavy blocks of granite on deck; the weight of one block never exceeded thirty tons. He exhibited a photograph of the obelisk which showed water near by and a plan of the deck of his bark, and said: " I will moor my vessel here, lower the stone down on her deck, and then sail. When we reach New York we will not be in any hurry to set it up, for we will cart it about the country and make a good thing out of it exhibiting it to the country folks." The objections to this plan were: 1st. His bark could not get within a mile of the obelisk, afloat, as the shore is fringed with sand-banks and reefs that extend out this distance. 2d. His bark could not have remained in the position he pointed out, even if she could have got to it, as the bay is exposed to the prevailing northerly wind and a heavy surf almost continuously breaks on the shore. 3d. His bark was only four hundred tons capacity, and the obelisk weighs two hundred and twenty tons. It would have been interesting to witness, from the deck of some other vessel, the performances of the bark at sea with the obelisk on her spar-deck. 4th. There was not room enough anywhere on the deck of the bark for the obelisk.

The next proposition was that the obelisk should somehow be got on the bottom of the bay with chains under it; these were to be taken on board of a steamer, and the obelisk lifted by them until it was suspended under the keel; in this position it was to make the sea-voyage. No plan was submitted for getting it on the bottom of the bay; and no arrangement was proposed for securing the services of mariners for the voyage.

Another plan was to encase the obelisk in wood enough to float it, and then tow the mass without steering it. Elaborate drawings and interesting computations accompanied this proposition; but no provision was made for getting the mass afloat, nor was any thing said about the management of the towing vessel in a sea-way. In order to get it afloat, launching ways half a mile in length would have been necessary, and their construction through the surf impossible.

For lowering the obelisk the French method was the only precedent. The English operations began with the obelisk lying on the sea-shore. There is no record of how the ancients lowered theirs; and it is probable that obelisks were never removed from an erect position, and that only those that had fallen were removed from where the ancient Egyptians placed them. The French method is fully described further on. It has the advantage of being subjected to the severest test at a moment when the breaking of any essential part of the system would have been least likely to result disastrously to the obelisk; and the conspicuous disadvantage of multiplication of parts essential to safety, and division of responsibility at the critical moments. In devising a new plan for lowering the obelisk it was essential that the turning structure should be made available for lowering and erecting; that it should be made in pieces of moderate weight and dimensions for facility of transport and handling; that it may be erected and taken apart without destroying it; that it should be adaptable to dimensions of the obelisk varying considerably from those given in books, which did not agree; and that it may have some value for other uses after the obelisk had been erected.

The accompanying drawings (Plates ii and iii) present a front- and a side-view of the structure. The first shows the obelisk clasped at its centre of gravity in a pair of trunnions; these rest on steel towers having masonry foundations. The towers are formed of I beams held in position by screw bolts through angle plates, flat plates, angle and channel bars. The horizontal steel beams forming the bottom of the structure rest on wooden beams which lie on the top of the masonry foundations. The wooden beams were designed for increasing or diminishing the height of the towers to correspond with that of the centre of gravity, which could not be determined until accurate measurements had been made of the obelisk. The heaviest pieces of the turning structure are the trunnions; each one weighs twelve thousand five hundred and seventy pounds; next to these are the pillow-blocks, each weighing three thousand seven hundred pounds; the head-pieces weigh seventeen hundred and fifty pounds each; and the beams vary from thirteen hundred and sixty to eleven hundred and ninety pounds each.

The device for lifting the obelisk clear of the pedestal and transferring its weight to the turning structure was a system of screws and turn-buckles. Tie-rods connected the lower edges of the trunnion-plates with beams under the bottom of the obelisk. Each tie-rod was in two sections, and on each end of each section there was cut a screw. The two sections were connected by a turn-buckle, and the upper and lower ends of the rods were held in position through the trunnion-plates and heel-beams by large nuts. As there were four tie-rods on each side the system comprised thirty-two screws, each with a diameter of three inches, which were capable of lifting at least double the weight of the obelisk with a large factor of safety.

To prevent the obelisk from slipping through the trunnions after it was horizontal, lips were cast on the inside vertical edges of the trunnions, to carry heavy iron plates; these were held in position by three steel bolts on each side, passing from one trunnion to the other, which also served as additional support. The trunnions were further held in position by three iron bolts on each side, making twelve in all. These bolts were not tightened until the obelisk had been lifted clear of its supports and high enough to allow the heel to swing clear of the pedestal when turning, as it was necessary, in order to lift it, that it should pass freely through the trunnions.

Although the section of the obelisk through the centre of gravity was found by computation to be strong enough to support the weight of the ends, with additions of twenty-eight tons suspended at the centre of gravity of each end, it was determined not to take any risk, in view of the length of time the syenite had been exposed to atmospheric influences and the possibility of deterioration. The simple device of trussing the ends of the shaft with steel cables was adopted as being most effective. Thirty tons of the weight of each section was in this manner transferred to the point of suspension. The truss and verticals are shown on Plate iii.

For lowering the obelisk to the ground after it was horizontal two plans were devised, and the selection left to circumstances. One was by means of an inclined plane, the other by means of hydraulic pumps placed on stacks of timber built up under the ends. The inclined plane would have been adopted if the obelisk had been transported overland to the port for embarkation; but as this was not permitted, the plan adopted was that shown on Plate iii. The hydraulic pumps were fitted with lowering valves, designed by Richard Dudgeon, of New York, which permitted a descent so gradual that it could not be detected without measurement. When the weight of the obelisk had been transferred from the turning structure to the stacks of timber, by lifting it with the hydraulic pumps clear of the pillow-blocks on which the trunnions rested, the turning structure was removed and the descent effected by removing layers of timber alternately from the tops of the stacks and under the pumps. The obelisk rested on the two top piles of each section while the hydraulic pumps were being lowered by removing the timber from under them.

There remained only the land transport of the obelisk to provide for to complete my plans for its removal from Alexandria. For this there were abundant precedents successfully applied in ancient and modern times. Of these the most ingenious is the method devised by Count Carburi, who was employed under the name of

THE STAGING

November 5, 1879.

Plate VI

Lascari, to move the pedestal of the statue of Peter the Great from the forest of Karelia to St. Petersburg. The mass that was actually moved measured, approximately, twenty-one feet in height and breadth and thirty-eight in length, and weighed about six hundred tons. The route by which it was transported was over a hill and across a marsh to the river bank; thence by river to the city quay, and thence again by land to the site. The total distance is forty-two thousand two hundred and fifty-feet, of which fifteen thousand is over land. The essential feature of Carburi's plan was the substitution of cannon-balls for the ordinary wheels or rollers and metal grooves for the ordinary tracks. A roadway was made across the marsh, and over this the mass of rock was moved, by tackles and capstans worked by two hundred men, a distance of six hundred feet per day.

Carburi's system was adopted. And in order to insure the obelisk against possible injury during its overland transport, and especially over yielding ground, two iron trusses were designed to form a carriage or cradle into which it was to have been lowered and to have remained until it was embarked.

REMOVING THE OBELISK FROM ALEXANDRIA.

On August 4, 1879, execution of the foregoing plans was begun. A contract for the construction of the turning structure and transporting cradle was entered into with the firm of John A. Roebling's Sons, of Trenton. Lieutenant Seaton Schroeder, U. S. Navy, having previously accepted the position of assistant, was granted leave of absence by the Navy Department. A foreman for iron-work, Mr. Frank Price, of Glen Cove, New York, and one for wood-work were engaged; and on August 24th Lieutenant Schroeder, the foreman carpenter, and I sailed for England on the "Arizona," leaving Mr. Price to follow on the steamer that took the machinery.

Every possible effort to charter an American steamer was made in the interval between August 4th and 26th, but not one available for the work could be secured.

We reached Liverpool on September 4th, and spent the ensuing two weeks in fruitless efforts to charter an English steamer. The rates demanded for charter were equivalent to a purchase, and generally the explanation that the obelisk was to be embarked on the vessel in the manner proposed caused a sneer or a smile. As steamers could be purchased at any time, it was finally decided to make no further effort to charter one, but to wait until every thing was ready for embarking the obelisk before purchasing one.

From England we travelled through France and Italy to Trieste with the intention of purchasing timber at Trieste. There we found that there would be no advantage in purchasing and shipping the timber to Alexandria, where, we were assured, there was an abundant supply on hand at rates less, if any thing, than it would cost to make especial shipment. We returned to Venice, sailed on the steamer "Ceylon" on October 9th, and arrived at Alexandria October 16th. The foreman carpenter having been sent by steamer direct from Liverpool had arrived about two weeks earlier. In this interval the Alexandrians had learned that the obelisk was really to be removed, and for the first time in many centuries it became an object of interest.

The French waited about twenty-five years and the English nearly seventy-five before removing the obelisks they had selected for removal. There was a feeling in Egypt that the Americans would certainly require a century to perfect their arrangements; and although it was well known that the obelisk had been given to the United States, no one, not even the Khedive, believed that it would be removed.

Our arrival was the signal for the beginning of an agitation by the foreign residents to prevent its removal. Violently abusive articles were published in newspapers, meetings were held, and petitions to the Khedive were circulated for signature; threats of personal violence against any one who attempted to commence the work of removal were made openly and by letter, and every other means of frightening us resorted to. One incident of this nature that occurred on the day after our arrival is recalled, in order to contrast it with another that occurred on the day of our departure seven months later. On both occasions I was passing through the street frequented by the younger merchants and brokers as a rendezvous, on my way to the telegraph office; on the first, I was greeted with a storm of hisses and a succession of choice epithets; on the last, scores of these very men crowded around me, congratulating me on my final success and wishing me a pleasant and safe voyage.

Removal of the New York Obelisk.

After having established ourselves at Alexandria in apartments near to the site of the obelisk we went to Cairo, and at an hour previously appointed, accompanied by Vice-Consul-General Comanos, we had an audience of the Khedive. He received us very cordially, and made inquiries about the plans for removing and transporting the obelisk, cautiously and delicately expressing anxiety that it should not be taken down unless we were sure of removing it. This, we assured him, there was no reason to doubt. After a long and very frank discussion about European influences on Egyptian affairs, he promised that orders would be sent to the Governor of Alexandria to formally deliver up the obelisk. Visits were made to all the Ministers, who received us very kindly, and offered, in the usual Eastern manner, to do all sorts of things, which we well understood as without meaning. Riaz Pacha, Minister of Foreign Affairs and President of the Council of Ministers, gave directions that the order to the Governor of Alexandria should be made out without delay. The following is a translation.

To His Excellency the Governor of Alexandria: In the time of the ex-Khedive the Egyptian government gave Cleopatra's Needle, now standing on the sea-shore of Alexandria, to the United States of America, to be erected in the city of New York. His Excellency Chérif Pacha, who was then Minister of Foreign Affairs, communicated the fact to the United States Consul-General in a dispatch dated May 18, 1879. An American officer having been sent here to receive and remove the said Cleopatra's Needle, and His Highness the Khedive having confirmed the gift by a decree, I hasten to instruct you to deliver that monument immediately to the said officer, and to offer him the same assistance for removing it from its site and embarking it as was offered at the time of removing the other obelisk that was given to the English government. All expenses will be paid by the officer of the United States.

(Signed)   MOUSTAPHA RIAZ, *Minister of Foreign Affairs.*

We returned to Alexandria by the first train after the receipt of this order, and on arrival there we lost no time in presenting it to the Governor, and as soon as he had read it we urged him to execute it at once by a formal transfer of the obelisk. This was all accomplished within three days after our arrival. Considering with whom we were dealing there was reason for great satisfaction at the promptness with which possession of the obelisk had been secured. As long as it remained in the control of the Egyptian government there were reasons for anticipating pressure from the European consuls and resident foreigners to prevent its transfer; but the transfer was effected so quickly and so quietly that these gentlemen had no time to act in concert and with effect before it was too late. To their protests and petitions subsequently presented, the Khedive and his Ministers answered: "Too late; Cleopatra's Needle is the possession of the United States officer sent to receive it." The efforts of foreign residents were then directed to preventing its removal.

Although the Governor had formally transferred the obelisk, he had stipulated that work should not be commenced for a day or two, and kindly suggested that the interval could be profitably spent in making our preparations. After a lapse of four days another visit was paid to him, and he authorized us to commence operations, and excused the delay on the ground of a legal complication about the land around the obelisk that he had been obliged to enquire into.

At noon on October 27th, a force of laborers having begun clearing away the ground, an incident occurred that is related in the following letter.

ALEXANDRIA, *Oct.* 28, 1879.
H. E. The Governor of Alexandria.

Sir: I regret extremely that it has become once more necessary for me to have recourse to your good-will and your duty to assist me in prosecuting the work with which I am entrusted by the government of the United States. Yesterday, having received authority from you, I set some men to work to remove the paving stones that surround the obelisk, the owner of the stones making no objection whatever. Another individual arrived, however, and ordered the work stopped. Arriving myself a few moments afterward, I learned that the man claimed possession of the ground and would allow no one to work there. He also added that if we persisted he would apply to the Italian Consul, whose janissaries would be sent to eject us from the premises. Not recognizing his right to interfere, but not wishing to bring about such a disturbance, I went to see the Italian Vice-Consul, accompanied by the Consul of the United

THE OBELISK ENCASED AND STAYED.

The Hoisting Shears with Trunnions suspended to them

Plate VII

States, to ask an explanation. He informed me that any Italian subject occupying a property belonging to him had a right to his protection, and that he would protect him, even by force of arms. I thought it strange that he should dare to prevent by main force what your Excellency had authorized me to do; but before notifying my government that the Italian Vice-Consul had defied the orders of the Egyptian government, and that I am thus stopped in the execution of a work with which I am charged, I thought it best to try to arrange it amicably, so as not to trouble your Excellency. During the dispute on the ground I had offered to the *soi-disant* proprietor to pay him a rent, just as though it really belonged to him; but he refused point-blank to rent the ground to me, and informed me through his lawyer that he would not permit the operations for removing the obelisk. Nevertheless, I begged the Italian Vice-Consul to try his best to settle the matter, and he promised to give me an answer by four o'clock this afternoon. If he does not succeed I shall be obliged to request your Excellency to protect me against the Italian janissaries. Failing that, I shall be compelled to telegraph to my government that I have been forcibly ejected, and that Egyptian authority has failed to protect me.

I beg your Excellency to so direct affairs as to enable me to begin operations at once, because it is needless to say that if the matter should take an official form between the two governments the situation would only become more grave.

I am, sir, with great respect, your obedient servant,

(Signed)   HENRY H. GORRINGE, *Lieutenant-Commander U. S. Navy.*

In a subsequent interview with the Governor, he explained that the legal complication he had been investigating, that caused the delay in authorizing us to begin work, was the claim that the land around the obelisk was the property of some Italians; and in further explanation he related the circumstances substantially as follows:

An Italian having been granted authority by Mohammed Ali Pacha, then ruler of Egypt, to build a bathing establishment on the sea-shore near the obelisk, was unfortunate enough to have his property destroyed by the sea during a gale. He subsequently made a claim against the Egyptian government for compensation for the damage done by the sea; and in order to secure himself against a possible adverse decision on his claim, he took possession of the land surrounding the obelisk and erected a shanty on it. This claim was still pending when the international courts were organized for the trial of causes between foreigners and the Egyptian government and between individuals of different nationalities. It was regarded as so absurd that difficulty was experienced in getting it placed on the docket, but the Italian Consul persisted, and it was finally so placed in the belief that it never would be pressed for trial by the government, and certainly not by the claimants.

Four fifths of the claims of foreigners against the Egyptain government have no firmer basis than the one here cited, and at least four fifths of the foreign residents of Egypt have claims that are handed down in wills to heirs, just as this one was, the original claimant having died several years ago. Their attorney had kept himself well informed of the proceedings in connection with the removal of the obelisk, and had in concert with others deliberately planned the prohibition of the work in order to prevent its removal.

The Governor expressed surprise at the presumption of the Italian Consul, and requested time to communicate with the Minister of Foreign Affairs at Cairo. I notified U. S. Vice-Consul-General Comanos by telegraph of the circumstance, and urged him to confer with the Italian Consul-General about it; and pending answers from the Governor and Mr. Comanos, I notified the Italian Consul that a suit for damages for £15,000 would be instituted against whoever attempted to interfere with the work of removing the obelisk, and that I limited the time for amicable settlement, by acceptance of my proposition to lease the ground, to four o'clock P. M. of that day.

In reply to this the Italian Consul informed our consular agent that the claimant had accepted my offer to lease the ground, and proposed to appoint arbitrators to fix on a suitable sum. This was agreed to, arbitrators were selected, and the lease effected before night. Although there could have been no question as to the result of a determination to proceed without leasing the land, it was deemed advisable to get absolute control of the ground that must necessarily be covered with the works, so as to have a right to exclude from it undesirable persons.

Removal of the New York Obelisk.

On the morning of October 29th work was begun by one hundred Arabs, varying from ten to seventy years of age, divided into three gangs. The middle-aged dug and filled baskets, the old lifted them to the backs of the young, who carried them to the shore and emptied them into the surf. By November 6th an excavation of seventeen hundred and thirty cubic yards had been completed. It had laid bare the pedestal and steps, and made a space large enough to construct a caisson in which to transport the obelisk to the port for embarkation. Several interesting fragments of statuary, a number of coins, and a few scarabee and other antique objects were found by the workmen, to whom liberal rewards were paid for each article delivered. Men accustomed to the work were employed to search the beach for other small objects that having escaped detection would probably be washed up by the surf. In this way many interesting bronze fragments were recovered.

The base of the obelisk and the position of one of the metal supports are shown on Plate iv, on the right. This is copied from a photograph taken at the time the London obelisk was being removed. One corner of the obelisk is shown, supported by a piece of stone that had been substituted for one of the metal supports. The corner diagonally opposite to it was supported in exactly the same manner, two of the metal supports having been removed. The two remaining ones were badly mutilated. Their condition is shown on Plate v, which is a photograph of one metal support in two positions and the other in one position. They had been cast in the form of sea-crabs, but when we uncovered them all the legs but one, and all the claws but a part of one, had been broken off and removed, doubtless for the value of the metal.

Plate iv also shows the excavation and the condition of the base and steps when they were uncovered. The masonry on top of the pedestal around the base of the obelisk, shown in the picture on the left, was put there about the time the London obelisk was removed; owing to inferior mortar and other causes it was loose and gave no support to the shaft. Another feature in the picture to the left is the reft in the base of the obelisk, that has been misrepresented as a crack in the shaft, received during its transportation. It is in reality a vein of hornblende, the outer part of which has been decomposed, leaving an irregular shallow notch nowhere exceeding an inch in depth. But for this photograph, made before the obelisk had been lowered, there might have been some question as to the origin of this defect, which is now very noticeable from the drive in the Central Park, the dirt having been washed out of it.

The bottom of the lower step was found to be nearly at mean sea level; as the foundation could not have sunk so nearly uniformly, it is certain that there has been a subsidence of the ground since the obelisk was erected; and if the level of the lower step was at the same height as the surface is at present, this subsidence is about seventeen feet in nineteen hundred years. Down to the level of the water there was nothing but loose earth and sand, mixed with all sorts of fragments of columns and statuary and pottery. In several places remains of old walls were met with. Surrounding the steps were fragments of a mosaic pavement, composed of alternate squares of white and dark marble. The sea end of the pit was left open down to the remains of an ancient massive wall that ran nearly parallel with the shore and close to the water. This wall served as a breakwater for the pit when the surf was high.

While the excavations were in progress another attempt was made to prevent the removal of the obelisk, through a creditor of the Egyptian government who applied to the International Court to sieze it and keep possession until his claim had been paid. Before serving the writ enquiries were made as to the probable result of doing so. On being assured that no notice would be taken of the writ, and that all the resistance possible would be offered to any use of force to take possession of the obelisk, the Court withheld the writ. The object of this proceeding was to arrest the work, get the obelisk into court, and keep the case pending until the attempt to remove it had been abandoned. It is inexplicable that the proposition should ever have been entertained; and yet it was not only entertained, but the process was actually begun, and would undoubtedly have been pushed but for prompt action that gave assurance of a determination to resist. The United States flag was conspicuously displayed on the obelisk to indicate ownership; and the means of defending it was provided and arranged in a manner that carried conviction to any one that had been in doubt about our sincerity and our determination to defend it and remove it.

TURNING THE OBELISK.

December 6, 1879

Soon after this affair had quieted down some of the consuls-general in Cairo, at the instigation of some resident European archæologists, made an attempt to have the work of removal suspended until the matter could be referred to their governments. It appears that by the terms of a convention entered into with several of the European powers, the Egyptian government agreed to prevent the exportation of any object of antiquity. No attention had been paid to this convention when the English removed the fallen obelisk; and its provisions were commonly violated by the consuls and archæologists themselves in the shipment of articles to Europe. Besides this, the *firman* that gave the Egyptian government existence stipulated that it should not make treaties with foreign powers, and it is clear that the convention in question was unauthorized. Fearing that the pressure on the Khedive and his Ministers might become more than they could resist, negotiations were commenced through a prominent, and at that time powerful, Pacha in Constantinople, whom it had been my good fortune to befriend, to insure the prompt confirmation of the gift by the Porte, in case of necessity.

To put an end to these annoyances I determined to push the work of removal forward as rapidly as possible by working night and day, so as to get the obelisk off its pedestal. Every effort was devoted to this end, and it was accomplished within a month from the day the turning structure arrived.

PREPARATIONS FOR TURNING THE OBELISK.

While the pit was being dug a staging was erected around the obelisk for sheathing it with planks, in order to protect the hieroglyphs from injury. (Plate vi.) The sheathing was held together by iron bands, similar to the hoops of a barrel. The top band was heavier than the others, and had a loop at each angle, into which were shackled four steel wire cables. These were secured to anchors at suitable distances from the base of the obelisk, and tightened so as to support it until it was secured in the turning structure. The masonry and concrete piers on which this was to stand were commenced as soon as the pit was dug, and in order to have them dry quickly hydraulic cement was used. These piers are shown on Plates ii and iii. As soon as the staging had been removed four long spars were placed in position, opposite the angles of the obelisk, to form derricks for hoisting the pieces of the turning structure into position. Plate vii illustrates the plan adopted for supporting the obelisk, the sheathing banded around it, and the hoisting shears with the trunnions suspended to them. For convenience in placing the trunnions on the pillow-blocks, they were hoisted first and left hanging until the turning structure had been erected.

The machinery and material for removing the obelisk were shipped from New York on the steamer "Nevada," of the Guion Line, which sailed on October 7th, and arrived in Liverpool on October 19th. There they were transhipped on the steamer "Mariotis," which sailed on October 27th, and arrived at Alexandria November 11, 1879. Preparations had been made for their prompt disembarkation and transport from the port, through the town, to the side of the obelisk; and this was completed in four days. The trunnions were the only pieces that gave trouble, owing to there not being a truck in the city suitable for their transport. They were, however, placed on the best truck obtainable, which was hauled by Arabs, who wisely selected the Christian Sabbath for the day to move them, owing to the diminution of traffic on that day.

The Arabs were very noisy and attracted a large and increasing crowd, who followed the procession through the town. For this an American missionary roundly abused us from a borrowed pulpit, and took advantage of the occasion to denounce the removal of the obelisk as a work of the Devil. This act of "Christian charity" was of no consequence, beyond the amusement it afforded the editors and readers of local newspapers, who seized on it with much eagerness as evidence of the prevailing sentiment of Americans. In explanation of the missionary's condition of mind on the subject it may be well to state on his own authority that he wanted the money that was being spent on the removal given to his mission. In connection with this question of Sunday-work, which was commented on in a rational manner by many friends, it is well to recall the fact that the Mohammedan and Christian Sabbaths are on different days. It was impossible to observe both; and a respect for the opinions of both sects led to the rule that work would be carried on without intermission, and that the workmen were at liberty to select their own Sunday and observe it in their own fashion. Arab Mohammedans and Maltese and European Christians formed the majority of the men employed. The former spent Friday, their Sabbath, in a rational manner, sleeping during the early part of the day, attending services at the mosque at noon, and devoting the afternoon to social intercourse and amusement. The Christians, almost to a man, would devote the thirty-six hours from Saturday evening to Monday morning in drinking, gambling, fighting, and other excesses, and return to work drunk, sleepy, and bruised.

By December 2d the turning structure had been placed in position, and so admirably were the several parts fitted that it was not even necessary to ream out a bolt hole.[1] The process of lifting the obelisk clear of the pedestal and disengaging the metal supports or crabs occupied us until the evening of December 5th. With the bolts that clamped the trunnions together loosened so as to allow the obelisk to pass freely up through them, levers inserted in the turn-buckles of the tie-rods were turned simultaneously with the nuts on the upper and lower ends of the tie-rods. Some anxiety was caused by the buckling of the heel-beams, due to imperfect bearing against the bottom of the obelisk. After this had been provided against by wedges driven in the vacant spaces, the lifting was successfully and easily accomplished. The operation of lifting, here briefly described, will be made clear by referring to Plate ii, where the turn-buckles in the tie-rods C are shown inside of the steel towers, about midway between the trunnions B, and the heel-beams D. And on Plate iii the ends of the tie-rods are seen through the brackets on the trunnions and also through the ends of the heel-beams.

Before turning the obelisk horizontal the steel wire-rope truss A, shown on Plates iii, vii, and viii, was placed in position and tightened by means of screws and nuts to an estimated strain of sixty tons ; thereby relieving the section of the obelisk through the point of suspension of this amount of the weight of the ends, and insuring it against fracture when it was horizontal. Plates vii and viii also show a stack of timber piled to receive the upper section of the obelisk should the tackles that were provided to keep control of the turning unexpectedly give way. These tackles were led from a strap round the bottom of the obelisk to posts led into the masonry towers. They were, theoretically, capable of raising fifteen tons. New rope and blocks of the best quality obtainable in Alexandria were purchased expressly for the purpose. The rope previously purchased had been so treacherous, and had parted so many times with inadequate strain, that it was deemed prudent to provide a safeguard against the obelisk revolving past the horizontal. The upper section was known to have a preponderance of three and a half tons of weight, given it to facilitate the operation of turning.

TURNING THE OBELISK.

On the morning of December 4th an attempt was made to pull the upper end of the obelisk over by means of tackles. This attempt failed, owing to the further bending of the heel-beams, which caused the bottom of the obelisk to bind against the top of one of the crabs. The impression prevailed that the turning structure had settled and was therefore of inadequate strength to sustain the weight. Several engineers and others strongly advised abandoning the attempt to place the obelisk horizontal in the manner proposed ; and letters were received protesting against the destruction of so valuable a monument by any further attempt to remove it. These expressions did not affect in any way the confidence I felt in a speedy termination of this, the first stage of the work, although they caused me great chagrin, and aroused every one associated with me in the work to an extra exertion in order to prove them senseless.

Removing the crabs was rendered very difficult by the lead which had been poured into the mortices in the pedestal while molten. The angles of the dowels of the crabs had notches in them (see Plate vi), and the bottom of the mortice was larger than the top. These were devices of the Roman engineer to prevent the removal of the crabs, and they were very effective. The process of lifting the obelisk, already described,

---

[1] The contract for this work was sublet by John A. Roebling's Sons to the Phœnix Iron Works of Trenton, to which all credit is due for its admirable execution.

THE OBELISK HORIZONTAL.

December 6, 1879.

Plate IX

Removal of the New York Obelisk.

was again resorted to, and having raised it clear of the crab the bottom was pushed over to seaward until the obelisk was in the position shown on Plate viii. In this position it remained seventeen hours without affecting any part of the structure in which it was suspended.

Rumors of a possible demonstration by the foreign residents when the obelisk was to be placed horizontal had been circulated until they reached Rear-Admiral Aslambekoff, of the Russian Imperial Navy, who was in the port of Alexandria in his flag-ship the "Minim." He was aware of the feeling that existed among the foreigners, and while unable to land an armed force for our protection, he landed a large force of unarmed trained seamen for the purpose of enclosing the grounds in a cordon of effective men and affording any assistance that was needed at a critical moment.

His Excellency, Zulficar Pacha, Governor of Alexandria, the Egyptian officials, and a few acquaintances were notified that the turning demonstration would take place at 9 A. M. of the 6th. But his Excellency did not arrive until 11 A. M. As soon as he had reached the platform provided for invited persons, the word was given to slack the tackles. A large crowd of Greeks, Italians, and other Europeans had gathered in the vicinity, and occupied every available spot from which the movement could be seen. While we were waiting for the Governor, the crowd was noisy and at times unruly when they were prevented from going within the inclosure. But at the instant the obelisk began to move there was absolute silence and stillness. As it slowly turned not a sound but the rendering of the ropes around the posts and an occasional creak of the structure could be heard. Immediately following a creak louder than any previous one, the motion was suddenly arrested, then there was a sharp snap—one of the tackles had parted. Instantly the order was given to slack the other tackle rapidly, using it merely to retard the motion and not to arrest it; but the man attending the fall had lost his wits, and instead of slackening, he held it fast and it very soon broke. The obelisk was at that moment about half over; it moved slowly at first, and then more and more rapidly, until it struck the stack of timbers, rebounded twice, and came to rest in the position shown on Plate viii. There was intense excitement; many of the Arabs and Greeks about the grounds had fled precipitously when the obelisk began to move rapidly; and when it rested on the stack of timber uninjured there arose a prolonged cheer, which was the first friendly manifestation shown by the Alexandrians.

The explanation given for the breaking of the first tackle by the man attending it was, that he looked up to see what the noise was, and in doing so involuntarily checked the passage of the rope through his hands; this brought the whole strain on his tackle and caused it to break. The other man was properly giving his whole attention to the command, and was unconscious of the accident until he saw that his companion had fled precipitately from under the obelisk, leaving him alone. Surely his loss of self-control was excusable. It was to provide against such contingencies that the timber stack was built. The two upper tiers of plank were crushed; aside from this no loss or injury to any person or any thing resulted from the successful accomplishment of the first essential feature of the work of removal.

Simultaneously with the preparations for turning, other equally important parts of the work were being pushed forward; notably the construction of a wooden box or caisson in which the obelisk was to be carried by sea to the port, and the clearing away of ruins from, and grading of the sea-bed along, the route over which it had to be launched. By way of explanation it is necessary to recall the fact that an iron truss-cradle, moving on cannon-balls instead of wheels, in channel irons instead of on an ordinary rail, had been designed, made in the United States, and brought to Egypt for transporting the obelisk overland to the port for embarkation. The distance overland was less than a mile; and the route was over comparatively unfrequented streets, except for a short distance across what was once the ancient causeway connecting Eunostos Island with the mainland, and what is now an accumulation of sand and debris, occupied by the most important part of the city. An examination of Plate x will make this clear.

Soon after our arrival at Alexandria an unofficial application was made to the Governor for permission to move the obelisk along the proposed route. A conference ensued during which the Governor stated, in effect, that in consideration for keeping the streets paved and clean the government had transferred all control of them to the foreign merchants. He agreed to ascertain the probable result of an application made to these merchants and to inform us. Several days afterward he advised us not to make the application until every other method of getting the obelisk to the port had been tried and had failed. It appears that the foreign merchants had determined not to allow the obelisk to be moved through the city, giving as a reason the probability of its crushing in the sewers. Guarantees of repairing all damage done were of no avail; the transporting cradle, costing $5,100, had to be thrown away, and the expensive and very dangerous method of sea transport in a wooden caisson a distance of ten miles was the only resource. The expense was least of all in the construction of the caisson, which cost only $2,200; it was chiefly in the preparations for launching it over a shallow bank cumbered with heavy blocks of syenite and granite; the massive submerged foundations of one of the famous palaces of Alexandria were directly in the way. These obstructions could only be removed by means of divers, a serious undertaking in smooth water, and a most discouraging and almost hopeless task to accomplish on an open coast on which the surf was breaking two thirds of the time. Diving operations were commenced on November 5, 1879, and continued, whenever the sea would permit, until March 18, 1880. A pier with derricks for lifting out the blocks had to be constructed. The estimated weight of material removed is one hundred and seventy tons. The pieces ranged from three to seven tons in weight. In Alexandria competent divers are scarce, and in order to retain those we employed they had to be paid whether at work or not. The cost of this submarine work was nearly $4,000. It will be shown hereafter that the cost of the caisson and submarine work necesssary for launching it were inconsiderable and unimportant when compared with the cost of launching and the imminent danger involved in the operation of getting it afloat, due to the displacement of the ways by the surf.

Plate iii shows the frame of the caisson in course of construction, and Plate viii shows the end sections nearly completed in the pit. The floor timbers of these sections were made to form a part of the timber stacks on which the obelisk was lowered, as shown in Plate iii. Work on the middle section could not be commenced until the pedestal, steps, and foundation had been removed; and their removal could not be accomplished until the turning structure had been released and taken down, and its foundation piers demolished.

LOWERING THE OBELISK.

The preparations for releasing the machinery and for lowering the obelisk from its elevated position, forty-three feet above the bottom of the pit, into the caisson are illustrated on Plate iii. After the obelisk had been placed horizontal, the upper section was temporarily supported on two spars under the pyramidion. The stack of timber placed to receive it was then removed. After several experiments in building the stacks, the plan illustrated in Plate iii was finally adopted. Planks three inches thick, nine inches wide, and sixteen feet long, were piled in groups of three, at right angles to each other, up to the level of the top of the pedestal; the lengths were then fourteen feet for two thirds the remaining height, and finally twelve feet for the remainder. Heavy timber, diagonal shores were placed against the sides and ends of the piles to insure stability. Oak beams were slung by iron rods under the obelisk, and fastened to it at the points against which the pistons of the pumps were to bear; and other beams were placed on top of the piles for the pumps to stand on, so as to distribute the bearing over the whole pile uniformly. The tops of the stacks were cut down through the middle to give room enough for the pumps to be worked,—(see Plate iii),—the ends being left to receive the weight of the obelisk when it was necessary to shift the pumps down. The pumps were fitted with lowering valves, an indispensable substitute for the ordinary method of tripping the plunger when releasing the strain from the piston. By means of these valves the liquid in the cylinder is allowed to escape to the chamber as rapidly or as slowly as the operator pleases, thereby allowing the piston to descend at any desired speed.

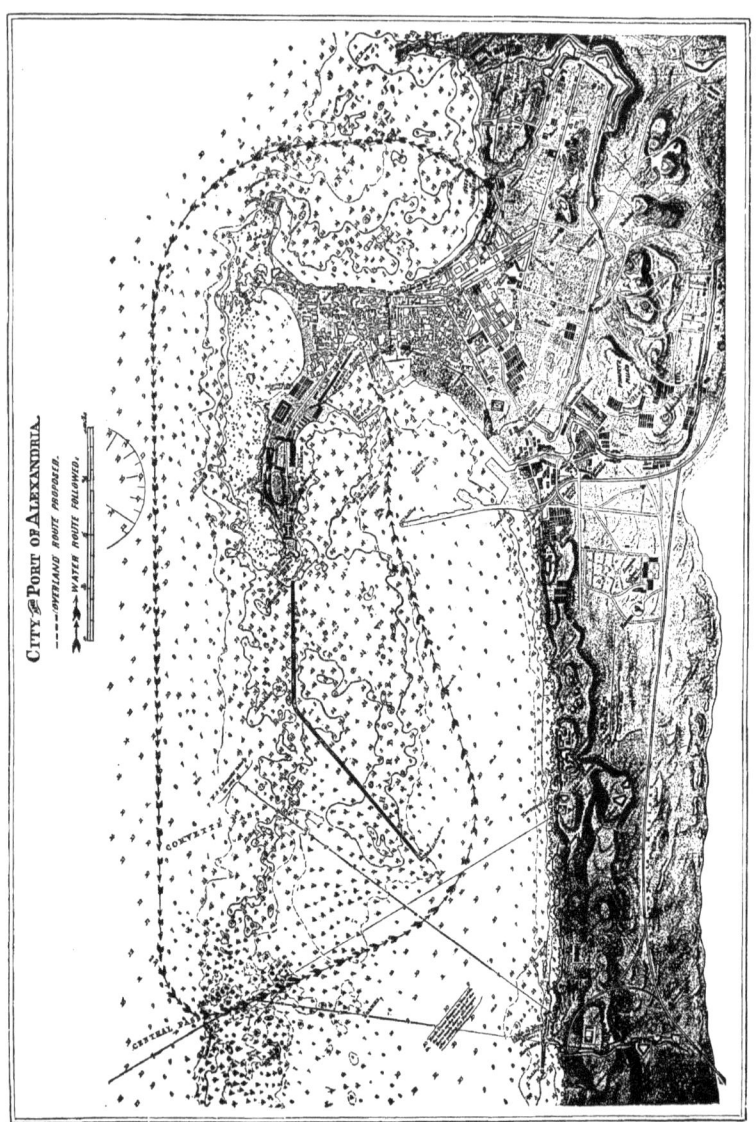

Very great inconvenience resulted from the use of small instead of large timber for the stacks, and it may well be asked why small timber was used. Relying on the order of Riaz Pacha to the Governor, to "offer him (the officer sent to remove the obelisk) the same assistance for removing it from its site and embarking it as was offered at the time of removing the other obelisk that was given to the English goverment," and knowing that the timber used by the English was still in the government store-house, no effort was made to find other timber until the time for lowering the obelisk had nearly arrived. Application for the loan of government timber was made. The officer in charge happened to be a European, and he managed to evade the order, even after it had been reiterated, by delays and other means, until it was too late. The obelisk was ready for turning, timber for lowering it had to be provided, and the only kind available was the soft planks that were bought at an exorbitant rate. Here again the vicious obstruction of Europeans failed to retard the work, and had no other effect than to increase the cost of its execution. In this instance the unnecessary expense for timber amounted to $4,300.

The operation of releasing the turning structure was very troublesome, owing to the elasticity of the stacks. The total compression in the forty-three feet was twenty-two and a half inches under the weight of the obelisk. As soon as the weight had been transferred to the stacks, the towers and trunnions were removed, and demolition of the masonry piers commenced.

The operation of lowering was as follows : The pistons of the pumps were forced out to within four inches of their limit of fourteen inches ; blocking was then supplied to whatever space intervened between the caps and the oak beam under the obelisk ; the piston was then forced out the remaining four inches, or as much as was needed to lift the obelisk clear of the blocking on the ends of the stacks, on which it had been landed while the trunnions and towers were being removed ; nine inches of this blocking was then gradually taken away, while the pistons of the pumps were allowed to descend slowly ; when nearly down to their limit, removing the blocking was stopped, and the obelisk once more rested on it with the pumps free. The planks that were parallel with the direction of the obelisk had to be sawed in two places to allow of removing the middle section so that the pumps might be lowered nine inches. Those that were laid in the other direction could be removed without being cut. When the pumps had been lowered the process above described was repeated. The average rate of lowering was about three feet per day. It must, however, be remarked that owing to the height of the stacks and to insure safety, work was not carried on simultaneously at both ends.

It was difficult to maintain uniformity of pressure on the pistons ; and instead of pumps capable of sustaining sixty tons each, it would have been much better to have had them capable of sustaining one hundred. Considerable delay resulted from the disabling of three of the pumps ; the system was new to the mechanics of Alexandria, and restoring the pumps to efficiency was a tedious and expensive process.

Demolishing the foundation piers without blasting was also troublesome, the cement having set to a degree entirely unexpected. As soon as they had been demolished the pit was enlarged on the east side, and the pedestal steps and foundation moved out from under the obelisk and placed in the enlargement. The pedestal was raised clear of the steps by driving steel wedges under it until there was room enough for the end of a bent steel bar or link to be inserted. (See Fig. L, Plate xi.) Hydraulic pumps acting on the upper part of this bar or link then raised the pedestal clear of the steps and held it suspended until channel irons and cannon balls could be placed underneath. The pedestal was then lowered on top of the channel irons and balls. It was moved with the greatest ease over a track of channel irons prolonged to the position assigned it. A section through the pedestal and channel iron tracks with the balls in position is shown on Plate xi, Fig. M.

This plate also shows the position in which each piece forming the steps and foundation was found, and gives the form and dimensions of all the essential pieces of the structure, including the pedestal. The curious features of the foundation are the forms and positions of certain pieces of syenite, and the marks and characters that are cut on other pieces that occupy the axis and east angle of the structure.

Whatever their significance there is something striking in their arrangement, and almost any explanation is more reasonable than the assumption that it was accidental.

THE MASONIC EMBLEMS.

The pieces forming the steps and all but four of those inclosed by them are a hard limestone of grayish-white color. Three of the four exceptions are syenite from the same quarry as the obelisk and pedestal (Plate xi, Figs. A, B, C); the other one, E, is soft limestone entirely free from discolorations and as purely white as the best statuary marble. The foundation below the lower step is composed of soft sandstone blocks, rough-hewn and of irregular form, with three exceptions; these three had been carefully dressed and had had figures cut in relief on the sides (Figs. P, G, H). Of the three pieces of syenite, two, A and B, are carefully cut and had been polished; the other, C, is rough and irregular, the upper part having been gouged by tools into an unnatural and conspicuously uneven surface. One of the polished pieces, A, is an imperfect cube, that is, the height is less than the sides in measurement; the other is of remarkable shape, more easily comprehended from the drawing B on Plate xi than from any possible description. The upper part is hewn to form a long and a short arm, at right angles, similar to the mechanic's tool called a builder's square, or in French *l' angle*. At the junction of the lower part with the vertical faces of the arms there are three beads, or convex surfaces of unequal dimensions; and around the lower edges of the sides there is a concave surface or groove. The assumption that it had formed a part of some ancient building, from the ruins of which it was taken to fill up a vacant space under the obelisk, would not be reasonable, chiefly because its form is unsuited for such a purpose, as will be very evident by examining the drawing. With reference to the rough piece of syenite there are two proofs that the roughness and irregularity were intentionally given to its upper surface: one of these is the tool marks; the other is its singularity in this respect, every other piece of the steps and foundation had the upper and lower surfaces dressed to give a good bearing for the layers above and below.

Assuming that the forms of these pieces of syenite, in connection with the fact that they are syenite while all the other pieces are limestone, have some significance, an explanation may be sought in their actual and relative positions. The polished cube occupied the east angle of the upper tier, and stood on the end of the long arm of the polished square; this extended across the S. E. face of the structure parallel with the inner edges of the second tier or lower step; the short arm extended half-way across the S. W. face, and touched the rough block of syenite which occupied the west angle of the same tier. If there is any thing within the limits of our knowledge and understanding that serves to explain the forms and arrangement of these three pieces it seems unreasonable to reject it until some better explanation is offered. One striking peculiarity existed in the manner of laying the polished cube. While every other part of the structure was laid in white mortar, this one was placed on yellow cement, and the spaces around it were not filled in, as all other spaces were, with fragments of hard limestone and white mortar.

The piece of white limestone was found on the lower part of the piece of syenite out of which the square was cut. The cube of syenite (A) rested partly on the long arm of the square (B,) and partly on the piece of white limestone (E). On the block of hard gray limestone adjacent to it (D) an *iron trowel* and a *lead plummet* (K) were found. These implements could not have been left accidentally by the workmen who built the foundation, for the trowel is firmly cemented to the surface of the stone. They are not modern, and could not have been placed where they were found at any time after the re-erection of the obelisk, B. C. 22.

After removing all the pieces forming the steps and those enclosed by them, numbering in all forty-three, two tiers of the foundation were removed. The only piece of the first tier that was dressed occupied the east angle. This piece is shown on Plate xi, marked H. Two of the sides have a figure in relief, extending through the middle, that resembles a snake in form. At the angle of these sides are two spiral figures in relief also resembling snakes. The upper part of the stone at this angle projects above

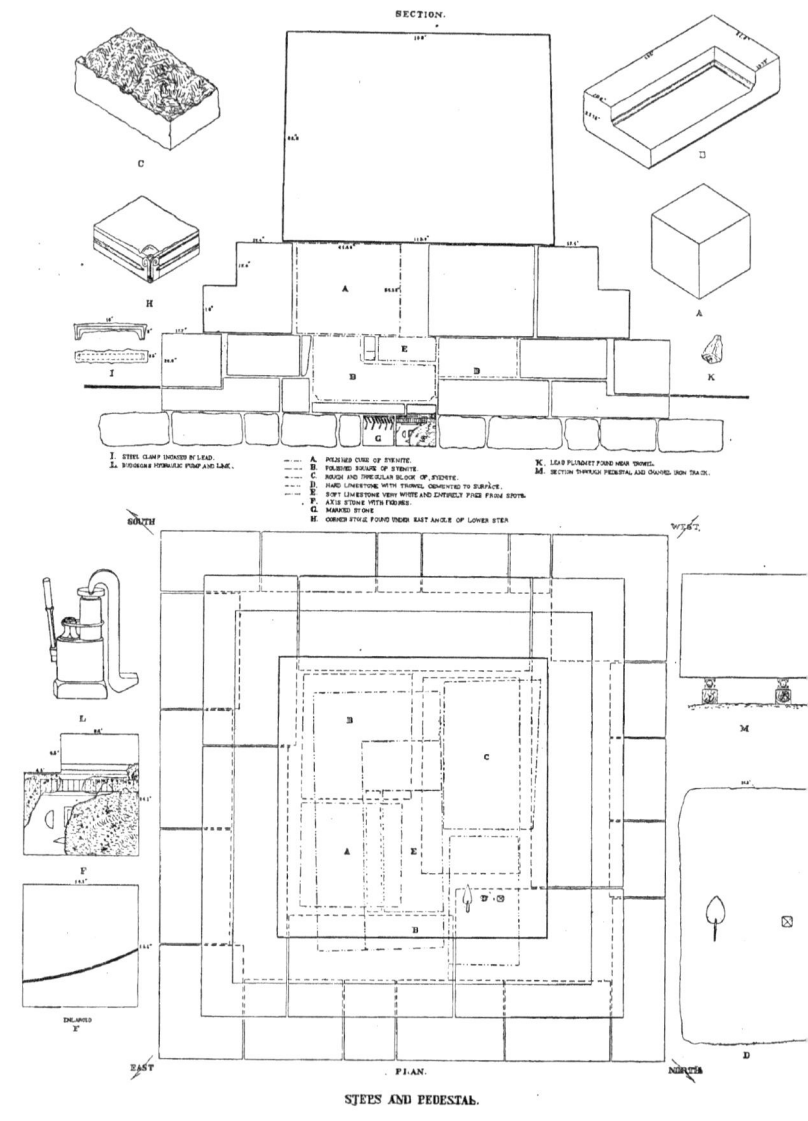

STEPS AND PEDESTAL.

the surface; and where the spirals meet there is an angular recess below it. The projection and recess form a group of three miniature steps above the spirals. In the face of the stone that was found adjacent to this one there is a diamond-shaped recess. No other mark was found on any piece of this tier.

In the tier next below, all of the pieces were rough and irregularly laid except two; one marked F in Plate xi occupied the axis of the structure, and the other marked G was adjacent to it. One face of the axis stone F has had a group of lines and a group of figures carved on it, the latter in relief; and another face has an arc of a very large circle extending across it. As far as it is possible to distinguish the group of lines they *may* be divided into three parts. The upper part appears to consist of three parallel lines of unequal length; the middle part consists of two parallel lines, the interval between them divided into equal spaces as if to form a scale; the lower part has a line forming with a part of the lower line of the scale, as far as it can be traced, a figure resembling the cubit measure of the ancient Egyptians. One of the group of figures resembles a builder's square, or angle; another is the segment of a circle or a semicircle; both of these forms are hieroglyphical characters; the other is more like a spherical triangle than any thing else; it is manifestly a part of some figure that is nearly obliterated.

The marked stone G adjacent to the axis stone F has one of its sides carefully dressed, the others being rough. On the dressed side there are two rows of parallel grooves about one eighth of an inch in depth and the same in width; the upper row contains nine groups with three grooves in each, and the lower row five groups with three grooves in each. The grooves are cut diagonally across the face of the stone in two directions; every alternate group of the upper row intersects one of the lower row, and forms with it an obtuse angle. A glance at the drawing will make this clear.

The rapid inflow of water prevented excavation below the lower tier shown on Plate xi, which appeared to be the last one that was composed of large stones.

The foundation and steps were removed with great care; each piece was measured and numbered as it was lifted out, and a corresponding number marked on a drawing made at the time, of which Plate xi is a reproduction.

The striking similarity between the forms and actual and relative positions of the pieces here described and those of the emblems of Freemasonry, led to the appointment of a committee of Freemasons, by the Grand Lodge of Egypt, to examine them; and after discussion and deliberation, the following conclusions were announced: The polished cube found in the east angle corresponds with the Masonic emblem designated the Perfect Ashler. The polished square corresponds with the emblem of that name. The rough block found in the west angle corresponds with the Rough Ashler. The stone with figures resembling snakes is emblematic of Wisdom. The axis stone is the Trestle-Board; and the marked stone adjacent to it bears the Master's Mark. The two implements, the iron trowel and lead plummet, are also emblematic of Freemasonry. It is worthy of record that the Masonic character of the foundation had been affirmed before either of these implements was discovered. The piece of soft white limestone that was found under the polished cube (E, Plate xi) has been regarded as the symbol of Purity, and as having been placed in the centre of the eighteen pieces forming the lower step to designate the word of the eighteenth degree.

Mr. Gaston L. Feuardent, of New York, unquestionably the most expert archæologist in the United States, was asked to examine the axis stone (F), and express an opinion as to the meaning of the figures and lines on it. The following is his reply:

"I have no doubt that the stone with the relief inscriptions, found in the lower tier of the foundation of the obelisk, was placed there entirely by accident among the rough stones forming the lower strata. If the people who built the foundation had desired to bury there some record, they would not have selected a mere fragment, but would have, as they usually did, placed there a record made and shaped in the most intelligible manner.

"The actual preservation of the iron trowel and the lead weight shows how little damage was suffered by the objects placed in the foundation; and there is ample evidence in the appearance of the stone itself, its uniformity of color, and its shape, to show that it was found in the same condition as when it was originally placed there, except a few scratches accidentally and recently put on it. Therefore I believe that the workmen took a fragment from some monument and placed it where it was found, after having cut it into shape to fit the place.

"I believe that a wrong interpretation was given to the characters cut in the stone, on account of the position it occupied in the foundation; that is to say, that its deciphering was attempted while keeping the stone in its horizontal position instead of placing it vertically as ought to have been done.

"The many vertical and horizontal lines on the side of the stone represent to me part of the original ornamentation, forming a kind of frame, of which the other portions are lost. The two hieroglyphic signs now existing at the middle of the stone represent to me (first) half a sphere and (second) the top part of a figure which originally represented three sides of a square, and these signs are meant to represent in hieroglyphics the word 'Temple.'

"I see clearly that most of the surface of the inscribed side of the stone was damaged or taken away before being placed in the foundation, and the many accidents appearing on the present damaged surface of the stone must have led to false interpretation in its deciphering, as is frequently the case in reading ancient inscriptions found on monuments in a poor state of preservation."

The conclusions of Mr. Feuardent are entitled to the greatest weight. It will be noted by instructed Freemasons that he interprets the hieroglyphical figures that still remain on the surface, distinct enough to be recognized, as meaning "Temple"; and it is a remarkable coincidence that figures of these particular forms should have been used to designate the word "Temple." Freemasonry is believed to be the modern representative of an order or society that was founded by the ancients engaged in the construction of temples, and the whole speculative fabric of modern Freemasonry is based on the operations of builders.

As differences of opinion on all subjects of interest are inevitable, there are some Freemasons who regard the arrangement and forms of the pieces of the base of the obelisk as having no Masonic significance. Those who do not belong to the Order are hardly capable of judging.

THE CAISSON.

Completing the caisson and lowering the obelisk into it occupied but a short time after the foundation had been moved out of the way. The caisson with the obelisk in it had to be placed on the launching ways, which were laid at an inclination of seven per cent., and extended out a distance of one hundred and ten yards from the low-water line of the shore to a depth of seven feet. Plate xii illustrates the form of the caisson and the method of securing the obelisk in it. The caisson was nothing but a large box eighty-three feet long, twenty-two feet wide at one end, thirty feet wide at the other end, and eleven feet deep on the outside. It was given two keels and two keelsons; the former to act as guides in launching, the latter to form a bed for the obelisk to rest on, and both to give it additional strength. The dimensions were determined by its weight with the obelisk in it, and the depth of water at the end of the launching ways, which was about seven feet at mean level of the tide.

LOWERING THE CAISSON ON THE LAUNCHING WAYS.

The accompanying figure illustrates the method of lowering the caisson with the obelisk in it on the launching ways. It was pivoted at the point (A) of intersection of its keels with the launching ways, which were laid in sections. The pivot was an oak beam, rounded on the lower side to fit into the curves of the pillow-blocks (C) of the turning structure, that had been placed on the blocking (D) underneath the caisson. The aggregate weight of the caisson and its contents was three hundred and seventeen tons. To provide adequate bearing surface for the pivot, it was found necessary to excavate some distance below the water-level, and pack pieces of heavy timber close together over an area twenty-five feet square. A similar bearing surface or foundation (E) was provided for the hydraulic pumps (P) that were to lower the sea end of the caisson to its position on the ways. The difficulties of this operation were much increased by the contracted space in which the work must be done, the want of light, and above all the encroachment of the sea. The break-water had necessarily been removed to place the launching ways in position; and the surf almost continuously poured a large volume of water into the pit. Powerful pumps were kept at work without reducing the water-level to any great extent.

I regard this part of the work, that is, the operation of placing the caisson on the launching ways and launching it, as attended with more embarrassments and risks than any other. We were restricted

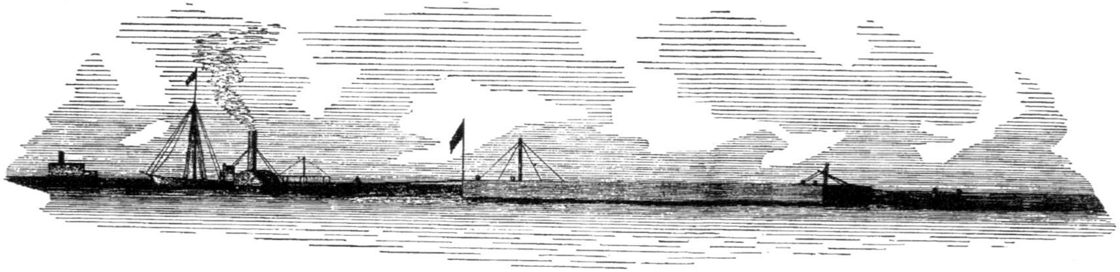

CAISSON AFLOAT

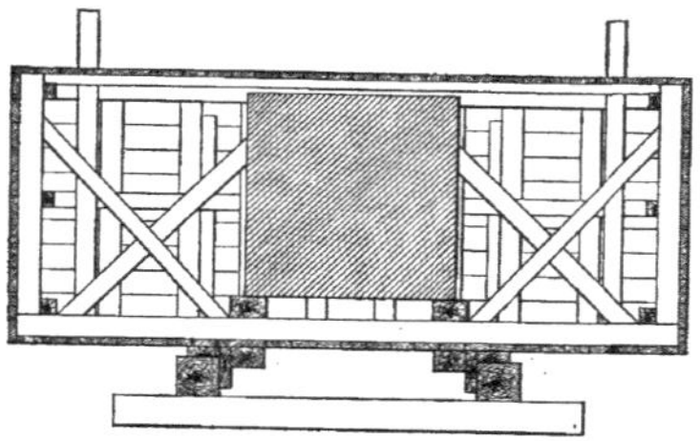

SECTION THROUGH CAISSON AND OBELISK

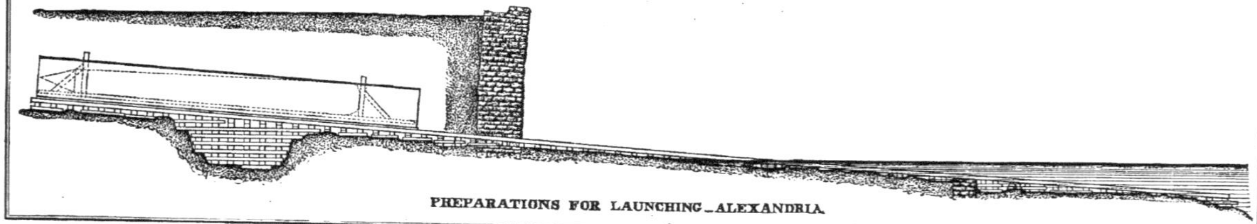

PREPARATIONS FOR LAUNCHING—ALEXANDRIA

Plate XII.

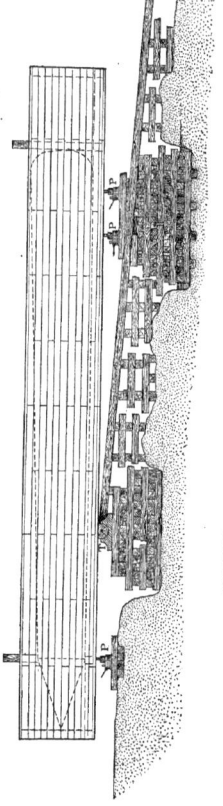

PIVOT FOR LOWERING CAISSON ON LAUNCHING WAYS.

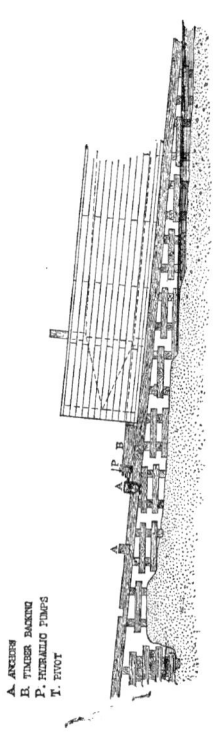

ANCHOR FOR HYDRAULIC JACKS TO PUSH CAISSON AFLOAT.

A. ARCHES
B. TIMBER BACKING
P. HYDRAULIC PUMPS
T. PIVOT

Removal of the New York Obelisk.

to an inadequate space for carrying on the work conveniently; we were operating on an exposed coast in the stormiest season (March), with the sea breaking dangerously at least two thirds of the time; and we were without sufficient hydraulic power to lower the sea end of the caisson without great risk. Hydraulic pumps available for the work could not be obtained nearer than New York City, and it was not possible to have those that had given out satisfactorily repaired in Alexandria.

RÉSUMÉ OF OPERATIONS FROM DECEMBER 6TH TO MARCH 18TH.

The time that had elapsed from December 6th, when the obelisk was placed horizontal, to March 18th, when it was ready for launching, was occupied in building the stacks of timber for lowering it, releasing the turning structure, lowering the obelisk from a height of forty-three feet, demolishing the foundation walls of the towers, removing the pedestal, steps, and foundation to make room for building the caisson and placing it on the ways, and building and laying the ways. It was not possible to carry on these different operations simultaneously. Their accomplishment in less than ninety working days, with an almost continuous surf breaking on the shore, constantly embarrassing and frequently suspending work, seems at this interval of time to have been very expeditious. The diving operations, already alluded to, for clearing a track for the launching ways, were carried on continuously when the state of the sea would permit; but it was a common occurrence for one day of heavy surf to destroy the results of many days' work. Nothing more disheartening can be imagined than to witness the destruction in a few hours of the results of many days of costly labor without the possibility of preventing it. The foreign merchants of Alexandria, who forced on us the sea transportation of the obelisk to the port by withholding their consent to its passage through the city, must have felt a grim satisfaction in witnessing the consequences of their decision. The worst result of their refusal was the difference in cost of the work, amounting to about $21,000.

LAUNCHING THE CAISSON.

There was every reason to feel assured that the caisson would slide down the ways after having been started. An abundance of lubricant was used on the ways to facilitate it, and every precaution taken against fouling of the sliding surfaces. A final examination of all parts, including those submerged, was made on the morning of March 18th, and at 11 A. M. of that day the lashings that held the caisson were removed. A powerful tug was waiting to tow it around to the port. The smaller hydraulic pumps, which had been placed in position to give it a start, were brought into action, and under pressure from them the caisson began to move very slowly at first, then more rapidly, and after it had slid a distance of twenty feet it abruptly stopped sliding. A tow-line was run out to the tug, and two anchors were planted off shore with cables leading to the caisson. The combined force of the tug and threefold purchases on the cables did not move it an inch. At this critical time the sea, which had been smooth, began to rise rapidly, and the tug was obliged to seek shelter in Alexandria harbor. By dark the sea had become so rough that all efforts to get the caisson afloat had to be suspended. By the next morning the sea had moderated, and our efforts to push the caisson into the water were renewed, in the belief that it would slide of its own accord if it could be started with rapid motion. But in this we were mistaken; there was no alternative to pushing it inch by inch down the ways with the hydraulic pumps until it was afloat. This tedious process lasted until March 31st, with frequent intervals, during which operations had to be suspended on account of the surf. One of these, on March 21st, caused us much anxiety. The caisson had by that time been pushed down the ways to a position where it was about half water-borne. In this position the sea end was liable to be raised by the waves, thereby causing it to thump heavily on the ways, with liability of breaking the obelisk and the almost certainty of displacing it and destroying the caisson. To provide against these dangers, water was admitted to the caisson and the sea end was strengthened by shoring the frames against the obelisk so as to resist the vigorous blows of the waves as they broke over it. When the gale subsided, an examination showed that no damage had been done. The water was pumped out of the caisson, and pushing it down the ways was resumed. Finally, on March 31st, at 10 A. M., our efforts were rewarded, and by 3 P. M. the caisson was safely moored in the port of Alexandria, having been towed around by the Peninsular and Oriental Company's tug "Ausari." Plate xii, *A*, illustrates the method adopted for pushing the caisson afloat with the hydraulic pumps (P) applied to the ends of the keelsons (K). The anchor against which the pumps bore was a timber beam let into a slot cut in the upper part of the ways and held in place by chain lashings. The beam had to be shifted when the caisson had moved about ten feet; the space between the pumps and beam was filled with blocking, which could not be held in place when it exceeded ten feet in aggregate length. The force required to move the caisson varied unaccountably from about one hundred tons pressure down to not less than ten. The cause of all this difficulty was subsequently ascertained to be the stripping of the sliding ways, doubtless through the presence of some hard substance that had been washed in by the surf during the storm of March 18th.

PURCHASE OF THE STEAMER "DESSOUG."

While the operations of lowering the obelisk and launching the caisson had been progressing, preparations were being made for embarking the obelisk on the steamer "Dessoug." This vessel had been purchased from the Egyptian government expressly for transporting the obelisk to New York. She is an iron steamer built in England in 1864 for the Egyptian government, and had been employed chiefly in the Egyptian postal service between Alexandria, Smyrna, and Constantinople. Extravagance and corruption in the service had caused the withdrawal of several of the steamers employed in it, the "Dessoug" among them. The service had never been a profitable one to the Egyptian treasury. When the financial administration of Egypt passed under the control of a European commission, abolishing the service altogether was contemplated; but the influence of the European employés effected a compromise, and it was finally determined to continue the service under the management of Europeans, as long as it did not sink money and draw the deficiencies from the Egyptian treasury. To insure this result superfluous vessels and useless material were sold from time to time for any thing they would bring. Very soon after our arrival at Alexandria, and while still negotiating for the charter or purchase of English and Italian steamers, my attention was attracted to the "Dessoug," then lying dismantled in the arsenal, chiefly by the fulness of her form, and particularly of her bow-lines. Measurements were made, which satisfied us that there was just height enough under the lower-deck beams to embark the obelisk, and length enough to get it entirely into the fore compartment, between the collision and coal-bunker bulkheads; and as this was an exceptionally advantageous feature of the vessel her purchase was determined on. Her engines and boilers were known to be in bad condition, but her hull was perfect; her hold was filthy, and she had been neglected to a degree that cannot be imagined. To refit and repair her, a long time and a large expenditure were necessary, which made it essential to purchase her at a low price. To effect this it was decided not to make an offer at once, but to treat the matter with apparent indifference. The result was the commencement of negotiations by the Assistant Postmaster-General, as we would term him here, which gave me a very decided advantage in conducting them. After several informal conferences an offer of £5,000 sterling was made in writing to the Postmaster-General, who affected to regard it as a joke, and suggested that the matter be treated seriously as to price, adding that other negotiations were pending for the purchase of the "Dessoug." A firm of shipbrokers who had been trying to charter or sell me a vessel had been informed of my negotiations with the Egyptian government for the purchase of a vessel, and had made an indefinite offer for the "Dessoug," with a view to being bought off by me. One member of the firm proposed to withdraw his offer if he was paid a commission of ten per cent. on the purchase-money. This was treated in a

EMBARKING THE PEDESTAL.

way it deserved; and in order to bring matters to a crisis formal notice was given to the Ministry at Cairo that my offer would be withdrawn at noon of December 3, 1879, unless it had been formally accepted before. The government then accepted the offer of the brokers, and demanded a guarantee of payment within a specified time. As they had no use for the vessel except to sell her to me, they offered her to me for £6,000. They were informed that the "Dessoug" would not be purchased from them under any circumstances. They could not give the guarantee demanded, and when the time allowed them had lapsed, I was notified that I could have the vessel on the payment of £5,100 sterling. The money was promptly paid, and the transfer effected on December 3d. It cost nearly as much more to refit, repair, and clean the "Dessoug"; and this work was carried on under the immediate supervision of Lieutenant Seaton Schroeder, U. S. N., simultaneously with that of lowering and launching the obelisk, to which I gave my personal attention. Pending the negotiations for the purchase of the "Dessoug," one other of the government vessels laid up in the arsenal was sold. Before the transfer from the government to the purchaser could be effected, a warrant was issued by the court taking possession of the vessel, or the money paid for her, in the interest of some one who had a claim against the Egyptian government. To avoid a repetition of this inexplicable performance in the transfer of the "Dessoug," the conclusion of the purchase and time fixed for transfer were kept secret. The transfer was effected in the office of the Director of the Postal Service, whose representative accompanied me on board, and hauled down the Egyptian flag, while I hoisted United States ensigns to the mast-heads and peaks. The Arabs in immediate charge of the vessel looked on in amazement at this performance. When ordered to gather up their personal effects and leave the vessel, they made no protest, but deferred their departure until they had prayed fervently and impressively. That a seizure of the "Dessoug" had been arranged for there can be no doubt, but no serious attempt was ever made to execute it. A notice in Arabic, Greek, Italian, French, and English was posted on each gangway, prohibiting any one from going on board without a pass from Lieutenant Schroeder, at the peril of their lives. Several persons approached the gangways in boats near enough to read the notice, but made no attempt to board the vessel. Any such attempt would have been met by force, if necessary. In justification of this course it must be conceded that the court had no right to issue a warrant to seize the property of an American citizen, unless it was for debt or violation of Egyptian law. Neither of these causes existed, and as there was no one on whom I could call for protection, I was bound to protect my property myself, with all the means in my power.

The nationality of the "Dessoug" was a delicate question to settle. Under the laws of the United States she could not be registered as an American vessel. Sailing under the Egyptian flag would have involved serious risks and embarrassments, especially in connection with the crew. The British or other European flag would have been more objectionable from every standpoint, especially in the evasion of laws relating to ownership. There was no other course than open defiance of law, which the circumstances fully justified; and I determined to make the voyage from Alexandria to New York without registry or nationality, thereby taking the risk of having my steamer seized by any vessel of war at sea, or by the authorities of any port I might be obliged to touch at. Gibraltar was the only port that it was desirable for me to touch at, and there only for coal. Personal acquaintance with the chief military and naval authorities there gave me confidence that the ship's papers would not be too closely examined. To remove all risk I made arrangements for taking in coal from lighters awaiting our arrival on the eastern side of Gibraltar Peninsula, in the event of any hesitation to admit us to the port.

The following is the only "document" I should have been able to produce, had the "ship's papers" been demanded.

ALEXANDRIA, 2d *December*, 1879,
12 o'clock noon.

In consideration of the sum of £5,100 sterling paid by Captain Gorringe, the Director-General of Posts, duly authorized by the Egyptian government, transfers the S. S. "Dessoug," with her equipment, into his possession, and recognizes that he is the sole proprietor from this moment.

The Director-General of Posts,

CAILLARD.

THE EMBARKATION OF THE OBELISK DELAYED.

One of the conditions of the purchase of the "Dessoug" was that the government floating-dock should be used for embarking the obelisk as soon as it was ready for embarkation. The English cylinder containing the London obelisk had been placed in the dock for repairs prior to its departure from Alexandria, and a charge only for actual expenses incurred, was made. The order of Riaz Pacha, the President of the Council of Ministers, that we should have the same privileges as the English, was reiterated, at my request, in relation to the use of the dock, and every precaution possible was taken to ensure admittance to it as soon as the obelisk arrived in the port. It arrived on March 31st, and was all ready to enter on the next day. But the Egyptian official, who had control of the dock, had other plans; he ordered several small river steamers to be hauled in, which was done without a word of warning to us; and before we could appeal to Cairo the dock was pumped out and plates torn off the bottoms of the steamers, so that they would not float and could not be ordered out by the Ministry. The steamers were of such a size that hauling them out of water, on shore, would have cost less than it did to dock them. The conduct of the official cannot therefore be excused on any ground.

Nearly five weeks elapsed before the dock was again disengaged. The caisson containing the obelisk was, however, placed in it on April 12th, by lowering the dock to a depth of seven feet, which did not affect the small steamers beyond washing out their filthy holds and destroying some of the vermin for which they are justly celebrated. The official referred to, fought hard to prevent even this being done, and would not yield, in spite of peremptory orders from the Ministry in Cairo, until I had consented to the docking of another vessel before the "Dessoug" was placed in the dock. This I had to do, as the caisson was leaking badly and there was danger of its being sunk by accident or design as long as it was afloat. As soon as it was in the dock it was demolished, not so much to advance the work of embarkation as to insure the obelisk not being removed from the dock until it had been embarked in the "Dessoug."

There was a widespread belief in Alexandria that the obelisk could not be embarked in the manner proposed, and this had doubtless influenced the action of the official, who spoke of the embarkation as something that would either entirely destroy the dock or at least occupy it to the exclusion of all other business for a very long time.

TRANSPORTING AND EMBARKING THE PEDESTAL AND STEPS.

It had been intended to use the caisson that took the obelisk to the port, for removing the pedestal and steps. To avoid delay and utilize the time we were obliged to wait for the dock, we chartered a lighter that had been used in the construction of the breakwater of Alexandria harbor, and hauled her up on the same ways that the caisson was launched on. After the lighter had been hauled up and carefully blocked, the pedestal was raised by the hydraulic pumps to the height of her deck, and moved on it in the same manner as it had been moved aside from under the obelisk, by placing it on cannon-balls. The steps and foundation and the pieces comprising the turning struc-

EMBARKING THE OBELISK.

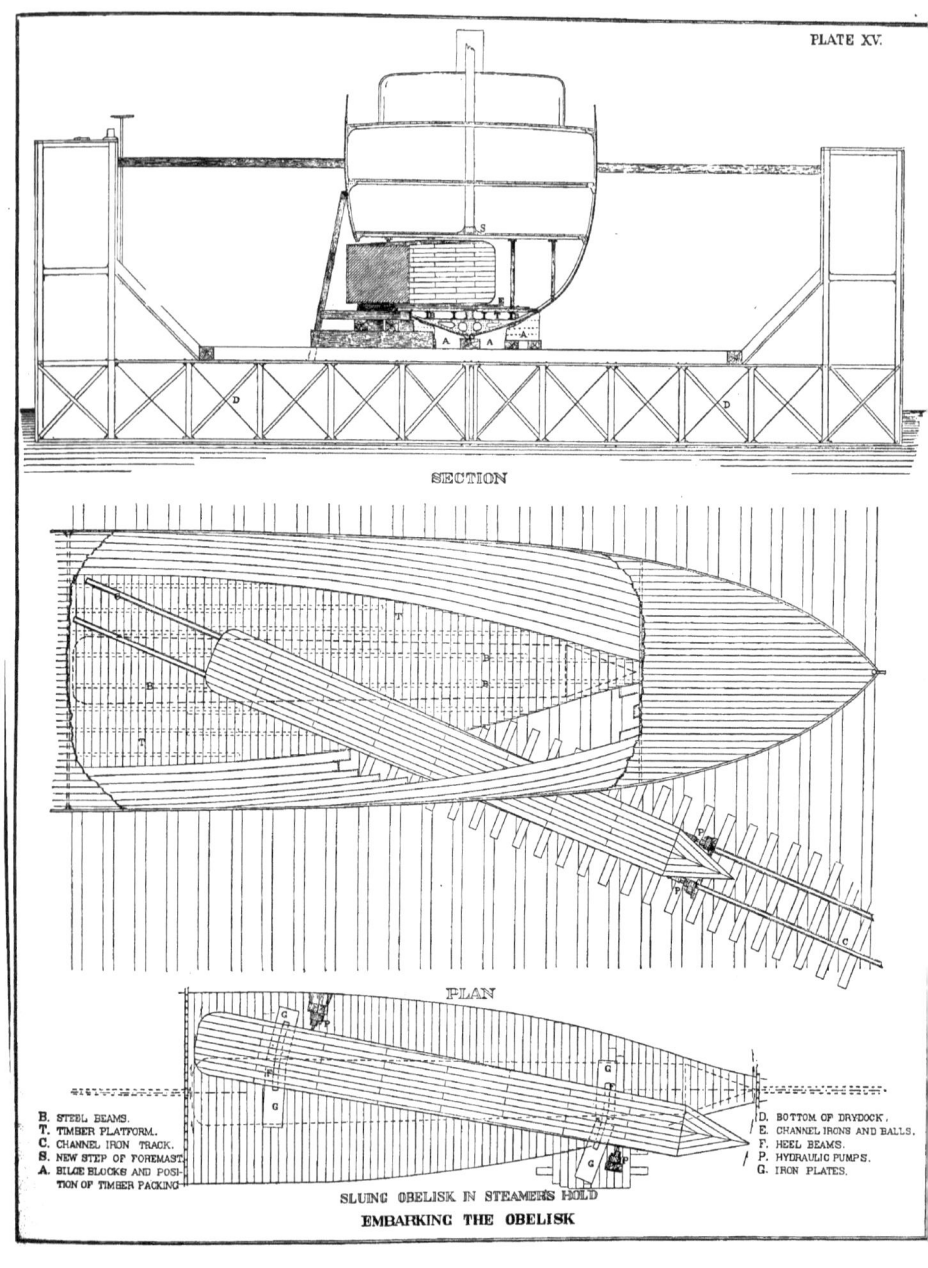

Removal of the New York Obelisk. 25

ture were also placed on the deck of the lighter, which had been designed to sustain a load of two hundred tons. The aggregate load placed on it was one hundred and seventy tons. Every thing having been secured for the trip by sea around to the port, the lighter was successfully launched and towed around on May 1st.

The pedestal weighs nearly fifty tons. It had to be placed in the after-hatchway, on an iron frame or stand that had been prepared for it and constructed so as to distribute the weight over a larger area than that of the side or base. There was just room enough in the hatchway to admit the pedestal sideways. To get it into the ship it had to be turned over on its side first, and then lifted thirty feet above the deck of the lighter to clear the bulwarks of the "Dessoug." The most powerful crane in Alexandria was one on the arsenal quay, capable of lifting only thirty tons. Besides this there was a floating steam-derrick capable of lifting twenty-five tons. Before incurring the expense of rigging special shears, it was determined to try lifting the pedestal simultaneously with the crane on shore and the derrick afloat. To insure proportionate distribution of the weight between the crane and derrick, a computation was made to determine the displacement of the floating derrick at different angles of the plane of the deck of the float with that of the water, and a mark was placed on the float at the point to which it would be submerged when sustaining a weight of twenty-two tons on the hoisting chain. This enabled us to insure no more than twenty-eight tons weight on the shore crane by keeping the mark on the float at the water level, which was made possible by the more rapid lifting purchase on the floating derrick. (See Plate xiii.)

The pedestal was slung with four parts of steel-wire cable, one and a half inches in diameter, capable, theoretically, of sustaining three times its weight. The lighter was hauled under the purchases, between the floating derrick and the quay; the purchases were hooked to the wire cable on one side of the pedestal, which was quickly turned over, and gradually lifted clear of the lighter without indications of excessive strain on any thing. The lifting continued until the pedestal was thirty feet in the air and high enough to clear the steamer's rail. The lighter having been hauled out, the stern of the steamer was being hauled under when a sharp sound was heard and the pedestal was observed to be oscillating. It was known positively that nothing had touched it to cause oscillation or vibration. If it had fallen while the steamer's stern was under it the destruction of that end of the vessel would have been the result. The "Dessoug" was hauled ahead as rapidly as possible; when her stern was well clear and nothing remained between the pedestal and the water, an examination was made, and one of the four parts of the steel-wire rope with which it was slung was found to have stranded. Only two of the seven strands remained uninjured. The pedestal was then lowered in the full expectation that it would fall into the water, whence it could be recovered without serious difficulty. But the two strands held on; and the lighter having been hauled underneath, the pedestal was once more safely landed on her deck. The cause of the stranding of the wire rope has never been explained. On the day following, May 6th, the pedestal was slung with a part of the "Dessoug's" bower chain cable, by which it was hoisted to the requisite height; and after the steamer had been placed in position, it was lowered into the hatchway and landed on the stand without incident. (See Plate xiii.)

EMBARKATION OF THE OBELISK.

During the four months that elapsed between the purchase of the steamer and arrival of the obelisk in the port, preparations had been made to embark the obelisk with dispatch. A platform had been constructed in the forehold by bolting the steel beams (B, Plate xv) of the turning structure to the frames of the vessel, and building on it a timber bed (T, Plate xv) on which the channel-iron tracks (C, Plate xv) could be placed in any direction desired. The steel beams gave great additional longitudinal strength to the hull, and served to distribute the weight of the obelisk over the whole structure. Without them the weight would have been concentrated on the keelson. Other preparations consisted in removing the single row of stanchions that held up the lower deck from over the keelsons, and substituting for them two rows, one on each side, over the bilge keelsons. The foremast was unstepped, and that part below the lower deck cut off. A new step on the lower deck was provided and the mast replaced. The frames that had to be removed to make the aperture for admitting the obelisk had all been cut, and the pieces for replacing them had been shaped, drilled, and fitted to their places with screw bolts. The plates above the water-line had been removed, and a large supply of tools provided for cutting off and driving out rivets, and for replacing them.

On May 10th the "Dessoug" entered the dock. A foreman shipwright from Glasgow had been brought to Alexandria expressly to superintend the opening and closing of the aperture. Three gangs of thirty men each, of Arab boiler-makers, had been selected and engaged; and as soon as the vessel was high and dry the work began, and was carried on without intermission day and night, each gang working eight hours, until the aperture had been opened. About seven thousand rivets, sixteen frames, and thirty plates had to be removed from the starboard bow to make the aperture large enough to admit the obelisk at the angle of 21° with the keel, the greatest angle at which it could be embarked without turning it twice during the embarkation. (See Plates xiv and xv.)

When the caisson containing the obelisk had been placed in the dock, it was placed at this angle with the axis of the dock. And when the "Dessoug" was hauled in, her bow was hauled up to the proper distance from the base of the obelisk, and held there until it had landed on the keel blocks; so that, when the dock had been pumped out, the relative positions of the vessel and the obelisk were exactly as they were designed to be.

While the aperture was being opened, gangs of carpenters were engaged in packing timber under the forward run of the steamer's hull, and under the track of the obelisk, so as to prevent straining of the frames. (Plate xv.) Only those who were engaged in this work can realize the difficulty of shaping the timbers to fit closely to the iron, and this consumed a large part of the time occupied in preparing to embark the obelisk. It was so thoroughly executed, however, that not one rivet or seam admitted a drop of water after the vessel was afloat, a result not even dreamed of. It was expected that the vessel would leak freely in all seams under the track of the obelisk, and extra provision had been made to pump out the water during the voyage.

The space that intervened between the obelisk and the aperture was bridged over with heavy timbers, supported on very long oak beams laid on the flooring of the dock, directly over the trusses D, Plate xv, that extended across the bottom of the dock. The bed of the track was thus a continuous one from where the obelisk had been landed on the dock, through the aperture, and into the hold. As soon as this track had been completed, the obelisk was raised by the hydraulic pumps, and while suspended on them the channel irons and cannon-balls E were placed under it on each side, near the edges. Soft wood was packed in between the upper channel iron and the obelisk to insure uniform pressure on the balls. The obelisk was then landed on the channel irons. The balls were $5\frac{1}{4}$ inches in diameter, and placed at intervals of 18 inches. Plates xiv and xv give a better idea than can possibly be given in words, of the general plan for embarking the obelisk. Plate xiv is taken from a photograph made while the obelisk was actually in motion, and just as its base was entering the aperture.

The power employed for moving it was two hydraulic pumps (P) pushing against the outer end, and at no time was it necessary to exert more than five tons pressure in order to start it. The time occupied in opening the aperture, laying the track, blocking under the vessel, and placing the obelisk on the channel irons and balls, was ten days; the time occupied in embarking the obelisk was eight hours.

Removal of the New York Obelisk.

The ship's frames were replaced as fast as there was room for them to be fitted into position, and almost as soon as the point of the pyramidion was within the vessel the last frame was up and riveted.

As soon as the obelisk was entirely inside of the hold it was lifted clear of the track, which was then removed from under it. There was hardly room enough to lift the weight clear of the channel irons; the work of removing them and the balls was tedious and trying beyond description. There was so little room to spare that all operations inside of the vessel were greatly embarrassed and delayed.

Plate xv illustrates the apparatus for turning the obelisk to parallel with the steamer's keel, with the axis directly amidships. The bending of the heel beams of the turning structure, it will be remembered, had caused me much chagrin when the weight of the obelisk had been transferred to them (see page 14). The bent keel beams (F) were utilized in the arrangement of the "turn-table," shown under each end of the obelisk in this figure. The obelisk was landed on them, with soft wood intervening to prevent injury to the edges; underneath the keel beams were the iron plates G, also belonging to the turning structure. These are shown on Plate ii in the position they were used while turning the obelisk horizontal in Alexandria, and on Plate xxviii while placing it on its pedestal in New York. Their function in the operation (illustrated on Plate xv) of turning the obelisk parallel with the keel was simply to reduce friction. The arrangement of this "turn-table" occupied two days. When it had been completed, hydraulic pumps (P, Plate xv, lower figure) were applied to the two ends of the obelisk, in opposite directions, and the obelisk was moved into position in three quarters of an hour. Shores were set between the ship's side, where the pumps rested, and the dock, to form anchors for the pumps to work against. The force exerted in turning the obelisk was equivalent to about twenty tons.

PREPARING FOR THE VOYAGE.

On June 1, 1881, three weeks from the day the vessel entered the dock to embark the obelisk, she was floated out with the obelisk on board. She was immediately hauled under the arsenal shears, to re-embark her ballast and equipments that had been removed prior to entering the dock, and to embark the pieces forming the base and steps of the obelisk. The largest of these pieces weighed seven tons, and the smallest nearly a ton. A force of the best shipwrights that could be hired in Alexandria was engaged shoring and stowing the obelisk for the sea-voyage. To obviate all risk of breaking the obelisk by the working of the ship, it was placed on a bed of Adriatic white pine, very spongy and soft, and ten feet of the extremities left without support. To prevent it from moving laterally, a system of horizontal, diagonal, and vertical shores were fitted into the hieroglyphs, and driven against the stringer-pieces of the steamer's hull; and the vacant spaces between the deck beams and the upper face were packed with wood so tightly that the wedges had to be cut out after our arrival in New York. The diagonal shores from the lower edges of the side faces were notched on the outboard ends, which were driven astride of the webs of the lower deck beams, and then shored up from the wing stringer-pieces. This alone made it impossible for the obelisk to move in any direction, and I have no hesitation in stating that the vessel might have laid on her "beam ends" without causing the obelisk to break adrift.

A judicious distribution of the pieces forming the steps and base, the ballast, and the pieces forming the turning structure, and other heavy material, brought the vessel to a good trim, and insured easy motion in a sea-way. Additional coal-bunkers were provided by building bulkheads between the upper and the second decks.

Providing a crew and securing a reasonable rate of insurance for the voyage had been the cause of endless trouble and negotiation from the day the vessel was purchased until the day she sailed. As there are no commercial steam-vessels of the United States trading to Mediterranean ports, I was obliged to send to Great Britain for officers and engineers, and to Trieste for a crew. The chief engineer, a Scotchman, had been in the Egyptian postal service, and had served several years on the "Dessoug" while she was employed in that service. He was engaged the day after the steamer was purchased, and remained on full pay during the five months and a half that elapsed between that date and our departure. He was supposed during this time to be engaged in thoroughly examining, overhauling, and repairing the machinery and boilers, having been provided with skilled mechanics to assist him. Yet he allowed a serious flaw in the shaft to escape detection. The first and second officers, the second and third engineers, and three quartermasters were sent for, to England. The first and second officers turned out to be confirmed drunkards; the latter so bad that he had to be dismissed to prevent him from killing himself. He fell twice from the second deck into the hold, and twice overboard, while drunk. The engineers were useful, hard-working, hard-drinking men. The quartermasters would do credit to a pirate's crew. The number of men who solemnly enlisted for the voyage and speedily deserted before it began, was forty-eight. Despairing of being able to secure a crew in Alexandria, I sent my power of attorney to Trieste, to a ship-agent there, with authority to enlist the requisite number, and, in addition, to make a contract with each one for the voyage. I relied on having these men arrive upon the day the vessel was ready for sea, and on getting away from the port before they had time to think about it. They arrived, however, the day the vessel was floated out of the dock. All but three remained. One man that had been shipped in Alexandria, named Jacob Zuratich, a Delmatian, stuck to the vessel throughout. It was his influence over his countrymen from Trieste that made them remain by the vessel and undertake the voyage. As the "Dessoug" had no nationality, deserters could not be arrested. But four of the crew, besides the quartermasters, could speak or understand a word of English. It must be evident that, considering the circumstances, commanding the "Dessoug" was not the most desirable and comfortable of occupations. Without the means of legally enforcing discipline, the only available method was the summary one.

The embarkation of every thing but coal was completed by June 7th. On the 8th the vessel was hauled away from the quay and moored to buoys. On that day and the next, five hundred tons of coal were taken on board. On the 9th and 11th I visited Cairo to take my leave of the Khedive and his Ministers, and to thank them for not having yielded to the pressure and influence exerted by foreign residents to revoke the gift, and for their steadfast friendship throughout. They expressed the greatest gratification at the successful removal and embarkation of the obelisk without damage, stating that otherwise it would have been embarrassing to them.

On my return to Alexandria the only thing remaining to complete our preparations was the final arrangements for insurance. The underwriters had yielded gradually from their demands for twenty-five per cent. premium down to five per cent., at which they stuck. I had insisted that the marine risk was not an extraordinary one if the general average clause was omitted and their liability for damage limited to total loss, and I gave notice to my London agent that I would pay no more than two per cent., and make the voyage without insurance if this rate was not conceded. After holding out for five per cent. until the day before our departure, the agents telegraphed to Europe that the steamer would certainly proceed to sea without insurance on the next day. This brought me a great many acceptances of two per cent., and insurance was effected by telegraph at this rate in a number of selected companies. Finally, at 2 P.M., of Saturday, June 12th, the moorings were cast off and the "Dessoug" steamed out of port amidst the sounding of steam-whistles, the cheers of ships' crews and boatmen, and a general dipping of colors. One gentleman who had watched our work with close attention bade me good-by, saying that he hoped we had good boats, well equipped and provisioned. A boat load of the Arabs who had been employed on the work all the time we were in Alexandria accompanied us to the entrance of the port, and hastily took their departure when the vessel began

DISEMBARKING THE PEDESTAL

to feel the swell and to roll. To Lieutenant Schroeder and myself the open sea, with the comparative rest and relief that it brought, was acceptable and enjoyable beyond expression.

THE VOYAGE.

The wind freshened and the sea increased gradually as we drew away from the land. The behavior of the vessel was most satisfactory; her pitching motion was slow and easy, her rolling exceptionally gentle. Perfect confidence in the efficiency of the stowage and the ability of the steamer to make the voyage with no greater risk than is involved in any similar voyage, was quickly acquired by the crew, who settled down to the monotonous routine of an ordinary merchant-steamer. The head-wind and sea continued for four days. During one night it blew a moderate gale, and while off the coast of Algiers we experienced violent squalls, accompanied by intense electrical discharges. Passing Malta at noon of the 17th, we ran close in to attract attention, so as to be reported to the Maritime Exchange in London. Having no distinguishing signal or registered number, the name of the vessel had been painted on the bows and stern in letters two feet long. At 8.30 P. M. of June 22d, we anchored off Gibraltar, having steamed 1,738 knots, and averaged almost exactly seven knots per hour. The only unpleasant feature of this passage was the leaking of both boilers in every furnace, which prevented them from making adequate steam. There was no excuse for this condition of the boilers. The chief engineer had been allowed all the labor and material he wanted to put them in efficient condition, had expended enough to do so, and had reported them thoroughly repaired. Immediately after our arrival at Gibraltar the fires were hauled, and as soon as the boilers had cooled off sufficiently, a force was put on to repair them. This work detained us three days, during which we took in five hundred and fifty tons of coal. A large number of people visited the ship to see the obelisk, among them Lord Napier of Magdala, the Governor, and his staff, accompanied by Lady Napier and a number of other ladies.

We sailed from Gibraltar at midnight of June 25–26th, having on board a total dead weight of 1,470 tons, not including fixtures of the vessel, drawing 15 feet forward and $17\frac{1}{2}$ feet aft. On the following day we experienced a fresh breeze from the northward, and a heavy beam sea which caused the vessel to roll deeply. On June 30th we passed through the Azores, the weather having been variable and at times disagreeable. On July 6th, at 8.30 P. M., when 1,500 miles from New York, with a smooth sea and a moderately fair wind, the engines came to an abrupt standstill after a short interval of unusual and noisy performance. Examination showed that the after-crank shaft had broken through an old flaw or crack in the after-web. Fortunately, the breaking of the shaft was the only damage done, and there were two spare sections of shaft on board, one of which belonged to the after-engine. Boring the large holes in and fitting the brasses to the new section, occupied all the men that could work at it, night and day, until July 10th. Connecting the engines took two days more. On July 12th we started ahead again under steam.

A curious incident in this connection is the persistency with which I insisted on having this section of the shaft delivered to me from the arsenal in Alexandria. According to the terms of purchase, "all equipments and spare articles on board and in store, that properly belonged to the 'Dessoug,' were included." This section of the shaft was in store, and it took me four months to get the authorities to deliver it. They had no use for it, and it appeared to them as if I had not; but it belonged to me, it was an excellent thing to have on board, and I never ceased demanding it until it was delivered, five days prior to our departure from Alexandria.

During the six days we were replacing the broken shaft the progress of the vessel, under sail alone, toward New York was seventy-six knots. At this rate it would have taken us one hundred and twenty days to complete the voyage. On the day following the accident we communicated with and purchased some bread from the Austrian bark "Nettuno" of Perzagno, Captain Emilia Zucovich, twelve days out from New York, bound to Constantinople, with a cargo of petroleum. The following telegram was delivered to the captain, with the request to send it from the first port he touched at:

SECRETARY OF THE NAVY, WASHINGTON, DISTRICT OF COLUMBIA, UNITED STATES OF AMERICA.

Steamer "Dessoug," with obelisk, broke crank shaft July 6th, latitude $37°$, longitude $47°$. Spare shaft is being fitted; probable detention ten days. Until repairs are completed will try to keep between parallels $37°$ and $38°$.

The dispatch reached Washington about two weeks after the "Dessoug" reached New York, having been sent from one of the Azores.

An incident occurred on July 10th which caused me more anxiety than any thing else during the voyage, much more than the breaking of the shaft. The weather had been squally, with heavy rain all day. Water-spouts were seen to form and dissipate without completing the column several times during the day. One formed directly to windward of the vessel, and after appearing to dissipate, it suddenly reformed much larger than before, and began moving directly toward us. Every precaution was taken to cover the hatches and skylights and open the bulwark ports, so as to exclude the water from below. After watching it closely it was evident that we were in for a deluge unless the course of the vessel could be changed. This was impossible owing to the lack of wind, which had in the meantime entirely died out. There was nothing to do but to await the deluge calmly, for we had no cannon to fire and break the spout. It kept us in suspense for about five minutes, and then abruptly changed its course, passed about fifty yards ahead of us, and broke with some noise about a thousand yards from the vessel. The danger feared was in the probable bursting in of our decks by the weight of the column of water which appeared at least fifty feet in height.

On July 13th, 14th, and 15th we experienced a westerly gale, which blew very hard from S. W. during the night of the 14th and day of the 15th, with a high sea that almost arrested our progress entirely. The behavior of the vessel was exceptionally good, as far as her motion was concerned, but she shipped two seas, among many others, which did considerable damage to boats and skylights. Very close watch was kept of the obelisk and its fastenings, but not the least motion was detected in any thing connected with them. With the fullest confidence that the vessel was able to stand any weather, she was held to her course and driven through the gale as hard as the boilers would permit, so as to reach port on the day set for our arrival—not later than July 20th,—and to avoid the usual but needless anxieties experienced by landsmen when vessels are overdue.

On the morning of July 19th we took on board Pilot Murphy, from N. Y. Pilot-boat A. M. Lawrence, No. 4. On that evening we stood in toward Fire Island, and made a pre-arranged signal which caused us to be reported in New York. At 2 A.M. of July 20th we anchored off Staten Island, at the Quarantine Station, and after having been granted pratique, moved up the Hudson and moored off Twenty-third Street during the afternoon. The crew and officers were promptly discharged, excepting three Arabs, who had been brought over, at their own urgent request, as cabin servants. One of these, a boy named Hassan, was an object of as great curiosity as the obelisk. During the ten days from July 20th to 30th the "Dessoug" was thrown open to visitors. On one day seventeen hundred and eleven persons visited the vessel between 7 A.M. and 8 P.M.

SELECTING THE SITE.

Before our departure from the United States in August, 1879, the spot on which the obelisk was to be erected in New York had been selected, after due deliberation, by Mr. F. E. Church, Mr.

TRUCKING THE PEDESTAL

Removal of the New York Obelisk.   31

W. H. Hurlbert, and myself. Mr. W. H. Vanderbilt had expressed a preference for the Central Park, in the vicinity of the Metropolitan Museum. In order to avoid needless discussion of the subject, it was decided to maintain the strictest secrecy as to the location determined on. The site that was adopted, the spot on which the obelisk now stands, is perhaps the worst one within the city limits for getting an obelisk to. It involved a much larger expenditure for transport by land, as it was a more difficult route than any other site that had been proposed. The other sites most warmly advocated were the circles at the intersection of Fifth and Eighth Avenues and Fifty-ninth Street, at the S. E. and S. W. entrances to the Central Park. The reasons given were: the ease with which the obelisk could be reached by the public, the desirableness of having it stand on level land, and the advantage of having it near some building. The objections were: the probability of having the obelisk surrounded by tall buildings, towering above it and dwarfing it by contrast; and the certainty that these buildings would not have one feature in common with the sublime architecture represented by the obelisk. There can hardly be found a wider separation of architectural design than an ancient Egyptian temple and a modern New York building. The best site for the obelisk was the one that insured its isolation, and this consideration resulted in the selection of the Graywacke Knoll. The objection that it would not be easy of access does not seem reasonable, in view of the prevailing opinion and hope that the Central Park will be at no very distant day what its name implies, and the assumption that the obelisk will stand where it is long after this has been realized. Few persons will deny that the Graywacke Knoll is the best site within the limits of the park. It is near the Metropolitan Museum of Art and Antiquities, with which the obelisk is intimately associated; it is close to the favorite drives and walks; it is a mass of solid granite that affords a natural and imperishable foundation on which the obelisk will stand erect until it is pulled down by man or thrown down by some violent convulsion of nature; and it is one of the highest points on Manhattan Island, without the appearance of being elevated.

At the regular meeting of the Board of Commissioners of the Department of Parks on May 5, 1879, a communication was presented from the Honorable Henry G. Stebbins, in behalf of the gentlemen interested in the removal of the obelisk, asking that the site they recommended may be formally selected by the Department. This was unanimously agreed to, and the desired permission duly recorded. Soon after the arrival of the "Dessoug" this decision of the Board was reconsidered, and the question remained unsettled until July 27th. On that day, after discussion and examination of the other sites urged on the Board, a final decision was reached, designating the summit of Graywacke Knoll as the spot upon which the obelisk was to stand.

DISEMBARKING AND TRANSPORTING THE PEDESTAL.

Circumstances made it easy to select a landing-place and a route for the obelisk. The rapid tidal currents and short intervals of slack water made a landing on the East River shore undesirable, although the grades are more uniform, the route more direct, and the distance less. The steep slopes on the North River shore abreast of the park have but one break, and that is through Ninety-sixth Street. At the foot of this street, therefore, the obelisk had to be landed. But it was not possible to move the pedestal by truck over the roadway of this Street, and another landing-place had to be found for it. The wharf at the foot of Fifty-first street was finally selected, and the "Dessoug" moored alongside of it on July 31st. The derrick belonging to the Dock Department of the city had in the meantime been loaned by the Dock Commissioners, on condition that all expenses incurred by the Department would be paid by me. Discharging the foundation and steps was begun on August 1st, and on the 4th the pedestal was lifted out of the steamer and landed on the dock by the derrick with an ease and rapidity that contrasted strangely with its embarkation in Alexandria.

The accompanying Plate (xvii) shows the pedestal suspended to the derrick. While so suspended the steamer was hauled ahead, and when she was out of the way, the arm of the derrick was swung around, and the pedestal landed on the wharf, as near as possible to the shore. From this point it was moved by sliding it on heavy timbers (skids) to a convenient place about five hundred feet distant, there to await the partial rebuilding of a truck that was to carry it to the Central Park. This truck was the only one in the city capable of sustaining a load of fifty tons that was suitable for moving the pedestal. It belonged to the firm of W. B. Smith & Sons, who made a reasonable offer to move the pedestal foundation and steps to their destination, and with whom I contracted to do that work.

Plate xviii illustrates the method of suspending the pedestal on the truck. Difficulty was experienced in several places in keeping the wheels from sinking into the pavements. They had only to sink nine inches for the chain slings, by which the stone was suspended to the beams, to touch the ground. Whenever this occurred the slings had to be slackened until the truck was released, and the wheels placed on timber laid on the pavement, and the stone again suspended. Thirty-two horses in sixteen pairs were attached to the truck for hauling it. The first forward movement was invariably given by hydraulic pumps applied to the tire of the rear wheels. As soon as the truck was in motion the horses were started and kept going on a slow trot until the wheels again sank into the pavements. The route was through Fifty-first Street to Fifth Avenue, through Fifth Avenue to the Eighty-second Street east entrance to the park, where the truck was dispensed with. Thence to the site the pedestal was moved on greased skids. This stone is the largest and heaviest moved on wheels of which there is any record, and excepting the obelisk it is the largest ever moved through New York City.

THE FOUNDATION.

It was not until August 5th that any action was taken by the Department of Parks to prepare the Graywacke Knoll for the foundation. On that day four laborers of the Department commenced removing the young trees that stood on it and clearing away the surface. A few days later the work was suspended without apparent reason. The invariable custom of the Department had been to prepare foundations for the reception of monuments and statuary contributed by individuals to the adornment of the city. In this case the custom was violated. Anxious that the foundation should be prepared before winter set in, I sought almost daily at the Department for the requisite authority to proceed with the work at my own expense. This was withheld until August 27th, and then granted under onerous conditions that involved a large increase in the cost of the work of placing the obelisk on the site assigned it.

The earth having been removed from the top of the knoll, the surface of the granite was levelled and the cavities filled with cement. A thin layer of this was then laid over the granite, and the foundation was replaced exactly as it had stood in Alexandria, each piece in the same relative position to the others, and to the points of the compass. Instead of leaving the interstices vacant as the Romans had done, they were filled with the best cement obtainable, thus making the structure as solid a mass as the granite on which it stands and as the syenite that stands on it. Each piece was bound to the other by iron and steel clamps similar to those that had been used by the Romans, which we had necessarily removed when taking the foundation apart in Alexandria.

A number of lead boxes of different shapes and sizes had been prepared to fit into available spaces enclosed by the steps, and into these were placed the various articles contributed by the Departments in Washington and by individuals. The boxes were carefully soldered up and completely encased in cement, so as to exclude air from their contents. Applications for space in them came from all over the country. Some were evidently prompted by vanity, others by a hope of advertisement, but the majority were based on a common-sense desire to perpetuate some examples

LAYING THE CORNER-STONE.

Plate XVIII a

of our civilization. I made an effort to secure a complete telephone system, but failed. I asked the representative of the American Bible Society to contribute the New Testament, or any part of it, in all the ancient and modern languages and dialects into which it had been translated and published. He referred me to the book-store where I could buy them. I did buy them; and they were carefully deposited in a lead case, where they will be preserved for an indefinite period. One of the persons connected with this Society displayed much zeal in the effort to have the names of the officers of the Society deposited with the New Testament. He did not succeed. I made application to the United States Coast and Geodetic Survey for standards of the weights and measures of the United States for deposit. I also asked for specimen copies of the publications of the office. Both were refused without assigning a reason.

The Departments at Washington contributed the following named articles which were duly deposited in copper cases hermetically sealed, enclosed in lead cases carefully soldered, and these again in a mass of cement:

THE DEPARTMENT OF STATE.—A copy of Federal and State Constitutions, colonial charters, and other organic laws of the United States. Congressional Directory for 1880. Fac-simile of the Declaration of Independence. Revised Statutes of the United States, 1878. Statutes relating to the District of Columbia and post-roads, XLIII Congress, 1873-4. Copies of papers on file in the Department, relating to the presentation, by His Highness, Ismaïl I, Khedive of Egypt, of the obelisk to the city of New York.

THE TREASURY DEPARTMENT.—A full set of medals of the Presidents of the United States. A full proof set of the silver and minor coinage for the year 1880. A collection of documents and engravings selected from those on file in the Department.

DEPARTMENT OF THE INTERIOR.—Official Register of the United States, 1879. Compendium of the Ninth Census, 1870. Report of the Secretary of the Interior, and accompanying documents, 1879. Report of Commissioner of Education, 1877. Catalogue of publications of Hayden's surveys. Register of the Department of the Interior, 1880.

WAR DEPARTMENT.—Official Army Register, 1880, corrected to September 17th. Signal Office International Bulletin. Tri-daily weather maps. Monthly weather record for July, 1880. General order announcing death of General Myer.

NAVY DEPARTMENT.—Navy Registers for January and July, 1880. Report of the Secretary of the Navy for 1879. Report of the " Polaris' " cruise in the Arctic regions. Model of the " Hartford's " propeller while Admiral Farragut's flag-ship. Silver medal for Arctic discoveries, 1818-25, presented by Queen Victoria to officers and seamen of the navy. Silver medals commemorating naval victories of the War of 1812. Model of an improved anchor.

THE SOCIETY FOR THE PREVENTION OF CRUELTY TO ANIMALS, through the President, Henry Bergh, furnished a parcel of documents relating to the Society.

ANGLO-SAXON LODGE, NO. 137, contributed a complete set of the emblems and jewels of the Order of Freemasons, in silver.

Mr. WILLIAM HENRY HURLBERT contributed a small box, the contents of which is known only to himself, and a gold plate on which is engraved the essential facts relating to the removal of the Alexandrian obelisk to New York.

A copy of Webster's Unabridged Dictionary, the works of William Shakespeare, New York City Directory, a map of the city, Telegraphic Determination of Longitudes in the West Indies, Nautical Almanac for 1880, Haydn's Dictionary of Dates, Wilkinson's Egypt, an Encyclopedia of Mechanics and Engineering, and a Compendium of Electricity and Magnetism, were among the books selected to fill vacant spaces in the boxes. Photographs of the different stages of the work of removing the obelisk, similar to those published in this volume, were also placed in the largest box. Specimens of all the

34   *Removal of the New York Obelisk.*

metals used in the industrial arts, different kinds of screws, samples of boring and cutting tools for wood and iron, several sizes of steel-wire rope, and a hydraulic pump, were among the articles deposited. The hydraulic pump was made and contributed by Richard Dudgeon, of New York, and was identical in form and system with those used for lifting and lowering the obelisk. It was encased in a lead jacket, the lead having been run into a mold containing the pump, while molten, so as to insure exclusion of the atmosphere and moisture.

By October 10th the foundation and steps were laid and in place with the exception of the polished cube of syenite (Fig. *A*, Plate xi), which was reserved for the Masonic ceremonies of laying the foundation-stone, this being the last piece to be placed before the pedestal was moved into position.

THE MASONIC CEREMONIES.

Most Worshipful Jesse B. Anthony, Grand Master of Masons in the State of New York, accepted the invitation to lay the corner-stone with Masonic ceremonies, and after consultation with the Commissioners of Public Parks, fixed October 9th as the date. The following order had been issued.

OFFICE OF THE GRAND MASTER OF MASONS IN THE STATE OF NEW YORK,
TROY, N. Y., *September* 16, 1880.

To the Masters, Wardens, and Brethren of the several Lodges in New York, Brooklyn, and vicinity, Greeting:

Having accepted an invitation to lay the corner-stone of the Egyptian obelisk about to be placed in Central Park, New York City, the ceremonies of which will take place in the afternoon of Saturday, October 2d,[1] it is desirable that the fraternity of Free and Accepted Masons should generally unite in recognition of the compliment paid our Society in thus becoming connected with the noble enterprise of placing this historical monument of Egypt in the metropolitan city. You are therefore most earnestly requested to support the officers of the Grand Lodge on this occasion, and make it a memorable event in the annals of the craft in the Empire State.

I have appointed Right Worshipful E. M. L. Ehlers as Grand Marshal of the Day, who will issue the necessary orders incident to the parade, and due publicity will be given to the same. All lodges proposing to parade will please report promptly to the Grand Marshal at Masonic Temple, New York.

Fraternally, JESSE B. ANTHONY, *Grand Master.*

In accordance therewith special meetings of the different lodges and commanderies in New York and vicinity were held and arrangements effected, resulting in the promulgation of a programme by the Grand Marshall.

The number of Freemasons that paraded for the ceremony was nearly nine thousand. It is estimated that from Fifteenth Street to the Eighty-second Street entrance of the park not less than thirty thousand people were on the sidewalks. The disciplined and orderly appearance of the paraders drew out much favorable comment. Each commandery and division was headed by a band, so that there was music at several points in the procession all the time. As the entrance to the park was approached the crowd grew denser, and in the park itself it was so great that the policemen were practically useless in keeping the spectators out of the spaces reserved for the ceremonies. The column having marched to the base of the obelisk, opened ranks three deep, and faced in. The line then extended to Sixtieth Street, where the Grand Master and the Grand Lodge officers left the carriages, and, preceded by Apollo Commandery and Anglo-Saxon Lodge, marched through the line to the platform on the Graywacke Knoll, from which the ceremonies were conducted. The Masters and Wardens of the lodges followed then, and the Marshals took charge. The ranks were closed, and the commanderies were massed on the west side and the lodges on the north and east sides, while the south side was crowded with spectators, some occupying as a vantage-ground the 43-ton pedestal of the obelisk at the foot of the knoll. When order had been obtained the Grand Master addressed the brethren as follows.

"BRETHREN: We have assembled to-day for the purpose of laying the corner-stone of the foundation which is to again support the ancient monument known as Cleopatra's Needle. The occasion is one of which, as a

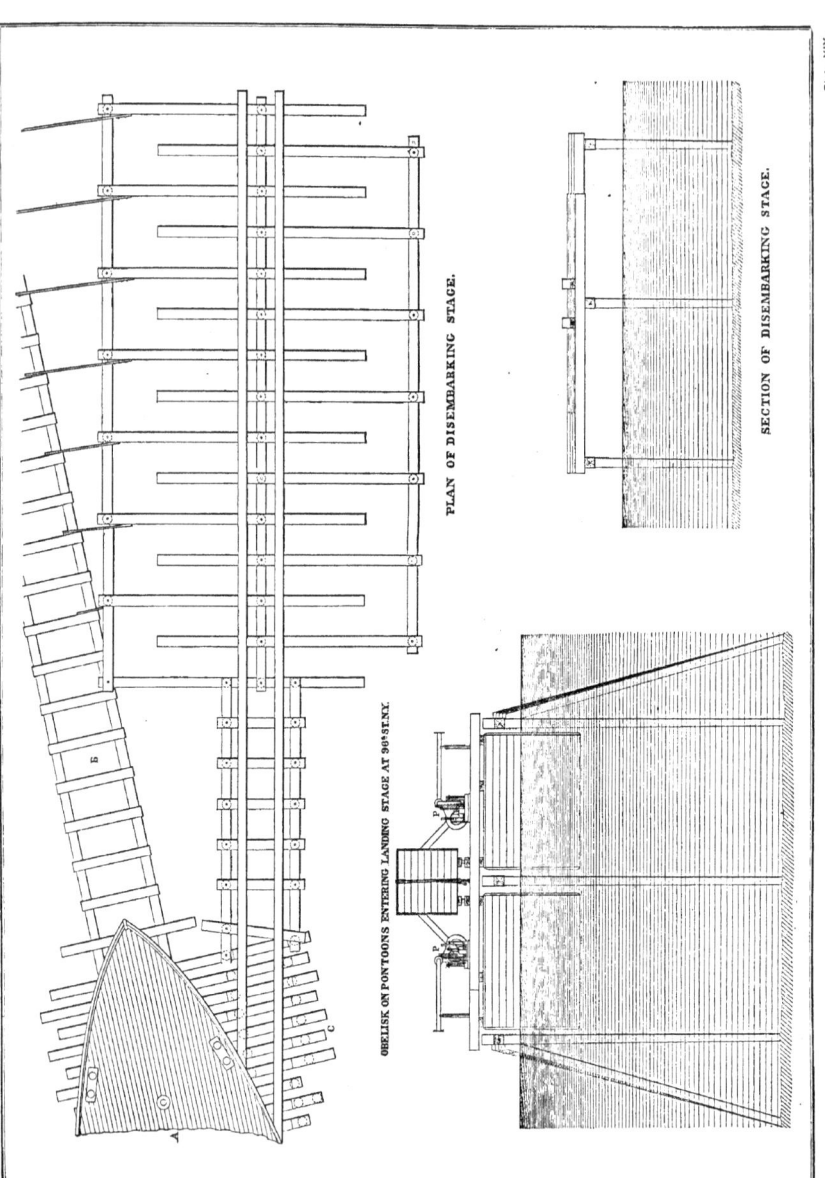

fraternity, we may well be proud, and while it is but true we engage in a labor which has been the custom of our fraternity from time immemorial when such service has been requested, yet as a matter of history connecting our Society with the national character of this work, we may regard it as the event of a lifetime and its record of great importance to our history as a craft. Coming thus publicly before the world as members of an organization which commends itself to the favorable consideration of all candid and unprejudiced minds, it is creditable to you that as individual members, as lodges, and as commanderies you have responded so nobly to the call and by your presence given your assistance to the work. The work is before us, and in accordance with our earliest Masonic lesson we will, before entering upon this undertaking, unite with Rev. and R. W. Bro. C. H. Hall, Grand Chaplain, in an invocation to the Deity."

The usual ceremonies having been concluded, the Grand Master delivered the following address:

"BRETHREN: Standing as we do upon ground which is ever to be memorable from the associations connected with the historical monument about to be replaced upon its original foundation, of which we have to-day laid the corner-stone in accordance with our forms and ceremonies, you will pardon me if in my remarks I depart somewhat from the usual course on such occasions. The importance of this labor to our history as a craft; the honor conferred upon our fraternity by thus being linked with the national importance of this successful achievement of the removal, transportation, and yet to be accomplished fact of again placing the obelisk on the foundation-stone; the universal interest in this addition to the monuments which adorn and beautify this city; the fact that this monolith represents to us the work of the operative workmen of centuries ago, and recalls to our minds most prominently the history of the past, demand that we turn our thoughts beyond the events and occurrences of the present moment to the ages that are gone, of which this obelisk is a venerable relic. This monument in its associations brings forcibly before us that period of which at present, we know so little and of which the researches of the scholar, the calculation of the astronomer, the study of the rocks by the geologist, and the skill of the engineer, are each year adding to our information and startling us with wonderful results. This trophy comes from that land, the history of which, was long lost in the mist and obscurities of ancient fable and tradition,—a land of wonderful creations of human power and genius, that has been, and long will continue to be, a place of interest and curiosity to the learned. Egypt itself is a book of history,—one of God's great monumental records, on the face of which He has written with His own hand many of the strange events of the past. It was the birthplace of literature, the cradle of science and art, the garden and garner of the world. The people of those days excelled in many respects the advanced growth of the present century. Could we but know that which time will yet unveil, we should be astonished at the revelation and ashamed of our littleness. The Supreme Master, the great Architect, in the design upon the eternal trestle-board, traced each cycle of the progress of the universe, inspired the people with the idea to be worked out, and in His wisdom, even though ages have intervened, the prophecy or design has been or will be fulfilled. 'The ways of the Almighty are indeed wonderful.' Let us for a moment consider some points in the history of Egypt which are intimately associated with the principles of our fraternity as a society of workmen, or as conservators of the liberal arts and sciences. In the branches of decorative art and the science of architecture they were undoubtedly far in advance of us at the present day, and could we bring to light that which is buried from our sight by the devastations of war, the sacking of the old cities, could we open the grave made by the growth of years we should be struck with awe and astonishment at the wondrous magnificence of ancient times. The character of Egyptian architecture is that of massive grandeur and severe simplicity, as exhibited in the sculptors' well-defined outlines and in the colossal dimensions of their temples and the enormous blocks of material employed in their construction. The great object of the builders seems to have been that the strength and durability portrayed in the prodigious magnitude of their structures should seem to typify their greatness. The architectural types of all other structures of antiquity sink into insignificance when compared with those of Egypt. The Egyptians were the first to observe the course of the planets, and their observations led them to regulate the year from the course of the sun. Among the immense structures erected by the Egyptian workmen, the pyramids were the first that claimed the attention of the outside world, and while it is conceded that they were generally constructed to serve as tombs for some monarch, yet it is also thought that they were designed for astronomical purposes. For while we cannot suppose that they were intended as places of observation, there are many things in connection with them—their position, the exact angle at which they were built, varying in accordance with their situation as regards the longitudinal lines, together with the peculiar position of the opening or entrance into them—which induce us to believe that the shadows cast into the interior were made the basis of useful calculations. Let us consider them a moment, and while we have reference particularly to the pyramids—and in the illustration that which is termed the great pyramid,—yet the application is pertinent to other monuments erected by this ancient people. They are so intimately linked together that it is impossible to completely separate them. The pyramids were built for a purpose and built in all respects with some peculiar and symbolic reference. Every stone and every line had some allusion or reference to something which should yet be accomplished. The exactness with which these calculations have been verified proves that they were no accidental allusion, and while it seems incredible to us that prophecies can be foretold in the block, lines, and exact situation of the pile of stone, yet we cannot shut our eyes to the fact that they have been proven to be true after the closest scrutiny and investigation of the leading minds of the world. The labors of the ancients in the science of astronomy cannot be despised. If the ancient philosophers groped where modern minds have seen more clearly, the events of time have proven that they appreciated the fact that the sun, planets, and stars were governed by fixed, immovable laws, and that there could be no variation from the great plan designed by the Almighty. The Egyptian priesthood 2,500 years before Christ had their calendar and periods proportioned to the processional cycle of the equinoxes. Tables have accumulated for over 3,000 years which now enable astronomers to predict with certainty the exact position each star in the solar system will occupy at a given moment. There may be a slight deviation of dates, but not sufficient to invalidate the fact that they had a correct knowledge of the laws governing the operation of the solar system.

"The great pyramid is more than science. It is the embodiment of a great revelation. 'The measurements, joint lines, and minute but exact markings, calculated at the rate of one pyramid unit or inch a year, agree with the past events of history, which must have been a prophetic revelation when built into its chronological passages.' If they have been correct in the past the inference is that they will be in the future. The investigations of astronomers have demonstrated the fact that the great pyramid was designed as an astronomical stone clock or ancient observatory, erected by inspiration of the Most High; for it cannot be attributed to accident that at exact periods of time of long intervals between—a thousand years and over—a certain star, the time-keeper of the ancients, is in such a position as to shine down the entrance passage of the great pyramid. This event is calculated by astronomers to occur during the coming year at a time which corresponds with the record engraved by the mystical lines on the stone. Jeremiah proclaimed: 'The great, the mighty God; great in counsel and mighty in works, which has set signs and wonders in the land of Egypt,' standing even unto this day. As we march along the cycle of time each one has added some discovery, or brought before us the fact that in many respects we have not yet equalled the position then occupied by the arts and sciences. In the former ages of the world, not having the art of printing—the power of the press at the present day—they wrought their lessons in the shape of the monuments of stone, and we cannot ignore the fact that the peculiarities of those ancient monuments, in the shape of the stone, numbers composing the same, the peculiar position, or the mystical inscriptions to be found thereon, were for a wise purpose. They were intended to tell their story at a future day and draw the veil from the past for the information and wonder of the present. Such a fact demonstrates that the lessons of the stone monuments erected in the land of Egypt, by inspiration undoubtedly from the Supreme Ruler, cannot be ignored, but demand of us the closest investigation. What we are in search of is truth. It is the mystical reward ever before the Masonic student, and every thing which in any way aids us in our progress in that direction should be carefully weighed and considered in all its aspects before we accept or reject the evidence thus brought before us. We should not, because of any previously conceived opinion, discard them hastily; neither, on the other hand, should we allow imagination to warp our judgment. The ancients were proficient in the science of mechanics, and as far advanced, if not farther, than we are at the present day in the knowledge of the use of the forces of water used as an adjunct to the labors of man. They were fully acquainted with the laws of hydraulics, and must have utilized that branch of science in their work. It is impossible for us on an occasion like this to examine in particular the various departments of art and science of which Egypt was the home. They were a wonderful race, combining within themselves all the branches which adorn, beautify, and add to the reputation of a people when directed in the right channel. Their works, whether the obelisks, pyramids, temples, palaces, tombs, or other structures, were all on a colossal scale. It has been a wonder to many how the ancients could have moved the immense blocks of stone used in the monuments of ancient times, but it can be no longer, for while they did not have all the appliances of mechanical skill extant to-day, yet they were thoroughly acquainted with the laws and forces of nature, adapted them to their wants, and rendered them serviceable in their vast undertakings. The advance which has been made in science by the present generation is in the utilization of electricity, and more especially in the line of chemistry, the combination of different elements to create a new source of power. The steam-engine is simply the application of chemistry in utilizing the elements of water in the form of units of steam, in conjunction with mechanical appliances.

"Egypt abounded in obelisks, or monoliths, as they are termed, and they were erected to commemorate some particular event, perpetuate the reputation, or hand down to posterity the glory, of some great monarch. They were erected in great numbers, and many of them have been removed to Europe to add to the trophies of some city. That of which we have to-day laid the foundation-stone was one of two originally located at Heliopolis some 3,400 years ago, and afterward, 23 years B. C., removed to Alexandria, where they received the name of Cleopatra's Needles. One of these now adorns the city of London, and the other will add to the attractiveness of this place and recall to our minds, by its allusions, the important lessons of past centuries. You will pardon me if I have devoted too much time to this part of my address; but in considering the work of to-day, the foundation of the result yet to be attained, my thoughts have turned instinctively to the past, of which this obelisk is to me a reminder. We cannot gaze upon it without desiring to know of the land whence it came, the status of the people, and especially of the evidences of skill of the operative workmen of those times. This is especially true when we consider that our Society was originally of the operative character, and that as the reward of the labor of one of our brethren of the present, discoveries have been made in the removal of the obelisk from its Eastern home which, in the judgment of many, seem to have an allusion to

DISEMBARKING THE OBELISK.

Plate XX

Removal of the New York Obelisk.

the fraternity of which we are members. Masonry may be divided into two periods: the operative and speculative. It was originally a school of architecture and a promoter of the sciences. In its operative character Masonry applied the unlimited resources of architectural skill to develop Divine ideas through symbolized stone. It awakened the emotional element of the people in the exquisite temples of worship, and it elevated their aspirations in art productions of wondrous beauty and uniformity. These guilds travelled from place to place engaging in the work, and in all sections is to be found that uniformity of detail which demonstrates that they were combined into societies to carry out a well-defined and arranged system. There have been operative societies in all ages of the world. They flourished in Egypt and we see their handiwork in the monuments, temples, and pyramids of that day. We find traces of them among the Greeks, in the introduction of peculiar characteristics of architecture into Rome. We find at one time that the home of the arts and sciences was located in the Orient, especially at Byzantium. We find it perpetuated in the Roman colleges instituted by Numa Pompilius. We find it carried into Britain with the Roman conquerors. It is generally conceded that Masonry as an operative science came from the East, was incorporated with the guilds of the Middle Ages, and subsequently constituted an essential part of Masonry of the present day. We cannot be expected to enter into minute detail, and we sketch the outline only for the purpose of presenting the proposition, that we can justly claim that the foundation of our speculative organization rests upon and is the natural outgrowth of the ancient operative corporations of the Middle Ages, and they in turn derived their origin from the still older societies banded together for the same purpose. I do not claim that all societies of the past engaged as operative bands were Masonic in their nature, for we know that they combined religious forms and ceremonies in many of the most remote, which are entirely foreign and antagonistic to Masonry of the present; but I think that we can fairly claim that the various points which these societies present in common, and which in some respects are to be found in our Society as at present organized, cannot have been the result of accident or the work of chance. Our Society is the natural outgrowth of these societies, and while we build for a nobler purpose and a higher ideal, yet the object which each endeavors to perpetuate and promote is in spirit harmonious. In its early history the operative workmen by all the resources of their art outlined and perfected Divine truths in the sculptured stone. They wrought out in granite blocks the thoughts and aspirations of their day. They worked for a wise purpose, and were actuated by a combined policy. Every object was designed to develop some great idea or to perpetuate some event of importance. They left the traces of their work behind them, and in the temples, pyramids, monuments, and other results of their labor do we find the distinctive marks of the craft. The marks of the workmen upon their work trace their progress, and the similitude to be found in the mystical marks proves that, in some respects at least, they must have possessed a common knowledge and been actuated by the same purposes. This is one of the essential points which have been demonstrated to us by the discoveries made at the exhumation of the foundation of this obelisk. We find delineated there certain emblems which are to be found in common use among the operative craftsmen of the Middle Ages, and it is an evidence that these marks are definitive mementoes of a systematic labor. They are suggestive of a connection which may have existed by regular sequence between the Eastern and Western builders. I do not, however, consider that we should regard these marks as being symbolic, for while such an inference may be drawn, yet the geometrical outlines should not be accepted without qualification. We find that they labored with the same tools that are preserved in our Society and regarded by us in a symbolic sense as teaching moral lessons. Now, brethren, let us consider for a few moments these discoveries with reference to Masonic history.

"I touch upon the point because it has been so prominently brought before the public in connection with this obelisk, and especially because in the judgment of many they seem to have a direct allusion to our fraternity. In considering these discoveries from a Masonic standpoint we must eliminate from our minds the Masonry of to-day as now organized. 'History,' says Cicero, 'is the light of truth. It differs from symbolism in that we expect and demand that it should be conclusive, that each link should follow the other in regular order, and when thus presented we should accept it as true.' It is a common remark that all history is uncertain, and if this be true in its full extent there would be little use in attempting to show the value of that which cannot be known with certainty. But although many events, or rather the minute circumstances of such events, are uncertain, the most valuable part of history rests upon visible monuments, such as pillars, edifices, heaps of stones, etc., erected upon the occasion of remarkable events. These monuments attracting the attention of the rising generation would naturally cause such inquiries concerning their origin and use as would long preserve the knowledge of the transactions to which they refer. It is questionable to my mind whether we are to confine ourselves to the historical rule—that is, to limit our views to that which can only be proven by indisputable facts and consecutive links to be true. Should we not take a broader ground and look to the principles which antedate the time assumed for the origin of Masonry as at present constituted? There can be no question but that in the secret societies of Egypt are to be found some elements now embraced in the principles or symbolism of Masonry of the present, and yet, notwithstanding this, I am not prepared to state that we should consider that Freemasonry existed in those days. We cannot honestly claim, because of such traces, that those societies or institutions were Masonic in their nature. In the annals of our craft there have been handed down to us much that is mythical and traditionary in its nature, and many of the old writers on Masonic history have in the support of their theories given us much that is visionary. We all know that when we enter the field of speculation there is really no limit to the extent it may be carried. Cast your eyes upon the fleeting clouds of the firmament as they pass along, give the imagination full play, and you create many fantastic and strange pictures; curb the imagination, look again, they are after all only clouds. Do not understand me as detracting in the least degree from the importance of these discoveries. They may have within them elements which may prove much, but I do not think we should hastily decide that they are conclusive.

"The antiquity of Masonry in its principles we must with one voice concede; for the spirit of our institution includes all that is good and elevating to the human race, and, as a system of morals, ranks with religion, leaving each one in that respect to be governed by the dictates of his own conscience and in accordance with his peculiar belief. I should be glad if from the discoveries which have been, or may yet be made, we might be able to successfully trace the history of our institution back through the past, for we all have a particular veneration for age. It is a principle which is imbued into our feelings at early childhood and grows with our years. In the proper regard which we have for antiquity do not let us rest upon and be content with that; the present is given for our field. We are to improve our opportunities, labor in the carrying out of the vital principles of our organization, and by so doing make a record which shall endure through the ages to come, so that when the monuments and temples have crumbled to dust, the good deeds of Masonry shall stand out on its escutcheon brighter and brighter with the passing years. The effect of these discoveries will be productive of one result at least. It will awaken new zeal in the student, and it is possible that some things which may now seem to be curious may lead to further discoveries which will demonstrate a connection between the ancient and modern that we are not yet prepared to admit. You will understand that I am expressing individual views. When I first heard of these discoveries I gave them no consideration whatever, and while I have had no opportunity to thoroughly examine them, yet there are some peculiarities which seem to me worthy of the careful consideration of the Masonic student. Let them be tested by the crucible of time, which may yet eliminate the dross and present the truth in its purity. The world we live in is made up of the occurrences of the past, and it is the work of the investigator, the geologist, the astronomer, the philosopher, and the student in any specialty, to examine, to dig out, to look into, to consider, and to analyze that which has been covered up by the operations of nature or the lapse of time. Every year presents new facts, develops new truths, which enlighten and render intelligible many things which have for ages been shrouded in darkness, or subject to the claim of speculation. Our world, which seems complete in itself and is remarkable for its achievements, appliances, and results, has passed through wonderful changes; and while we boast of the intelligence of the nineteenth century, yet when we uncover and bring to light the buried treasures of the past, we find that even with our boasted superiority we do not equal the skill of the ancients. The monuments of the past are to be considered by us as representatives of some grand historical event in the history of those nations, or as memorials of their knowledge perpetuated in the form of stone. The history of the world has not yet been written, neither has the history of Masonry, and even though 'the mills of God grind slowly,' yet all incongruities will finally be reduced to an even and consistent nature, and the almighty power of truth shall prevail. In conclusion, brethren, there is nothing done in Masonry that is not for a purpose and is not designed to impress its lessons upon us. What is the design upon the trestle-board to-day? What has been brought prominently before you on this occasion? What thought is uppermost in your minds? Is it not that a man's work in this world lives long after he has laid down the implements of labor, and that his influence does not entirely cease with the termination of life's powers? This obelisk erected thousands of years ago is not without its lesson to us of to-day. The ancient workman did not build for an age, but for eternity. So with us, brethren; we may not consider that our efforts amount to much of themselves, but nevertheless every one has his influence, and in a greater or lesser degree we contribute to the aggregate whole. Let it be our endeavor therefore to lay the foundation of character on a broad, sure, and deep foundation; let it be such as will bear the application of the plumb, square, and level; let us continue to build upon that foundation a character which is above reproach in the sight of Him Who ruleth all things. And, when finally we have completed our task, erected a monument of moral grandeur and symmetry, achieved something which is for the welfare and advancement of the human race, then in after years the coming generations will treasure our memory, imitate our example, point to our deeds, and draw inspiration from our age as worthy of their veneration. Such a monument will be more enduring than even that of stone; and the chiselled record, long after the tracings upon the stone shall have become obliterated, will stand out in its original sharpness, telling of grand enterprises and noble works, which are the real monuments of a successful life. Let us therefore labor faithfully in the present, looking forward to the reward promised to him who performs his whole duty, and the past, present, and future of each and every one will entitle him to the salutation: 'Well done, good and faithful servant.'"

The benediction was then pronounced by R. W. and Rev. Brother J. Bradford Cleaver, Grand Chaplain, and the ceremonies were concluded.

The only thing remaining to complete the structure on which the obelisk was to stand was to move the pedestal from its temporary resting-place near by on the west side of the foundation to its

CROSS SECTION THROUGH OBELISK AND PONTOONS.

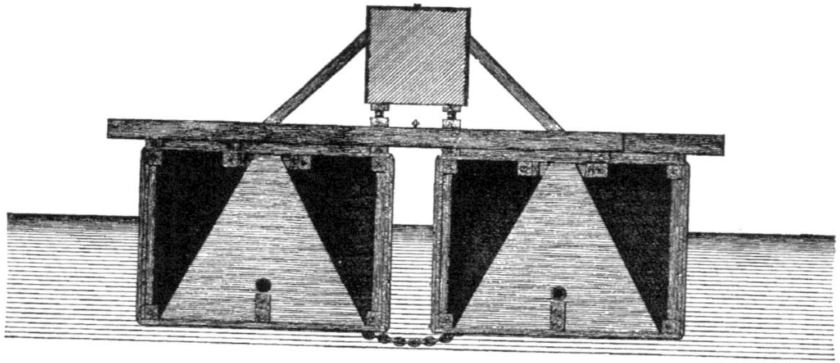

SIDE ELEVATION OF OBELISK AND PONTOONS.

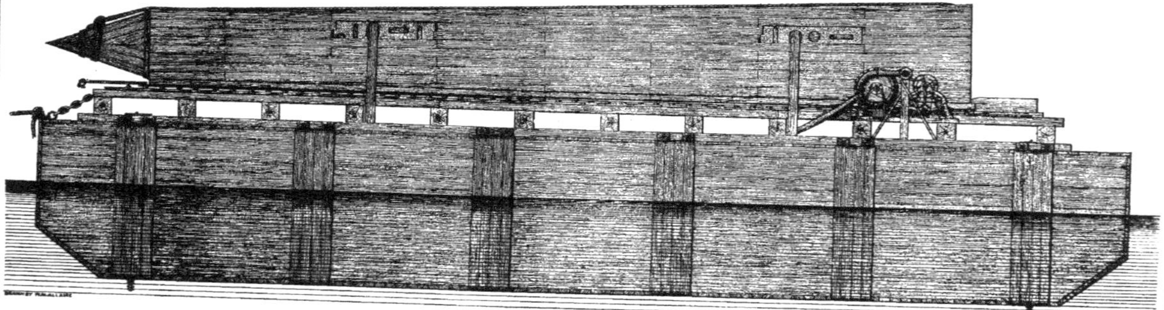

Plate XXI.

proper position. This was accomplished on October 11th. Building the masonry piers for the turning structure (Plates xxvii and xxviii, G) was pushed forward rapidly. By November 30th the turning structure was erected on them ready for the obelisk.

DISEMBARKING THE OBELISK.

Almost the first thing that occupied my attention on arriving in New York on July 20th was the arrangement for disembarking the obelisk. It was very soon discovered that there was only one dry dock at or near the city in which it could be disembarked by reversing the plan of embarking it. The owners of this dock had also discovered this fact. On opening negotiations with their representative it was evident that they were prepared to dictate their own terms for the use of the dock without regard to the customary charges. They had the right to fix on whatever price they pleased and make their own conditions for the use of their property. They fixed on a price in excess of that charged for other steamers, and made the condition that I must give security for any injury that might result to their property from disembarking the obelisk. These terms contrast strangely with the arrangements made by the Egyptian government, which gave me the free use of the dock in Alexandria for an indefinite period, without conditions as to injury, and charged only for the actual expenditure of fuel and labor in raising and lowering the steamer. I offered the dock owners the same rates as were paid by other steamers, and proposed the appointment of a commission of experts to watch the operation of disembarking the obelisk and decide what amount of damages, if any, should be paid them resulting therefrom. The answer to this was to the effect that unless I accepted their terms and conditions at once they would not agree to take the "Dessoug" on the dock at any fixed date, according to turn, but would leave the disembarkation of the obelisk to some time when there was no immediate demand for the dock. Without replying, I left the office, determined to devise some other plan for disembarking it.

At first I thought of taking the "Dessoug" to Philadelphia or Baltimore, disembarking the obelisk in the spacious dry dock in either of these cities, and bringing it to New York on floats by canal. Negotiations with the dock owners or their representatives developed the same feeling as that existing in New York as to extra charges. Besides this there would have been no end of obstacles to be overcome in connection with the Customs authorities and navigation laws. The "Dessoug" had neither register nor nationality, and could not leave the port of New York. The next plan that suggested itself to my mind was the construction of a marine railway at the foot of Ninety-sixth Street, North River, where the obelisk was to be landed on Manhattan Island, on which to haul the "Dessoug's" bow out of water, and then haul the obelisk out of her hold on to the shore. This was found to be impracticable on account of the Hudson River Railway, which skirts the shore, and the abrupt increase of depth close to the river bank. Besides these objections were the cost, and the condition exacted by the Dock Department, that the structure should be entirely removed and the piles *pulled out* after the disembarkation of the obelisk. Removal would have cost almost as much as construction.

Disembarking the obelisk while the "Dessoug" was on a marine railway was entirely practicable and as easily accomplished as if the steamer were in a dock. But getting the obelisk afloat with moderate expense after it had been disembarked, so as to remove it to the foot of Ninety-sixth Street, was the difficult problem to solve. After having almost despaired of being able to accomplish my object without yielding to the demands of the dock company, I reached a solution that may be summed up in the word *tide.* I determined to make the rising tide lift the obelisk and the falling tide land it. There would be no lack of power.

Before communicating my plans to any one, I visited incognito all the marine railways on the shores of New York Bay, and fixed on a new one at Staten Island as the best adapted to my purpose. An illustration and advertisement in the *Daily Graphic* had attracted my attention to it. The proprietor had no knowledge of my plans until the terms of an agreement had been entered into for the occupation of his slip. Had he then changed his mind I had two other marine railways in view, the proprietors of which were ready to accept my offer. Every thing was arranged satisfactorily. The " Dessoug's " bow was hauled out of water on August 21st, at Lawler's Marine Railway, on the east shore of Staten Island. Iron shipwrights had been engaged; and the work of opening the aperture was begun on August 22d, and completed on the 29th.

While this was in progress a disembarking stage on piles had been prepared adjacent to the marine railway to receive the obelisk. Plate xix illustrates the plan and section of the disembarking stage, and shows the relative positions of the steamer's bow (A), the marine railway (B), and the disembarking stage and its approach (C). Two rows of piles were driven from a point close to the railway right under the aperture in the steamer's bow, to a distance of seventy feet, and at an angle with the line of the railway equal to that at which the obelisk had to leave the steamer's hold. Capping and cross-beams were placed on these piles, to form the approach to the disembarking stage. The latter comprised three parallel rows of piles, twenty feet apart. The centre row had double the number of piles in the outside rows. Over each pile of the outside rows and every alternate one of the middle row heavy cross-timbers were placed; and on these, longitudinal pieces were laid to form the bed for the channel iron tracks, prolonged into the steamer's hold. This arrangement of the cross-timbers was due to the impossibility of purchasing suitable timber long enough to extend across the whole width of the staging. The spaces between the rows could not be reduced in width, as suitable pontoons of less than twenty feet beam could not be obtained. The staging and approach were given the same incline as the platform in the steamer's hold, which was the same as that of the marine railway.

The obelisk having been slued inside of the steamer, in identically the same manner as it had been slued in Alexandria, to the angle at which it was to be disembarked, it was raised, and the channel iron tracks and cannon-balls placed under it. It was moved outward about fifty feet by a *pulling* hydraulic pump, when, to hasten the disembarkation a fourfold purchase of six-inch rope was applied to it. The hauling part of the purchase was taken to the engine of an ordinary floating pile-driver, secured to the end of the disembarking stage, as shown on Plate xx. The time occupied in making the aperture in the steamer's bow, building the stage and its approach, sluing the obelisk in the hold, raising it, and placing the track under it, and preparing to disembark it, was two weeks. The time occupied in disembarking it was fifty minutes.

The report that the obelisk was to be disembarked brought down to Staten Island a crowd of spectators, who occupied every available spot from which a view of the work could be obtained.

REMOVAL FROM STATEN ISLAND TO MANHATTAN ISLAND.

On September 13th the pontoons, that had been prepared for the operation of lifting the obelisk from the staging, were placed under the cross-timbers and between the rows of piling at low tide. Water was let into them to prevent their rising with the flood tide. On the following day they were pumped out. As the tide rose they naturally rose with it and lifted the obelisk. About two hours before high-water the cross-timbers were clear of the capping, and the obelisk was once more afloat. Owing to lack of space the positions of the pontoons had not been properly adjusted. It was found that they did not float on even keels. To effect this adjustment they were hauled fifteen feet toward the shore; and water was admitted to them while in this position, so as to land the cross-timbers sustaining the obelisk on the capping this distance from their original positions. This operation consumed the short interval of high-water, and nothing more was attempted until the 16th. The wind on the 15th was such as to cause a considerable sea in the bay, in which it would have been imprudent to float the obelisk on the pontoons. The delay was utilized in removing the approach to

THE OBELISK CROSSING THE HUDSON RIVER RAILROAD.

the disembarking stage, and clearing a passage for the caissons to be hauled out of the slip directly astern, instead of ahead first and then astern as had been intended.

In the forenoon of September 16th, every thing being ready and the weather favorable, the pontoons were pumped out at low-water and adjusted to their proper position under the obelisk. The rising tide caused them to gradually raise the cross-timbers clear of the capping on the piles until the weight of the obelisk had been transferred from the stage. At high-water, 4 P.M., they were hauled out of the slip into the bay, bearing the obelisk on their decks (see Plate xxi). The next half hour was spent in lashing them together by means of chains passed through the wells in each and under their bottoms, as shown in Plate xxi, cross-section through obelisk and pontoons. The side elevation of obelisk and pontoons on this plate shows the pumps that had been placed to free the pontoons of water, and the method of securing the obelisk by shores from the recesses of its hieroglyphs to the decks of the pontoons.

A landing-stage had been prepared for the obelisk at the foot of Ninety-sixth Street, North River, identically the same in principle as that at Staten Island. The steamer "Manhattan," belonging to the Dock Department of the city, was in readiness to tow the pontoons from Staten Island. The steamer "Rescue" of the Coast Wrecking Company was in attendance to escort it. She was provided with powerful pumping machinery and the necessary flexible hose to convey steam from her boilers to the pumps on the pontoons. And in order to provide against all contingencies she towed one of the Wrecking Company's schooners, also provided with steam boilers and pumps.

The time of high-water at the foot of Ninety-sixth Street is about two hours later than at Staten Island. The distance is twelve miles. At 4.55 P.M. the "Manhattan" started ahead with the pontoons in tow. As she proceeded up the bay, tugs and steamers diverged from their courses to greet the strange object with vigorous and prolonged blasts of their steam-whistles and the cheers of their passengers and crews. We reached the landing-stage at Ninety-sixth Street at 7.15 P.M.. The evening was very dark and it seemed as if it would be impossible to adjust the pontoons between the rows of piles. After one or two failures, owing to the swiftly running tide, this was finally accomplished. Plate xix shows the obelisk on the pontoons just entering the landing-stage. As soon as it was in position the valves of the pontoons were opened to admit water to them, and in a few minutes the obelisk had been finally landed on Manhattan Island. As it settled down on the staging the piles swayed, owing to their great height; but as soon as the whole weight was on them they remained steady and the staging became stable.

CROSSING THE HUDSON RIVER RAILWAY.

The Hudson River Railway tracks skirt the river bank at the point where the obelisk was landed; passenger trains pass at very frequent intervals, the longest time between trains being an hour and a half about noon. To have blocked the road at this point for more than two or three hours would have involved serious loss and much serious inconvenience to travellers. Preparations for transferring the obelisk from the landing-stage across the track to the roadway of Ninety-sixth Street, comprised the placing of heavy timbers across the street and others at right angles to them for the channel iron tracks to rest on, and adjusting these to a uniform grade. The frequent passage of trains and the rugged surface of the unpaved street delayed this work until September 25th. The temporary bridge across the railway tracks had been prepared with care, every piece hewn and cut to the proper size, marked, and its position well understood by the workmen. Strong anchors had been sunk deep down into the rip-rap of the street, and made secure by chain-cable backing to large iron bolts let into holes drilled in the solid rock on the south side of the street. The pulling purchase was rove and overhauled; the hauling part was led to the drum of the engine of a floating pile-driver moored to the wharf adjacent to the landing-stage. Nothing that could be thought of that would

42   *Removal of the New York Obelisk.*

facilitate and hasten the crossing was neglected. Orders had been given by the railway officials to stop all trains at 11 A. M. Immediately after the passage of the last train that was allowed by, the temporary bridge was thrown across the track; in one hour and twenty minutes subsequently the obelisk was resting on the roadway of Ninety-sixth Street and the track was entirely clear of obstruction. The freight train seen in Plate xxii was delayed twenty-five minutes. The regular passenger trains were not delayed at all.

THE LAND TRANSPORT.

The landing-stage had necessarily been built at an angle with the direction of Ninety-sixth Street, a wharf at the foot of that street preventing its construction in any other way. The first operation after having moved the obelisk across the Hudson River Railway was that of sluing it to the direction of its route. This was done in identically the same manner as it was slued when embarked and disembarked. The route that was followed from this point to the site in the Central Park is shown on Plate xxiii: Eastward through Ninety-sixth Street to the West Boulevard; southward through the West Boulevard to Eighty-sixth Street; eastward through Eighty-sixth Street to the Eighth Avenue entrance of the sunken road across the park; eastward through this sunken road to Fifth Avenue; southward through Fifth Avenue to the Metropolitan Museum gate facing Eighty-second Street; then westward through the park to the site. Notwithstanding its numerous turns, this route was the best one that could be followed, chiefly on account of the more uniform grades and the condition of the streets. The aggregate distance is ten thousand nine hundred and five feet; and the aggregate vertical lift from the level of the landing-stage to that of the axis of the trunnions of the turning structure was two hundred and thirty feet. This lift is not, however, the difference of elevation above water-level, which is one hundred and forty-seven feet. Eighty-three feet of the lift was due to the up and down grades of the streets, as will appear from an examination of the profiles on Plate xxiii.

The apparatus used for moving the obelisk across the railway, and invariably up to the time it reached the roadway of Ninety-sixth Street, is illustrated on the accompanying drawing, which is a section through it, showing the cross-timbers (A) that were placed on the ground to distribute the weight over a large area, the track timbers (B) on which the lower iron channel tracks (C) were placed and adjusted, the cannon-balls (D) and the upper iron channels (E) on which the obelisk rested. The great advantage of substituting iron channels and cannon-balls for the ordinary wheels, axles, and tracks, was in diminishing the friction to a minimum and increasing the resistance of the rollers to a maximum. There was, however, one difficulty experienced with this method that could not be overcome at moderate cost. The bottom of iron channels of ordinary dimensions was found to be insufficiently thick to resist the pressure, and the iron channels were literally split into two angle irons by the cannon-balls. To remedy this defect three-quarter-inch flat iron plates were riveted to the bottom of the iron channels, but even this was found to be insufficient. Every effort was made to procure iron channels of the required size with thicker bottoms, but none could be found nor could any be made unless machinery was made expressly to roll them. This was out of the question.

It became necessary, therefore, to change the method of moving the obelisk. Nothing offered so many advantages as the ordinary cradle, rollers and track of a marine railway, which were substituted for the iron channels and cannon-balls. The idea first suggested itself to me in Alexandria, during the embarkation of the obelisk, when the iron channels also split. The change was determined on at Staten Island, during the disembarkation, when it was found that riveting flat irons on the back of the iron channels was not effective to prevent the splitting.

The system in use on marine railways and adopted for the land transport of the obelisk is illustrated on Plate xxiv. It comprised a cradle (G) a ways (W) and rollers (R). The cradle is

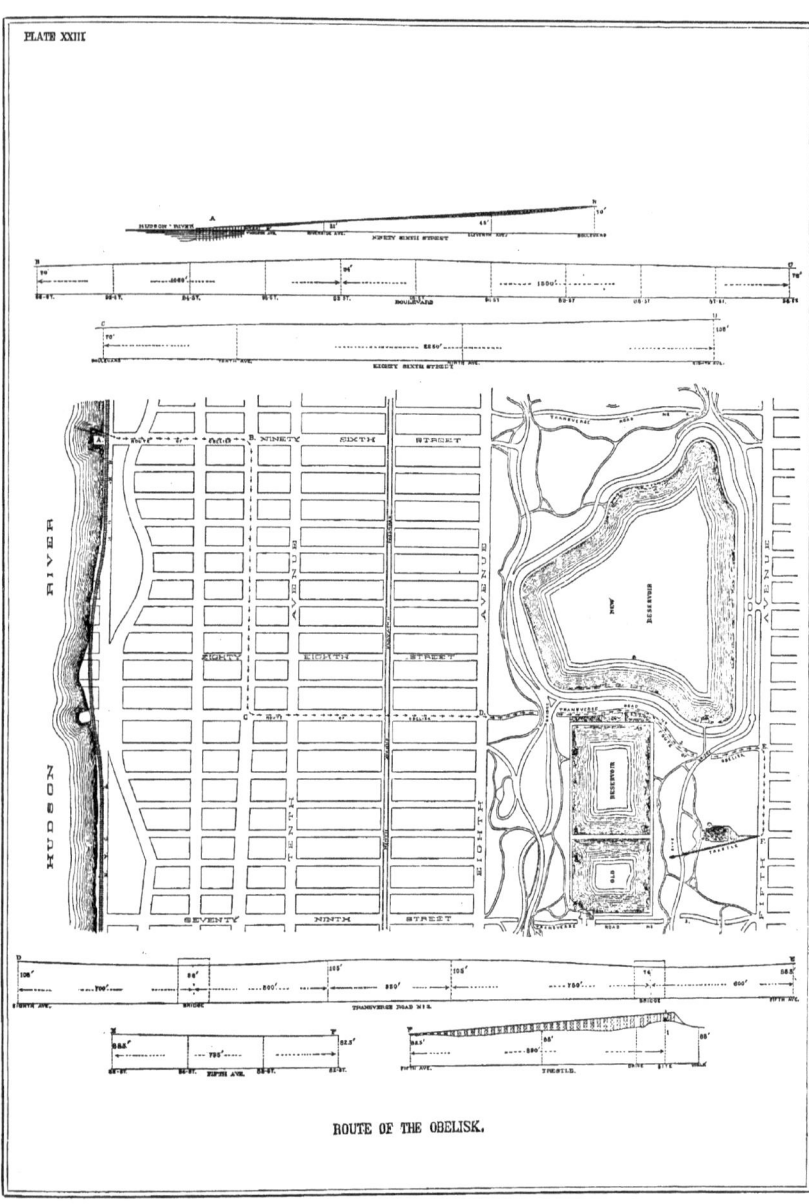

ROUTE OF THE OBELISK.

Removal of the New York Obelisk. 43

formed of two parallel beams, long enough to contain the obelisk and engine, about eighty feet, held together with through bolts, (I) and held apart by wooden struts, not shown on the drawing. Suitable fastenings were secured to the forward end of the cradle to hook or shackle the movable purchase block on. The lower faces of the cradle beams and upper faces of the ways beams were grooved through the middle and shod on each side of the groove with flat irons (H). The ways beams were kept independent of each other, to facilitate shifting them along the route after the obelisk had passed over them. The rollers were grouped in "boxes" of the form shown on the accompanying figure. The side pieces (P) were two-inch plank, twelve inches deep and six feet long, held together by wooden struts (S) having shoulders on the inside and keys through the ends. Iron thimbles (T) were let into the plank, to reduce the friction of the ends of the rollers (R). These rollers were cast with a flange around the middle, that fitted into the grooves of the cradle and ways beams and acted as a guide. The motive power of an ordinary marine railway is stationary. That of the obelisk railway was a pile-driver engine fastened to the forward end of the cradle and moving with it and, therefore, with the obelisk. It is evident that the rollers would travel over half the distance advanced by the obelisk and cradle, and that the ways were stationary. To have laid continuous ways from the river to the park would have been a useless expense. Six double lengths of ways beams and one and a half double lengths of roller boxes were provided. Gangs of men were employed grading the track ahead of the obelisk by placing cross-timbers and crib-work for the ways beams to lie on, others moving the timbers and other material ahead for the grading, others sinking anchors for the stationary purchase block to be shackled to, and picked men were employed placing the ways beams and adjusting them to the exact grade on which the next advance of the obelisk was to be made.

The preparations for the first advance lasted until September 30th. Rainy weather, difficulty in finding suitable men, and other causes delayed the work, and the obelisk did not reach the West Boulevard until October 27th. The distance from the starting-point, near the railway to the West Boulevard is twelve hundred feet; the difference of level is sixty feet, the grade being about one in twenty. For hauling the cradle with the obelisk and engine on it up this steep grade a fourfold purchase was applied to it. Six-inch manilla rope was used for the fall. The stationary block of the purchase was shackled to a length of bower chain-cable belonging to the "Dessoug," which served as a pennant, the other end of the cable having been fastened to an anchor sunk twelve feet into the roadway of the street. The hauling part of the fall was taken to the drum of the engine on the cradle. The traction to be overcome averaged about thirty-eight tons—that is, the strain on the purchase was equal to a lift of thirty-eight tons before the inertia, the tendency down the incline, and the friction could be overcome. To keep the cradle from descending in case the rope or any thing connected with the pulling purchase should have given way, men were stationed in the rear of the obelisk with large iron wedges, that were held close against the rollers. The least retrograde movement would have caught the points of the wedges; the weight of the large end of the obelisk would, in this manner, have been utilized as a brake.

A change of grade and turn of ninety degrees were the next things to be accomplished after reaching the West Boulevard. The former occupied a few hours. The hydraulic pumps were placed under the ways in spaces left vacant in the blocking, which was removed as soon as the weight had been suspended on the pumps. The lower end of the obelisk was thus lifted, whilst the upper end was lowered until the new grade had been reached.

Instead of lowering the ways on blocking they were lowered on large timbers placed diagonally across the street so as to form a plane on which the obelisk and its railway could be slued. Strips of half inch iron were placed between the ways timbers and diagonal timbers, to reduce friction. Powerful purchases operating in opposite directions were applied to the ends of the obelisk and its railway, and the whole slued around by November 3d, after six days and nights of tedious and unsatisfactory work.

It was evident that a more expeditious method of making the remaining eleven turns and part turns necessary in order to reach the site must be designed. The London obelisk was not turned or moved overland at all. The Paris obelisk had been turned by placing it on a pivoted cradle, an expensive and for my purposes an impracticable system. The turning apparatus shown on Plate xxiv I designed and arranged in time for the next turn from the West Boulevard into Eighty-sixth Street. The distance between these points, two thousand six hundred and fifty feet, with two changes of grade, was made in eight days. The ways beams were laid directly over the new turning apparatus, which was reached on November 15th. Twenty-two hours were occupied in preparing the blocking and four hours in effecting the turn.

The apparatus comprises two circles of iron channels, with cannon-balls between, and a hundred-ton hydraulic pump under the large end of the obelisk as a pivot, and two sections of iron channels bent to arcs of different radii under the middle and the small end. The upper channels of the two latter were long enough to project a little beyond the ways beams; the lower ones covered an angle of ninety degrees. A purchase was applied to the small end of the obelisk, and the power necessary to effect the turn was equivalent to that required for lifting only two tons. The end of the railway bearing the engine was allowed to slide on a beam shod with iron.

From the intersection of Eighty-sixth Street with the West Boulevard to the Eighth Avenue entrance of Transverse Road No. 3, the distance is two thousand two hundred and fifty feet, with ascending grades of one in thirty-seven and a half, and one in ninety. The entrance to Transverse Road No. 3 was reached on November 25th. An examination of the plan and profile of this transverse road on Plate xxiii will indicate, in a measure, the difficulties to be overcome in order to transport the obelisk through it. The distance from Eighth to Fifth Avenue is two thousand nine hundred feet, with a descending grade of one in sixty, followed by an ascending grade of one in fifty-six, a level, then a descending grade, of one in twenty-six, and concluding with an ascending grade of one in fifty. Besides these changes of grade, there were eight partial turns in both directions to be made, aggregating one hundred and seventy-three degrees of arc. To add to the difficulties of this part of the work, intensely cold weather alternated with heavy falls of snow, and the picked men gave out one by one from attacks of rheumatism and other effects of exposure. The time occupied in moving the obelisk through the transverse road was nineteen days. Work was carried on continuously night and day by two gangs, relieving each other at six o'clock, morning and evening. I made it a point to spend six hours of each day and five hours of each night personally superintending the work. And in order to give encouragement and hasten it, a bonus was paid for accomplishing a distance greater than that regarded by the foreman as a fair day's work under the circumstances at the time.

The turn southward down Fifth Avenue was made on December 16th. The distance to the Eighty-second Street entrance to the park is seven hundred and ninety feet, or a uniform down grade of one to one hundred and thirty-one. The obelisk reached the turning-point at the intersection of Fifth Avenue with Eighty-second Street on December 18th, and was turned on December 22d to the direction in which it was to be hauled over the trestle to the site. The greatest distance covered in one day was six hundred feet on November 11th in the West Boulevard.

The trestle extended a distance of eight hundred and ninety feet from the roadway of Fifth Avenue to the site. It had a uniform ascending grade of one in fourteen nearly. Plates xxiii, xxiv, and xxvii fully illustrate this ordinary form of trestle, which was composed of timber bents, braced together in the customary manner, standing on mudsills, the tops connected with exceptionally large stringer-pieces which formed the ways timbers of the obelisk railway. The highest bent was

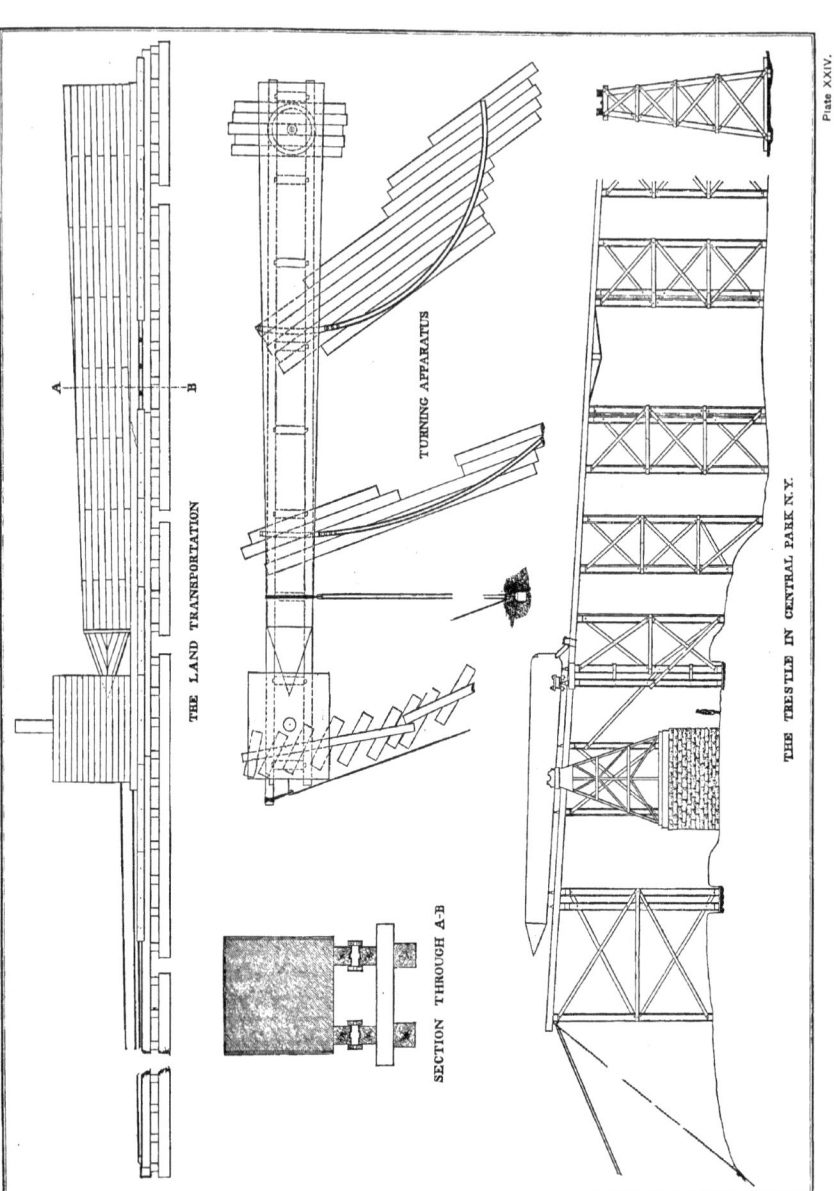

THE LAND TRANSPORTATION

TURNING APPARATUS

SECTION THROUGH A-B

THE TRESTLE IN CENTRAL PARK N.Y.

Plate XXIV.

Removal of the New York Obelisk.

forty-eight feet. The sizes of the timber for verticals, cross-pieces, and stringer-pieces varied from twelve to sixteen inches square, according to the height and other circumstances. It was commenced about October 1st, and completed just as the obelisk reached the lower end during the last week in December. Several sections of the "Dessoug's" bower cable were shackled together and extended along the entire length of the trestle; one end was secured to a large steel pin that had been let into a hole drilled in the rock a short distance west of the site. This served as a pennant for the pulling purchase, the stationary block of which was shackled into the links of the cable, and shifted farther along when the obelisk cradle had been pulled up to it.

A heavy fall of snow on December 28th, followed by intense cold, delayed the operation of hauling the obelisk up the trestle several days, and it did not reach its destination until January 5, 1881. On that day the centre of gravity was placed directly over the axis of the pedestal and foundation, and its long and tedious land journey was at an end. It had travelled 10,905 feet in 112 days, or at the rate of about ninety-seven feet a day.

SUSPENDING THE OBELISK IN THE TURNING STRUCTURE.

The cradle and engine were released by raising and suspending the obelisk on hydraulic pumps in the manner illustrated on Plate xxiv, lower figure. Double bents had been placed in the trestle, on each side of the turning structure, for the hydraulic pumps to stand on that were to raise the ends of the obelisk, and extra single bents were placed on the pedestal for other pumps to stand on to aid in lifting and supporting it. The aggregate lifting power of the seven hydraulic pumps used for this operation was four hundred and sixty tons, about double the weight of the obelisk. The apparatus used for applying two of the pumps to the large end was an iron yoke, shown on the lower figure in Plate xxiv, consisting of two wrought-iron beams, eight inches wide, six inches deep, and nine feet long, placed underneath and projecting on each side of the obelisk far enough to allow of two steel bolts, each three inches in diameter, to pass through the ends of each beam. The upper ends of the bolts passed through iron plates two feet long, six inches thick, and eight inches wide. The pistons of the pumps acted against the lower sides of these plates, which were adjustable to the requisite height by means of nuts screwed on both ends of the bolts.

Every thing having been cleared away between the lower side of the obelisk and the stringer-pieces of the trestle, the trunnions were hoisted by a pair of shears on one side and a boon derrick on the other, and carefully adjusted to the centre of gravity of the obelisk. Plate xxviii, enlarged section through the centre of gravity, illustrates the method of clasping the obelisk in the trunnion plates. Strips of very soft wood were placed against the stone to prevent injury by the iron; the plates P were then slid into position, between the lips E and the wood; the bolts H were rove through the lugs in the trunnion plates, and nuts screwed over the threads in both ends as tight as possible. The truss T, the same as that used in Alexandria, was then adjusted, as shown on Plates xxvii and xxviii, to support the ends of the obelisk. This work was completed on January 15th, and on that day the obelisk was lowered by the hydraulic pumps until the trunnions rested in the pillow-blocks and the entire weight had been transferred from the trestle to the turning structure. All supports were then removed from under the ends in order to test the turning apparatus and to determine whether or not the obelisk had been suspended exactly at its centre of gravity. The structure gave no evidence of weakness, and the obelisk turned easily in either direction.

The ancient Egyptians had invariably placed the obelisks they erected directly on the *pedestals*. The Romans had invariably mounted those they removed on metal supports, leaving a space between the obelisk and pedestal. My desire was to give the obelisk the greatest possible stability, while restoring it and its accessories as nearly as possible to the exact conditions that existed in Alexandria when I took possession of them. With this in view it was decided to mount the obelisk directly on

46 *Removal of the New York Obelisk.*

the pedestal, and place the metal supports under the corners. The bottom was imperfect from injuries received before I took charge of it, and not over two thirds of its area would come in contact with the pedestal. To give it a bearing surface equal to that which it would have if the corners had not been broken off, flanges had been cast on the bottoms of the crabs nearly equal to the difference of the area of the bottom of the obelisk as it is and as it was originally. Recesses R, Plate xxviii, end view of base, were cut into the rounded part of the bottom for the upper bearing on the crabs. These had been reproduced from plaster casts of the originals, perfected by Mr. Theodore Baur, sculptor, with great skill and feeling. The new crabs were cast at my expense in the Brooklyn Navy Yard, Commodore G. H. Cooper, U. S. N., Commandant, by permission of the Honorable Nathan Goff, Secretary of the Navy, under the immediate and careful supervision of Chief Engineer Charles H. Loring. Artistic moulders could not be found to complete this work. It was done mainly by the ordinary brass-moulders of the Navy Yard, to whose skill the results bear ample testimony. The metal is a bronze as nearly as possible the same as that of the crabs cast by the Romans nineteen centuries ago. The average weight of the new crabs is nine hundred and twenty-two pounds each.

The decision to place the bottom of the obelisk directly in contact with the pedestal necessarily involved a change of plan from the reverse method of raising it in Alexandria. The new plan is fully illustrated on Plate xxviii. Plaster casts were made of the sides of the obelisk close to the bottom. From these casts moulds were made that would allow for shrinkage of the molten metal, so that the clamps would fit exactly into the hieroglyphs and around the broken corners. Lugs (L) were cast on the outside faces of the clamps for the trunnion tie-rods (C) to pass through. The ends were also provided with holes for steel bolts (I) to pass through from one to the other. The weight of each was five thousand seven hundred pounds.

The clamps were hoisted and placed in position on January 18th. The bolts (I) passing through the ends were provided with threads over which nuts were screwed to bind them tightly against the stone. It is evident that the metal that fitted into the recesses of the hieroglyphs and around the corners of the obelisk would prevent the clamps from sliding toward the trunnions when the tie-rods had been placed in position and tightened. For the same reason the obelisk could not slip downward after it had been turned to a vertical position, until the tie-rods (C) had been lengthened by revolving the turn-buckles (K).

The work of demolishing the trestle had been proceeding rapidly, and by January 20th all the bents, except the double one, shown on Plate xxvii, under the forward end of the obelisk, had been removed.

The composition clamps had given the large end of the obelisk preponderance enough to overcome the friction of the trunnions in the pillow-blocks while the obelisk was horizontal. Tackles were led from both ends to suitable places to insure perfect control ; and by the forenoon of January 20th the obelisk was ready to be placed vertically on its pedestal. Noon of January 22d had previously been fixed on for the operation. To thoroughly test every thing and be reassured that there would be no unforeseen difficulty, an experimental turn was made at 11 o'clock P. M. of the 20th. The obelisk was then replaced in a horizontal position, and remained suspended on the turning structure through the violent gale of January 21st, that left its mark on so many things in and around New York.

RE-ERECTING THE OBELISK.
NOON JANUARY 22, 1881.

Long before the hour fixed on for turning the obelisk, spectators had occupied every available space in the park and its vicinity from which a good view could be obtained. In spite of the piercing cold wind and thick bed of snow that lay on the ground, ladies formed at least half of the

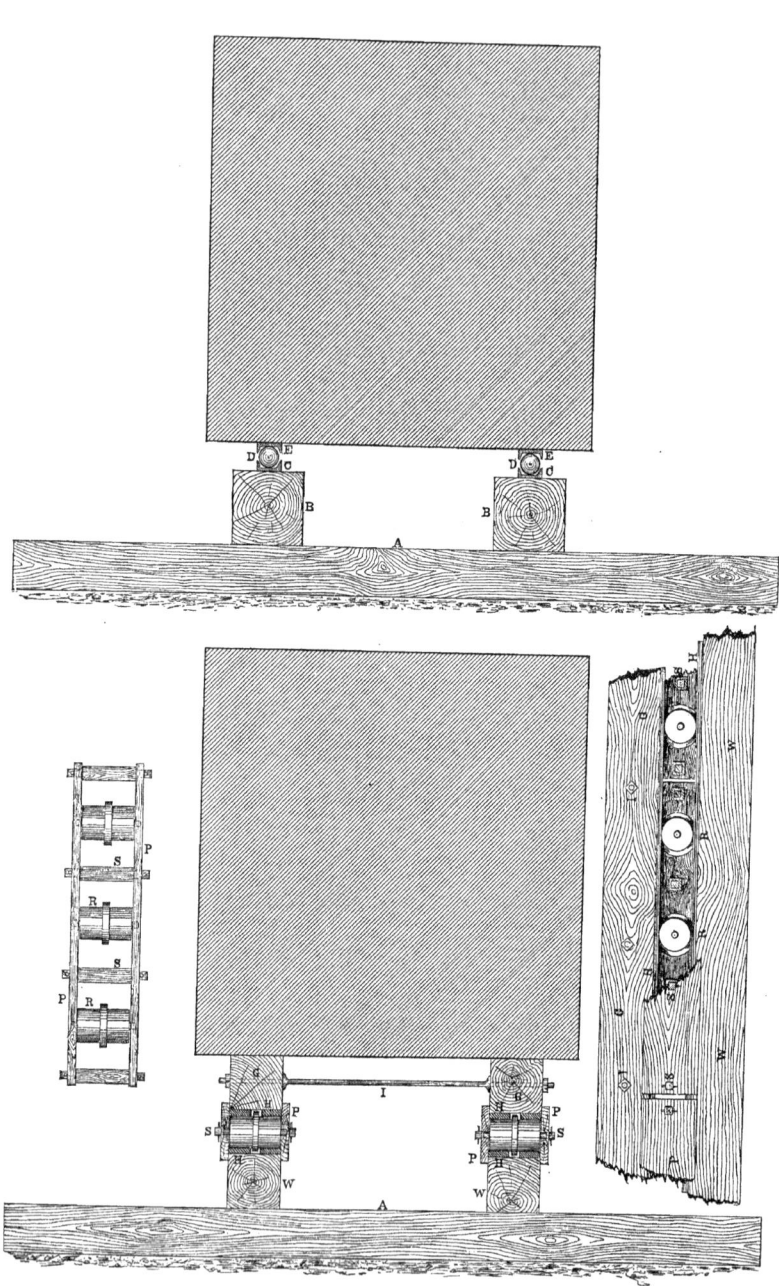

IRON CHANNELS AND MARINE RAILWAY.

Removal of the New York Obelisk. 47

ten thousand persons estimated as the number who witnessed the operation. A cordon of park-keepers encircled the immediate vicinity of the site, and with difficulty kept the crowd from encroaching within the space reserved for workmen. A platform had been erected on the north side of this space for the accommodation of distinguished persons and officials. A battalion of sailors and marines from the Navy Yard, Brooklyn, under the command of Lieutenant-Commander W. H. Whiting, U. S. Navy, and Captain Bishop, U. S. Marine Corps, had been ordered by the Secretary of the Navy to act as a guard of honor for the occasion. They arrived at the park headed by the Marine Band at a little before noon, and were paraded in double line on the north side of the site, enclosing the platform on three sides. His Honor, W. R. Grace, the Mayor, the Aldermen, and other officers of the city, many of the civil and judicial officers of the State, very many civil, judicial, army and navy officers of the United States, nearly all of the foreign consuls residing in New York, a large delegation of the members of the Grand Lodge, almost all the members of Anglo-Saxon Lodge in a body, and a large number of distinguished citizens and professional men, accompanied by their wives and families, having positions upon the platform, occupied nearly every inch of available space. Five thousand cards had been issued as a souvenir of the event, bearing on one side a picture of the obelisk as it stood in Alexandria, and on the other an announcement that it would be placed on its pedestal in the Central Park at noon of January 22d.

A few minutes before noon the Hon. Wm. M. Evarts, Secretary of State, the Honorable Nathan Goff, Secretary of the Navy, and Mr. William Henry Hurlbert, Editor of the *New York World*, drove up to the foot of Graywacke Knoll, dismounted, and took positions reserved for them on the platform. The men stationed at the fall of the down-haul tackle from the base, and those stationed at the fall of the lowering tackle from the top of the obelisk, had been previously instructed to haul down and slack away, respectively, when I held my hand up, and as long as it was held up, and to stop as soon as I lowered my hand. After a moment's conversation with Mr. Evarts the signal was given, and the obelisk slowly turned, the spectators preserving a silence that was almost unnatural. When the obelisk had changed from the horizontal to an angle of about forty-five degrees, I gave the signal to hold it in that position while Mr. Edward Bierstadt made a photograph for which he had made preparations. This seemed to break the spell that bound the spectators in silence, and when the signal was given to continue the turning there arose a loud cheer which was prolonged until the shaft stood erect. It is something to have witnessed the manipulation of a mass weighing nearly two hundred and twenty tons changing its position majestically, yet as easily and steadily as if it were without weight. It was to me an inexpressible relief to feel that my work was complete, and that no accident or incident had happened that would make my countrymen regret that I had been intrusted with the work of removing and re-erecting in their metropolis one of the most famous monuments of the Old World and the most ancient and interesting relic of the past on the American Continent. Only five minutes elapsed from the first signal to the time the obelisk was vertical. As it reached this position the Marine Band played the national airs while the battalion presented arms. Congratulations followed, and the spectators very soon dispersed.

After the grounds had been cleared the hydraulic pumps (*A*, Plate xxviii) were placed in position under the clamps (*B*) on each corner of the pedestal. The obelisk was once more supended on them, the bolts of the trunnions were slackened, the turn-buckles of the tie-rods revolved, and the obelisk lowered by the pumps and turn-buckles until it rested on the pedestal. Adjusting it so as to have the axis correspond with that of the shaft, heating the surfaces that were to come in contact so as to fit them for a thin layer of cement, and spreading this cement uniformly in the severe cold that prevailed during that afternoon, delayed the work until eight o'clock in the evening, at which hour the obelisk was finally landed on the pedestal and released from the turning structure. Fifteen months had elapsed from the day the work of removal began in Alexandria. In this time it had travelled five thousand three hundred and eighty miles by water, and eleven thousand five hundred and twenty feet by land; had been lowered thirty-nine feet, and lifted two hundred and thirty feet.

Removing the machinery, demolishing the foundation walls and workshops, and clearing away the debris from Graywacke Knoll, were all accomplished within ten days after the obelisk was re-erected. Placing and securing the crabs in position was a tedious process, owing to continued freezing weather, and occupied us ten days longer. To give the upper part of the metal a uniform bearing, molten lead was poured into the vacant spaces and caulked in around the edges. To render their removal impossible without destroying the pedestal, molten lead was poured into the mortices around the dowels projecting downward from the lower side of the flanges, through holes bored in them for the purpose. The crabs are not ornaments only; they serve to give the bottom of the obelisk a bearing surface on the pedestal nearly equal to the area of its base if the corners had not been broken off. To pull the obelisk over without first raising it clear of the pedestal would require a force applied to its centre of gravity equivalent to that required for lifting seventy-eight tons. The maximum pressure that could be exerted by wind blowing with the force of a hurricane on the obelisk would be equivalent to that required to lift fifteen tons. This pressure would be exerted uniformly over the whole of one face or its equivalent. The factor of stability is therefore very great. It would require an exceptionally severe earthquake, one that would leave very few buildings in New York standing, to render the obelisk unstable.

THE PRESENTATION CEREMONIES.

The ceremony of formally presenting the obelisk to New York City was fixed for February 22d, and the use of the grand hall of the Metropolitan Museum near by was tendered by the trustees for the purpose. A committee, of which the Honorable Henry G. Stebbins was Chairman, Messrs. Algernon S. Sullivan, John Taylor Johnston, Robert Hewitt, Jr., and Stephen A. Walker were members, had perfected all the arrangements and issued tickets of admission to the museum.

The following detailed account of the ceremony and incidents connected therewith is reproduced from the *New York World* of February 23d. It would be impossible for me to make a better record of the facts. It would be embarrassing for me to relate such as have a personal bearing, and it seems as if the record would be incomplete without them.

The tide in the direction of Central Park and the obelisk set in at noon, and at 2 o'clock had flooded the flat ground between the Metropolitan Museum of Art and Greywacke Knoll, upon which the obelisk stands, and all the walks and drives adjacent thereto, with people. Not a train on either of the elevated roads, not a car on the several street railways, but had gone up town after noon loaded down with passengers. At a rough estimate there were in the Central Park at 2 P. M. 20,000 people. It had been announced that the interesting ceremonies connected with the formal presentation to the city, through the United States government, of the Khedive's splendid gift would take place within the shelter of the Metropolitan Museum of Art, and that admittance to the museum could only be obtained by tickets. Nevertheless an unlimited number of people, a throng beyond the capacity of any ten halls in New York combined, went to the park, bent upon hearing the address of the Secretary of State, and on being close eye-witnesses of all the interesting details of the presentation. This fact is pleasant, inasmuch as it shows beyond peradventure that the people of New York are not insensible of the value and magnitude of Egypt's gift to America; but the immediate results were inevitable. To have opened the doors of the Metropolitan Museum, spacious as is that structure, to the throng which surged about it, would have been to produce a crush in which nobody could have lived. Early comers had, however, taken possession of the top steps leading to the two doors of the museum, and behind them, stretching away to the north and south, were solid lines of impatient citizens who blocked the broad stairways and the asphalt walks, and rendered it a matter of extreme difficulty for invited guests to extricate themselves from their carriages and gain a foothold anywhere in front of the museum building.

At 2.10 o'clock, a platoon of park policemen having meantime been pressed into service, the doors leading to the museum were opened and the holders of tickets were admitted. It was the crush of a favorite opera night ten times intensified. Presently, however, as the hopelessness of obtaining an entrance began to dawn upon the unticketed, the ways broadened and the invited company was ushered into the hall. At the east end of the main floor a platform capable of seating sixty or seventy persons had been erected. Facing this platform were

TRANSPORTING THE OBELISK

Plate XXV

a number of chairs reserved for the holders of special tickets. The intervening space between the reserved rows and the four walls of the building was quickly filled. It was a thoroughly amiable throng, however, which had taken possession of the building, and understanding that accommodations were of necessity limited, contented itself in good-humor. The scene through any one of the great windows in the front of the building would at this moment have done good to the gracious heart of his generous Highness the ex-Khedive Ismaïl. Clear cut against a cloudless sky rose the graceful lines of the monolith. Thousands of people, made very small by contrast with the towering shaft, crowded around its base and pressed one another on the sloping hill. Closer at hand, between the throng of devotees at the base of the monument and the Museum of Fine Arts, was a mass of carriages. Inside of the museum the only unoccupied space at 2.30 o'clock was the platform. The north gallery had been taken possession of by Theodore Thomas' New York chorus, and the south gallery, divided by a partition, gave seats to the one hundred common-school boys who were to receive copies of the medal struck in honor of the occasion by the Numismatic Society, and to a number of ladies whose avowed interest in the obelisk, as well as in the Museum of Art, entitled them to special privileges.

At a little after half past 2 P. M. Mr. Evarts, leaning upon the arm of Mr. John Taylor Johnston, ascended the platform. His appearance was the signal for an outburst of applause, which had not ceased when all the gentlemen who followed him had found seats. Immediately behind Secretary Evarts and Mr. Johnston were Chancellor Howard Crosby and Chief-Justice Daly, the former wearing the black silk faced with violet velvet robe of his office. The platform soon became fully occupied. His Honor, W. R. Grace, the Mayor, who was to receive the gift, was seated next to Secretary Evarts, who was to present it.

Mr. John Taylor Johnston, the President of the museum, presided. Mr. Evarts was given a seat at his right. President Barnard, with Lieutenant-Commander Gorringe at his side, sat on Mr. Johnston's left. Dr. Crosby, at the request of Mr. Johnston, began the ceremonies with prayer, as follows:

"Almighty God, our Heavenly Father, Who hast given to us a goodly heritage in this land of liberty and peace, and hast afforded us opportunity and means for growth in wisdom and knowledge, we desire to lift up our hearts to Thee with humble and grateful acknowledgment of Thy mercies and to ask for Thy continued favor. We thank Thee for the prosperity of our beloved city, for its health and thrift, for its wealth and enterprise, and for its institutions of charity and education. We thank Thee for the centres of refined culture Thou hast enabled our citizens to establish by which to elevate and enlighten the public mind, and now this day we do give Thee our hearty thanks that Thou hast permitted the enterprise which connects us with an extreme antiquity to be brought to a successful termination; and we pray Thee, most gracious Lord, that those who have been especially instrumental in forwarding this work may be rewarded by seeing its utility, both as an ornament and a teacher among us, adorning the city, while it contrasts our light and privileges with the darkness and tyranny of the older time. We beseech Thee, Almighty God, to accept our petition for Jesus' sake. Amen."

Next the hymn, written expressly for the occasion by Mr. Richard Watson Gilder, was finely sung by Mr. Thomas' trained choir in the north gallery, which was conducted by Mr. George F. Bristow and Mr. William G. Dietrich. The hymn, which had been adapted by Mr. Thomas to the music of Luther's hymn, "Ein' Feste Burg," is as follows:

> Great God, to Whom since time began
> The world has prayed and striven;
> Maker of stars, and earth, and man—
> To Thee our praise is given!
>   Here, by this ancient Sign
>   Of Thine own Light Divine,
>   We lift to Thee our eyes,
>   Thou Dweller of the skies—
> Hear us, O God in heaven!
>
> Older than Nilus' mighty flood
> Into the mid-sea pouring,
> Or than the sea, Thou God hast stood—
> Thou God Whom we 're adoring.
>   Waters and stormy blasts
>   Haste when Thou bid'st them haste;
>   Silent, and hid, and still,
>   Thou sendest good and ill:
> Thy ways are past exploring.
>
> In myriad forms, by myriad names,
> Men seek to bind and mould Thee;
> But Thou dost melt, like wax in flames,
> The cords that would enfold Thee.
>   Who madest life and light,
>   Bring'st morning after night,
>   Who all things did'st create—
>   No majesty, nor state,
> Nor word, nor world can hold Thee.
>
> Great God, to Whom since time began
> The world has prayed and striven;
> Maker of stars, and earth, and man—
> To Thee our praise is given!
>   Of suns Thou art the Sun,
>   Eternal, Holy One:
>   Who can us help save Thou?
>   To Thee alone, alone we bow—
> O hear us, God in heaven!

Removal of the New York Obelisk.

An introductory address by Mr. Henry G. Stebbins, the Chairman of the Committee of Arrangements, was to have followed the singing of the hymn, but Mr. Stebbins was not able, as will be seen by the following letter, to be present:

"2 WEST SIXTEENTH STREET, *February* 21st.

"A. S. SULLIVAN, Esq.

"DEAR SIR: I had hoped and expected until to-day to perform the duties assigned to me by the committee in charge of the arrangements in the formal presentation of the obelisk in Central Park to-morrow. I find myself, however, prevented by a sudden and severe cold, which forbids the carrying out of my purposes. I regret this the more because I have taken a special interest in the bringing here and in the location of an artistic memorial of an ancient civilization, which now fitly looks on the beginning of what I trust will become a great museum of art. This museum is destined to supply a permanent home for the trophies from all countries and of all periods in which art has flourished and left its memorials. I hope I may be allowed to express my conviction that the selection of the site for the obelisk will be more approved as its harmony with the surroundings and the security of its setting become more and more generally recognized. Liberality, enterprise, official aid, and private assistance have added a graceful and suggestive monument to our great out-door gallery. I hope that the successful placing of this interesting monument in such a relation to the future national gallery of America will encourage our wealthy citizens to enlarge the Art Museum and to fill it with all those treasures which so greatly increase the attractions of the metropolis.

"Yours, very sincerely,

"H. G. STEBBINS."

Mr. John Taylor Johnston then introduced Mr. Evarts, who was received with hearty applause, and who in the following address formally presented the obelisk to the city:

MR. PRESIDENT, LADIES AND GENTLEMEN: I responded with pleasure to the call of the committee to take such part in the installation of the obelisk as they in their judgment thought suitable. My relation to the occasion and my service before you are naturally and necessarily mainly official and ceremonial, for I have had no personal share in the first construction of this obelisk, nor in any of its movements since; and in the great transaction so creditable to ourselves and our age by which it has been acquired, by which it has been transported, and by which it has been placed on this site, I have had only an official and ceremonial share. I think it is something like twelve years ago that one of our distinguished fellow-citizens, the head of one of the principal journals of the country, being in the Mediterranean on the occasion of the opening of the Suez Canal, and being in the company of the Khedive of Egypt, learned from him that there was no insurmountable obstacle in Egyptian mystery or Egyptian pride against the obelisk's being sent across the ocean, if only an obelisk could be supposed capable of making the voyage. This idea, cherished for some years, at last began to put itself in the course of execution. In the first year, I think, of my administration of the Department of State some preliminary considerations on the subject were taken between that gentleman and myself; but it was not until the visit of our excellent and faithful Consul-General in Egypt, Mr. Farman, to this country in the summer of 1878, that full information was gained here of the conditions necessary and the prospect of success, and that full instructions were given to him on the part of the government as to his action in reaching the desired end. From that step the stages were easy and rapid, and in May, 1879, Mr. Farman informed the State Department that the consent of the then Khedive had been given to the transaction, and your distinguished fellow-citizen, Mr. Stebbins, was acquainted with the success of the measure to which from the beginning he had lent his name and influence. Thus it seemed as if every difficulty was overcome so far as the good-will of the Khedive was concerned, and the first step of our government for the transfer of the prize; but by one of the vicissitudes of government which abound in that land the Khedive suddenly abdicated, leaving his gift incomplete and leaving the country and the obelisk behind him, and there was somewhat of solicitude whether the incomplete gift would be assured to us by the approval and ratification of his successor. But the delicate and careful and faithful efforts of Mr. Farman were at last crowned with success, notwithstanding some obstacles on the part of jealous governments which thought it a shame that their capital should not hold all the obelisks, even if Egypt should be despoiled of them. When we arrived at that conclusion we went in search of a man of courage, skill, and knowledge of the sea, competent in the judgment of others and confident in his own ability, and we were fortunate in finding such an one in an accomplished officer of our navy, Lieutenant-Commander Gorringe, a man wholly fitted for the achievement of bringing the obelisk hither. And when I asked the Secretary of the Navy to grant him leave of absence, and desired to know whether his previous record had been such that this grand work, with all its risks and peril, could be entrusted to him, I got but one answer, and that was that whatever Gorringe undertook to do he would accomplish. Whether that was as well-deserved a reputation then as I supposed it to have been I know not, but I think that the wider circle of observers and the generous testimony of his fellow-citizens will now give warrant, that whatever Lieutenant-

OBELISK CROSSING THE MAIN DRIVE IN CENTRAL PARK.

Copyright, 1881, by HARRROUN & BIERSTADT, New York

Plate XXVI

Removal of the New York Obelisk. 51

Commander Gorringe undertakes to do he will accomplish. Lieutenant-Commander Gorringe reached Alexandria on the 21st of October, 1879. He procured a vessel and began the opening of her sides, or her bow or her stern or whatever was most useful, in order that the obelisk might be trundled into it on cannon-balls. He left with it about June, 1880, and met with a disaster at sea that was enough to wreck the vessel had he not been provided with a shaft to replace the broken one. He reached here some time about the 25th of July, and then the labor of the land passage began, which was incomparably greater than that of the transport across the Atlantic. By slow stages the obelisk traversed its way along our crowded thoroughfares, and finally reached a position to be elevated on its present pedestal on the 22d of January last. The foundation had been prepared previously, and the laying of its corner-stone had been accompanied by imposing ceremonies under the charge of the Masonic institutions of this country, that institution finding most interesting records to show that the Free and Accepted Order of Masons existed in Egypt at least 1,800 years ago. Now the communication of these facts leaves only one thing to be added, and that is that an obelisk cannot work its own passage across the Atlantic. Somebody must pay for it, and such an one had been found in your very public-spirited fellow-citizen, a man furnished with abundant means to carry out whatever he should undertake in a financial direction. When he was first approached on the subject, Mr. Wm. H. Vanderbilt made the immediate and generous response, that he would bear the expense of the undertaking, desiring his name not to be mentioned until a time should come when it could properly be announced. His presence was expected here to-day, but we are deprived of it by some casual infirmity which detains him from us. These facts, the voyage of this obelisk and the provision for the expense thereof, show, I think, a munificence unexampled, great advance in opportunities and means of such transportation, and great skill, energy, and economy. The expense of the transfer has been a little over $100,000, and Lieutenant-Commander Gorringe has contributed his services as his part of the great work.

"This is not the first obelisk that has left its home in Egypt to seek new scenes; but never before perhaps has the transfer been as voluntary on the part of the Egyptian government as now. These obelisks, great and triumphant structures, having for their inscription nothing but the official pomp of their founders, mark a culmination of the power and glory of Egypt, and every conqueror has seemed to think that the final trophy of Egypt's subjection and the proud pre-eminence of his own nation could be shown only by taking an obelisk—the chief mark of Egyptian pomp and pride—to grace the capital of the conquering nation. The first was taken by a conquering Assyrian monarch, of great mark in his time and remembered through all the ages since, known better to us and more easily by the Greek name of Sardanapalus. He took an obelisk to Nineveh when that empire was the mistress of the world, and that obelisk made the first great voyage like this which our obelisk has taken. Although there are no records of the precise route which the Assyrian took for his obelisk, yet it is very apparent that it was taken to the Red Sea, and then down the Red Sea into the Indian Ocean, and then through the Persian Gulf to the mouth of the Euphrates, and thence to Nineveh, beyond the navigation of the river. This route must have included some 1,500 miles of water transport. We are somewhat at a loss to understand how the methods and vehicle for such a transportation could have existed at that age. We have but little record of that; but as the obelisk undoubtedly got to Nineveh and could not get across the desert by land, it must have made this circuitous route of 1,500 miles. The next power which assumed to take obelisks from Egypt was the Roman State in the times of the emperors, and they took as many as fifteen, one after the other, and twelve of them now remain in Italy. This brings us to the period close upon the Christian era and to the time of the first famous Cæsar, Julius, and his successors, when Egypt, subject and abject, yielded up the treasures of its art and of its faith to the conquering spoiler. Next comes the Eastern Empire, having Byzantium as its capital, and it, too, demanded contribution of the wealth of Egypt,—the contribution of obelisks to mark the domination of the city of Constantine,—and Byzantium, now Constantinople, still contains two obelisks thus taken. This closes the list of transportations in ancient times. All subsequent removals of obelisks have been within this century. The French and British, as all know, made Egypt a battle field, and the famous naval battles of the Nile and the famous battles in which Napoleon and Abercrombie measured their strength are familiar to us all. Egypt recognized her obligations to England, and offered an obelisk to England—then the great power of the earth,—but its very transportation—the expense thereof—seemed so serious that the gift remained lying on the sand at Alexandria, and no attempt was made for its transfer until 1877. This was completed in 1878. British ingenuity in the architecture of naval vessels and in navigation and in engineering had only taught Britons that the obelisk could not be carried in the hold of a ship, and the experiment was made of building a vehicle around the obelisk that could float it and float itself, and could be towed by steamer so arranged as to give the crew an opportunity of saving themselves, so that when it came to a choice between the sinking of the obelisk and the sinking of the crew the steamer could be cut loose from the tow. The experiment was not such as to encourage imitation by us even if Commander Gorringe had not had that faith in a ship which had been his cradle from his youth, and had not thought that if a ship could carry all the men and all the armor and all the cargoes that modern civilization burdens it with, it could carry the obelisk. The caisson, or whatever it was called, in which the English obelisk was inclosed was abandoned in mid-ocean, and the experiment, delayed for fifty years from the time the gift was made till the courage and skill were found to undertake it, stood disappointed in its accomplishment. Some adventurers of the sea, picking up the abandoned obelisk, towed it in and afterward libelled it in the Admiralty Court and received £5,000 for executing what the original arrangement had failed to accomplish. The French obelisk was given by Mehemet Ali to Charles X, though Napoleon had long before planned the taking of one to Paris. In 1831, just fifty years ago, Louis Philippe undertook the transportation, and placed the obelisk where so many good Americans have seen it, in Paris, in Place de la Concorde. It is indisputable that the expenses of this transfer across the Mediterranean, or around by the Bay of Biscay, whichever way it went, were nearly $500,000, or about five times as much as our enterprise, under the execution of Commander Gorringe, cost.

"Our obelisk is here. It is here—and now, Mr. Mayor, I have the honor to transfer to the keeping of the city of New York this great and ancient monument. May it stand upon its site a perpetual monument, an emblem of Egypt, a witness and teacher of that most ancient civilization, to be cherished by this great modern city in the present and the future, as a pledge and an evidence of the constant friendship of the ex-Khedive Ismaïl, of his son Tewfik Pacha and of the Egyptian government to the government and people of the United States. What is our obelisk? How came it here? What shall it teach us and what shall we say to it while it remains with us? This obelisk was one of two at the Temple of Heliopolis, a few miles from Cairo, and was one only of the numerous structures of this character that the great King Thothmes III raised in glory to himself and in honor to his god. Great temples, great monuments in other forms as well as in obelisks, marked his reign. He was the greatest king that Egypt had ever seen. He had united Upper and Lower Egypt into one kingdom. He had conquered other nations and extended the Egyptian frontiers to the ends of the earth. He was a patron of the arts, a lover of learning, had all the kingly virtues, was full of devotion to religion, faithful to Egypt, a magnificent king and conqueror. He was of the age that saw the exodus of the Hebrews from Egypt. He was of the age in which Moses was born. He appears in the long line of history with the greatest conquerors of the world—with Alexander, with Cæsar, with Napoleon. He lived in a stage of society at a period in the world's advancement when the gulf between the king and the people was vast, and in the proportion in which he was vast and magnificent they were abject and poor. This obelisk, then, standing there in front of that temple for fifteen hundred years, saw all the famous men of other countries seeking the learning of the Egyptians in this temple, the great school resorted to by great statesmen and philosophers of the ancient world. No doubt, passing under the shadow of this obelisk, Moses came to know all the wisdom of the Egyptians. In this same temple Solon and Thales and Plato learned the wisdom that made them the benefactors of the world. Transferred to Alexandria to grace the triumph and illustrate the supremacy of the Cæsars, our obelisk witnessed there on the shores of the Mediterranean—in the great city founded by the Greek who carried the arms of Europe to the Indus—the rise, fluctuation and fall of great schools of philosophy, the fortunes of a mighty mart of commerce, and the final disappearance of Græco-Roman civilization under the flood of Mahometan conquest. Cleopatra got more credit for this needle, or rather this needle has got more credit from Cleopatra than the fact justifies. It was not erected in front of the temple or palace of the Cæsars until six years after her death, and whatever the glories were that Cleopatra and Cæsar shared together in the Egyptian splendor of those days at Alexandria, this obelisk and its contemplation were not among them. Yet it formed a part of Roman splendor and domination in Egypt, and while they took as many as they pleased, fortunately this was left, as being associated with Roman glory in Alexandria, in front of the palace or temple of the Cæsars. The other was thrown down, but this one stood wherever it was placed from the time it was so placed until, standing, it was taken down to be removed. This, then, is the genius of this obelisk—the faculty of staying where it was put. It never has been prostrated by time or casualty. It never has been broken by clumsiness or blundering. It never has been out of good hands. First, those of Thothmes and his engineers; second, of the Cæsars and the Roman masters of mankind; and, third, of Mr. Hurlbert and Mr. Stebbins and Commander Gorringe and Mr. Vanderbilt. What, then, is the lesson, what the teaching that this obelisk is to give us? Hitherto, in ancient times, each one was transferred from its home in Egypt, at a time of the strength and pride of the nation that took it, as spoil. These obelisks have looked down and waited, not in vain, for the same strife, for the same ruin which they had witnessed in Egypt. Rome, mistress of the world, in the sight of the obelisks planted in the great city, was taken and sacked by Northern barbarians, its empire dispersed, its learning, its civilization obscured, its power as an empire never again restored. The obelisks of Byzantium saw the last Constantine perish under the tide of Asiatic barbarism. Assyria within our obelisk's lifetime has fallen as an empire—by successive conquerors has been trampled in the dust. Asia still holds its obelisks, if you can only find them, but they have been buried in the ruins of Nineveh, which has hidden them from all modern explorers. Sooner or later, then, in the experience of ancient times, the obelisks have had their revenge, if they cherished any affection for Egypt and felt any humiliation in her degradation and their transportation. If these obelisks could only tell of the glories in which they have assisted, if they could only remember all they saw and only narrate all they remember, what teachers they would be! How they would smile at modern strength and glory and at the pride of one hundred or one thousand years as indicating strength and permanency and endurance! How they would say, whatever else may be the forms through which civilization and population, governments and power of nations are to pass, there is one common grave of ruin in which they are all to be buried.

"Turning to modern obelisks we see what has happened within the brief time in which one of them for

TURNING THE OBELISK

Plate XXVII

half a century has stood in the Place de la Concorde. In this fifty years it has seen the monarchy followed by the empire, and that empire yield to the republic. But observe how little those forms of government—how little those great men of the earth—are in the action of modern civilization. How has France been humbled? The pride of domination and dynasty has fallen, but France—greater, richer, freer, more noble and prosperous than ever—stands the same, and this obelisk in the great place of Paris has seen only those little perturbations upon the surface without one stone falling from another in the great structure of the French nation. The English obelisk has not been there long enough to gather much experience about the prosperity of our great mother country. It has so far witnessed only the agitations of the Irish Land League, though who can tell what those may yet portend? While we all feel solicitude and sympathy for her fate, we feel that as a matter of pride, next to ourselves, the mother country of our republic should bear a high place among the nations of the world. But you will say at once that in England any transposition of force—of stated power—would pass for little. It has been a long time since the institutions of England depended upon its monarchy, and it has been a long time since the monarchy has formed one of the vital institutions of the country. Now, here—what shall we say of the prospects and assurances by which we may hope in our system of society, in our system of religion, in our system of government, to outlast the obelisk, if the obelisk is to wait for our ruin? At the very time that Thothmes was rearing these great monuments of his power, a feeble Hebrew infant, doomed to death from his birth in expectation of the race becoming too formidable and too much oppressed, uttered a feeble cry from the bulrushes when the daughter of Pharaoh disturbed his sleep, and Moses has come here long before this obelisk; Moses, the greatest law-giver that the world ever saw—Moses with his ten commandments—is in possession of the churches, and of the schools, and of the literature, and of the morals of society. Egypt is represented not only here but throughout our system of civilization by the cry of the infant Moses, heard throughout the whole modern world. Twenty-two years after this obelisk was raised at Alexandria by the Romans to mark their perpetual dominion, there was born in the neighboring and subject province of Palestine another infant, destined also to death from His infancy—Christ the Saviour, a name before which all kings and rulers and conquerors, all dynasties, all principalities and powers have fallen in obedience; and before this obelisk from Alexandria had reached our shores we had heard the name of Christ, and the religion of Christ has been made the basis of our civilization, of our national strength, of our national permanence. I do not deny that we may see slow corruption. I do not deny the possibility of popular failure. I do not know but you may become weary of well-doing, and scoff at Moses and the prophets, and fall away from the name of Jesus. Who indeed can tell what our nation will do if any such perversity is possible of realization; and yet this obelisk may ask us, 'Can you expect to flourish forever? Can you expect wealth to accumulate and man not decay? Can you think that the soft folds of luxury are to wrap themselves closer and closer around this nation and the pith and vigor of its manhood know no decay? Can it creep over you and yet the nation know no decrepitude?' These are questions that may be answered in the time of the obelisk, but not in ours."

At the conclusion of Mr. Evarts' address, Mayor Grace, who was seated just behind President Barnard, arose to respond on behalf of the city, and, bowing to Mr. Evarts and the ladies upon the platform, said:

"SIR: On behalf of the city of New York it affords me great pleasure to receive from the Khedive of Egypt, through the kindness of very public-spirited gentlemen, the great historical monument which now adorns our Central Park. The generosity of the donor is extreme. He sends us to be placed in our midst a most valued and valuable monument of an older era, as if to remind us of the instability of nations, of our own youth, and of the greatness of the past. The civilization in the midst of which this monument was constructed presents a most perfect contrast to that of our day and country. The social constitution of Egypt, based as it was upon caste, has nothing in common with that newer notion which lies at the bottom of the modern state— absolute equality of opportunity, absolute equality before the law. As time has proved the enemy of the old social form and the friend of the new, it may be hoped that the stability which was wanting to the one may not be so to the other. Strangely enough, that civilization whose bond was community of blood, and of which the city was the parent and the centre,—the pre-Christian civilization,—was that which afforded the least stability to the city, while that which regards universal liberty as the groundwork of society, and holds the city as only a constituent part of a larger political whole, is the most favorable to municipal development. As our city grows in its liberties it continues in the true spirit of conservatism to save all of value in the past, and so a historical monument which will serve to bind us to antiquity as does this great obelisk—which has been safely brought here only by the exercise of ingenuity and engineering skill—is something of which the city of New York should be, and, I assure you, will be proud."

Mr. A. S. Sullivan then rose to present the medals struck in commemoration of the occasion. "On behalf of the American Numismatic and Archæological Society of New York," he said, "I have now to fulfil a commission without which our proceedings would almost fail to express in rounded proportions the significance, the utility, and the beauty of these stately ceremonies. Yonder cuts the Western sky a memorial stone which has hitherto been a beacon under an Eastern sky. While, as I speak, its shadow, from the sinking sun, moves toward us, it seems to people this museum, from the dim past of the Orient, with weird myths and mysteries and splendid legends. That monolith was an emblem of Deity. The kings and priests who set it up have been mummies for thirty centuries, and their sun-worship is giving place to the adoration of the '*Lux Benigna et Divina*' of the true revelation. Their monument has been moved to the new continent to be an ever-speaking witness to the continuity and unity of human thought. It is the fittest of all possible sentinels at the portal of our future great archæological temple. An appreciative token of the liberal financial donor, Mr. William H. Vanderbilt, and of the skilful and indefatigable engineer, Lieutenant-Commander H. H. Gorringe, U. S. N., to whose mediary agency we owe this souvenir of Egyptian methods, has been stamped upon medals to commemorate this occasion medalically, artistically, and historically. The first impressions from the die in silver, in the name of the distinguished society already named, and in view of this assembly, I now deliver to Mr. Vanderbilt and to Lieutenant-Commander Gorringe, whose great services to the cause of art and historic enlightenment are hereby recognized by all the educational circles of New York and America."

As he spoke Mr. Sullivan removed from its paper folds a long flat box of handsome workmanship, which he handed unopened to Commander Gorringe amid the applause of the audience. Commander Gorringe, hearing cries of his name from all parts of the hall, signified by a gesture to Mr. Johnston his disinclination to speak. Mr. Sullivan, saying that the absence of Mr. W. H. Vanderbilt was deeply regretted by him and, he had no doubt, by all present, also handed a box, similar to the one presented to Commander Gorringe, to a gentleman who took charge of it for Mr. Vanderbilt. The medals contained in these boxes were similar in character to those which were immediately afterward presented to the boys from the public schools, wrought only in more precious metal. Mr. Sullivan then addressing the hundred boys, who had risen to their feet and whose bright faces were turned attentively toward him, continued:

"But there remains the closing and not the least important feature in the design of this celebration. I turn to the gallery above us and I see one hundred faces of as many bright boys of New York and who represent the one hundred thousand children who crowd her public schools. My lads, you are welcome participants in our ceremonies. It is, perhaps, the first time in the history of New York that the children have been formally given a station in great public movements, but I hope it will not be so hereafter. We wish you to grow up with the feeling that the monuments, the museums, the schools, the libraries, the statues, the public institutions, the churches, the parks, and all the agencies that look to the improvement and the refinement and the health of the people, to the honor and virtue and morals of the city, to its public spirit and its civic pride, to its good repute and its magnificence, are a trust which you are soon to assume. They are now to influence and educate you, and we beg you to cherish them continuously. Let your book-studies be associated with all these sentiments. Meditate upon them with love. Determine to take a part in the community for its good, and that New York shall be better for your having lived in it. Revere such benefactors of mankind as dear old Peter Cooper, and ever remember that 'a good name is better than riches.' In the hope that this day shall be a great teaching day to all the children of New York, and lift them forward on an ascending plane, I address you as the representatives of all of them. I also present to you a medal which, as a talisman, shall ever remind you of the beauty and the duty of good citizenship. The motto upon the medal is taken from a Latin poet, and is '*Discipulus est priori posterior dies*,' and may be translated, 'To-day must learn from yesterday.' I entreat you to observe in your lives the lessons, the wisdom, and the examples of experience.

As the crowded condition of the building rendered it impracticable for the boys to come down to the platform to receive their medals Mr. Sullivan handed them over to the care of a teacher appointed by President Walker, of the Board of Education, to receive and distribute them. Each medal was encased in heavy paper made into the shape of a little book, which books contained upon their outside covers a copy of the inscription on the pyramidion of the obelisk and the seal of the American Numismatic and Archæological Society in the name of which the medals were presented, together with the following inscription : "Presented to ———on behalf of the American Numismatic and Archæological Society of the City of New York, by Robert Hewitt, Jr." The inner covers of the books contained the following memoranda:

"The object of this medal is to commemorate the erection of the Egyptian obelisk in the Central Park as having an educational meaning for the people, and to recall to the present and future generations that the history of the ancients may be studied to profitable account.

"An aphorism borrowed from the poet Publius Syrus has been placed upon it as conveying this idea. The legend is, '*Discipulus est priori posterior dies*,' which may be freely translated, 'Let the future profit by the lessons of the past.' In the field the obelisk is seen a little toward the right; in the background the sun is represented rising over the sea, being an allegory recalling the ancient association of the obelisk with the worship of the sun, and at the same time also representing a part of the arms of the State of New York. In the lower field of the medal are represented the shields of the United States and New York City, grouped; that of the United States being surmounted by the American eagle, and that of New York resting on the scroll bearing the word 'Excelsior.' These two shields, grouped with laurel, are meant to represent the recipients of the gift from Egypt, forming, in all, a trio emblematic of the East and the West."

An inner border, ornamented with stars, representing the States of the Union, separates somewhat the legend from the subject, and the ground of the outer circle, on which the motto is placed, is filled in with the conventional lotos, cut in low relief under the lettering, appropriately suggesting a souvenir of Egypt.

TURNING THE OBELISK.

Plate XXVII a

Removal of the New York Obelisk.

The reverse side of the medal bears the following inscription:

> PRESENTED TO THE
> UNITED STATES
> BY
> ISMAÏL, KHEDIVE OF EGYPT,
> 1881.
> QUARRIED AT SYENE
> AND ERECTED AT HELIOPOLIS BY
> THOTHMES III.
> RE-ERECTED AT ALEXANDRIA
> UNDER AUGUSTUS.
> REMOVED TO NEW YORK
> THROUGH THE LIBERALITY OF
> W. H. VANDERBILT,
> BY THE SKILL OF
> LIEUT.-COM. H. H. GORRINGE, U. S. N.

The bronze crabs placed at each corner of the obelisk are the substitutes of the original ones placed there by the Romans; they bear the following legends, which it seems appropriate to reproduce here as matters of historical record:

First crab, first claw:

(*Outside.*)   (*Inside.*)
L. Η ΚΑΙΣΑΡΟΣ   ANNO VIII
ΒΑΡΒΑΡΟΣ ΑΝΕΘΗΚΕ   AVGVSTI CAESARIS
ΑΡΧΙΤΕΚΤΟΝ ΟΥΝΤΟΣ   BARBARVS PRAEF
ΠΟΝΤΙΟΥ   AEGYPTI POSVIT
    ARCHITECTANTE PONTIO

(*Reproduced from the original.*)

Second claw (cartouch of Thothmes III):
Quarried at Syene, Egypt; erected at Heliopolis, Egypt, by Thothmes III in the sixteenth century B. C.
Second crab, first claw:
Removed to Alexandria, Egypt, and erected there B. C. 22 by the Romans.
Second claw:
·Removed to the United States of America A. D. 1880, and erected in New York City January 22, 1881.
Third crab, first claw:
Presented to the United States Government by Ismaïl, Khedive of Egypt.
Second claw:
Rutherford Burchard Hayes, President; William Maxwell Evarts, Secretary of State of the United States.
Fourth crab, first claw:
The cost of removing from Egypt and placing on this spot this obelisk, pedestal, and base, was borne by William H. Vanderbilt.
Second claw:
Lieutenant-Commander Henry H. Gorringe, United States Navy, designed the plans for and superintended the removal and re-erection.
The singing of "Old Hundred" followed the presentation of medals and terminated the ceremonies.

The following are the names of the medal recipients:

William H. Vanderbilt.
Lieutenant-Commander Henry H. Gorringe, U. S. Navy.
Matthew Francis Farrell, Thomas G. Killeen, Clifford Bishop, Clarence G. Christie, George E. Clark, Eli Schreyer, George Cornell, Edward A. Bruen, Richard Schumacher, William Mitchell, John E. Timmons, Jesse Rosenthal, Josiah Ramsey Wray, William Klottman, Max Joseph Zahed, Adam Kellerman, Samuel J. Koplik, Herman O. Bohlen, Charles Keller, Saly Frankenberg, Frank Pokarny, Diederich F. B. Winter, Floyd S. Neely, Charles Geigerman, Julius Charles Bernheim, John McKie, William A. Painter, Hugo Reichart, Charles Strodl, Frederick Biermann, Julius W. Müller, Gabriel Ettinger, Herman Kaufman, Alexander Donald, Henry L. C. Wenk, Julius Reinecke, Edward P. Shields, Andrew Wieland, Herbert Joseph Carr, Robert J. Dyatt, Peter C. Brady, George H. Huneke, Samuel S. M. Pettit, Charles Knapp, William Arthur Gage, George Philip Kohlman, Michael Stern, Charles H. Overbeck, Henry A. Sherman, Theodore H. Banks, Frank B. Poor, Julius Grunow, Charles Schalkenstein, William L. Saulpaugh, Horatio N. Flanagan, Samuel Linderman, Charles E. See, John W.

56   *Removal of the New York Obelisk.*

Wood, Henry H. Jackson, Frank Jones, Julius Rogaliner, George G. Isaacs, Joseph P. Hannigan, Eugene O'Brien, Reuben Muller, James Cavanagh Brady, Henry Powell, William O. Holly, Daniel Quinn, William A. Dabbie, Frederick H. Cumming, Robert E. Dowling, James Houghton Strong, Eugene Henry Hœber, Robert Fitch Shedden, Joseph Jacob Myers, Charles Warren Holton, Herbert C. McKenzie, Charles W. Irving, Cornelius Carbonell, Adam F. Pentz, Martin Strauss, Benjamin Veit, David A. Pollor, Thomas William Timpson, George Urstadt, Charles Ellworth Atwater, Henry M. Walter, William C. Littlewood, Frank Loomis Eckerson, Arthur J. Lawrence, David Willard Lamberson, Samuel Whitney Dunscomb, Charles Alexander Clinton, William Russell Bennett, Garret Schenck Roome, William C. Guth, Alfred W. Pinneo, David D. Jacobus, Abbert Finkelstein, Emlin Frecklin.

It remains only to state the cost, to complete the record of the removal of the obelisk.

The actual net expenditure for material and labor for the whole operation aggregated eighty-six thousand six hundred and three dollars ($86,603). Of this sum fifty-seven thousand eight hundred and seventy-one dollars ($57,871) were expended on the obelisk, and twenty-eight thousand seven hundred and thirty-two dollars ($28,732) on the pedestal, steps, and foundation. The incidental and contingent expenditures, in which are included interest, commissions for use of money, and *backsheesh*, amounted to fifteen thousand nine hundred and seventy-three dollars ($15,973) additional. By *backsheesh* is meant the various amounts paid to different persons whose good-will was necessary to success, and whose ill-will would have involved delays and lawsuits that would have been ultimately more costly. The total cost was therefore one hundred and two thousand five hundred and seventy-six dollars ($102,576). Mr. Vanderbilt had agreed to pay seventy-five thousand dollars ($75,000) when the obelisk had been re-erected in Central Park,[1] and subsequently agreed to pay the cost of removing the pedestal, foundation, and steps. After the obelisk had reached New York he advanced forty-five thousand dollars ($45,000) to defray current expenses of completing the work. In February, 1881, after the obelisk had been erected, he paid the balance, making a total of one hundred and three thousand seven hundred and thirty-two dollars ($103,732) paid by him. The difference, eleven hundred and fifty-six dollars ($1,156), was the net profits derived from the fulfilment of my agreement.

As to the steamer "Dessoug": The money to purchase, refit, and operate her was advanced by two friends, under an agreement with me that I was to have absolute control of her until the obelisk had been disembarked. In consideration for this I agreed to pay them thirteen hundred pounds sterling (£1,300, $6,327) "for freight and other charges for transporting, from Alexandria to New York, the obelisk, its pedestal, and foundation, and the materials used in removing them." I was also "to pay all expenses incurred in loading, stowing, and discharging the obelisk and pedestal." I further agreed to sell the steamer to the best possible advantage for their sole benefit and to guarantee them against loss. These terms were exceedingly liberal compared with the proposals for charter of other steamers that had been made me.

After the obelisk had been disembarked at Staten Island, the aperture in the "Dessoug's" bow was closed and she was towed to the Brooklyn Navy Yard, where Commodore G. H. Cooper, the Commandant, had kindly offered me space to lay her up.

A favorable opportunity to sell the steamer to a foreign company, to ply between New York and West India ports under foreign register and flag, occurred very soon after the obelisk had been disembarked. It seemed, however, desirable that the vessel, identified as she was with the work of removing the obelisk, should have an American register. To accomplish this a special act of Congress was necessary. Soon after Congress met I visited Washington and conferred with Mr. Darius Lyman, Chief of Navigation Division, Treasury Department, who drew the following:

JOINT RESOLUTION authorizing the inspection and issue of an American register to the Egyptian steamship "Dessoug."

Resolved by the Senate and House of Representatives of the United States of America in Congress assembled, That the Secretary of the Treasury be, and is hereby, authorized to issue an American register to the steamship

---
[1] See Correspondence, p. 5.

PLATE XXVIII.

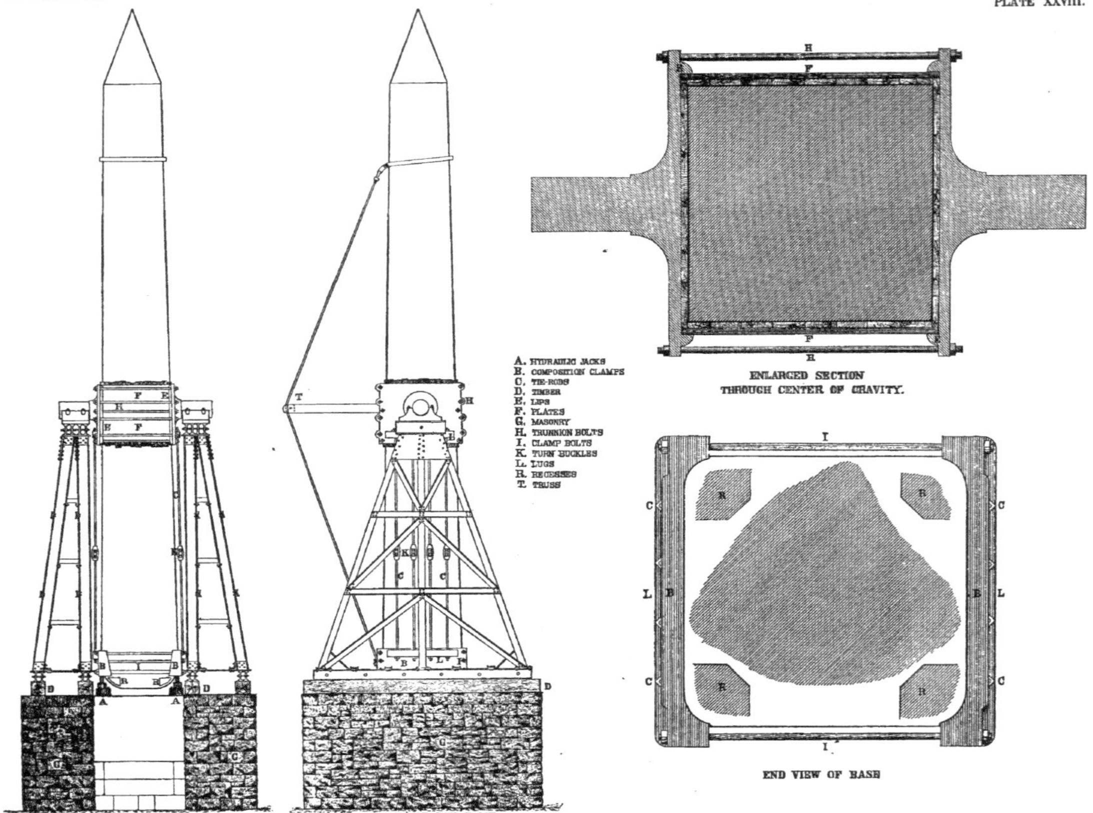

ENLARGED SECTION
THROUGH CENTER OF GRAVITY.

END VIEW OF BASE

A. HYDRAULIC JACKS
B. COMPRESSION CLAMPS
C. TIE-RODS
D. TIMBER
E. LEGS
F. PLATES
G. MASONRY
H. TRUNNION BOLTS
I. CLAMP BOLTS
K. TURN BUCKLES
L. LUGS
R. RIGGERS
T. TRUSS

LOWERING ON THE PEDESTAL.   SIDE VIEW OF THE SAME

PLACING THE OBELISK ON ITS PEDESTAL IN THE CENTRAL PARK JANUARY 22ᴰ 1881.

"Dessoug," of Egyptian nationality but of American ownership; and that the inspection of her machinery and hull shall be restricted by the inspectors of steam-vessels simply to the inquiry as to their safety for the conveyance of passengers, without reference to the mode or place of their construction; and that a special certificate of inspection may be issued for said steamship.

I took a copy of this to the Honorable William M. Evarts, Secretary of State, who gave me the following letter to Senator Matt W. Ransom, of North Carolina, and Representative John H. Reagan, of Texas, chairmen respectively of the Senate and House Committees of Congress.

DEPARTMENT OF STATE, WASHINGTON, *Jan.* 5, 1881.

SIR: I have the honor to bring to your attention, and, through your committee, that of the Senate, the eminent propriety of procuring the passage of an act granting an American register to the steamer "Dessoug," purchased by Lieutenant-Commander H. H. Gorringe, of the United States Navy, and employed by him in the successful transportation of the obelisk known as "Cleopatra's Needle" from Alexandria, Egypt, to New York.

The circumstances under which the obelisk was presented by the government of Egypt to the city of New York are so familiar that I need merely advert to the brilliant service rendered by Lieutenant-Commander Gorringe, involving the assumption of considerable personal risk on his part, and notably so in the purchase and alteration of a sea-going steamer for the transportation of the monolith.

The sentiment of national pride naturally felt in this successful achievement, coupled with the international character of Mr. Gorringe's service, makes it fitting that some appropriate action should be taken by Congress in the premises, and in no way could this be more appropriately done than by permanently identifying the vessel in question with the country and flag to which she has rendered so signal a service.

I am informed that the prominent merchants and ship-owners of New York are in favor of some such recognition of what Lieutenant-Commander Gorringe has done in behalf of their city, and that the course suggested would not be opposed by any conflicting shipbuilding interest.

The accompanying draft of a bill has been prepared as suitable to the desired end, subject to the consideration and approval of your committee, to which I earnestly commend it.

I have the honor to be, sir, your obedient servant,

W. M. EVARTS, *Secretary of State.*

The resolution was passed by the Senate on January 28, 1881; by the House on February 1, 1881, and approved by the President on February 8, 1881. Senator Francis Kiernan and Representatives Anson G. McCook, of New York, John G. Carlisle, of Kentucky, and W. C. Whitthorne, of Tennessee, together with the chairmen of the committees, were chiefly instrumental in pushing it through the crowded calendar of an expiring Congress and against a decided opposition to its passage that was unexpectedly developed. To strengthen their efforts four petitions for the passage of the resolution, signed by several hundred members of the Produce Exchange and other commercial bodies of New York, were presented at different times to Congress while the measure was pending. These petitions were prepared and circulated chiefly through the efforts of Mr. T. H. Parker, President of the Produce Exchange, Mr. W. H. Paton, and Mr. Marvelle W. Cooper, merchants of New York.

The "Dessoug" was sold to the Ocean Steamship Co. |of Savannah, for a less sum than that offered for her by the foreign company. This fact is recorded in order to prove that the value of the vessel was not enhanced by granting her an American register, as was stated in some of the newspapers at the time and has never been denied.

The following was introduced in the House of Representatives by the Honorable Abram S. Hewitt, of New York, passed unanimously by that body, called up in the Senate by the Honorable T. F. Bayard, of Delaware, and passed unanimously there :

JOINT RESOLUTION tendering the thanks of the people of the United States, to His Highness, the Khedive of Egypt, for the gift of an ancient obelisk.

Whereas, the Khedive of Egypt presented to the United States the ancient Egyptian obelisk known as Cleopatra's Needle, which has been removed and re-erected in the city of New York, thus placing in the possession of the people of the United States one of the most famous monuments of the Old World and one of the earliest records of civilization ; Be it therefore,

Resolved by the Senate and House of Representatives of the United States of America in Congress assembled, that the thanks of the people of the United States are hereby tendered to His Highness, the Khedive of Egypt, for a gift which only the oldest of nations could make and the youngest can most highly prize.

APPROVED, *January* 12, 1881.

THE NEW YORK OBELISK

CHAPTER II.

THE ARCHÆOLOGY OF THE NEW YORK OBELISK

SYMBOLISM.

IN the ancient Egyptian mythology the Supreme Creator was worshipped through His attributes as they appeared to men's minds. The sun was regarded as more nearly representing Him than any other apprehensible object. The religion of the Egyptians was, therefore, essentially sun-worship. Almost endless was the variety of their deities—endless as the variety of the Creator's attributes. They worshipped these deities much as a great many people of the present time bow to and adore inanimate representations of their spiritual conceptions. The main difference is that the objects adored by the Egyptians as representing the attributes of the Divine Creator were invariably the creations of nature,—man, and other animals, birds, reptiles, and fishes, while the objects adored by many devotees of the present day are invariably the creations of man. On the subject of ancient Egyptian belief the reader is referred to the many works in which it is discussed more fully and instructively than the author is capable of discussing it. James Bonwick's "Egyptian Belief and Modern Thought" is an admirable résumé of the subject.

An obelisk appears to have been symbolic of the highest attributes of nature,—generation and reproduction, that is to say, re-creation. There is no evidence that it was an object of adoration in itself. Obelisks invariably bore the sculptured representations of the gods to whom they were dedicated and of the kings who erected them. Both were worshipped. The assumption that an obelisk was itself an object of adoration seems to be founded on the sculptures on scarabee, representing human figures in the attitude of adoration before an obelisk. On one scarab there is engraved a sphinx and two men kneeling, one on either side of an obelisk, which bears the prenomen of Thothmes III. Parker states that the kneeling figure "on each side of the obelisk is the king,—Thothmes III, in a royal garment, worshipping the obelisk." If this were correct we would have the anomaly of the king worshipping himself. The relation of the kings to the gods is aptly compared by Bonwick to the attitude of the heads of certain Christian sects toward the founders of Christianity.

Infallibility and supreme power over the world and its inhabitants were claimed by the Pharoahs as they are by the Popes and Patriarchs. The claims of the latter in this regard were acknowledged for a few centuries, those of the former for many. The Egyptian kings assumed divine power and prerogatives, personated the Deity, were adored while living, and worshipped after death. Obelisks seem to have borne the same relation to the living kings as did the pyramids to those who had passed from life to a state of transition or inaction termed death. Some of the early sculptures in Egypt represent an obelisk surmounting a pyramid. Belief in the resurrection explains this association. Re-creation, as represented by the obelisk, springs from and rises out of the transitory condition called death, symbolized by the pyramid. As obelisks were originally erected only on the east bank of the

Nile and pyramids only on the west bank, the one has been regarded as allegorical of the rising, as the other is of the setting sun, aptly representing the living and the departed monarchs.

The sacred character of the obelisk is proven by its invariable association with the Egyptian temples. In this respect the obelisk and sphinx are alike. The temples were not complete without them, yet they formed no part of the temple; they were exterior accessories—a part of the system of Egyptian architecture as it embodies the profound thought of the Egyptian religion. This association of the obelisk and sphinx leads naturally to another conclusion as to their significance. The sphinx is believed to have been designed to represent the highest development of physical and intellectual force, the body of a lion, combining activity, grace, and strength, with the head of a man, the most intellectual of created beings. The obelisk is believed to represent the most essential and mysterious power of nature,—that of re-production.

In the museum of the Louvre, in Paris, there is a series of engraved scarabee that tend to confirm this view. The gradual development from the original to the existing form of an obelisk, through the earlier periods of Egyptian progress from barbarism to civilization, is clearly shown.

The obelisk seems to have been the special representative of the king and sovereign pontiff in Egyptian sacred architecture. On the shaft are engraved his titles, a record of his victories, and an assertion of his supreme power over the lives and property of his subjects. On the surmounting pyramidion are representatives of the gods conferring these titles and powers on the king, who is frequently represented as a sphinx. Every thing tends to associate the obelisk with king-worship as its material purpose, and with the power of generation and re-creation as its symbolic meaning.

The obelisk is not exclusively Egyptian. Essentially the same form is found in Assyria, Persia, and India, and even in America, although not well enough defined in the latter to be beyond question.

Bononi and others have identified the idol which Shadrach, Meshach, and Abednego declined to worship as an obelisk. "It was not only a representative of the divinity of the sovereign himself, but bore idolatrous emblems. To bow to it was an acknowledgment of the false gods and a recognition of Nebuchadnezzar as a god. * * * Captain Selby found near Babylon, on the 'Waste, of Dura,' the remains of a pyramidal column, which some identify as the image once covered with gold."[1] The proportions are those of an obelisk.

Obelisks represent in Egyptian sacred architecture exactly the same idea as church towers with surmounting steeples represent in that of to-day. The tower corresponds to the shaft of the obelisk, the steeple to the pyramidion. The form and proportions are different because modified by the fancy of man through centuries; but it is a striking fact that if these relics of the distant past are traced through their modifications we return to the obelisk. The position with reference to the temple or church is identical; and while it is customary at the present time to place but one steeple on churches, the two towers are preserved, and stand, as did obelisks in Egyptian architecture, one on each side of the entrance to the sanctuary of the temple or church, of which they form an essential part.

The material of which obelisks were made, red syenite, may have had a symbolic reference to the color of the sun's rays as seen by the Egyptians through the hazy atmosphere that pervades the valley of the Nile. Red syenite was also the hardest substance available for making them; and this was chosen from the quarries of Syene, where there is a stratum unequalled for its uniformity and freedom from cracks and veins of foreign matter, thereby enabling the architect to set no limit to the dimensions save that necessary for safety of removal and transport.

FORM.

An obelisk is a monolithic quadrilateral shaft terminating in a pyramidion. The proportions are not fixed; they vary even in those erected in one reign. The size and proportions were probably

---

[1] Bonwick, p. 300.

Archæology of the New York Obelisk.

determined solely by the mass that had been removed from the quarry. The sides of many are not even of uniform dimensions. The obelisks of Luxor have a slight curvature of two of the faces, in which they differ from all others.[1] The earlier obelisks are generally more slender than the later. The proportions vary from eleven times to eight times the width at base for total height. The New York obelisk which belongs to the first period of Egyptian renaissance is nine times its width at base in total height. It is impossible to find any two original authorities who give the same dimensions for any one Egyptian obelisk. The table in Chapter V is the result of a careful compilation of the data available for determining the dimensions of the obelisks recorded in this volume.

It is worthy of note that the shaft of the New York obelisk would come to a point if it was twice as long as it is; that the height of the pyramidion is equal to the width of the shaft at the bottom; and that the width of the top of the shaft is two thirds that of the bottom. How far these features may extend to obelisks generally cannot be determined until accurate dimensions are known.

The sides of the shaft are inscribed with vertical rows of hieroglyphical characters. The faces of the pyramidion contain figures and inscriptions. All are in *intaglio relievo*. Every part of the surface was originally polished. Some of the obelisks in Egypt, notably those of Usortesen and Hatasou, retain a high polish still. If the translations are correct the inscriptions have little historical value. Those on the pyramidions are unquestionably dedicatory; the translations of those on the shaft are little more than "a monotonous list of official epithets and magniloquent titles." One noticeable feature of Egyptian obelisks is their durability, amounting almost to indestructibility. They have experienced vicissitudes at the hands of man, and have passed through convulsions of nature that would have destroyed almost any thing else. Doubtless many have been destroyed; the wonder is that one remains. Every conquest of Egypt of which we have any record, from that of Asshurbanipal B. C. 662 to that of Napoleon in this century, has been followed by the removal of one or more obelisks from their original positions to others designated by the conquerer in and out of Egypt. There can be no better proof of the interest they excite and the curiosity they arouse. Their symmetrical form attracts the eye as their associations fascinate the mind. Their presence leads inevitably to historical research. What is the obelisk? Whence came it? What manner of people created it? How was it cut? What machinery moved it? What is the meaning of the characters engraved on it? These are among the questions that arise in the minds of Americans as they stand before the New York obelisk. The result of its removal to this country will be chiefly educational. The erection in this city of a monument, so simple in form, and yet so grandly impressive in its outline and proportions, may be to arrest the tendency of our architecture to extravagance of detail. That grace and elegance may be achieved by simplicity is one of the artistic lessons unlearned in America, but forcibly taught by the obelisk.

Of the three characteristic forms of Egyptian monuments—the obelisk, the sphinx, and the pyramid —the first is the only one that has been universally adopted. It is a curious evidence of the force of habit, and the imperishable influence exerted over the world by early Egyptian civilization, doctrines, and beliefs, that the obelisk is to-day the most common form of sepulchral monument. While the scarab symbolized resurrection itself the obelisk symbolized the power behind resurrection,—that of re-creation, and thus becomes the most appropriate of all forms to mark the graves of those who believe in a future state.

THE INSCRIPTIONS.

Plate xxx, the four faces of the pyramidion, is a reproduction of *squeezes* made directly from the obelisk. The figures and inscriptions were blackened on the squeezes, which were then photographed. We have therefore an absolutely accurate copy of the figures and hieroglyphical characters that remain after twenty-five centuries of exposure to atmospheric influences. The vacant

---
[1] See Chapter III.

62   Archæology of the New York Obelisk.

spaces in the upper rows of hieroglyphs in the oblongs under the sphinxes, and between the oblongs and the seated figures in the two upper squares, indicate where the hieroglyphs have been obliterated.

The Rosetta stone[1] furnished a key to the meaning of certain characters and groups in hieroglyphical writings. This has been made the basis of all translations. While it must be admitted that there has been an approach to correct rendering in modern languages of many of the hieroglyphical writings and inscriptions, it is certain that the grouping of characters and their values in different relative positions are not as yet sufficiently understood to warrant accepting the translations as accurate. It is also certain that the Egyptian mind had reached a stage of development in all branches of human knowledge far beyond that indicated by the translations of the inscriptions on the monuments. To accept as accurate the translation of the inscriptions on the New York obelisk given further on, would be equivalent to assuming that Thothmes III and Ramses II were a pair of vainglorious fools. Is such an assumption consistent with the marks on the world's history that were left by these men? The achievements of Thothmes III in war and the results of his consolidation of the Nile States into one empire are unequalled in modern history. Ramses II was for many centuries before Christ what Cæsar is to the Christian era. Men combining the superior qualities of these monarchs could not have left such incomprehensible nonsense for posterity to judge them by, as that assumed by Chabas and Brugsch to be the meaning of the hieroglyphs on the New York obelisk.

The meaning of the sculptures on the pyramidion of the New York obelisk affords a good example of the imperfect knowledge of the subject even of the most eminent Egyptologists. According to Birch[2] the vignettes or squares represent Thothmes III as a sphinx adoring Ra and Tum, two deities of Egyptian mythology. According to Chabas[3] "the pyramidion represents a square vignette in which is figured the king seated on a throne before the sphinx of Hor-em-akhou Harmachis, upon a pedestal," to whom the obelisk was dedicated.[4] According to Brugsch the sculptures on the pyramidion represent the god Ra, and the king, Thothmes III, seated on a throne, before them the sphinx, emblem of the physical and intellectual force.

The squeezes of the pyramidion were made by Mr. H. de Morgan, who has kindly furnished me for publication the following explanation and translation that he has reached after prolonged study and careful comparison of the sculptures with the figures of identified deities in Egyptian mythology.

In the left hand upper square of Plate xxx the god Atum,[5] seated, presents to the king, Thothmes III, the sceptre and *crux ansata*. The former is the emblem of authority, the latter is the emblem of life. Thothmes III is represented as a sphinx. He extends one hand to receive the emblems and with the other presents an offering.

What remains of the hieroglyphs in this square has been literally translated by Mr. de Morgan as follows : * * * giver, Ra-men-Kheper, gracious God, lord of the world, giver of life, beloved by Tum, master of the world. The word Ra-men-Kheper is enclosed in an oval with a line tangent to the lower end, that is known as a cartouche. It is the prenomen of the king, Thothmes III.

On the upper right square the god is Ra.[6] Enclosed by the oblong under the sphinx are the

[1] Discovered in 1799 by Captain Bouchard, an engineer officer of the French army.   [2] Parker, p. 43.
[3] Records of the Past, vol. x, p. 22.   [4] The great sphinx at Gizeh was dedicated to Harmachis.
[5] Atum was especially the god of Heliopolis. The great temple there was called "the house of Atum," as a church is called "the house of God." He is described as "the source of life," and in the Egyptian ritual there is the following: "I am Atum making the heavens, creating beings, self-created, lord of life." Wilkinson (p. 178, vol. iii) states that he was "one of the principal deities of the second order of gods." Bonwick (p. 94) assumes that he was the "*rising sun*," while Rawlinson (vol. i, p. 347) asserts that Atum represented "the sun as he approaches or rests upon the western horizon just before and when he sets."
[6] Ra, like Atum, was one of the sun-gods of Egyptian mythology. Ra appears to have chiefly represented the mid-day sun. To describe Ra in all his phases would be equivalent to writing a treatise on Egyptian gods. It is recorded of Ra that he was "born of Neith, but not engendered"; also, that he came from the side of his mother. There is a striking similarity between the Ra of Egyptian mythology and the Son of Christianity. Ra seems to have formed the connecting link between the spiritual and material world. He was almost universally worshipped throughout Egypt. He is commonly represented as having a hawk's head, and above this is a sphere, or disk, to designate the sun. It is inexplicable that the

THE FOUR FACES OF THE PYRAMIDION.

Egyptian Obelisk, Central Park, New York.

Archæology of the New York Obelisk. 63

titles and prenomen of the king, that have been translated thus: Son of the sun, Ra-men-Kheper, Strong Bull, Horus. One character is wanting. The horizontal and vertical lines under these titles represent the royal standard. The hieroglyphs between the sceptre and oblong of this square are partly obliterated; those that remain mean nothing in themselves. The horizontal row on top is also incomplete; what remains indicates that they have essentially the same meaning as the hieroglyphs similarly situated in the left upper square.

In the lower left-hand square the inscription on top is nearly complete. It has been translated thus: Giver of life, Ra-men-Kheper, gracious god, master of the world, giver of life, Horus-Ra, lord of the world, god, lord of heaven. The group of hieroglyphs between the sceptre and oblong signifies that the king makes presents to Ra.

In the lower right-hand square there is apparently nothing wanting. The inscription on top reads: Ra-men-Kheper, king of lower and upper Egypt, master of the world, gracious god of Heliopolis, king, giver of life, stability, and power, beloved of Atum, lord of Heliopolis, gracious god, lord of the temple. The inscription between the oblong and seated figure reads: He made presents of libations to Noun, who has made him giver of life.

It is probable that the sculptures and hieroglyphs on the four faces of the pyramidion are simply dedicatory to the two gods, Ra and Atum; to Ra as god of heaven, and Atum as god of Heliopolis. It would not be straining a point to render the inscription on top of the lower left square thus: Ra-men-Kheper, king by divine right, master of the world, with power over life (dedicates this) to Horus-Ra, god of the universe (or of earth and heaven). The characters under the sphinx are probably simply the king's name and titles. Those between the god and king explain their attitudes. In the lower right square the inscription would be in perfect keeping with those of modern times if it were translated thus: Ra-men-Kheper, king of united Egypt, master of the world, high-priest of Heliopolis, with power over life and property, dedicates this to beloved Tum, god of Heliopolis and gracious lord of the world.

Plate xxxi, the four sides of the obelisk, will enable the student of hieroglyphs to seek a more satisfactory translation than the author can furnish. The translation of Chabas is as follows:

NORTH SIDE.

LEFT.	CENTRE.	RIGHT.
The kingly HORUS, Strong Bull, Beloved of the goddess, Ma, the King of Upper and Lower Egypt, RA-OUSOR-MA-SOTEP-EN-RA,[1] Lord of panegyries like his father,[2] PTAH TOTANEN, Son of the Sun, RAMESSOU MERIAMEN. Ra has generated him to adorn festively Heliopolis to furnish abundantly the temples of him who generated him. The lord of the two lands RA-OUSOR-MA-SOTEP-EN-RA,[1] Son of the Sun, RAMESSOU MERIAMEN, (invested with life) stability and happiness.	The kingly Horus lifting up the Hat; (White Crown,) the King of Upper and Lower Egypt, Golden Hawk, who has struck the kings of all lands approaching him; after the commandment of his father, RA. Victory over the entire world, and valiance of sword are at the mouth of his hands for the extension of the limits of Egypt, the Son of the Sun, THOTHMES, Vivifier.	The kingly HORUS, Strong Bull, Son of TUM, the King of Upper and Lower Egypt, the Lord of Diadems, who protects Egypt and chastises the nations. Son of the Sun, RAMESSOU MERIAMEN, king, warlike, who has acted with his own hands, in the face of the whole earth, the Lord of the two lands, RA-OUSOR-MA-SOTEP-EN-RA,[1] Son of the Sun, RAMESSOU MERIAMEN, the stable.[3]

head of Ra on two of the four faces of the pyramidion should have been so nearly obliterated, while the head of Atum has been so well preserved. It is barely possible that the head of Ra may have been gilded, while that of Atum was only polished like the rest of the surfaces, and that this gilding may have been the cause of the obliteration.

[1] Prenomen of Ramses II.   [2] Lord of Festivals.   [3] Inscription incomplete.

64   *Archæology of the New York Obelisk.*

EAST SIDE.

LEFT.	CENTRE.	RIGHT.
The kingly HORUS, The Strong Bull, Son of Kheper-Ra,[1] the King of Upper and Lower Egypt, RA-OUSOR-MA-SOTEP-EN-RA, Golden Hawk, of abundant years, (very) victorious, Son of the Sun, RAMESSOU MERIAMEN, who issued from the womb, to take the crowns of the sun; whom the sun generated to be (the) sole Lord, Lord of the two lands, RA-OUSOR-MA-SOTEP-EN-RA, Son of the Sun, RAMESSOU MERIAMEN, the splendor of OSIRIS, like the sun.	The kingly HORUS, Strong Bull, crowned in Thebes, the Lord of Diadems, whose royalty is expanded, like (that of) the Sun. (Beloved of TUM, Lord of Heliopolis, Son of his loins, THOTH created him, THOTHMES.)[2] They created him in the great abode, from the perfection of their limbs, so that he will make an extended royalty for centuries. The King of Upper and Lower Egypt, RA-MEN-KHEPER, Beloved of TUM, the great god, and the gods of his circle, giving all life, stability, and happiness like the sun for ever.	The kingly HORUS, Strong Bull, Beloved of MA, the King of Upper and Lower Egypt, RA-OUSOR-MA-SOTEP-EN-RA, (who is) a sun, generator of gods, Possessor of the two lands, Son of the Sun, RAMESSOU MERIAMEN, a noble youth of kindness like ATEN[3] blazing from the horizon. Lord of the two lands, RA-OUSOR-MA-SOTEP-EN-RA, Son of the Sun, RAMESSOU MERIAMEN, the splendor of OSIRIS, Vivifier.

SOUTH SIDE.

LEFT.	CENTRE.	RIGHT.
The kingly HORUS, Strong Bull, Son of the Sun, the King of Upper and Lower Egypt, RA-OUSOR-MA-SOTEP-EN-RA, Golden Hawk, ... Son of the Sun, RAMESSOU MERIAMEN[4]	The kingly HORUS, Strong Bull, crowned in Thebes, the King of Upper and Lower Egypt, RA-MEN-KHEPER.[4] . . .	The kingly HORUS, Strong Bull, Beloved of MA, the King of Upper and Lower Egypt, RA-OUSOR-MA-SOTEP-EN-RA, (who is) a sun, generator of gods, ... Lord of the two lands RAMESSOU MERIAMEN.[4] . . . .

WEST SIDE.

LEFT.	CENTRE.	RIGHT.[5]
The kingly HORUS, Strong Bull, Beloved . . . the King of Upper and Lower Egypt, RA-OUSOR-MA-SOTEP-EN-RA. Lord of panegyries like his father Ptah, Lord of . . . RAMESSOU MERIAMEN.[4]	The kingly HORUS, Strong Bull, crowned in Thebes, the King of Upper and Lower Egypt, RA-MEN-KHEPER.[4]	

[1] The Creator.
[2] "This cartouch is very curious and interesting, as the phrase is calculated to form the name of Thothmes with the last word of each column."
[3] The solar disk.   [4] Remainder illegible or not translated.   [4] Remainder illegible or not translated.   [5] Illegible.

THE FOUR SIDES OF THE OBELISK.

Plate XXXI

Archæology of the New York Obelisk. 65

The following is the translation of Brugsch Bey, first published in the *New York Herald* of February 22, 1880. Dr. Brugsch thus describes the sculptures on the pyramidion: On the north face, corresponding to the lower left square of Plate xxx, "King Thuthmes[1] III is represented as a sphinx, with the head and arms of a man. He is offering two vases of wine to the Sun-God On. His body rests on a sort of pylon, decorated with the titles:—

> "The Strong Bull,
> Who manifests himself
> King
> In the Thebaïd,
> The Son of the Sun:
> Thutmes.

"Over the body may be read:—

> "The Gracious God,
> Lord of the Two Worlds,
> King of Upper and Lower Egypt,
> Ra-men-kheper." . . . . .

On the west face, which corresponds with the lower right square of Plate xxx, Dr. Brugsch says:— "The representation and the text inscribed upon the pylon are the same as those on Face A," which is the preceding. He states further that "The inscriptions engraved over the sphinx and the figure of the god are not sufficiently distinct to here read them." In which he is manifestly in error.[*]

The sculptures and inscriptions on the south face, corresponding to the upper left square of Plate xxx, he regards as illegible.

On the east face, corresponding with the upper right square, he states that "The representation and the text inscribed upon the pylon are the same as those on Face A. The Sun-God is this time called '*Hormakhu*'—that is, the Harmaïs or Harmachis of the Greeks.

"The King's titles are:—

> "The Gracious God,
> The Lord of the Two Worlds:
> Ra-men-kheper.

"The offering to the god is indicated by the inscription:—

> "Gift of Wine."

NORTH SIDE OF SHAFT.

TEXT OF THE LEFT-HAND LINE.	TEXT OF THE CENTRE LINE.	TEXT OF THE RIGHT-HAND LINE.
Horus: the Strong Bull.	[*Name of the Royal Standard.*]	Horus: the Strong Bull.
Friend of Justice.	Horus: Magnified and Enlightened by the Crown of Upper Egypt.	The Son of Tum.
King of Upper and Lower Egypt.		The King of Upper and Lower Egypt.
Lord of the Periods of Thirty years.		Ra-user-ma.
Like his Father Ptah-Tanen [*the God of Memphis*].	[*The Official Standard.*]	The Chosen one of the Sun.
The Son of the Sun: Ramessu Meri-amun[*] [*that is to say, the Friend of the God Amon of Thebes*].	The King of Upper and Lower Egypt: Ra-men-kheper.	Lord of the Diadems of the Vulture and of the Serpent.
		Protector of Egypt.
The Sun created him.	[*The Title of the Victorious.*]	Chastiser of Foreign Nations.
To Cause Great Rejoicing in the City of On, and to fill with Riches the Sanctuaries of his Creator.	The Golden Horus.	The Son of the Sun, Ramessu Meri-amun.
	The Strong of Arm,	The Conqueror,
	Who beat the Kings of Foreign Nations	Who with his Own Arms Performed Great Deeds

[1] Thothmes.   [*] See Plate xxx.
[*] In the Greek lists of Manethos containing the names of the Pharaòhs this name *Meri-amun* is written *Miamun*.

66   *Archæology of the New York Obelisk.*

NORTH SIDE OF SHAFT.—(*Continued.*)

TEXT OF THE LEFT-HAND LINE.

The Lord of the Two Worlds:
   Ra-user-ma.
The Chosen One of the Sun.
The Son of the Sun: Ramessu
   Meri-amun,
Who gives Life of all Stability and
   Purity
To-day as ever after.

TEXT OF THE CENTRE LINE.

Who were numbered by hundreds
   of thousands,
For his Father, the Sun-God Ra,
   ordained for him
Victories over all Lands.
Mighty Power
Was concentrated at the points of
   his hands
To widen the Boundaries of Egypt.
   [*The Family Name.*]
The Son of the Sun
Thutmes . . . . .
Who gives Life of all Stability and
   Purity
To-day as ever after.

TEXT OF THE RIGHT-HAND LINE.

In the face of
The Entire World Assembled.
The Lord of the Two Worlds:
   Ra-user-ma,
The Chosen one of the Sun.
The Son of the Sun: Ramessu
   Meri-amun,
Who gives Life of all Stability
   and Purity
To-day as ever after.

EAST SIDE.

TEXT OF THE LEFT-HAND LINE.

Horus: the Strong Bull,
Son of the Sun-God Kheper [*that
   is, of him who exists*].
The King of Upper and Lower
   Egypt,
Ra-user-ma,
The Chosen One of the Sun.
The Golden Horus:
Rich in Years; Grand in Victories.
The Son of the Sun: Ramessu Meri-
   amun.
He came out from the Belly,
To receive the Crowns from the
   Sun-God Ra,
Who created him to be the Sole
   Monarch.
The Lord of the Two Worlds: Ra-
   user-ma,
The Chosen One of the Sun.
The Son of the Sun: Ramessu Meri-
   amun.
The Reflected Splendor of
The God Tum
Like the Sun.

TEXT OF THE CENTRE LINE.

[*Name of the Royal Standard.*]
Horus: the Strong Bull,
Who manifested himself as King in
   Thebaïd.
   [*The Crown Title.*]
The Lord of the Diadems of the
   Vulture and of the Serpent.
His Kingdom is as lasting as is
   the
Sun in the Heavens.
[*The Family Name, enclosed in an
elliptical circle and containing a
curious allusion to the meaning of
the name Thutmes.*]
The Creature of the God Tum,
   Lord of the City of On,
The Son who came out from his
   Belly, and whom
The God THUT *formed.* [MES.]
They created him in the Grand
   Hall [*of the Temple of On*]
After the model of their own body,
Being conscious of the Great Deeds
   he was to accomplish ;
He, whose Kingdom should be of
   long duration.
   [*The Official Title.*]
The King of Upper and Lower
   Egypt,
Ra-men-Kheper,
Friend of the Great God Tum, and of
The Circle of his Divinities.
He who gives
Life of all Stability and Purity
To-day as ever after.

TEXT OF THE RIGHT-HAND LINE.

Horus: the Strong Bull,
Friend of the Sun-God Ra,
The King of Upper and Lower
   Egypt.
Ra-user-ma,
The Chosen One of the Sun.
He has taken possession of the Two
   Worlds.
The Son of the Sun: Ramessu Meri-
   amun,
A handsome and Kind-Hearted
   Youth ;
He is as resplendent as is
The Solar Orb in the Horizon.
The Lord of the Two Worlds ;
   Ra-user-ma,
The Chosen One of the Sun.
The Son of the Sun : Ramessu
   Meri-amun.
The Reflected Splendor of
The God Tum
Who gives Life.

Archæology of the New York Obelisk.

SOUTH SIDE.

TEXT OF THE LEFT-HAND LINE.	TEXT OF THE CENTRE LINE.	TEXT OF THE RIGHT-HAND LINE.
[*So effaced as to be illegible.*]	[*Name of the Royal Standard.*] Horus: the Strong Bull, Friend of the Sun-God Ra. [*The Official Title.*] The King of Upper and Lower Egypt, Ra-men-kheper . . . . \ .	Horus: the Strong Bull, The Companion and Friend of Justice. The King of Upper and Lower Egypt: Ra-user-ma: Lord of the Periods of Thirty years, Like his Father, the God Ptah; Lord of the White Wall [*name of the Citadel of Memphis*]. The Son of the Sun: Ramessu Meri-amun. The God: the Divine Being. The Terrestrial Star of the City of the Sun-God Ra, Which is sustained by the deeds of The Lord of the Two Worlds: Ra-user-ma. The Son of the Sun: Ramessu Meri-amun, Who gives Life.

WEST SIDE.

TEXT OF THE LEFT-HAND LINE.	TEXT OF THE CENTRE LINE.	TEXT OF THE RIGHT-HAND LINE.
Horus: the Strong Bull, Friend of Justice. The King of Upper and Lower Egypt; The Son of the Sun; The Creature of the Gods, Who [has taken possession of] the Two Worlds. The Son of the Sun: Ra-user-ma Meri-amun; The Friend of the City of the Sun; Never before was done what he did for the City of On. His Memory is forever fixed in the City of Tum [*Pitum*]. The Lord of the Two Worlds: Ra-user-ma. The Chosen One of the Sun. The Son of the Sun [*Ramessu Meri-amun*] Who gives Life.	[*Name of the Royal Standard.*] Horus: the Strong Bull, Who manifested himself as King in the Thebaïd. [*Official Title.*] The King of Upper and Lower Egypt: Ra-men-kheper, Who caused Great Rejoicing In the House of the Sun-God Ra— [*That is Heliopolis.*] Who created The Beauty of the Sun Disk; The Day when for the first time was made	Horus: the Strong Bull, The Son of the Sun-God Ra. The King of Upper and Lower Egypt Ra-user-ma The Chosen one of the Sun. The Golden Horus: Rich in Years; Grand in Victories. The Son of the Sun: Ramessu Meri-amun. . . . . The Lord of the Two Worlds Ra-user-ma The Chosen One of the Sun, The Son of the Sun [*Ramessu Meri-amun*] . . . . . Like the Sun.

"At the foot of the four faces of the obelisk there is a horizontal line of text which reads: 'May he live! The gracious god: Ra-user-ma—The chosen one of the sun—The gracious god—Ramessu Meri-amun.'"

In explanation of the above it is well to "remark that all Egyptian kings had five distinct appellations, which were always preceded by five titles." These titles are:

1. The *Name of the Royal Standard*, preceded and indicated by the words, "Horus," or "*Horus, the Sun.*"
2. The *Official Title*, preceded by the words, "The King of Upper and Lower Egypt," or "Lord of the Two Worlds."
3. The *Crown Title*, preceded by the words, "The Lord of the Diadems of the Vulture and of the Serpent *Ouraios*."

4. The *Family Name*, indicated by the expression, " The Son of the Sun."
5. The *Title of* " *The Victorious*,' preceded by the words, " The Golden Horus."

On the north, west, and east faces, near the bottom, is the cartouch of Usorken I, in much smaller characters than the other inscriptions.

Dr. Brugsch expresses the opinion that Ramses II was the father, by adoption, of Moses. He states that of the names of Thothmes III, Ramses II, and Usorken I, inscribed on the New York obelisk, " each marks a distinct historical period." Thothmes III, the period of expansion and conquest about sixteen centuries before Christ; Ramses II, the Sesostris of the Greek writers, who lived about three centuries later, the period of Egypt's greatest power and splendor; and Usorken I, who reigned about 933 B. C., the period of decline. Usorken was probably of Assyrian origin.

HISTORICAL.[1]

The obelisk now standing in Central Park is of the fine syenite of the Assouan quarries. It was formerly the companion of the obelisk now standing on the Thames Embankment. The pair were originally erected by Thothmes III [xviii dynasty, sole reign, B. C. 1591–1565, Lepsius], before the famous Temple of the Sun at Heliopolis, the New York obelisk being then the eastern of the two. According to Birch,[2] they were the second pair erected by Thothmes III at this temple; the obelisk now at Constantinople, together with its former mate, being the first pair.

Pliny, who seems to give names to the Egyptian kings according to his own fancy, says that these obelisks were the work of Mesphres. " There are two other obelisks which were in Cæsar's Temple in Alexandria, near the harbor there, 42 cubits in height, and originally erected by order of King Mesphres." " Mesphres, who reigned in the City of the Sun, was the first who erected one of these obelisks, being warned to do so in a dream; indeed, there is an inscription to this effect; for the sculptures and figures which we still see thereon are no other than Egyptian figures." [Pliny, Nat. Hist., bk. xxxvi, ch. 14.] It is needless to say that no such dream-record as this appears on the New York obelisk. By Mesphres, Pliny means, according to Birch, King Mephres or Mesphra-Thuthmosis of Manetho's xviii dynasty; that is, Thothmes I. Parker, p. 21, would identify this name of Mesphres with that of Pepi Merira. Cooper, however, with more charity for Pliny's minute acquaintance with Egyptian chronology, concludes that he intended Thothmes III.

Near the modern village of Matariyeh, five miles from Cairo, is the site of the ancient city of Heliopolis; the only Egyptian city, according to Osburn (Mon. Hist. of Egypt), which is mentioned in the book of Genesis (Gen. xli, 45).[3] Nothing now remains of the city except the standing obelisk, and rude mounds, the ruins of crude brick walls, enclosing, says Mariette, a space 4,560 ft. by 3,560 ft., and marking the vast open space or square in front of the ancient temple. But, in the days of Egypt's glory, it was a place of the highest renown. It was preëminently the "City of the Sun," the "abode of Ra" (Helios); it was also called "the home of the Phœnix" (Bennu), and An, whence its Hebrew name On.[4] Here was the far-famed Temple of the Sun, where originated the profound learning of the Egyptians. Hither came, as to the most sacred place, pilgrims from all parts of the kingdom. The greatest Pharaohs added to their titles that of " Prince of Heliopolis."

Wilkinson calls Heliopolis the university of Egypt, where were taught the speculative and mystic forms of Egyptian theology, philosophy, astronomy,[5] and all branches of practical science as then known. Here flourished a college of learned priests; a school of higher renown, according to Ebers, than even those of Saïs, Memphis, or Thebes. In this school Moses is said to have studied. Herodotus

---

[1] Kircher, Œdipus, vol. iii, p. 339. Norden, pl. viii, ix. Descr. de l' Égypte, Antiq., vol. v, pl. 32, 33. Lenormant, Musée, pl. xxix, xxx. Denon, pl. ix. Champollion, Monuments, t. iv, pl. ccccxliv. Burton, Exc. Hier., pl. li.
[2] Parker, p. 43.   [3] See Gen. xvi, 7. Shur, which Gesenius thinks to be Suez.
[4] On (Gen. xli, 45). In Jeremiah xliii, 13, it is called " Beth-shemesh," *i. e.*, " the abode of the sun,"—a name which the Septuagint here employs as the name of the temple. (W. Smith, Dict. of the Bible.) The Egyptians called the city Annu, *i. e.*, " pointed columns," or " obelisks." (Brugsch.)
[5] Astronomy and all branches of science were studied here.—*Wilkinson*.

has written its praises. Hither came Pythagoras, Plato, and Eudoxus for Egyptian training. It is thought that from the records preserved in the temple, Manetho collected his history of the ancient Egyptian kings.[1] At the period of the Ptolemies, Alexandria became the centre of learning; in Strabo's time, although the houses once occupied by the priestly scholars were still standing, the once famous college of Heliopolis was in ruins.

The renowed Temple of the Sun at Heliopolis was consecrated to the special worship of Ra, the mid-day sun, the god of creating light and life; and thence, secondarily, to the honor of those deities whom the Egyptian mythology brought into the closest connections with him, viz.: Tum, the setting sun, the god of the promised resurrection; Harmachis, the rising sun, the child-sun, the awakening of life out of darkness; Thoth, the deity of the moon, the god of measures and of the sciences; Osiris and Isis, the children of space (Nut) and time (Seb),—Osiris, the principle of quickening life,—Isis (Isis Hathor), the earth, as receptive of this quickening; and, with these, their son, the avenging Horus, the representative of the final triumph of life and truth over death and falsehood, Typhon.

Thus, at the great temple of Ra, the religious belief of the Egyptians clustered its deities like planets around the central sun, and in its combination of their several rites of worship with reference to Ra as the supreme, gave peculiar fame and splendor to the shrine of Heliopolis. "Proud Pharaohs," says Ebers, "who at Memphis confined themselves to offering a sacrifice to the deity Ptah, here, at Heliopolis, submitted in the Temple of the Sun to many ceremonies, and were initiated into the mysteries of the god."

The sacred animals venerated at this temple were the white or light-colored bull Mnevis (sacred to Ra, as Apis was sacred to Ptah), and lions of light-colored, lustrous skin,—sacred to Ra. Here, too, was the fabled home of the Phœnix, which dies in fire to rise again, and brings its ashes to Heliopolis once in every five hundred years. The Egyptians called the Phœnix, Bennou; in many inscriptions the temple is called the "house of Bennou."

There is no record of the first building of this temple, so great is its antiquity.[2] With the single exception of the shrine of Ptah at Memphis, it was the most ancient temple of all Egypt. "The building was as old," says Ebers, "as the Egyptian adoration of the sun."[3] It was so old that the most venerable myths had had time to gather around its ancient walls and take up their abode in its inmost sanctuary. In the wars of the gods, the Temple of the Sun had given asylum to the deities; Typhon and Horus, each wounded by the other, had been healed in the "great hall" of Heliopolis.

An ancient Egyptian manuscript now preserved in the Berlin Museum informs us that the temple was partly rebuilt by Amenhat I, of the xii dynasty, and finished by his son, Usortesen I. An interesting manuscript on parchment, procured by Brugsch at Thebes in 1858, and now at Berlin, records that Usortesen, in the third year of his reign, assembled the chief officers of his court to give their counsel as to erecting worthy buildings to the sun-god. The monarch's address dwells on the importance of monuments dedicated to the deities,—monumuents which alone can make the memory of a ruler eternal; the counsellors unanimously applaud the intentions of their sovereign; then follows the account of the solemn laying the foundations of the proposed structures by the king himself.

The existence of the present obelisk of Heliopolis, says Brugsch, proves that the building, under Usortesen, had reached the great pylons, before which it was customary to erect these giant shafts.[4]

It was the daughter of a priest of this temple,—the "Priest of On," Potiphera, *i. e.*, dedicated

---

[1] Long, Egypt. Antiq., i, 26. This history of Manetho is lost, except his lists of kings.
[2] Cooper (p. 22) says it was "founded" [built] by kings of the first six dynasties.
[3] According to Manetho, the bull Mnevis was first worshipped here in the reign of Kaiechos, the second king of the ii dynasty. W. Smith, Dict. of the Bible, and Manetho in Wilkinson i, 18.
[4] Brugsch, Hist. of Egypt, i, 130.

to Ra, that the Pharaoh, who according to Rawlinson, was of the xvii dynasty and the last of the Hyksos, gave Joseph to wife.[1]

The great conqueror and builder, Thothmes III (xviii dynasty), restored or enlarged the ancient temple. An inscription referred to by Brugsch[2] shows that he surrounded it with a stone enclosure in the forty-seventh year of his reign. But, especially, he adorned it with new and splendid obelisks; of these three now exist, though far removed from their original site, viz.: the large obelisk at Constantinople, the obelisk of London, and the obelisk of New York.[3]

Around the shrine of the sun-god were erected many other obelisks.[4] According to Ebers, the greater part of the obelisks removed by the Cæsars to Rome, Alexandria, and Constantinople, were from Heliopolis. Besides the monoliths of Constantinople, London, and New York, there are four others still existing which originally stood at Heliopolis, viz.: three in Rome, the obelisk of the Piazza del Popolo, that of the Vatican, and that of Monte Citorio; and one in Florence, that of the Boboli Gardens. The inscription on the London monolith mentions "the house of the Phœnix." The inscription on the shaft of the Piazza del Popolo speaks of the king (Seti I) as "filling Heliopolis with obelisks." In the inscription of King Piankhi (F. C. Cook's translation, Records of the Past, ii, 98) the temple is called "the temple of obelisks." Even so late as the time of Abd-el-Lateef there were so many remains of these monuments that he speaks of them as "innumerable."

Seti I (xix dynasty) was also a builder or restorer of the temple of Heliopolis, and erected, at least, a pair of obelisks, of which one, that of the Piazza del Popolo, still exists.

A very remarkable model of the Temple of the Sun, bearing the cartouch of Seti I (see Plate xxxii), discovered at a village near Cairo in 1875, is now in the possession of the author of this volume. It is believed to be the most ancient architectural model, or plan, known to exist, and has been pronounced by Professor Brugsch to be the most important historical discovery made in Egypt for many years.

The model is of granite; it is 44.25 inches long, 34.65 inches wide, and 9.25 inches deep. It shows the double flight of steps ascending to the level of the sanctuary: on either side these steps are, first, sockets in which were formerly set models of the great sphinxes guarding the entrance; higher up, on either side, are marked the positions of the statues of the king and of two great obelisks. At the top of the steps are again, on either side, sockets for two smaller sphinxes. Beyond these are marked the positions of the two great pylons; in front of these pylons were set tall masts or flag-staffs; on the inner sides of the pylons are seen holes marking the place of the double gate of the sanctuary, beyond which monarchs and priests alone could pass. Farther on are shown the positions of the great walls enclosing the sanctuary, within which were preserved the morning and the evening barges of the god.

On three sides or edges of the model are sculptures representing the monarch presenting offerings to the deity, and inscriptions in finely cut hieroglyphics. The signification of the separate hieroglyphs has been given by Brugsch, but the arrangement or collocation of words in the following translation is as given by Hon. W. J. Shaw, of San Francisco (see his article in the *Overland Monthly*, May, 1875): "This good model in stone, he (the king) has made of the temple illuminated by the two spheres. Horus, the Sun, his father, to this moment has made the gods gracious. The two tall slender towers are made of mest stone. Of metal are the great doors. Of white stone are the two pylons, but grayish in their external appearance. Joyous were the spirits of heaven at Heliopolis!

---

[1] But Wilkinson (1. 30) says that Joseph arrived in Egypt during the reign of Usortesen I.
[2] Brugsch, Hist. of Egypt, i, 403.
[3] Brugsch (i, 404) says that Thothmes III erected obelisks before the great *wings* of the temple. According to an inscription in the Temple of Assassuf, the height of a pair was 108 Egyptian ells, or 186 feet.
[4] Pliny (Nat. Hist., bk. xxxvi, ch. 14) states that the first obelisk was erected by Mesphres, at Heliopolis, and that Sesosthes erected four in the same city.

ANTIQUE MODEL OF THE TEMPLE OF ON (HELIOPOLIS).

Copyright, 1881, by H. H. GORRINGE, New York.

Plate XXXII

Archæology of the New York Obelisk. 71

At Heliopolis the sphere of heaven is illuminated! The two obelisks are of polished porphyry (?). Gifts were presented: first, to Ra-Hor-Chuti[1]; secondly, to Tum, master of the two worlds of Heliopolis; thirdly to Khaparah in his barge, and to Horus, the Sun of the two illuminated spheres, the good god, the grand master of the heavens in the midst of his celestial palace. The King, part of the Sun, the Sun stable in justice, arrived and worshipped thee, O Tum! and presented incense to thee, and green cosmetic for the eyes, and oil coming from the eye of Horus. The King (cartouch of Seti I), part of the Sun, the Sun stable in justice, came and adored thee, O Tum, and thee, O Khaparah, and thee, O Horus, sun of the two illuminated regions, and filled you all with adorations." According to Shaw the following inscription also appears: "The gracious god (Seti, I) has made this monument to his father the Sun, to Tum, and to Khaparah. He has made to his father a splendid sanctuary, comparable to the sphere of heaven, to the place of repose, to the place of the two regions, and of the masters of Hun; and it is united in the interior like Tum to the heavens."[2]

In the time of Ramses III (xix dynasty) the possessions of the temple were immense. The celebrated Harris papyrus records the costly presents of this monarch to the shrine, and his restorations at Heliopolis: "I built its temples which were gone to decay; I sculptured their gods in their secret shapes, of gold, silver, and all precious stone, an eternal work. I made thee great statues of granite, figures of Tum."[3] The number of priests, together with their subordinates and servants, attached to this temple is estimated, in a census made under this reign, at no less than 12,913.

A remarkable account of a royal visit to this shrine, and showing how far up the Nile its fame had ascended, is given in the "Inscription of Piankhi Mer-Amon," discovered in 1863 at Gebel Barkal, the site of the ancient Napata, in Ethiopia.[4] Piankhi, who about 750 B. C.,[5] obtained sovereign power at Napata, and established thence his suzerainty over all Egypt, descended the Nile, subduing in battle and in siege the native Egyptian princes who ventured to resist his supremacy, until, flushed with victory on victory, he approached the sacred spot of Heliopolis. Although the account of this monarch's visit to the Temple of the Sun has only preserved to us a description of the edifice in the most general terms, yet the account is enough to give us an idea of the great importance attached by the Egyptians to this famous shrine. Piankhi's visit is described as follows:[6] "When he approached in order to enter the temple of the Sun-God Ra, the chief of the temple greeted him with respectful greeting, and the singing priests read the holy words to keep evil from the King. And the King completed the consecration, putting on the fillets, and purifying himself by incense and holy water. Then he received the wreaths of the Benben chamber[7] and brought them forward, mounting the steps to the great window[8] to behold Ra in his Benben chamber.[9] The King stood there all alone; he drew back the bolts, opened the doors, and beheld his father Ra in the splendid Benben chamber, and the morning bark of Ra and the evening bark of Tum. After this he shut the doors, laid sealing-earth upon them, and pressed upon it his own royal seal, thus commanding the priests: 'I have set my

---
[1] Harmachis (?).

[2] It is to be hoped that some eminent Egyptologist may be able to furnish a more satisfactory translation from the plate.

[3] Records of the Past, vol. vi, p. 53.

[4] Translation in Brugsch's Hist. of Egypt, vol. i, p. 128; also in Records of the Past, vol. ii, p. 79; and Mariette, Notice des Principaux Monuments, etc., p. 295.

[5] Rawlinson's Egypt, ii, 437. Brugsch [on *Card*] says 8th or 9th century B. C. (Cook, in Records of the Past, ii, 79, says xxii [22d] dynasty; not so, apparently, according to Bædeker's Egypt, p. 91.)

[6] Brugsch, i, 128.

[7] Cook, Records of the Past, ii, 98, translates this: Wreaths "from the Temple of Obelisks." Note by Brugsch: "The word Benben, in the old Egyptian, has the same meaning as the Greek word *pyramidion*. The Benben, accordingly, had the form of a small pyramid, and was venerated in the temple of On, with devotion like that paid to the Omphalos in the temple of Delphi."

[8] "The great shrine." Cook.

[9] "Temple of Obelisks." Cook.

72   *Archæology of the New York Obelisk.*

seal; no other of any kings shall any more enter in.' While he stood there they prostrated themselves before his majesty, saying : ' O thou, always increasing in empire, may affliction never come to the divine Horus, the friend of the town of On.' "

More than seven centuries after this visit of King Piankhi, the Greek geographer Strabo[1] wrote a description of this temple as a type of all Egyptian temple buildings (Brugsch). "Heliopolis," he says, "has an ancient temple constructed after the Egyptian manner, bearing many proofs of the madness and sacrilegious acts of Cambyses, who did very great injury to the temples, partly by fire, partly by violence. In this manner he injured the obelisks, two of which that were not entirely spoiled were transported to Rome. The plan of the temples is as follows :—At the entrance into the temenos (sacred enclosure) is a paved floor, in breadth about a plethrum[2] or even less; its length is three or four times as great, and in some instances even more. This part is called the dromos, and is mentioned by Callimachus ; ' This is the dromos, sacred to Anubis.' Throughout the whole length are placed on each side stone sphinxes, at the distance of twenty cubits or a little more from each other, so that there is one row of sphinxes on the right hand, and another on the left. Next after the sphinxes is a large propylon, then on proceeding farther another propylon, and then another. Neither the number of the propyla nor of the sphinxes is determined by any rule. They are different in different temples, as well as the length and breadth of the dromos. Next to the propyla is the naos, which has a large and considerable pronaos ; the sanctuary in proportion ; there is no statue, at least not in human shape, but a representation of some of the brute animals. On each side of the pronaos project what are called the wings. These are two walls of equal height with the naos. At first the distance between them is a little more than the breadth of the foundation of the naos. As you proceed onward, the [base] lines incline toward one another till they approach within fifty or sixty cubits. These walls have large sculptured figures, very much like the Tyrrhenian (Etruscan) and very ancient works among the Greeks."[3]

The precise history of the decline of Heliopolis is not known. Mariette raises, without answering, the question : When did this decline begin ? The fury of Cambyses [B. C. 525-521] did not entirely destroy it; for although Strabo, who visited Egypt B. C. 24, found it a deserted city, yet the temple could be seen and described in all its parts. So late as the time of Abd-el-Lateef, who wrote in A. D. 1201 (De Sacy), the Arabian physician could still speak of it as a small city, with ruined but still standing walls, which it was easy to see were the walls of a temple ; for there were those "large and terrible idols of hewn stone, each of which is thirty cubits high, with limbs in proportion." The gate of the city—perhaps the pylon of the temple described by Strabo—was still preserved. The figures and fragments seen by Abd-el-Lateef were covered with reliefs and hieroglyphics. " There is hardly a stone," he says, "without writing, or sculpture, or figures." What has become, asks Ebers, of these enormous quantities of stone which were seen so lately by Abd-el-Lateef? and his answer is that they have been carried away to be used in the building up of Cairo, so near at hand.

Resuming the history of the New York obelisk, there is no record that it had been thrown down by Cambyses when he destroyed the temple of Heliopolis, but it is very probable that it shared the fate of many others and lay prostrate among the ruins for five centuries, from the conquest of the Persians in the sixth century before Christ to that of the Romans in the first century B. C.

The inscription on one of the bronze crabs that supported the New York obelisk while it was in Alexandria (see Plate v) is the only record that exists of its removal. This simply states that it was erected at Alexandria in the eighth year of Augustus Cæsar, corresponding to 22 B. C., by Pontius the architect, while Barbarus was Prefect. From other records we learn that the pair, hereafter to be known as the London and New York obelisks, were placed in front of the Cæsareum or Temple of the Cæsars.

---

[1] Visited Egypt B.C. 24.   [2] About 100 feet.   [3] Strabo, bk. xvii, ch. 1.

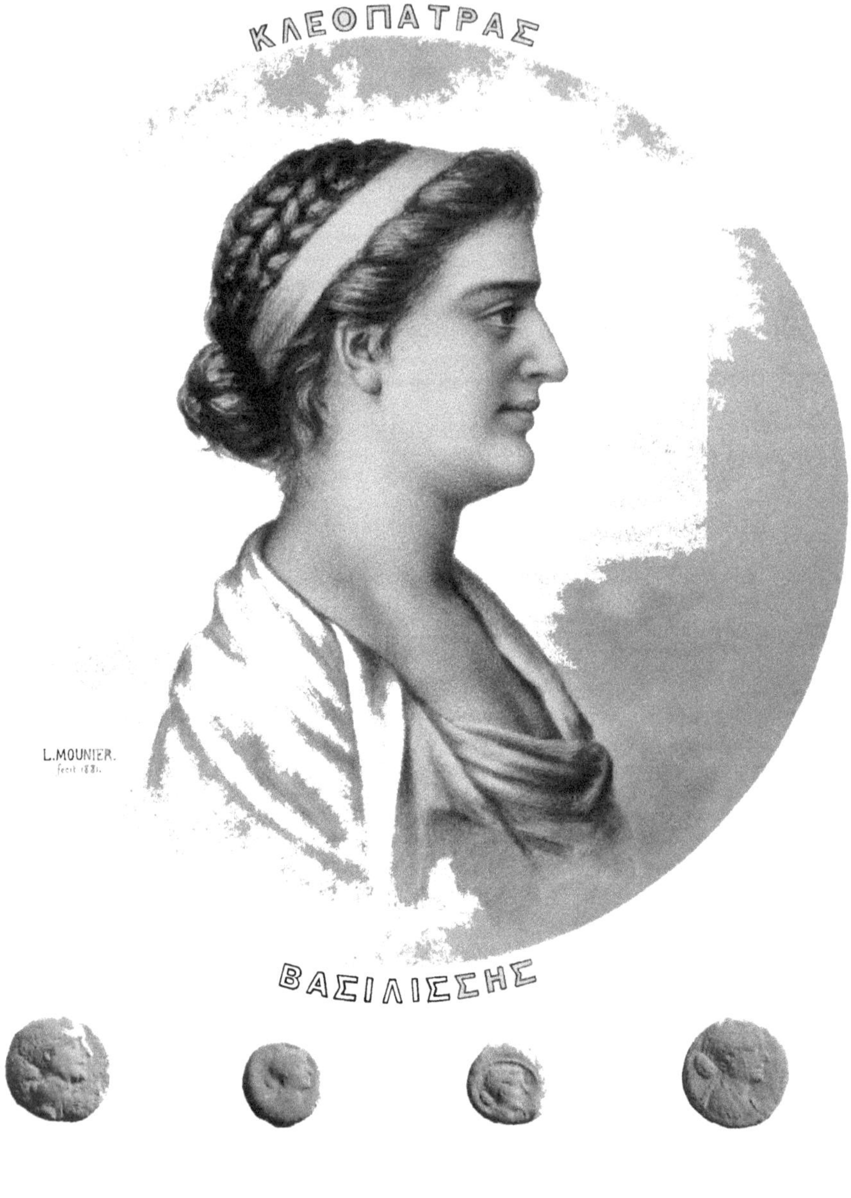

ΚΛΕΟΠΑΤΡΑΣ

ΒΑΣΙΛΙΣΣΗΣ

Archæology of the New York Obelisk.

This temple was one of the most imposing structures of ancient Alexandria, and the monument of imperial Roman pride and power in the newly subdued province of Egypt. A sacred grove surrounded it, a library was attached to it, it was adorned with colonnades and enriched with paintings and statues. Here divine honors were paid to the emperors, even in their own lifetime. The building may have been begun by Cleopatra, after the birth of Cæsarion; it is certain, however, that it was completed by the Alexandrians in honor of Tiberius. In A. D. 336, during an insurrection of the pagans, it was burned down; at a later period it was rebuilt. The date of its final destruction is unknown.

In modern times the New York and London obelisks have been known as Cleopatra's needles. Tradition has associated them with that famous queen of Egypt, whose charms are said to have conquered the austere Pompey, the immortal Cæsar, and the brilliant and dissolute Anthony, but failed to captivate the crafty Octavius. Since the discovery by Mr. Dixon of the inscription on one of the bronze crabs that supported the New York obelisk in Alexandria, archæologists have assumed that she had nothing to do with removing them, as she had been dead about eight years when they were re-erected. Traditions cannot be disposed of by assumptions; there is every reason to believe that Cleopatra ordered the removal of the obelisks. Revolutions and invasions during the latter part of her reign probably delayed their re-erection. After her death there was no one but the conquerors of her kingdom to perpetuate her name. Considering the times and circumstances, it was natural that the Roman Prefect should have been silent as to their removal. But it is probable that the other crabs bore inscriptions which recorded all the facts. Until some proof is offered that the tradition is without foundation, it would seem reasonable to accept it and pay our tribute to a beautiful and captivating woman by associating her name with two of the world's most interesting monuments.

The accompanying plate is a portrait photographed directly from her coins, and finished as any other portrait would be by an artist, who has endeavored to be faithful to the original. The four coins reproduced below the portrait were found under the obelisk in Alexandria very much defaced and corroded. These coins, struck from different dies, manifestly give us a true representation of Cleopatra's profile.

It has been said that these two obelisks were used at Alexandria as gnomons, and reference is made to a concave dial found at the base of one of these shafts, and now preserved in the British Museum. Sharpe[1] mentions a marble dial, now in the British Museum, which was found, as he says, in front of the temple of Alexandria; it was, however, constructed for a horizontal gnomon.

Although the present London obelisk had fallen from its pedestal,[2] yet our obelisk remained standing where the Roman engineers had placed it, before the Temple of Cæsar, until the time of its removal to New York,—almost exactly nineteen centuries. Of later years it had inclined a little from the vertical. For hundreds of years it was a landmark, known as "the standing obelisk," or, *par excellence*, as "Cleopatra's Needle" (it is so called by Paul Lucas, Norden, Baron de Tott, the Description de l' Egypte, Lepsius, Schnaase, Sharpe, Long, etc.), although our English neighbors have recently appropriated this title to the monolith now on the Thames Embankment.

For the earliest notices by different chroniclers of the two obelisks at Alexandria, the reader is referred to the account elsewhere given of the London obelisk. The Arabian geographer Edrisi, whose book was completed A.D. 1154, not merely mentions these monoliths, but professes to give also a translation of their hieroglyphs. Among the many fanciful and wholly conjectural interpretations which were given to hieroglyphic inscriptions before the days of Champollion, none is so extraordinary as this. The following is taken from the French translation of Edrisi by Jaubert: "Near this city (Alexandria) are seen two obelisks. You see on them inscriptions in Syrian characters. The author

---
[1] Sharpe's Hist. of Egypt, vol. ii, p. 96, together with his explanation of Fig. 44, in vol. ii, p. 5.
[2] For probable date of its fall see article on the London obelisk.

of the Book of Marvels states that they were cut in the mountain of Tarim, or Iarim, at the west of Egypt. You read on one of them as follows: 'I, Ia'mor ben-Cheddad, I have built this city, at a period of life still remote from old age,—my death not appearing to be near at hand, nor my hair blanched with years. At an epoch when stones were as clay, when men knew no other master than Ia'mor, I have built the colonnades of the city, I have brought in its water, I have planted its trees; I have desired to surpass the ancient kings who governed it in my construction of admirable monuments. I (therefore) sent Thabout ben-Mara, of the tribe of A'd, and Makdam ben-el-O'mar ben-Abi Reghal, the Thamoudite, to the red-colored mountain of Tarim. They took thence two blocks of stone, which they brought here on their backs; and since Thabout's side was broken, I gave up to his service the people of my kingdom. Fedan ben-Djaroud el-Montefeki; erected for me these shafts in a time of prosperity.'"

The Arabian physician Abd-el-Lateef, writing in 1201 (De Sacy), merely mentions that he saw the two obelisks near the sea. From this time a long period elapses without any especial record of these shafts, until the visit of Petrus Bellonius to Alexandria in the middle of the sixteenth century A. D.[1]

The plate of Kircher, published in 1652, shows our obelisk as square and unbroken to the base. Paul Lucas, visiting Alexandria in 1714, found the lower portion of the shaft buried to the depth, as he estimates, of twelve feet. In 1718, the French Consul Le Maire is reported to have excavated the obelisk to its pedestal. Sicard, in his Nouveaux Mémoires (vol. vii, published in 1729) found the base concealed from view, but notes that the shaft rests upon a granite pedestal, according to the account given by Le Maire. Thomas Shaw, who visited Alexandria about 1730, found the base hidden from sight, but repeats the account of Le Maire's excavation: According to Le Maire, he says, "the bottom of the shaft was not square, but was hemispherical in shape, and was exactly fitted into a socket of corresponding form cut in the upper surface of the pedestal."

Norden, travelling in Egypt in 1737-38, found that the base of the shaft was buried in the earth. Pococke, in Egypt, 1737-39, repeats the account of Le Maire: "It has been found," he says, "by digging under ground that the bottoms of the obelisks were rounded and let into a plinth, as the Egyptians used to place their pillars." Dominique Jauna, in his history published in 1747, reports that the pedestal cannot be seen, since it is covered with sand. Van Egmont and Heyman[2] state that the pedestal of the standing (New York) obelisk is "a flat, square plinth, eight feet on each side and six feet in depth, formed out of a single block of greyish marble or granite, which projects fourteen inches on every side beyond the base of the obelisk." The visit of Niebuhr, in 1761, adds nothing to our information. Baron de Tott (Mémoires sur les Turcs, 1785) found that the base of the standing (New York) obelisk was buried out of sight, but judged from his examination of the base of the fallen (London) obelisk that each shaft originally stood upon four bronze cubes or dies.[3] Zoega, in his "De Origine et Usu Obeliscorum," published in 1797, has in mind the accounts of Le Maire and of Baron de Tott, when he says that it is probable that the foot of the shaft is inserted into the upper surface of the pedestal, and is perhaps made firm by means of bronze bars.

The authors of the Description de l' Egypte report that the shaft had been excavated to its pedestal by M. Conté,[4] but at the time of their own examination it was again buried from sight. Their plate shows the shaft, with its pedestal, resting upon three steps; no bronze crabs are to be seen, but the obelisk is represented as supported or propped upon its pedestal by fragments of stone.

---

[1] See description of London obelisk.   [2] Travels translated from the Dutch and published at London in 1759.

[3] Mr. Feuardent's comment on this is that the Baron saw the remnants of the metal supports attached to the (London) obelisk, and that they were probably already broken, since he calls them "cubes" or "dies."

[4] I cannot learn at what date M. Conté excavated the pedestal. I have gone through the 5 vols. (9 vols. in 5) of the text of the Description, etc., without finding a word on Alexandria. The above statements are taken from the brief explanation of the plates. "When the French army was at Cairo, the base was laid bare to its lowest foundation."—Long, Egyptian Antiquities, vol. i, 300.

Archæology of the New York Obelisk.

Denon,[1] in his Atlas, published 1829, presents us with a very neat and draughtsman-like delineation, in which the pedestal with its three steps appears to have been drawn with the fidelity of an eye-witness; unfortunately, however, for our reliance on his accuracy, the base of the shaft is represented as square, unbroken and flush with the surface of the pedestal. Lenormant, in his Musée, published in 1841, copies the plate of the Description de l' Egypte, and adds the following : " The obelisk rests upon a block of granite, which is 6 [Fr.] ft. 1 in. high, and 8 ft. 10 in. in diameter ; this pedestal is itself supported by three granite steps, which project on every side. The base of the monolith, its corners being broken, and being of an irregularly rounded form, is sustained upon its pedestal by a sort of mason-work (maçonnerie), which compensates for its inequalities and maintains the stability of the shaft. This masonry, of more recent date, was intended to replace the *piédouches* (bracket-pedestals) of bronze which anciently supported the monolith while isolating it from its pedestal."

At the time of the removal of this obelisk to New York, it was found that, at some period since its erection at Alexandria, the corners at the bottom of the shaft had been broken and irregularly rounded. Pontius had mounted it on bronze supports, one under each angle, firmly. soldered with lead into mortices drilled upward into the shaft and downward into the pedestal, each bar projecting from the body of a bronze crab about 16 inches in diameter. One of these crabs had been seen in position by Mr. John Dixon, when, on the removal of the London obelisk from Alexandria in 1877, the base of our obelisk was exposed. Two of the crabs only, both broken, were found by the author of this volume ; the other two had at some previous time been carried off by plunderers. (See Plate v.) Upon the only remaining claw of the two crabs that were found by the author there are two inscriptions, on one side in Greek, on the other in Latin, which fix the date of the re-erection in Alexandria.

The only satisfactory explanation that has been given of the adoption of the form of a crab for the metal supports on which the Romans mounted the obelisks in Alexandria, is that of Mr. Gaston L. Feuardent, in a paper read before the American Numismatic and Archæological Society on January 15, 1881, which is as follows :

In examining these interesting fragments of bronze, the discovery of which has resulted in establishing the true history of the obelisk now in New York, as well as that of the one in London, and does away with the legend which brought the name of Cleopatra in relation with their erection at Alexandria, we cannot help inquiring into the reasons that led the Romans to select the " crab " to support the venerable monolith. We know that the ancients were most careful in their dealings with subjects relating to religion, and every detail in their figurative works had meaning. In the case of the erection of the Alexandrian obelisk in the Roman time, prudence must have been observed by the conquerors in order not to offend the superstitions of the vanquished Egyptians, especially when they related to a class of monuments which, from immemorial time, were regarded in Egypt as being divine symbols.

Therefore, we may feel certain that the " crabs," placed by the Romans under the obelisk, were well chosen to give satisfaction both to the Roman and Egyptian peoples.

I am astonished that—since they were first mentioned by Dickson—no European archæologist has attempted to explain why they were placed as found.

We know, however, that the "crab" is constantly brought in connection with the worship of Apollo in ancient times, and we remember it was principally at the beginning of the Roman Empire that Apollo-Phœbus was distinctly identified with the " Sun." So, in Egypt, where the native Pantheon was already assimilated to the Greek mythology, it must have been regarded as quite natural that an attribute of Apollo, the Sun-God, was employed to support the symbol of Ammon-Generator, which takes a material shape and is visible in the form of the " Sun."

Here is a coin of Croton, struck in the sixth century B. C., on which you will see a " crab " in connection with the " tripod " of Apollo. You will remember also the fable of Hercules killing the hydra, where the "crab" is represented as an instrument of the hatred of Apollo against Hercules. The demi-god is in the act of fighting the hydra, when an enormous " crab " bites him at the heel; Hercules kills the " crab," which is placed in heaven by Juno, and where it becomes in the Zodiac, the sign called " Cancer." Many antique monuments represent the relation of the " crab " to the worship of Apollo, and to come back to our favorite pursuit,

---

[1] Denon died in 1825.

Archæology of the New York Obelisk.

"Numismatics," there is that beautiful and highly artistic coin of Amphipolis, on which is represented the bust of Apollo, full face, with a large "crab" resting on his neck.

You will find in the *Revue Numismatique*, of 1863, an article by M. Dupré, in which that coin is engraved; and in the text, the scientific development of this question. In recalling to my mind that article, the idea came to me to suggest to you that these images of the "crabs" are one more proof of the steady and constant aim of the ancient conquerors of the world to try to assimilate to their own beliefs the religion of the peoples they had vanquished, and by so doing, to make them more easily friendly to themselves; while, since the Mediæval times, the idea of conquerors has always been to impose their own faith on the less fortunate peoples; and perhaps in this remark we may find an explanation of the comparatively facile assimilation of annexed countries with that of the Greeks and Romans.

For convenience of the reader the inscriptions and translation are reproduced here with the notes of Mr. Feuardent, which are of the greatest interest:—

(*Inscription.*)

L.[1] H ΚΑΙΣΑΡΟΣ
ΒΑΡΒΑΡΟΣ ΑΝΕΘΗΚΕ
ΑΡΧΙΤΕΚΤΟΝ ΟΥΝΤΟΣ
ΠΟΝΤΙΟΥ

ANNO VIII
AVGVSTI CAESARIS
BARBARVS PRAEF
AEGYPTI POSVIT
ARCHITECTANTE PONTIO

(*Translation.*)
In the eighth year
of Augustus Cæsar
Barbarus[2] prefect
of Egypt placed.
Pontius architect.

The shaft supported on the bronze crabs had been placed by the Roman architect Pontius on a plinth of syenite, which stood on a base with three steps of hard limestone. The foundation was a mass of concrete capped with masonry up to the level of the pavement. A drawing (Plate xi) and description of these will be found in Chapter I. The plinth and base were removed to New York and restored exactly as they were constructed by Pontius; the only instance, with the exception of the small obelisk of Corfe Castle, in which an Egyptian obelisk, transported from its home in Egypt, has ever been accompanied by its original pedestal and steps. There is no positive proof that these were removed with the obelisk from Heliopolis by the Romans, but there are good reasons for such an assumption.

---

[1] This sign is like the Roman letter "L," and is of frequent occurrence in the Græco-Egyptian inscriptions. It is to be found in the coins of the Lagide dynasty as early as the time of Ptolemy Soter, when the Latin language could not yet have been introduced into Egypt. It represents the first letter of the Greek word "$Λυκάβαντος$" meaning," of the year," for it is the genitive of the word "$Λυκάβας$." It is supposed to be a demotic ideographic sign, and certainly represents the word "year."—G. L. F.

[2] The presence of the name of Prefect Barbarus in connection with the eighth year of Augustus seems to contradict the suggestion made by Mr. F. Feuardent, in his *Numismatique de l'Égypte Ancienne*, that P. Rubrius Barbarus was prefect in B. C. 13; Barbarus was in power in Egypt at least ten years before that date; and Mr. G. Feuardent's authority, viz.: the inscription of Philae (Wescher: *Bullet. Instit. Archéol.*, 1879) appears to have misled him.

I have not been able to compare this question of the time of power of Barbarus, as written on the obelisk "crab," with the list of prefects published by Franz, in his *Corpus Inscriptionum Græcorum*.

In regard to the corresponding date of the eighth year of Augustus with that of the Christian era, I suggest that it was during the year B. C. 22 that the obelisk was erected at Alexandria. This date of the eighth year cannot correspond with the "Actian Era," and then it must be that of the reign of Augustus himself. Therefore, the *Anni Augusti* having begun in the year of Rome 725 (A.U.C.), or B. C. 29, the eighth year of Augustus falls at B. C. 22. I do not follow Censorinus, who makes the Cæsarian era begin at A. D. 27.—G. L. F.

CHAPTER III.

REMOVAL OF THE LUXOR OBELISK TO PARIS.

BY LIEUTENANT SEATON SCHROEDER, UNITED STATES NAVY.

TO the first Napoleon is attributed the original thought of endowing Paris with an Egyptian obelisk. That which sixteen years of war and the continental blockade forbade his undertaking, his royal successor began. By order of Louis XVIII the French Consul-General in Alexandria commenced and successfully completed negotiations with the Viceroy of Egypt for the cession of one of the Alexandrian monoliths. The gift was cheerfully made and Cleopatra's Needle now standing in Central Park, New York, became the property of France. No steps were taken to remove it during that reign, however, nor is it now known what were the causes that so postponed the enterprise.

The mere nominal possession of so noble a work of art also seemed to satisfy the dignitaries of the succeeding government for some years, until letters from MM. de la Borde and Champollion (the younger) recalled the apparently forgotten gift. Drawn to Egypt by their love of the sciences those gentlemen could not fail to be struck by the beauty of monuments so utterly unappreciated by the listless Arabs, and they succeeded in firing the enthusiasm of friends at home. Baron d' Haussez, Minister of Marine, spurred on by Baron Taylor, whose rank, studies, and tastes lent weight to his opinion, quickly became interested in a project that would shed lustre as well on the reign of his master as on himself, under whose administration it would be carried out. An additional plea was not wanting when it came to asking the Chambers for the necessary funds. Regarded by Napoleon simply in the light of a monument to the campaign of 1799, the obelisk had recently acquired a value of a far different nature; the Egyptian Museum, just founded by the king, Charles X, and bearing his name, coveted it as a specimen of antique art.

In November, 1829, the Minister wrote to M. de Cerisi, a French officer then in charge of the naval constructions of Egypt, asking for information regarding the dimensions and weight of the monolith, and also his advice as to the best means of lowering and transporting it. Another officer on duty in the fleet in the Levant was instructed to consult with M. de Cerisi on the subject.

In the meantime Champollion, travelling through Egypt, had seen the obelisks of Luxor, and, in a letter which was afterward shown to Baron d' Haussez, descanted on their greater beauty, and advised making an attempt to secure them even if at the sacrifice of the one in Alexandria. The opinion of so eminent an authority was immediately accepted, and his advice acted on soon after.

The first plan of removal discussed in Paris was that of M. Besson, a French officer serving in the Egyptian navy. He proposed a method similar to that used by the ancient Romans. A raft would be built in Karamania, 110 feet long and 45 feet broad, and towed up to Thebes. The obelisk, encased in a huge wooden cylinder, fastened with iron bands, would be placed on the raft, leaving only one half of its diameter above the surface. This would then be towed to the Gulf of

Toulon, and the Needle there transferred to a seaworthy vessel specially built to bring it to Havre, whence it would be taken to Paris by a number of the small craft usually employed in the navigation of the Seine.

This plan, as is easily seen, was very complicated, and Baron Tupinier, Director of Ports, showed its faults most clearly to the Minister of Marine, whereupon a commission was formed, composed of MM. de la Borde, Tupinier, Drovetti, Taylor, Briet, de Mackau, and de Livron, with Baron d' Haussez as president. These gentlemen, after a long discussion, recommended that Baron Taylor should be sent to Egypt to consult with Besson and de Cerisi on the best plan of removal, as well as to obtain the cession of the two other newly coveted obelisks. The friendly disposition of Mohammed Ali was so well known as to leave little doubt of his consent. The approval of King Charles was immediately obtained, and on the 6th of January, 1830, Baron Taylor was duly invested with the royal authority to wait upon the Pacha, to negotiate the cession of the Luxor obelisks, and have Cleopatra's Needle transported to France. A credit of $20,000 was opened to defray the expenses of the mission, and the brig "Lancier" was detailed to convey him to Egypt.

These preliminaries settled, attention was again bestowed upon the methods of executing the various operations, and a plan advanced by Baron Rolland was approved by the Minister of Marine, who ordered the construction of the "Luxor" even before the departure of Baron Taylor on his mission. The "Luxor" was an immense barge of such build as to ascend the Nile, receive on board one of the obelisks, and bring it to Paris. That is to say, the task set the constructors was to produce a vessel that could navigate two rivers and the high seas, should not draw over six and a half feet with the obelisk in, should pass under the bridges across the Seine, and should be strong enough to take the enormous weight while lying on a beach. Of course M. Rolland had to depart from the usual rules of naval architecture; the proportion of length to breadth was very small, five keels were fitted, and the necessary longitudinal and transverse strength obtained by multiplying fastenings and ties. The result was an immensely strong craft, shaped like a parallelopipedon with rounded angles; three masts were given her. It is perhaps needless to add that the material of which she was built was wood; iron shipbuilding in those days was a thing of the future. The launch took place at Toulon on the 26th of July, 1830, and M. Mimerel, naval constructor, and M. Verninac de St. Maur, also of the navy, were detailed to take charge of the work, the former having charge of all operations on shore, and the latter being in command of the vessel afloat.

Meanwhile Baron Taylor reached Egypt after many delays, had an audience with the Pacha, and succeeded in the principal object of his mission. It was not without difficulty, however, as Mr. Barker, the British Consul, had labored indefatigably, and finally obtained the cession of the Luxor obelisks to England. The skilful diplomacy of M. Taylor, added to the Viceroy's desire to please the French envoy, soon suggested a way out of that difficulty, and Mr. Barker was offered the magnificent obelisk of Karnak in place of those of Luxor, which he accepted. Then came the news of the events of July, 1830, and intrigues were commenced to have the gift withdrawn. But M. Taylor and the French Consul-General, M. Mimaut, were determined to retain ownership of the obelisks, whatever might be the action of the new government in the matter of taking possession of them. They had no difficulty in persuading the Pacha that his gift had really been to the French nation and not to the person of the king, and therefore the Revolution could afford no reason for withdrawing his gift. The following letter from the Egyptian Prime Minister to Count Sebastiani, the new Minister of Marine, finally confirmed the cession.

Removal of the Luxor Obelisk to Paris.

ALEXANDRIA, *November* 29, 1830.

EXCELLENCY:

His Highness, the Viceroy of Egypt, has received from M. le Baron Taylor the dispatch of which he was the bearer, from the Secretary of State for the Navy and Colonies, to negotiate in the name of H. M., the King of France, and obtain one of Cleopatra's Needles at Alexandria, and particularly the two obelisks of Luxor, which form a part of the ruins of Thebes.

His Highness, the Viceroy, has charged me to express to your Excellency the pleasure he feels in showing his gratitude to France for the numerous marks of kindness and friendship that have been manifested to him at different times, and which have been recently renewed on the part of his Majesty, the King of the French, through M. le Consul-General Mimaut.

I am ordered by His Highness to place the three monuments at the disposal of H. M., the King of the French, and your Excellency is requested to tender them to His Majesty in the name of H. H., the Viceroy, Mehemet Ali Pacha.

It is very flattering to me to be the interpreter of the wishes of my prince on this occasion, and I beg your Excellency to accept the assurance of my most distinguished consideration.

(Signed) BOGHOZ JOUSSOUF.

On the 25th of June the transport "Dromadaire" had arrived at Alexandria for the transportation of that Needle. But as she had not brought all the material, especially wood, needed for the various operations, it was necessary to send to Karamania to supply the deficiency, and delays arising from these circumstances resulted later in abandoning the idea of removing that obelisk.

The change in the government of France had caused no abatement in the desire to erect the obelisks in Paris. Count Sebastiani inherited his predecessor's enthusiasm in the matter, and the equipment of the "Luxor" was pushed rapidly forward. The sum of $60,000 already appropriated being nearly all expended, partly in the construction and equipment of the "Luxor," partly in M. Taylor's mission, a further credit of $40,000 was asked and granted.

A change, however, had to be made in the detail of officers to take charge of the work, as M. Mimerel found that the state of his health was such as to compel him to yield the honor to another, M. Apollinaire LeBas, Naval Constructor, was chosen to take his place, and it was this officer that lowered, embarked, and afterward re-erected the monument that towers up to such fine effect in the Place de la Concorde. By a singular coincidence of name and stature, M. LeBas was a man of very diminutive proportions, and the smallness of his size appeared in striking contrast with the magnitude of the operations he was called upon to plan and execute. His skill and energy, be it said, proved in inverse proportion to his height.

M. LeBas was left perfectly unhampered as to the mode of procedure in lowering and embarking the obelisk, but was provided with every thing that study and good judgment could point to being necessary. He was also authorized to select a master carpenter, and a number of other carpenters, smiths, caulkers, joiners, stone-cutters, etc., from the dockyard, and the "Luxor" was provided with several picked boatswains. Amply equipped and manned, the transport finally made sail from Toulon on the 15th of April, 1831, under the command of M. Verninac de Saint-Maur.

The novel craft behaved at sea much as was expected; with a fair wind she made as much as eight knots, but when close-hauled her progress was crab-like. Fortunately, the weather was propitious, as a rule, and on the 3d of May the anchor was dropped in Alexandria harbor, off the Viceroy's palace. Although anxious to proceed with all haste to Upper Egypt to examine the ground and prepare a bed for the "Luxor" before the inundation, M. LeBas was detained here three weeks, waiting for the consul to come from Cairo and arrange for an audience with the Pacha. Mohammed Ali was most cordial, however, and by his evident desire to further in every possible way the success of the undertaking, removed to a considerable degree the disagreeable impression caused by this first apparently ominous delay. All formalities were quickly finished; the party were transferred to a fleet of swift *cangiahs* and on the 19th of June they started up the Nile from Rosetta, leaving the "Luxor" to follow with most of the material.

The month that took them to reach their destination was mainly characterized by difficulties and vexatious ¦delays purposely caused by the *raïs* or captains of the *cangiahs* who naturally, perhaps, were anxious to spin out the time as much as possible. The passengers humorously, and not inaptly, compared them to the average fiacre-driver of Paris, who takes such smiling advantage of a green traveller that may have engaged him by the hour. The governor of Cairo on hearing of their conduct placidly ordered them to be whipped, but graciously countermanded the order when so requested. He had simply directed that the difficulty should be settled according to the custom of the country, and was perhaps not a little astonished when the foreigners interceded in behalf of the culprits. Poor Arabs! sinned against perhaps more than sinning, their lot was hard under the rule of the great Mohammed Ali; nor has it been greatly bettered since that time. But it is pleasant to chronicle the opening of a vista of improvement, shining in the light of an earnest and just administration. Since the present enlightened prince, Tewfik Pacha, has occupied the vice-regal throne, it has required less optimism to foretell brighter days in Egypt's future.

A greenish tint in the water, announcing the commencement of the annual rise, warned our friends bound up to Luxor that no time was to be lost. At their request *kavasses*, or body-guards, were detailed to accompany the expedition, to stir up the *raïs* when they seemed inclined to lag; and sail was again made on the *cangiahs*. Atfyh, Beni-Soueyf, Abou Girgeh, Mellaoui, Siout, Kene, and the wonderful ruins of Denderah were passed successively, and as the Gamouleh bend was rounded, the gigantic vestiges of the ancient city appeared on all sides, gorgeously tinted by the slanting rays of the setting sun. On the right were the ruins of Quournah, of the Memnonium, the Valley of Tombs, and the temples of Medinet-Abou; to the left, the temples of Karnak, with its colossal obelisk; and, farther on, the colonnade of the Luxor palace, with two granite obelisks guarding the immense gateway. The little fleet anchored immediately abreast the latter, and sailors, workmen, officers, and all scrambled on shore to make acquaintance with the two lofty, aged sentinels, one of which was about to desert his post after a watch of thirty-four centuries.

In glowing terms had Champollion written of the city of a hundred gates, containing palaces, sphinxes, and colossal monuments, all bearing witness to a past grandeur and subsequent decadence; enthusiastically had he weighed upon the superior beauty of the westernmost of the two ruddy monoliths, the one on the right hand in entering the Rameseion. But one thought alone actuated the enterprising little band whose fortunes we are following. For the moment they were interested only in a mass of granite weighing some 230 tons, which it devolved upon them to uproot and carry away. Mazacqui, the Italian stone-cutter, true to his instincts, saluted the stony giant with a professional tap of his hammer; something seeming to startle him, he repeated the blow, and, after listening attentively, exclaimed in the jargon only intelligible perhaps to travellers in Mediterranean France: "Moussou, la pietra, elle est félée, mais je ne crois pas qu' elle soit routta; Iou son est sano; on pourra l' enlever pourvu qu' elle tombe piano, ben piano."[1]

The fellow was right; the defect was patent, although unmentioned in any known work on Egypt. To some of the native officials the fact was no secret; during the short stay at Cairo, Krali Effendi, in speaking to M. LeBas, of the "Stones of the King of France," as he contemptuously called them, had stated that there was a fissure in that westernmost obelisk. But it had made no great impression on that officer's mind, because of the improbability of so serious a matter having escaped the attention of all writers on Egypt. Even Champollion, whose recent visit had led to the acquisition of these obelisks, had affirmed that the base of the westernmost was in a perfect state of preservation.

---

[1] "Sir, the stone is cracked, but I do not think it is broken; the sound is good; it can be removed if it falls softly, very softly."

The mason's blow, however, brushed away all doubts with no gentle stroke, and excavations soon revealed that a fissure extended to the base, twelve feet underground, and seemed to penetrate into the stone. Fortunately, as subsequent events proved, the strength of the mass was not seriously impaired, and special care does not seem to have been necessary to prevent undue strain on that lower part during the operations of lowering and erection. The monolith was simply disfigured to a certain extent; but that seam and the marring of the pyramidion are the only faults to be found with that beautiful shaft.

M. LeBas' orders were to bring home that western obelisk—"the one on the right hand in entering the Rameseion"; marred or not he had no alternative. An examination of the ground was commenced the day after they arrived, and two facts were quickly revealed: the plans that he had been maturing since leaving Toulon were impracticable under the circumstances, and new ones had to be devised; also the necessary excavations would require the demolition of some thirty miserable huts. A proposition was made to buy these, but the cupidity of the tenants was immediately aroused by the offer, and the answer was a flat refusal to sell. The Governor of Upper Egypt, on being apprised of the difficulty, sent his interpreter and an officer of his guard with orders to enforce immediate compliance with M. LeBas' wishes. Those two worthies naturally proposed to end the matter à la Turque, but were persuaded to desist, and a commission was appointed to appraise the buildings and decide the amount to be paid each proprietor. The scenes that ensued, as described afterward by M. LeBas, the shouting, the gesticulating, the noisy wrath of men, and the weeping of women, the apparent fury on both sides, can be imagined perhaps only by those who may have visited the bazars of the East; whatever be the article in question, whether rugs, rose-water, or, as in this case, houses, the progress and finale of the transactions are practically the same. Great was the astonishment of the strangers in Luxor, when, as the storm of anger and debate appeared to reach its height, there was a sudden hush, and Ibrahim, the interpreter, wiped his honest brow, and with a look of conscious pride at having faithfully performed a painful duty, said calmly, though hoarsely: "It is all arranged." The noise had ceased as by magic, and the various disputants all retired with abundant manifestations of respect and affection.

Will the reader be as shocked as were those Frenchmen on learning afterward that Ibrahim's wonderful zeal was all a hoax? The whole scenic effect—menaces on the one side, prayers and reproaches on the other—proved to have been slyly concocted and theatrically produced—for what? To ensure honest Ibrahim a fair commission on the sale!

The four sides of the obelisk faced respectively to N. W., N. E., S. E., and S. W., the first being turned toward the river. It was quickly decided, therefore, to lower it on its N. W. face and haul it to the barge. This vessel would be grounded at high Nile, and the obelisk embarked after the fall of the river; the following year the stream rising again would float the vessel and cargo, and the journey home would begin. The level of high-water was indicated by traces of the river at various points of the bank, and it was found that the "Luxor" could safely be brought to a distance of about 430 yards from the obelisk.

M. LeBas' intention at first was to lower the Needle all the way by one simple rotation on an edge of the base, as that was found to be approximately on a level with the bench-mark where the "Luxor" was to be grounded. A horizontal roadway would then be constructed to the bow of the vessel. This would necessitate an excavation of about 55,000 cubic yards, a work of some magnitude in itself, apart from the danger of encountering obstacles in the shape of ancient or modern masonry concealed underground, the removal of which might add enormously to the labor. In view of such possibilities he conceived the idea of two successive rotations; the first would be round the lower edge of the N. W. face as the axis, until the Needle should touch a second pivot on a higher plane than the base, and at such distance as to take approximately at the centre of gravity. Thus poised, the remainder of the descent would be easy, and that second rotation would at once lower the summit and raise the base to a plane above that of the pedestal. A considerable amount of excavation would thus be saved, and the advantage gained of a down grade to the river.

These essential points determined, it remained to devise the means of executing them. The only mechanical application of power available under the circumstances was fortunately that which suggests itself most readily to the naval mind, namely, the pulley. The result to be produced required two systems or series of tackles. One would pull the top of the obelisk over toward the river; the other would hold it in check and lower it safely, only beginning to act when the vertical through the centre of gravity should pass beyond the axis of rotation.

Pending the arrival of the material, all that could be done was to tear down the buildings that were in the way, and prepare the bed for the "Luxor" in such position that she could lie with her three masts in a line perpendicular to the face of the obelisk. The Nile was rising so fast by that time that the men working at that and at the foundation of the sliding-ways had to be protected from the water by movable dikes, that were shifted in as the work progressed. It had been announced in Thebes and the neighboring villages that laborers were wanted and would receive daily a fixed sum. Such novel news was hailed with acclamations by the *fellaheen*, and the work never flagged for want of unskilled labor. Four hundred men, women, and children were soon busily engaged with pick, hoe, and basket, and the usual songs were chanted, interrupted only by the cries of the sheiks: "Yalla! volet; Yalla! benti." (Go ahead, boys; go ahead, girls.) The heat of course was intense, and the dust suffocating, and the suffering on all sides very great; but many hands made light work, and matters progressed very fairly. On the 1st of August a number of ladders lashed together were raised along the face of the Needle, and soon after the sailors had the French ensign displayed from the top.

On August 13th all the *raïs* in the vicinity came trooping in to herald the approach of a huge craft which some compared to a floating mosque, and others to a feddam of ground.[1] It was the "Luxor," the manœuvring of which without a sound save that of the boatswain's whistle could not fail to amaze the noisy and simple-minded Arabs. On the 14th she anchored near by, and on the following day was placed in position, bows in, over the carefully prepared bed, by that time well under water. The ruins of a neighboring temple had then to be cleared out, roofed over and turned into quarters. A hospital was also prepared, and several other buildings erected for the various uses of a camp,— kitchen, bakery, storehouse, etc. The village quickly assumed a new aspect.

A staging was built to the top of the obelisk for the purpose of encasing it with wood and of measuring all its dimensions. As is perhaps known to all, the shape of the Needle is that of a quadrangular truncated pyramid, surmounted by a pyramidion, or small pyramid. The dimensions are as follows:—

	FEET.	INCHES.
Height of main shaft (truncated pyramid) - - - - -	68	6.8
Height of pyramidion (imperfect)[2] - - - - - -	6	4.4
Total height - - - - - -	74	11.2

[1] A feddam is about two thirds of an acre.

[2] If perfect, this pyramidion would be about eight feet in height. As the Egyptians never left such unfinished work, it seems probable either that the stone has worn away there, aided perhaps by superficial flaws, or that another material was substituted for the granite which was deficient. M. J. J. Hittorf, who some years later designed the new pedestal in the Place de la Concorde, and the other embellishments of that handsome square, argued powerfully in support of the latter theory, maintaining also that bronze, possibly gilded, appeared, from its nature, and the undeniable proofs of its analogous use in other Egyptian monuments, to be the material most suitable to supplying the given want. The fact of there being a small flat ledge at the base of the pyramidion certainly gives coloring to the idea, though it is still a mooted point among Egyptologists whether or not the ancients resorted to that means of perfecting their monuments.

Removal of the Luxor Obelisk to Paris.

		FEET.	INCHES.			FEET.	INCHES.
Base of main shaft	N. E. side	8	0	Top of main shaft	N. E. side	4	11
	S. E. "	7	11.3		S. E. "	5	2.2
	S. W. "	7	11.3		S. W. "	4	11
	N. W. "	7	11.3		N. W. "	5	2.2

These data give a volume of 2,948 cubic feet for the main shaft, and 54 for the pyramidion, or 3,002 in all. Assuming the specific gravity of the granite to be 2.66, the weight of the Paris obelisk is 222.28 tons,[1] neglecting loss from hieroglyphics.

A close examination revealed that all the sides of this monolith are not planes; the N. W. and S. E. faces as it stood at Luxor (turned respectively to the Seine and to the Madeleine in Paris) have a double curvature. Laterally both are convex, the versed sine of the convexity[2] of the former being 1⅜ inches, and of the latter 1⅛ inches; in other words, these two sides are rounded out, the middle of the rounding being 1⅜ and 1⅛ inches from an imaginary straight line across from edge to edge. The longitudinal curvatures are remarkable in that the N. W. face is convex, and the S. E. concave, in consequence of which all four longitudinal edges are curves convex to N. W.,—to the river Seine as the obelisk now stands. The versed sine of this curvature is very small, being only four-fifths of an inch for the N. W. face, and half an inch for the other.

It is a very curious fact that the sides of the other obelisk, still at Luxor, present the same peculiarity, the convexity of its edges also being turned toward the Nile. This can hardly be attributable to accident, or to the imperfection of the work of quarrying and dressing, but must be considered one of the many questions connected with these wonderful monuments that have yet to be solved.

As during the first contemplated rotation the entire weight of the obelisk would come on the edge round which it was to revolve, it was necessary to have that edge take on some comparatively soft material, which would act as a cushion and save it from being crushed. It was, therefore, *let in* to a heavy oak cross-log; this was carefully rounded on the outside so as to turn easily in a second timber hollowed to correspond; this bottom-piece rested in a mortise cut like a step in the top and side of the pedestal. Thus was formed a sort of hinge around which the rotation would be operated.

Of the two systems of tackles necessary to bring the obelisk safely from the vertical to the horizontal, we will first examine the apparatus for inclining the obelisk from the vertical.

This gear consisted of three capstans to which were taken the hauling parts of as many tackles. The fixed blocks of these tackles were taken to anchors planted in the sand, and the movable blocks to a cable fastened to the obelisk just below the pyramidion. The tackles were sixfold purchases of 6¼-inch new untarred rope, rove through sheaves 14 inches in diameter. Each capstan was fitted with sixteen bars, on each of which would be four men.

In hauling on a heavy sixfold purchase the strain on the hauling part is more than double that on the standing part, because of the friction and loss of power resulting from the numerous changes in direction of the various parts. Also, for the same reason, to overcome a certain weight at the movable block of a tackle of this size, the power applied to the hauling part must be one quarter that weight, and not one sixth. In the case under consideration the weight to be moved (to start the obelisk and appendages from the vertical) was found to be about 52,000 pounds. Assuming every man to heave on his capstan-bar with a steady power of 22 pounds, the mean leverage on each bar being 6½ feet, the power transmitted by each capstan to the hauling part of its tackle would be

---

[1] English tons of 2,240 pounds. M. LeBas assumed the specific gravity to be 2.70 and found the weight to be 225.87 tons.

[2] Mathematically speaking, the versed sine of half the arc.

Removal of the Luxor Obelisk to Paris.

about 5,120 pounds after deducting the loss by friction and by the angular lead of the fall away from the barrel. The quadruple gain in power by the sixfold purchases would increase that to 20,480 pounds exerted by each tackle, or 61,440 pounds in all,—nearly 10,000 in excess of the weight. In case of necessity a much greater power could be exerted by encouraging the men to put forth their strength; a man can exert a power of forty pounds on a capstan-bar for several hours.

The maximum power in an operation of this kind is only required at first, because the resistance or weight must decrease as the vertical through the centre of gravity approaches the axis of rotation. When that vertical reaches the axis equilibrium ensues, and after that the duty of the inclining gear is done, and it becomes necessary to check the mass and allow it to descend gently.

This required an entirely separate system of tackles, which we will designate as the apparatus for lowering the obelisk. It will be readily seen that a series of checking or lowering tackles leading to the top of the obelisk from any point on the ground would be at a favorable angle with it at first, but as the inclination from the vertical increased, the angle between them and the axis of the monolith would decrease, finally becoming so small as to bring upon them a strain greater than could be resisted by the means at hand. To obviate this difficulty recourse was had to a certain number of spurs or derricks to keep that angle practically constant.

First of all, excavations were made to the level of the pedestal, and carried toward the river only as far as the position of the second pivot. In this angle of the pit a heavy platform was built, from which rose a brick wall to support that second pivot and to prevent crushing in of the earth. On this platform was also the fundamental feature of the whole apparatus,—the axial beam of the spurs.

This axial beam, of which the lower part was rounded, was placed horizontal in the right angle formed by the vertical brick wall and the platform. On its plane face were stepped the eight masts or derricks, arranged in two equal groups, one on each side of the obelisk, and laid nearly horizontal with the heads on the opposite side of the obelisk,—away from the river. The heads of all eight, slightly converging, were connected by a double cross-piece, the entire fabric forming a trapezoid capable of rotating around its base. At that double cross-beam the head of each mast was permanently connected with the top of the obelisk by a standing cable or shroud, so that the top of the Needle in descending would pull the heads of the masts up correspondingly. The power for checking the descent would then be applied to these spurs' heads. For this eight heavy sixfold purchases were used, the movable treble-blocks being secured to the derrick-heads and shrouds, and the fixed double-blocks to a heavy framing worked around the pedestal of the other obelisk.

In lowering by these tackles it would be of paramount importance to always keep exactly the same strain on all the falls, and this it is impossible for eight men to do when acting independently. The difficulty was overcome by an ingenious though simple device. A large round log was prepared as a roller, with cleats or whelps bolted on to make the surface rough. The hauling parts of the tackles were taken to this roller, a groove being made for each so as to keep them separate; two turns of the ropes were taken around the beam to prevent their slipping or *rendering*. In this way the tackles could only be eased away by the revolution of the beam; the diameter being exactly the same in all the grooves, one revolution of the beam would slack all the tackles equally. It was only necessary to give them all an equal strain before beginning operations.

From the moment the centre of gravity passed outside the axis of rotation, the strain on the derrick-heads and thence on the tackles would increase from zero at the beginning to a maximum when the inclination of the obelisk would be greatest, that is, when it would reach the second pivot. This maximum power was found to be 209,100 pounds on the tackles, or 26,140 on each. By means of turns of the ropes around immovable posts and beams, friction was obtained sufficient to reduce the weight required at the end of each fall to about 28 or 30 pounds, or well within the command of the seaman attending it.

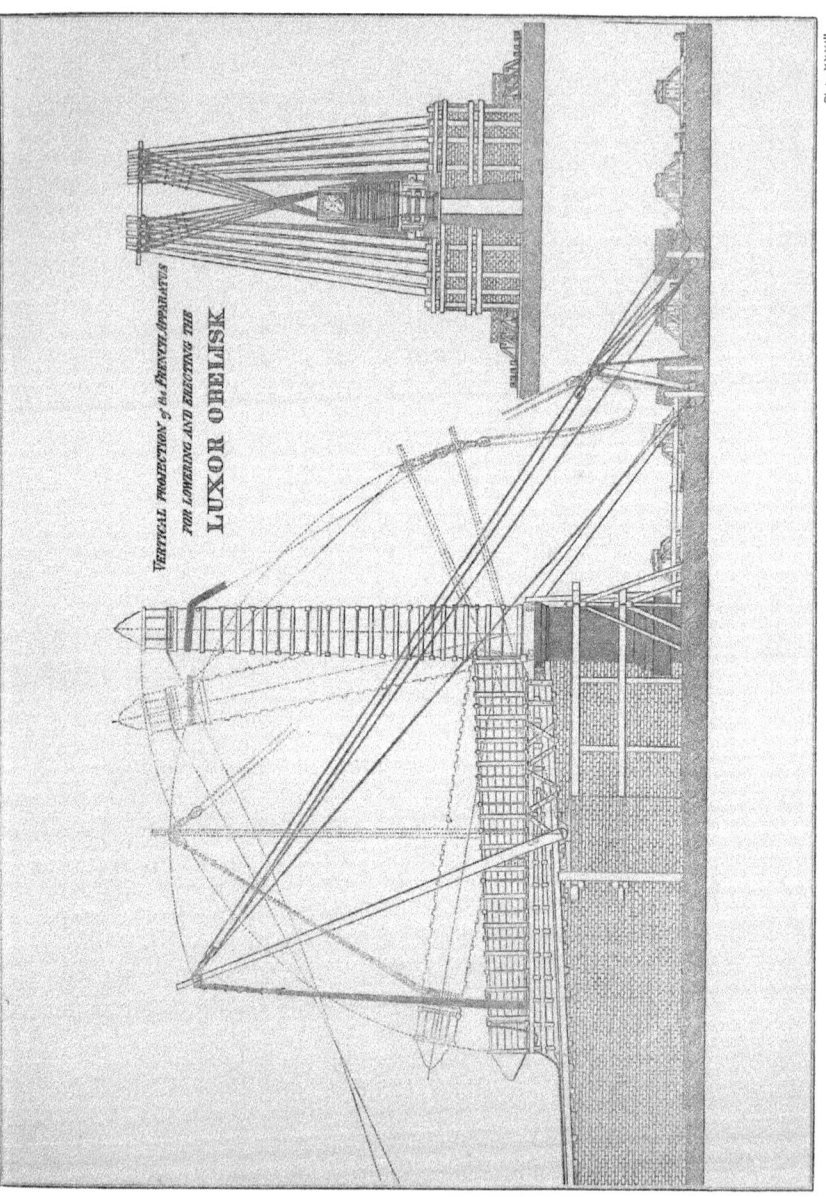

Plate XXXIII.

Removal of the Luxor Obelisk to Paris.

The inclination of the obelisk from the vertical would necessarily bring about an increase in the horizontal component of the thrust exerted by it on the pedestal. The thrust exerted by the derricks being in an opposite direction, the platform on which they were stepped was rigidly connected with the pedestal, and a part of the eastward thrust taken up. The strain on the pedestal being in excess of that on the platform, the resultant of the two opposing forces would be neutralized by the sand and earth against the southeast face of the plinth.

The two apparatus just described are similar to those used later in raising the obelisk again in Paris, the main difference being that in the latter operation only one rotation was performed, the edge of the base being the axis. Plate xxxiii therefore, represents the main features of both operations.

The child-like Arabs quickly adapted themselves to the new and extraordinary work going on, and a squad of expert long-sawyers was soon organized and trained. Thoroughly unacquainted with the tool at first, the more intelligent ones were made to practise on trunks of date-palms until their proficiency warranted leaving all such work to them under supervision, and the carpenters of the expedition were saved that labor and remained free to do more delicate work. In spite of the heat and dust every thing progressed satisfactorily. By the first of September the scaffolding was finished to the top of the obelisk, and the sheathing commenced. This was of 5 1-4 inch plank.

Shortly after, however, a terrible visitor made its appearance. Cholera, whose approach had been heralded step by step up the river, suddenly attacked the little colony. Fifteen of the seamen were soon in the extemporized hospital; the Arabs fared worse than the Europeans, many of them dying suddenly at the close of a day's work. Communication was also interrupted with Alexandria, and the hoped-for supplies of wood and other material had to be given up. Every thing looked dark indeed; but the gallant little band, far away from all help or encouragement, thrown entirely upon their own resources, struggled along with the work. A strict compliance with the régime prescribed by the surgeon was enforced, and daylight dawned ahead at last.

By the 1st of October the sheathing of the obelisk was completed, the axial beam of the derricks in place, and these all ready to be stepped. The shrouds were secured to the top of the obelisk and to the derrick-heads, the blocks *turned in*, and in short the whole apparatus prepared as described above.

Daylight on the 24th of October, 1831, found every one at his post,—Arabs at the capstan-bars, seamen at the lowering tackles; and as the first beams of the rising sun gilded the colossal statue of Memnon, the silence was broken by the words of command. The capstans went round, the tackles tightened, and the great mass slowly yielded, drawing after it the derrick-heads which had been fancifully decorated with little flags and palm branches. An angle of eight degrees from the vertical was reached when the whole came to a stand-still; the officer in charge of the capstans reported that their anchors were drawing through the sand. Orders were given to slack away more rapidly on the opposite side; this being done the rotatory motion recommenced, and very soon the centre of gravity passed beyond the plane of the axis and every thing devolved upon the eight picked men that controlled the movement. In twenty-five minutes from the time the first order was given to heave, the obelisk touched the beam that was to form the axis of the second rotation. Nothing had given way; so far perfect success had crowned the efforts put forth.

The first great suspense was over, but difficulties were seen ahead as great as had yet been encountered, if not greater. All the wood left for use, excepting the soft trunks of palm-trees, consisted of six joists, 23 feet long and 7 by 8 inches square, and a few pieces of plank. With this slender stock a timber way had to be constructed to the bow of the "Luxor" on which to slide the obelisk. There being no hope of obtaining the material written for, work had to be begun with what there was on hand. The six joists sufficed to form sliding ways 69 feet long, made in three parts capable of being disconnected. The joists were connected by heavy cleats at the ends, and rested on a flooring made of transverse pieces of planking spiked to their under side. The whole did not present enough bearing surface to ensure safety, and M. LeBas felt serious doubts as to its answering the purpose. So great were his misgivings, in fact, that he refrained from sending a report of progress until the end of the final operation.

While this work was being carried on an examination was made of the heel of the obelisk. It was found that the fissure that had so disconcerted M. LeBas was crossed by two dovetail-shaped mortises, filled with a yellowish dust, the remains of the wooden *dogs* which must have been driven in before the erection to prevent any possible widening of the crack.[1] The fissure therefore was, beyond doubt, a defect in the stone, as old as the monolith, the antiquity of which was itself well attested by the nomen and prenomen of Ramses II, sculptured under the heel. Various incisions were also found in both pedestals, and one of these in the eastern could not fail to attract attention. It was near and parallel to the N. W. side of the block, semicircular on section, and its axis lay exactly under that edge of the obelisk. It would seem quite credible therefore that it had served as a receptacle for a wooden axis of rotation in the erection. The fact of this groove being on the side next to the river, and it being known that that eastern obelisk was the first of the two erected, so that the other was not in the way, would also point to the possibility of its having been brought by water to the adjacent bank, and that in the transportation as well as the erection means had been employed perfectly similar to those used more than thirty centuries later in lowering and removing its fellow.

When the section of ways was completed the master carpenter reported that every particle of wood was used, and that if any thing should break he would be unable to repair it.

The centre of gravity being slightly beyond the new pivot, the second rotation would succeed the first without application of power, except to hold back. It being necessary to cast off the shrouds from the obelisk before it should touch the ways, two tackles were secured to the derrick-heads and to the pyramidion, near the point, and the shrouds removed. Before allowing the second rotation to take place it was necessary also to provide means to prevent the whole mass slipping and sliding back eastward when the lower edge should rise from the mortise in the pedestal, which would be sure to occur because of the checking tackles from the derrick-heads leading at such an acute angle with the axis of the Needle. To effect this a block of masonry was built on the pedestal, the side of it touching the heel of the obelisk and curved properly to coincide with the arc to be described by it.

These and all other minor details completed, the head of the monolith was allowed to descend and the heel to rise from the socket. The entire weight then resting on the log forming the pivot, compressed and ground it into the brick wall beneath, and made the latter also settle somewhat into the platform and earth. The monolith being lowered bodily by the amount of the compression, took on the end of the sliding ways; this, of course, sank into the ground under the pressure, and the timber road assumed a curve convex upward. As the point of the needle descended, the axis of rotation gradually changed forward up that curve until it reached the centre of gravity, when the whole system was in equilibrium, the Needle lying on an upward slope. Power was applied to raise the heel, four tackles from the derrick-heads being used, with the falls taken to small capstans. It was brought somewhat nearer the horizontal, but soon all efforts proved unavailing to move it. The cable that had been used for inclining it from the perpendicular was then taken round the heel, four heavy tackles clapped on the ends, and the falls taken to capstans manned by forty-eight men each, the object being to rouse the obelisk up the slope and out of the pit. This gear was ready on the 16th of November; they hove on the large capstans and at the same time on the vertical tackles on the heel, but to no effect. The men were cheered on, and hove with all their strength; the ropes stretched enormously, and finally two of the tackles parted.

---

[1] The Egyptians frequently resorted to this method of connecting blocks of stone; a number of the slabs in the temples of Luxor and Karnak are thus united two by two.

EMBARKATION OF THE FRENCH OBELISK.

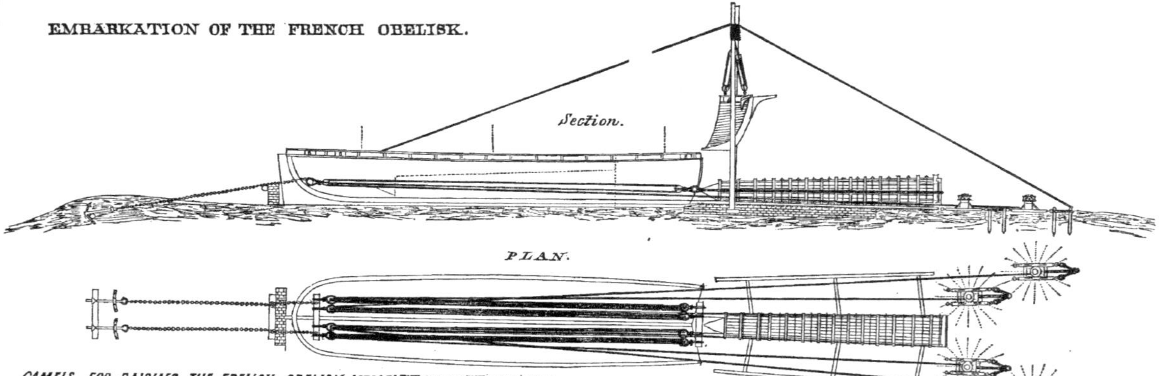

Section.

PLAN.

CAMELS FOR RAISING THE FRENCH OBELISK VESSEL TO CROSS THE NILE BAR.

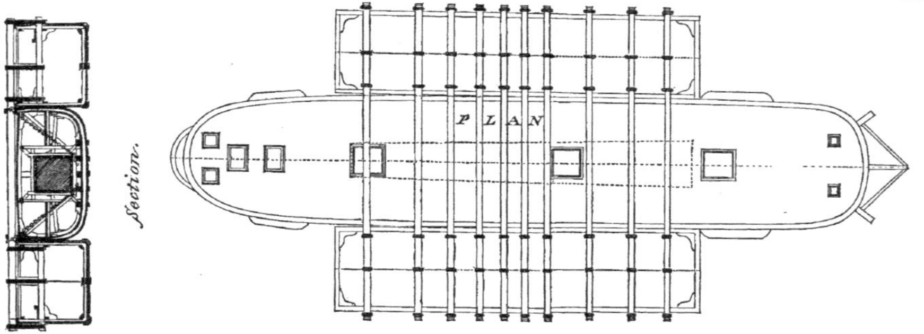

PLAN.

Section.

Plate XXXIV.

The loss seemed irreparable, and the cause seemed inexplicable as the power applied was double what was necessary to drag that weight. Something was evidently wrong, and it seemed most probable that some part of the sheathing of the obelisk had caught against the timber-work. The only way to get at it to examine it was to remove the log around which the rotation had been made. This was so ground into the wall that, although relieved of the weight there, it had to be cut out with chisels. Even the earth was so compressed that it had to be chipped away with tools, and the fragments were too hot to handle.

The cause of the trouble soon came to light. The sight that greeted them confirmed most emphatically M. LeBas' fears about the timber-work not having enough bearing-surface; every thing seemed to be in chaos. The immediate cause was that the first section of the ways had been thrown out of line transversely; the joists and traverses had all been broken in two; and the pieces of the latter, held down at the ends by the joists, but forced up in the middle by the earth, had taken against the cross-ties of the sheathing, thus blocking the obelisk completely. The only way to get at the traverses to clear them was by removing the earth from under that part of the planking; of course this had to be done very cautiously and slowly. The traverses were then forced down the sliding ways by wedges made from capstan-bars.

The tackles were rigged again as before, and in addition ten screw-jacks were applied to the heel of the obelisk. At the order the men hove on the capstans and screw-jacks together, and the ropes seemed to be reaching the limit of safety, when the obelisk gave a start and moved forward three feet with a jump. Every thing was upset again, joists and traverses broken, and further progress prevented; the same work had to be gone over again of removing the earth and forcing the planking down with wedges. This done, another pull was given with the same success, and with the same subsequent work. And so it went on with fresh complications each time, and with the additional feature that the obelisk forged somewhat to the right of the direct line in consequence of the lateral inclination of the ways. No attention was paid to that, however, until it was hauled entirely clear of the excavations. It was then no longer in any possible danger of breaking, as had been feared while the heel overhung the pit, and, moreover, it rested throughout its length on the remains of the sliding ways, compressing it less and making further progress easier.

Another section of ways had to be built, and to do this the derricks had to be sacrificed. When the time came to haul again small spurs were placed angularly against the side of the obelisk, and by their rigidity forced it back to the proper line of progress as it advanced. After that it was only a matter of time and patience to reach the "Luxor," the only fear being at first that the operation of embarking might not be completed before the rise of the Nile in the summer. As the event proved they might have spared themselves that anxiety, as the poor fellows had to remain there eight tantalizing months in idleness waiting for the rise.

When it came to opening the bow of the "Luxor" what seemed a simple task at first proved the opposite. The mere opening was not difficult, but the rebuilding afterward would be out of the question with the scanty stock of timber on board, none of which was of suitable shape. So instead of tearing down that part of the vessel it was carefully sawed off near the foremast, and triced up out of the way by means of shears. The following arrangements were then made for hauling the obelisk in.

Two anchors were planted astern of the vessel, and their chains passed inboard through holes cut in the counter. The ends of these were bent in the fixed blocks of four heavy tackles, the movable blocks being secured to a cable passed around the heel of the obelisk; the hauling parts were led to capstans. To save the stern from being cut through by the chains as they tightened, a brick wall was built close to the stern-post up to the height of the holes in the counter. Immediately forward of the vessel a stone causeway was also built, twenty-five feet long, to take the weight and save the timbers as the obelisk came in, and prevent their being thrown out of line at that critical moment.

On December 19, 1831, all was ready; one hundred and ninety-two men hove on the capstans, and in less than two hours the monolith was in its place on board. The joy and pride felt by all, especially by their enterprising leader, at the completion of that important operation may be imagined more easily than described; four months and a half of excessive toil, trial, and suffering were rewarded by complete success; the problem was solved. Among the natives the principal emotion was that of wonder; and when, a week later, the bow of the vessel had been lowered to its place, and even the marks of the saw were barely visible, their astonishment gave way to the usual superstitions, and these wonderful results were attributed to the *Afreets*.

To secure the bow every alternate plank that had been cut, both inside and outside, was removed, and a new one substituted spanning the cut. The keels had not been injured, but taken apart at the scarfs near the forefoot. Additional long breasthooks were worked in, and the scarfs of the keelsons strengthened by long heavy cleats. The wood used for all this was taken from the remains of what had served as derricks, platforms, capstans, and ways; the master carpenter, Elies, skilled by that time in economizing material, managed to make good use of stuff that would probably have been condemned as valueless in any dockyard.

Eight weary months had to be passed before the rise of the Nile would float the craft; we will pass over that period without remark, and with but a pitying thought for those who had to drag disconsolately through it.

In the early part of June a decrease in the transparency of the water, accompanied by oscillations in its level, announced that the annual rise was at hand. While the Arab women sang praises on the banks of the river, and the priests heralded the glad tidings from the mosque door, the Frenchmen set to and dug away the sand that had been piled up around their vessel and constantly wetted to protect it from the sun. On the 18th of August the "Luxor" floated, and on the 25th started down the river under the guidance of two pilots. As the anchor was dropped every evening progress was but slow, and Rosetta was not reached until the 1st of October, when it transpired that the pass which had been navigable twelve days before, was then closed. There seemed to be no help for it, and that entire month was passed in hoping for a slightly increased rise.

Plans were then made of *camels* to lighten the draught. Plate xxxiv gives an idea of these. The frames of the "Luxor" not being strong enough to stand the upward pressure from these caissons, it was decided that stout timbers should be passed across from one to the other, and the cables taken from them round the obelisk instead of round the vessel. The weight would be thus diminished by the amount of buoyancy in the camels, the draught diminished in proportion, and no strain put on the timbers of the transport.

The bad season had been reached, however, and the pilots asserted that this combination of vessels could not put to sea until the spring. The assurances of these men seem to have been given great weight, and their advice followed rather unquestioningly. The "Luxor" was laid up off Rosetta for the winter, and would probably have remained there that length of time but for a fortunate accident. A bark, loaded with oranges, had sunk near the mouth, and while raising her it was discovered that a pass had formed. Orders were immediately given to prepare for sea, and on the 1st of January, at eleven in the evening, after touching once or twice on the bar, the "Luxor" entered the Mediterranean and proceeded to Alexandria in tow of the steamer "Sphinx." Delayed there again by bad weather, the anchor was finally weighed on the 1st of April, and after a stormy passage compelling the captain to seek shelter at Rhodes, Marmara, Milo, Navarino, Zantes, and Corfu, the obelisk reached the port of Toulon during the night of the 10th of May, 1833.

A month's quarantine awaited the poor fellows there, after which M. LeBas, having completed the task allotted him, was summoned to Paris. After an interview with M. Thiers, then Minister of Commerce and Public Works, he was informed that the work of erecting the obelisk in Paris would be entrusted to him in the hope that he would successfully finish the operations he had so skilfully begun. But it was not until August that he was apprised of the decision, which was a pity, because, as will be seen, a whole season was nearly lost by slight delays.

While the "Luxor" was being examined in dock at Toulon, towed to Rouen, and thence up the Seine, preparatory work was begun in Paris. The Place de la Concorde having been selected as the site for the obelisk, the foot of the western ramp at the Pont de la Concorde was naturally chosen for the disembarkation. The river being still low, work was immediately begun to clear away that part of the bank preparatory to laying the ways on which the vessel would be grounded. M. LeBas' plan was to carry the slope of the ramp down so that the "Luxor" could be grounded at that angle, and the obelisk hauled directly out. But an inopportune strike among the workmen in Paris brought about a delay that compelled him to give that up. During the delay the river rose, and when work was resumed a timber-bed had to be built above water and sunk in place, the men working in water up to their armpits.

The surface of this bed was horizontal, and the obelisk, therefore, would have to come out of the vessel at an angle with the ramp. To overcome this difficulty a wedge-shaped cradle was built, the lower part resting on the ways, but the upper being horizontal and on a line with the keelsons of the "Luxor." The obelisk would be hauled on the cradle, and then cradle and all pulled up the ramp.

On the 23d of December, 1833, the "Luxor" was in place, but it was not until the following August that the falling of the river permitted opening the bow; on the 9th of that month two hundred and forty soldiers manned the capstans, and the obelisk was pulled out and landed on the cradle. On the following day the movable blocks of the tackles were shifted from the obelisk to the cradle, and by four that afternoon they both reached the quay at the head of the ramp.

The power required for this operation was computed to be about fifty-two tons, but the friction caused by a weight moving up an inclined plane, the surfaces being greased, is such an intangible quantity that it was decided to furnish nearly double that. Five sixfold purchases were rigged, each with its capstan manned by forty-eight men; the total effective power thus applied, granting each man to heave twenty-two pounds, was about ninety-four tons.

During the remainder of the journey of the obelisk to its future position in the centre of the Place de la Concorde, it had to change direction several times in both vertical and horizontal planes. To effect the former, for each slope or grade a cradle was constructed of wedge-shape similar to the one used on the ramp at the river bank, the upper surfaces of all being horizontal; on reaching the point where the change of grade occurred the obelisk was hauled from one to the other, thus remaining always horizontal. There were only two lateral changes of direction to be effected: one was just beyond the head of the ramp, to clear the ditch in the angle of the square; the other, almost a right angle, was where this second track met the direct one leading to the centre of the square. To perform these turnings the cradle was hauled until the centre of gravity was over the intersection of the two ways, where a stout pivotal stake had been driven; the cradle was revolved over and around that. Heavy cross-timbers connecting and filling the angle between the two ways supported both head and heel of the obelisk; being well greased the cradle slipped easily over them, and it needed no great power to pull the two ends in opposite directions. The usual pulleys were used for this.

All this work was sadly delayed by having to wait a long time for the pedestal. By a strange neglect it was not until after landing the obelisk that the design of the pedestal was determined. The granite was to come from Laber-il-dut, on the coast of Brittany, and in the original plan twenty-seven pieces were shown; but the contractor having discovered a rock in that bay, from which a block could be quarried sixteen feet long by ten square, the number was reduced to five. The total weight of the pedestal is about 236 1-4 tons. The "Luxor" and "Sphinx" were detailed for that service, and started as soon as the former could be floated again.

This neglect, causing such a great delay, seems inexplicable, and must have been due to some concatenation of circumstances, political or other, the record of which may have been swallowed in the graver events of those troubled times. However that may be, the obelisk lay inert for many months; it was not until the 8th of September, 1836, that it was placed on the last cradle, which was to carry it up the slope leading to the top of the pedestal.

This final ramp was built of masonry, with a rise of eight feet in a hundred. The intention at first was to use a steam-engine to haul the obelisk up this incline, and much enthusiasm was felt at the idea; but unfortunately the machine broke down in a preliminary trial, and the same old capstans and tackles had to be resorted to again.

An article that appeared in this connection, in the *Journal des Débats*, of October 16, 1836, is doubly interesting, portraying as it did the feelings akin to awe with which that motor, since become so familiar, was then regarded. The following is an extract:

"It is much to be regretted that sufficient precautions were not taken to ensure this engine working satisfactorily. The idea of inaugurating the steam-engine on so solemn an occasion was most happy. For a part of the public the steam-engine is of the unknown, a mysterious and formidable creation liable to explode like thunder. It would have been well to associate the monuments of antique art with one of the finest productions of the inventive mind of modern times. It would have been well to show two hundred thousand people one of these engines, so foolishly dreaded by the ignorant, seizing the obelisk of Sesostris, and raising it little by little with perfect regularity of motion, without the aid of a living being, excepting the one man charged with supplying coal to the furnace, the soul of the engine. These machines are destined to relieve man of all work that needs only brute force, and even, such is their perfection, of some work that may seem to demand guidance from an intelligent being. The steam-engine is one of the greatest triumphs of mind over matter; it is nature made captive, working for man, and in man's stand. It is nature enslaved; and it is the only slave, the only serf of the future."

The writer of those lines probably had as little thought of the future of the electric current as we now have of—what?

No difficulty was experienced in pulling the obelisk up the ramp; five hours sufficed to bring it close to the pedestal. Great care was then necessary. Advancing up the greased incline not steadily but in jumps of one to two feet at a time, it finally came to within an inch of the line that the edge of the base had to cover, and to make it come just to but not beyond that line was a problem involving delicate manipulation of a great power. To do it the tackles were stretched taut, and the capstans then stopped; with this strain on, the very slight movement required was imparted by giving two slight ramming blows to the Needle.

The *modus operandi* in erecting the obelisk was the same, reversed, as that of lowering it in Egypt, except that only one rotation was necessary and possible. As before, the edge of the base which was to constitute the axis of rotation was *let in* to a heavy beam of wood, rounded on the opposite side and free to revolve in a corresponding groove in another beam. This last rested in a step which unfortunately had to be cut in the top and side of the pedestal. M. LeBas proposed two ways of obviating the necessity of so disfiguring the plinth, but he seems to have been not entirely unhampered in the prosecution of this work, and the step was cut.

The gear for raising the point of the Needle consisted of ten derricks rigged as previously described. See Plate xxxiii. The derrick-heads were connected with the obelisk five feet below the base of the pyramidion by ten cables or shrouds; on the other side were frapped the movable blocks of as many seven-fold tackles, the hauling parts of which were taken to capstans. By heaving on these, the derricks would first be acted upon, and the power transmitted from them through the shrouds to the head of the obelisk.

During the contemplated rotation it is evident that a great and increasing weight would be thrown on the side of the pedestal supporting the axis; furthermore, owing to the angle at which the power was to be applied, the horizontal component of that weight would at certain periods of the ascent be very great, and constitute a lateral thrust that would inevitably overturn the pedestal if left unsupported. To prevent this two huge timber props were inclined against the outer face of the block, their upper ends being kept from slipping up by hanging-pieces bolted to timbers secured underneath all.

As regards the weight to be lifted and the consequent power to be produced, although the actual weight remained the same, yet the obelisk being now horizontal, the strain on the shrouds, derricks, and tackles at the beginning of the ascent would be greater than at the end of the descent in Egypt, when it still lay at a considerable angle with the horizon. With the derricks stepped as shown in the plate, the shrouds coming to the obelisk at nearly a right angle, the strain to be stood by them at first would be almost one half the total weight of the monolith, decreasing to zero as the vertical from the centre of gravity passed within the base. The tension on the shrouds, on account of the angle formed by the ropes and the derricks, was found to correspond to a maximum tension of about one hundred and three tons on the tackles, decreasing to zero during the ascent. Allowance made for friction, four hundred and eighty men heaving twenty-five pounds each on the capstans would produce a power of one hunred and thirteen tons. This could be easily increased if desired.

To secure the fixed blocks of the tackles the following plan was adopted: At a certain distance in rear of the pedestal two rows of heavy piles were driven vertically in a pit, and mortised into horizontal timbers, the whole being weighted with iron ballast. A similar fabric was constructed a few yards farther to the rear, except that one row of piles was considered sufficient. A row of spurs, somewhat similar to the hoisting derricks but much smaller, was erected on the first platform, and the long straps of the fixed blocks passing over those spurs' heads were lashed to both platforms. The ballast amounted to one hundred and two tons. It was estimated that the entire fabric would stand a strain of one hundred and ninety-one tons from the direction in which the tackles would pull, or about eighty-eight tons more than required.

By October 24th every thing was ready, and at noon of that day a preliminary pull was given to try the gear. It worked so well that M. LeBas was anxious to continue and complete the erection, but royal orders compelled him to defer it until the next day.

On the morning of the 25th an immense crowd gathered in the Place de la Concorde, the Champs Elysées, and the terraces of the Tuileries gardens. It was estimated that two hundred thousand people were present to witness the last stage of the formidable and protracted operations. A cedar box was placed in a cavity in the pedestal, containing a set of the gold and silver current coins of the realm, also two medals bearing the effigy of the king and the following inscription: "Sous le règne de Louis Philippe I, roi des Français, M. de Gasparin étant ministre de l' intérieur, l' obélisque de 'Luxor' a été élevé sur son piédestal le 25 octobre, 1836, par les soins de M. Apollinaire LeBas, ingénieur de la marine."

At half past eleven M. LeBas placed himself on the ledges of the pedestal, whence he could command a view of the entire scene of operations, and the artillerymen, under the command of Captain Meeunier, began walking round the capstans to the sound of the bugle; the immense power was gradually transmitted through the apparently intricate maze of rope, and the point of the Needle rose majestically in air. At twelve loud cheers greeted the arrival of the king, accompanied by the queen and members of the royal family, at the windows of the Ministry of Marine. The circular march at the capstans was continued, uninterrupted until a vibration was noticed in the whole fabric, accompanied by a cracking as of wood; but this was soon found to be caused simply by the great compression and not by the displacement of any parts. So M. LeBas resumed his place on the pedestal, and gave the order to heave at the double quick to pass the angle of forty-five degrees, in which position the strain on the pedestal was greatest. Forty-five minutes sufficed to bring the obelisk thirty-five degrees nearer the position of equilibrium, when another stoppage became necessary. The chains leading from the top of the obelisk toward the river, to hold it as the vertical passed within the base, had been fastened, or, in nautical parlance, *stopped* along the pyramidion to keep them out of the way. An order had been given to clear them the day before but had been forgotten, and it was necessary to do so now before the chains should tighten, because the *stops* in breaking under a heavy strain would cause a dangerous jarring. Two sailors immediately jumped aloft and released them, and the capstans were again started, but more slowly. Three turns were hove, then two, then one, then half a one, and so on until, the position of equilibrium being gently and slowly passed, the cables were seen to tighten and take the weight. The tackles on the chains were slacked carefully, and in three hours and a half from the beginning of the operation, and five years and a day from the time it was lowered in Thebes, the Egyptian obelisk rested safely and securely on the Breton rock that formed its new pedestal.

Brought from the silent ruins of the greatest city of the ancient world, to the brightest and gayest of modern capitals, this hoary monument now marks the spot where the equestrian statue of Louis XV once stood, and where that monarch's unfortunate grandson expiated the crime of royal misgovernment. Unmindful . perhaps of the dire associations called forth, but impressed by the delicacy of the operation just completed, the immense throng turned to their venerable sovereign and rent the air with prolonged *vivats*. National ensigns soon waved from the summit, and, as night approached, brilliant illuminations kept the base revealed to the numerous groups of promenaders. Nor was the general enthusiasm at all diminished by the distribution among the workmen that evening of 3,000 francs, presented by the king.

It was some time before all the gear was removed and the lofty shaft and pedestal exposed in their grand simplicity. As a protection against a climate so much more rigorous than that of its native land, the surface of the obelisk was covered with a concentrated solution of caoutchouc. Later, diagrams and inscriptions were carved upon the pedestal and handsomely gilded. On the side facing the Madeleine are illustrations in outline of the operations of lowering and embarking the monolith; on the side next the river are shown the apparatus used in its erection.

On the side turned toward the Tuileries gardens is the inscription:

"Ludovicus Philippus I, Francorum Rex, ut antiquissimum artis Ægyptiacæ opus, idemque recentis gloriæ ad Nilum armis partæ insigne monumentum, Franciæ ab ipsa Ægypto donatum posteritati prorogaret, obeliscum die 25. Aug. A. 1832 Thebis Hecatompylis avectum navique ad id constructa intra menses 13 in Galliam perductum erigendum curavit. Die 25 Octobris anni 1836. Anno reg. septimo."

Facing the Champs Elysées the inscription reads:

"En présence du Roi Louis Philippe Ier, cet obélisque, transporté de Louqsor en France, a été dressé sur ce piédestal par M. LeBas, ingénieur, aux applaudissements d' un peuple immense, le 25 octobre, 1836."

Models of all the apparatus used were also deposited in the Musée de Marine, and are still to be seen there.

As was stated above, five years and a day elapsed between the dates of lowering and re-erecting this obelisk. That seems a long time, and unreflecting critics may pass adverse judgment on the skill of M. LeBas. A word on this matter may therefore not be amiss. Returning for the nonce to Upper Egypt, we see that the obelisk was lowered and embarked in the "Luxor" in five months from the date of the arrival of the party, in spite of undeniably grave obstacles. There was then a forced delay of eight months before the rising Nile floated the vessel. Almost immediately on top of that, three months were thrown away waiting for an opportunity to cross the Rosetta bar, and fully two more in Alexandria waiting for fair weather before putting to sea. The worst delays, however, did not take place in Egypt. On the banks of the busy Seine the ebb and flow of waters was no more generous than in Thebes, and the "Luxor," floated over the bed prepared on the ramp at the Pont de la Concorde on the 23d of December, was not left high and dry enough for operations until the following August. The delay resulting from the neglect in not selecting a suitable pedestal in time was touched upon above ; for twenty-two months the monolith lay untouched, while its pedestal was being quarried, transported, and put in place. Surely those forty-two months lost cannot be laid reproachfully at the door of the officer who was merely given a suitable vessel, some spars and ropes, and told to go to Thebes and bring the Needle home and erect it again. Nor is it perhaps necessary to invite attention to the unadvanced state of the mechanical arts in that day as compared to the present time when steam, hydraulic and electric power are regarded as mere journeymen laborers.

The cost of the undertaking was apparently very great, though the exact figures are not known. The total expenditure is said to have been about two and a half millions of francs, or $500,000 ; in that, are included the expenses of Baron Taylor's mission, the maintenance of a numerous personnel, and the purchase, quarrying, and transport of an immense pedestal.

Regard being had for all the circumstances, the verdict of even the present rapid day must be that M. LeBas reflected honor on his country and his profession and richly deserved the meed of praise bestowed upon him at the time. On the 11th of November he received the following letter from the Minister of the Interior.

SIR: The erection of the Luxor obelisk has met with unanimous approval from the King and the public. It is with genuine satisfaction that I send you my congratulations on the success of this important operation.

A medal having been struck to commemorate the event, I send you two copies of it, one in silver, and one in bronze.

I have the honor to announce to you at the same time that I have decided to allow you, as indemnity for your cares in the prosecution of the work, the sum of 4,000 francs.

I have not forgotten, sir, the favorable mention you made of persons engaged in this work under your direction; gratuities in proportion to their services are granted them as follows:

To M. Lepage, Second Inspector, . . 1,500 francs. To M. Card, Storekeeper, . . . 300 francs.
" M. Heurteloup, First Inspector, . 1,000 "   " M. Morel, Boatswain's mate, . . 200 "
" M. Labrie, Carpenter's mate, . . 300 "   " M. Masqueron, Boatswain's mate, . 200 "
" M. Dacheux, Boatswain's mate, . 300 "   " M. Monot, Carpenter's mate, . . 200 "

I request that you will acquaint them with the fact of these sums having been awarded, and notify them that the payments will be ordered immediately.

Receive, &c.,

(Signed)   GASPARIN.

M. Lepage was further rewarded by being decorated with the cross of the Legion of Honor.

Nor did official recognition of M. LeBas' services end with the small donation mentioned in M. de Gasparin's letter. The king appointed him Director of the Naval Museum, which, together with the riband of the Legion of Honor conferred some time before, constituted a lasting memorial of his success.

For a record of this obelisk see remaining obelisk at Luxor, chapter vi. The original pedestal that was left at Luxor, where it now remains, was sculptured in very high relief with figures of the dog-headed ape, the god of sciences and arts. The Nile god, *incised* on two of its faces, is represented as bringing in the products of the country. Chabas, in "Traduction complète des inscriptions hiéroglyphiques de l'obélisque de Luxor, à Paris," gives the following translation of the characters on the Paris obelisk.[1] It is the latest and doubtless the best of the many translations that have been made at different times and published in Europe.

NORTH SIDE FACING THE MADELEINE.

Vignette: Rameses II on his knees offering two vases of wine to Ammon-Ra.
Cartouch of Rameses II: The master of the two worlds, OUSOR-MA-RA, Lord of the diadems. MEI-AMMON-RAMSES.
The god says to the king: "I give thee perfect health, I give thee life, stability and perfect happiness."

EAST SIDE FACING THE TUILERIES.

Vignette: The same subject as before.
Cartouch: The good god, master of the two worlds, OUSOR-MA-RA, Son of the sun, Lord of the diadems, MEI-AMMON-RAMSES, *vivifying like the sun.*

WEST SIDE FACING THE CHAMPS ELYSÉES.

Same offering.
Cartouch: The good god, master of the two worlds, OUSOR-MA-RA, Son of the sun, Lord of the diadems, MEI-AMMON-RAMSES, *vivifying like the sun eternally.*

SOUTH SIDE FACING THE PALAIS LÉGISLATIF.

Rameses II making an offering of water to Ammon-Ra.
Cartouch: The good god, OUSOR-MA-RA, SOTEP-EN-RA, Son of the sun, MEI-AMMON-RAMSES, *who gives life, stability and happiness, like the sun.* AMMON-RA tells him (to the king) "I give thee perfect joy."

NORTH SIDE FACING THE MADELEINE. CENTRAL COLUMN OF HIEROGLYPHICS.

The HORUS-sun, strong bull of the sun, who has smitten the barbarians, Lord of the diadems, who fights millions, magnanimous lion, Golden Hawk, strongest on all the world, OUSOR-MA-RA, bull at his limit, obliging the whole earth to come before him, by the will of AMMON his august father.

He has made (*the obelisk*) the Son of the sun MEI-AMMON-RAMSES "living eternally."

COLUMN OF HIEROGLYPHICS TO LEFT OF SPECTATOR.

The HORUS-sun, strong bull, the strongest (of the strongest) who fights with his sword, king of great roarings, master of terror, whose valor strikes the whole earth, King of Upper and Lower Egypt OUSOR-MA-RA, SOTEP-EN-RA, Son of the sun, MEI-AMMON-RAMSES whose dominion is twice cherished like that of the god inhabiting Thebes, King of Upper and Lower Egypt, OUSOR-MA-RA, SOTEP-EN-RA, Son of the sun, MEI-AMMON-RAMSES "the vivifier."

COLUMN TO RIGHT OF SPECTATOR.

The HORUS-sun, strong bull, the grandee of the triacontaerid fêtes, who loves the two worlds, king strong by his sword, who has seized both worlds, supreme chief whose royalty is great as that of the god TUM, King of Upper and Lower Egypt OUSOR-MA-RA, SOTEP-EN-RA, Son of the sun, MEI-AMMON-RAMSES. The chiefs of the entire world are under his feet; King of Upper and Lower Egypt, OUSOR-MA-RA, SOTEP-EN-RA, Son of the sun, MEI-AMMON-RAMSES "vivifier."

EAST SIDE FACING THE TUILERIES. CENTRAL COLUMN.

The HORUS-sun, strong bull, fighting with his sword, Lord of the diadems, who subdues (strikes down) whoever nears him, who seizes the ends of the world, Golden Hawk, very terrible, master of valor, King of Upper and Lower Egypt OUSOR-MA-RA, divine issue of his father AMMON, Lord of gods. Causing to be joyous the temple of the soul and the gods of the great temple in joy. He has made the obelisk the Son of the sun MEI-AMMON-RAMSES "living eternally."

COLUMN TO LEFT OF SPECTATOR.

The HORUS-sun, strong bull, Son of AMMON, how multiplied are his monuments! the very strong, beloved Son of the sun, on his throne, King of Upper and Lower Egypt OUSOR-MA-RA, SOTEP-EN-RA, Son of the sun, MEI-AMMON-RAMSES, who has erected the dwelling of AMMON (Thebes), like the heavenly horizon, by his great monuments for eternity, King of Upper and Lower Egypt, Son of the sun, MEI-AMMON-RAMSES "vivifier."

---

[1] Copied from vol. iv, "Records of the Past," London, 1875.

COLUMN TO RIGHT OF SPECTATOR.

The HORUS-sun, strong bull, beloved of the goddess TRUTH, king doubly cherished as the god TUM, supreme chief, delight of AMMON-RA for centuries; King of Upper and Lower Egypt OUSOR-MA-RA, SOTEP-EN-RA, Son of the sun, MEI-AMMON-RAMSES: what is heaven, that (such) is thy monument; thy name will be permanent like the heavens, King of Upper and Lower Egypt OUSOR-MA-RA, SOTEP-EN-RA, Son of the sun, MEI-AMMON-RAMSES "vivifier."

WEST SIDE FACING THE CHAMPS ELYSÉES. CENTRAL COLUMN.

The HORUS-sun, strong bull, beloved of the goddess TRUTH (MA) Lord of the diadems, who takes care of Egypt and chastises nations; Golden Hawk, master of armies, the very strong, the King of Upper and Lower Egypt OUSOR-MA-RA, king of kings, issue of TUM, one in body with him to perform his royalty on earth for centuries, and to render happy AMMON'S dwelling by benefactions. He has made (*the obelisk*) the Son of the sun MEI-AMMON-RAMSES "living eternally."

COLUMN TO LEFT OF SPECTATOR.

The HORUS-sun, strong bull, rich in valor, king potent by the sword, who has made himself master of the whole world by his strength, King of Upper and Lower Egypt OUSOR-MA-RA, SOTEP-EN-RA, Son of the sun, MEI-AMMON-RAMSES; all countries of the earth come to him with their tributes, King of Upper and Lower Egypt OUSOR-MA-RA, SOTEP-EN-RA, Son of the sun, MEI-AMMON-RAMSES "vivifier."

COLUMN TO RIGHT OF SPECTATOR.

The HORUS-sun, strong bull, beloved of the sun, king who is a great plague (to his enemies); the whole earth trembles in terror of him, King of Upper and Lower Egypt OUSOR-MA-RA, SOTEP-EN-RA, Son of the sun (MEI-AMMON-RAMSES), Son of MONT, whom MONT has formed with his hand, King of Upper and Lower Egypt OUSOR-MA-RA, SOTEP-EN-RA, Son of the sun, MEI-AMMON-RAMSES "vivifier."

SOUTH SIDE FACING THE PALAIS LÉGISLATIF. CENTRAL COLUMN.

The HORUS-sun, strong bull, very valorous, King of Upper and Lower Egypt OUSOR-MA-RA, SOTEP-EN-RA, eldest son of the king of the gods, who has raised him on his throne on the earth, like an unique Lord, possessor of the whole world; he knows him, as he (the king) has done homage to him by bringing to perfection his dwelling for millions of years, mark of the preference he had in the *Southern Ap* for his father, who will prefer him for millions of years. He has made (the obelisk) the Son of the sun MEI-AMMON-RAMSES "vivifier" eternal as the sun.

COLUMN TO LEFT OF SPECTATOR.

The HORUS-sun, strong bull, loved by the goddess TRUTH (MA), King of Upper and Lower Egypt OUSOR-MA-RA, SOTEP-EN-RA, Son of the sun, MEI-AMMON-RAMSES, Scion of the sun, protected by HARMACHIS, illustrious seed, precious egg of the sacred Eye, emanation of the king of the gods, to be the unique Lord, possessor of the whole world, King of Upper and Lower Egypt OUSOR-MA-RA, SOTEP-EN-RA, Son of the sun, MEI-AMMON-RAMSES "eternal vivifier."

COLUMN TO RIGHT OF SPECTATOR.

The HORUS-sun, strong bull, beloved of the sun, King of Upper and Lower Egypt OUSOR-MA-RA, SOTEP-EN-RA Son of the sun, MEI-AMMON-RAMSES king excellent, warlike, vigilant to seek the favors of him who has begotten him: thy name is permanent as the heavens; the length of thy life is like the solar disk therein (the heavens), King of Upper and Lower Egypt OUSOR-MA-RA, Son of the sun, MEI-AMMON-RAMSES eternal vivifier like the sun.

CHAPTER IV.

REMOVAL OF THE FALLEN OBELISK OF ALEXANDRIA TO LONDON.

BY LIEUTENANT SEATON SCHROEDER, UNITED STATES NAVY.

VIEWED in the light of modern associations, the London obelisk carries one back to the opening of the present century, when the struggle on the oft-disputed battle ground of Egypt resulted in favor of the British. Hence a tendency to regard it as a trophy of victory. It is more commonly looked upon, however, as a monument of Egyptian gratitude for the victories achieved three quarters of a century prior to its final rendition. In truth, the numerous episodes that occurred after the first, unsuccessful, attempt to remove it in 1801, were so varied as to leave little foundation for either sentiment. It certainly could have been with but diplomatic frankness that Mohammed Ali presented this obelisk to England in recognition of services rendered to Egypt at the beginning of the century, when at the same time he gave a handsomer one to the nation over whose forces gallant Nelson and Abercromby had won their victories. Moreover, as will be seen farther on, the opening negotiations for the cession of the Needle give scant coloring to the idea. Egypt's warlike ruler was possibly anxious to conciliate both the great Powers in question, while carrying out his ambitious schemes; but in neither case is it probable that he was actuated by any special feelings of gratitude.

The claims of the obelisk to respect and admiration stand upon a much firmer and more enlightened base than its prostrate presence near a battle field where some 17,000 troops were pitted against a force of about half that strength. In common with those that help adorn the At Meidan, Place de la Concorde, Central Park, and various piazze in Rome, this mighty monument of hoary antiquity is an enduring tablet whereon the hierologist may decipher the secrets of a remote past. From the carvings on its face we read of an age anterior to most events recorded in ancient history; Troy had not fallen, Homer was not born, Solomon's Temple was not built; and Rome arose, conquered the world, and passed into history during the time that this austere chronicle of silent ages has braved the elements. Furthermore, in the words of Dean Stanley: "It will speak to us of the wisdom and splendor which was the parent of all past civilization,—the wisdom whereby Moses made himself learned in all the learning of the Egyptians for the deliverance and education of Israel—whence the earliest Grecian philosophers and the earliest Christian fathers derived the insight which enabled them to look into the deep things alike of Paganism and Christianity."

Our first introduction to the modern history of the Needle is the attempt to remove it in 1801, when the battle of Alexandria placed it in the hands of the British forces. It being the eager wish of the army and the fleet to secure it in commemoration of their victory, officers and men subscribed their pay to the amount of £7,000; Lord Cavan entered into the project warmly, and Major Bryce, R. E. (afterward General Sir Alexander Bryce), made the plans for the operation. The monolith lay near its erect sister on the shore of the bay, just east of the peninsula on which stands the town of Alexandria. It was intended to build out a pier into moderately deep water, and from it introduce the obelisk into a vessel through the stern. A sunken French frigate was raised for the purpose, and the pier was partially built; but during a gale that arose the sea washed it away, and, as the army moved off shortly afterward, the project had to be abandoned.[1]

It appears, however, that they left a record of their victories there, to be unearthed many years after. The following is an extract from the *Bombay Courier* of June 9, 1802[2]:

"The pedestal of the fallen Needle of Cleopatra having been heeled to starboard, and a proper excavation made in the centre of the base stone, this inscription on a slab of marble was inserted, and the pedestal restored to its former situation. The Needle was likewise turned over, and the hieroglyphics on the side it had so long lain on found fresh and entire.

"In the year of the Christian era 1798, the Republic of France landed on the shores of Egypt an army of 40,000 men, commanded by their most able and successful commander, General Bonaparte. The conduct of the general and the valor of the troops effected the subjection of that country. But, under Divine Providence, it was reserved for the British nation to annihilate their ambitious designs. Their fleet was attacked, defeated, and destroyed in Aboukir Bay, by a British fleet of equal force, commanded by Admiral Lord Nelson. Their intended conquest of Syria was counteracted at Acre by a most gallant resistance, under Commodore Sidney Smith; and Egypt was rescued from their dominion by a British army, inferior in numbers, but commanded by General Sir Ralph Abercromby, who landed at Aboukir on the 8th of March, 1801; defeated the French on several occasions, particularly in a most decisive action near Alexandria, on the 21st of that month; when they were driven from the field, and forced to shelter themselves in their garrisons of Cairo and Alexandria, which places subsequently surrendered by capitulation. To record to future ages these events, and to commemorate the loss sustained by the death of Sir Ralph Abercromby, who was mortally wounded at the moment of victory on that memorable day, is the design of this inscription, which was deposited here in the year of Christ 1802, by the British army, on their evacuation of this country and restoring it to the Turkish empire."

The exact position of this pedestal is not at present known with certainty, although it was seen and greatly admired by many travellers in the early part of the century. It is presumably a block of the same massive dimensions as its sister now in Central Park, and probably lies a few yards southwest of the spot from where the latter was removed in 1880. During the progress of the excavations made for the removal of the New York obelisk, indications were found of the presence of large masses of granite in that relative position. Unfortunately, the fact of a Levantine stone-cutter's house, immediately over it, being somewhat undermined already, prevented making any farther investigations at that time. It is likely that this point will be settled before long. When the owner of that ground carries out his expressed intention of building upon it, the plinth, if where supposed, will certainly be encountered in laying the foundations. In that case the statement in the *Bombay Courier* may be corroborated and a most interesting relic secured to the British capital.

The first overtures for the peaceable possession of the Needle were made during the reign of George IV, by Samuel Briggs, Esq., British Consul at Alexandria, as is shown by the following extract of a letter written by him shortly afterward to the Right Honorable Sir Benjamin Bloomfield.

"UPPER TOOTING, SURREY, *April* 11, 1820.

"SIR: Having, on my late visit to Egypt, witnessed the stupendous labors of the celebrated Mr. Belzoni, and received from him the assurance that he could confidently undertake the removal to England of one of the granite obelisks at Alexandria; and the Viceroy of Egypt, Mohammed Ali Pacha, having frequently expressed to me his desire of making some acknowledgment for the handsome equipment of his corvette, the 'Africa,' and for the presents sent him by His Majesty on the return of that ship to Egypt in the year 1811, I was encouraged to submit to His Highness my opinion that one of the obelisks at Alexandria, known in Europe under the appellation of Cleopatra's Needles, might possibly be acceptable to

---

[1] It has been stated that lack of co-operation on the part of the fleet had much to do with the failure of this enterprise; but that seems hardly worthy of credence.
[2] Appendix to "Cleopatra's Needle and Egyptian Obelisks," by Erasmus Wilson, F.R.S.

Removal of the Fallen Obelisk of Alexandria to London.

His Majesty, as unique of its kind in England, and which might, therefore, be considered a valuable addition to the embellishments designed for the British metropolis. His Highness promised to take the subject into consideration; and, since my return to England, I have received a letter from his Minister, authorizing me, if I deemed it acceptable, to make, in his master's name, a tender of one of those obelisks to His Majesty, as a mark of his personal respect and gratitude."

The present was accepted, the prostrate Needle being specified as the one given. But no effort was made to remove it, and it appeared to be forgotten until the year 1832, when the propriety of making an attempt was discussed in Parliament, and supported by Joseph Hume, a sum of money being proposed for the purpose. That fell through, however. Some thirty years later it was suggested to erect it in Hyde Park as a memorial to Prince Albert, in recognition of his efforts to perfect the success of the Exhibition held there in 1851. That also came to nought. Finally, the attention of Lieutenant-General Sir James E. Alexander was drawn to the matter, and to his indefatigable zeal is due the presence of the obelisk now on the banks of the Thames. While in Paris in 1867, that officer, struck with the beauty of the tall shaft in the Place de la Concorde, was reminded that another obelisk, the property of the British nation, lay imbedded in the sands at Alexandria, and, furthermore, was informed that the owner of the ground where it lay proposed to break it up for building material. Determined to prevent such vandalism if possible, he labored hard, for several years, to arouse public interest in England, and to obtain the sanction of the viceroy for the removal of the Needle. In 1875 he went to Egypt, provided with an introduction from the Earl of Derby, Secretary of State for Foreign Affairs, to General Stanton, H. M. Agent and Consul-General, and, at a private audience with H. H. the Khedive, obtained the desired permission. Returning to England he was about to go into the city, and, with the help of Alderman Cotton, try and raise the necessary funds. But he was saved this trouble, for, on explaining the matter to his friend, Professor Erasmus Wilson, this gentleman, with a liberality up to that time unique, undertook the whole matter himself.

It was now only a question of the mechanical means to bring it safely across the seas and erect it. The various methods proposed from time to time are interesting from their number and variety, and a partial record of them, at least, properly attaches to the personal history of the obelisk.

Captain Boswell, R. N., appears to have been the first in the field, and plans, supposed to have been prepared by him in 1820, are now in the Royal United Service Institution, London. They provide for a large flat-bottomed vessel, including plans, and certain machinery for raising the obelisk on its pedestal.

Captain, afterward Admiral Smyth, R. N., also proposed two plans, in 1822. The first was similar to the one already tried in 1801, and Mohammed Ali Pacha offered to assist by building a pier expressly for the purpose; but no action was taken in the matter. Captain Smyth's other plan was to excavate and form a little dry-dock beneath the obelisk; build a lighter into which the stone could be lowered; then, by means of a canal cut for the purpose, float it out into the bay and tow it home.

General Alexander, not content with laboring to obtain possession of the Needle, thought out two methods of getting it afloat and transporting it. The first, which he described in a paper read to the Royal Society of Edinburgh in 1868, was based upon the desirability of avoiding the construction of a special vessel. His words were as follows: "A large Clyde lighter, raised upon, might transport it across the Bay of Biscay in summer; or, if an old ship, sufficiently seaworthy, is got, and the masts taken out of her, and the beams cut across, the obelisk might be taken alongside, raised, and lowered into her, iron beams being ready, with bolts and screws, to connect and secure the cut beams of the vessel, then towed by a steamer to England."

Removal of the Fallen Obelisk of Alexandria to London. 99

A few years later, however, he submitted detailed plans which involved the construction of a special iron vessel. First of all the obelisk was to be turned to point to the shore; rails would be laid on either side, and a carriage built upon them and over the Needle, which would then be suspended from it. To effect this, cross-rods would be inserted beneath the stone and connected with hanging-rods from the top traverses of the carriage; by digging away the earth the weight of the monolith would be taken by the carriage. The vessel was to be put together on launching ways, the rails continued in through the bows, the carriage rolled on board, the bows closed again, and the vessel launched.

In 1872 there was a way suggested that was not devoid of novelty. It was proposed to make the surface of the obelisk cylindrical by a filling-up of wood; it could then be rolled down into the water, suspended from heavy balks crossing the decks of two steamers lashed alongside of each other, and be carried off to England. The stone being slung in the water would be diminished in weight by nearly one half, so each vessel would have a large margin of carrying capacity for cargo.

The year 1873 was quite fruitful of ideas. The first in chronological order was that of Mr. J. L. Haddan, Director of Public Works, Aleppo, Syria, who suggested building up round the obelisk a solid, or partially solid, cylindrical casing of wood of such diameter that the timber thus applied would float the mass. Its cylindrical shape would make it an easy matter to roll it into the bay, whence it could be towed to the Thames. Hoisted then intact, packing and all, on to the embankment, either by the risings of several tides or by hydraulic jacks, it could be rolled to its site. Understanding that the weight of the obelisk was 284 tons, and taking into consideration the weight of bolts, bands, etc., Mr. Haddan estimated that about 320 tons of wood would be required, the diameter of the cylinder being about 20 feet and the length 72 feet.

The idea of incasing the obelisk in a sufficient quantity of wood to float it was also advanced later by a gentleman in Alexandria, who, undismayed by one failure, revived the plan in 1879, for the benefit of the New York obelisk,—with equal success.

In the same year as the preceding, Mr. W. A. Wharton, of the Bestwood Park works, near Nottingham, advocated building a strong timber carriage round the stone, to run on iron rails. This could easily be moved forward at the rate of a mile a day to the shore, when it would be run out as far as possible at low tide, the trucks, etc., taken off, timber of tramway loaded in the intermediate spaces, and the whole thing allowed to float, being made into a temporary boat in a few hours. Mr. Wharton was apparently unaware that the obelisk lay only a few yards from the water, and that there is no tide at Alexandria.

The following was proposed by a gentleman who prefaced his remarks by saying that he did not know the relative position of the Needle with regard to the water. The plan provided for a launching ways and cradle, built of wood and iron, by which the obelisk could be moved to the water's edge, capstans, screw-jacks, and small engines being used to effect the locomotion. Being at the water's edge, it was to be raised by hydraulic pumps, and an iron ship put together round it, such ship being built in England and sent out in pieces. The launch would be effected in the usual way and the vessel towed to England. The plan of disembarking was somewhat complicated. A dry-dock was to be built in the embankment, fifty feet longer than the vessel, the depth being thirty feet from the surface of the ground; the vessel, being hauled in stern first, would be cut apart, and the forward end drawn away, closed with a bulkhead, and floated out. The stern would then be cut off also so as to permit hydraulic jacks to get a bearing under the Needle, which would then be raised sufficiently to allow the middle section of the vessel to be drawn forward; that middle section would be again joined to the stern, the other open end closed by a bulkhead, and the whole floated out of the dock. The entire vessel could afterward be put together and sold for commercial purposes. The obelisk was then to be raised by the hydraulic jacks until above ground, the dock being built up after it. It would then be erected and afterward lifted vertically by the jacks, one under each corner, until at the proper height for the pedestal.

Removal of the Fallen Obelisk of Alexandria to London.

In 1876, in a letter to Lord Henry Lenox, First Commissioner of Works, Mr. Arthur Arnold suggested the possibility of shipping the Needle by constructing a railway on piles to such a distance from the shore as would admit the approach of a vessel capable of carrying it to England; suspended in slings from running gear it would be moved out until it hung over the intended position on board.

In the same letter Mr. Arnold recommended the adoption of another method, for which he gives credit mainly to Captain Methven, of the Peninsula and Oriental Company. After excavating round it the obelisk was to be strung from girders resting on the ground, and an iron vessel about 120 feet long and 6 feet draught put together in the space excavated beneath. A channel to deep water would be dredged or blasted, and when the vessel was ready the sea would be admitted and would raise it to its burden. The barge would be decked, given as much free-board as necessary, and towed to England.

On the subject of the transportation of the Needle being publicly broached, Messrs. King, Scotchmen, offered to perform the task. Their plan, and a most excellent one it was, avoided the construction of a special vessel, their idea being to bring the Needle home in a steam hopper-barge, such as are used for dredging. The obelisk would first be launched down a timber ways into the water, and then lifted up through the bottom of the hopper-barge. These vessels are large flat-bottomed screw steamers, having water-tight compartments running all round the hull; the large space in the middle for carrying the mud is furnished with a false bottom, in the form of trap-doors which open downward into the sea. One of these could easily have steamed to England, possibly under convoy.

Mr. John Walker, Chief Engineer of the Ramleh Railroad, in Alexandria, held that the best way was to haul the obelisk through the streets of Alexandria to the port, and put it on the deck of a well-laden ship.

Such are the broad features of most of the plans suggested to remove the obelisk. While in Egypt, however, Sir James Alexander had become acquainted with Mr. John Dixon, who had paid considerable attention to the subject of the monolith and its proposed transportation, and had brought his skill and experience as a civil engineer to bear on the practical points involved. Returning to England, Mr. Dixon had an interview with Professor Wilson, and not long afterward an agreement was entered into by them; Mr. Dixon, taking all risks, engaged to set up the obelisk on the banks of the Thames, and Mr. Wilson agreed to pay the sum of £10,000 on its erection. The contract was signed on January 30, 1877; and both performed their part.

The London obelisk is the first large one that was ever transported or erected under private auspices; all the more credit is therefore due to Professor Wilson, not only for securing the monument to his country, but for setting an example of liberality that has since been so generously followed in the United States. To Mr. Dixon, also, must be conceded the honor of being the first to assume the financial risks attendant upon such an undertaking; more is the pity that his enterprise, through unforeseen disaster, resulted in serious pecuniary loss.

The London obelisk was also the first one handled after the beginning of the great forward stride in the mechanical arts that has so distinguished this nineteenth century. All the phases of the various operations bore the impress of increased facilities in the utilization of iron and mechanical tools, and in the employment of steam and hydraulic power.

The main special difficulty in the removal of this particular obelisk lay in the fact that the bay, on the shore of which it was lying, was encumbered with shoals and exposed to gales. In consequence of this no ordinary sea-going vessel could lie there in safety, much less if brought near enough to the shore to take the obelisk directly on board. Therefore, either a special vessel had to be built which could be handled on the shore and then launched and towed away, or the obelisk would have to be carried to the harbor and there embarked in a suitable vessel.

Removal of the Fallen Obelisk of Alexandria to London.

Mr. Dixon elected in favor of the former method. His general plan of operations was to construct an iron cylinder of adequate size in England, ship it to Egypt in pieces, put it together round the monolith, roll it into the sea, and tow it to London.

The design of a vessel is generally made to meet the requirements of the service on which she will be employed at sea. In this particular case, however, the builders had the novel experience of constructing a seaworthy craft in which every thing had to be subordinated to the one prime feature that would enable her to be launched by rolling down the beach. That is to say, the vessel had to be perfectly cylindrical; stability and other desirable qualities had to be obtained mostly by internal arrangements. Were the axis of the Needle to coincide with the axis of the cylinder, it is evident that when once started rolling in the water, it would keep on almost indefinitely, retarded and finally stopped only by the *skin resistance*. By bringing the centre of gravity of the Needle below that axis, the vessel would be in a state of stable equilibrium; that is to say, however much the wind and sea might careen it over, the action of gravity would bring it back to the vertical; and this would obtain until the vessel were actually upside down. The lower the weight, the greater the righting force, and therefore the greater stability, but also the more violent rolling motion. It was decided to place the centre of gravity of all weights about nine or ten inches below the axis of the cylinder, or, in the phraseology of a naval architect, to give the vessel a meta-centric height of that number of inches. The bed for the obelisk, however, was placed only four inches below the centre of gravity of the cylinder, it being the intention to have sufficient ballast in the bottom to lower the centre of gravity the remaining five or six inches.

In order to ease the pitching motion as much as possible, the bed of the obelisk was also prepared so that it would lie with the thick end forward. The centre of gravity of the Needle being at about one third its height from the base, and being naturally placed in the centre of the vessel (in regard to its length), the upper or longer end would extend farther from that centre, or nearer to the end of the vessel, than would the larger and shorter end; therefore putting the latter forward would throw less weight into the bows than the small end would bring. The lines of the bow were also made as full as was consistent with a reasonable expenditure of power in towing.

Such was the vessel designed by Mr. Dixon, with the help of Mr. B. Baker, to whom he gives credit for much assistance. Her construction was entrusted to the Thames Iron Works Company. The length of the "Cleopatra," as she was subsequently christened, was ninety-three feet, diameter fifteen feet; she was divided into ten compartments by nine water-tight bulkheads, with two intermediate reverse angle-iron frames in each compartment, carried right round to ensure the stiffness of the plates. To prevent all possibility of rupture of the Needle in consequence of any deflection in the length of the vessel, caused by the waves or by rolling down to the water, elastic timber cushions were provided at all the bearings, which would allow a possible deflection of four inches before bringing any undue strain on the stone. This was greatly in excess of any probable contingency, for the calculations showed that the strength of the hull was such that the maximum strain that could be experienced at sea would cause a change of form of less than one eighth of an inch.

Captain Henry Carter, of the Peninsula and Oriental Company, was selected to command the "Cleopatra." He remained in England to inspect the vessel when completed, and then proceeded to Alexandria to assist Mr. Waynman Dixon in the preliminary operations.

The total length of the London obelisk is sixty-eight feet five and one half inches, including the pyramidion which is seven feet six inches high[1]; the width at the base is seven feet ten and one half inches and seven feet five inches, on adjoining sides, tapering to five feet one inch and four feet ten inches at the base of the pyramidion.[2] Assuming it to be a perfect block these dimensions give a cubic

---

[1] The pyramidion is imperfect; the point is broken off.
[2] Erasmus Wilson.

Removal of the Fallen Obelisk of Alexandria to London.

measurement of 2,517 feet; and the specific gravity of the stone being 2.66, the weight of the monolith is found to be very nearly 186½ tons, neglecting loss from hieroglyphs and the marring of the heel and edges. That marring of the heel, to the extent of breaking off large masses at the corners, cannot be attributed to the present age. The fractures are also too irregular to admit the theory that they were purposely broken off to facilitate the operation of raising the Needle. It seems probable that in the Middle Ages the obclisk was erect, and, like its fellow, now in New York, sustained by bronze crabs.[1] To get at these the lower corners may have been broken off and the shaft itself felled. But this is a matter of conjecture. Not so, though, with the marring of the edges. The hammer of the conscienceless relic-hunter is answerable for most of that. A writer in *All the Year Round*, October, 1859, relates the evidence of his own eyes, as follows: "The last time the writer saw it (not very long ago), a Briton was sitting upon it, knocking off enough of the inscribed stone for himself and fellow-travellers with a hammer. The writer expostulated with his brother Briton, and reminded him that that wonderful relic of bygone days did not belong to him, but had been handsomely presented to the British nation, and therefore belonged to it. 'Well, I know it does,' he answered, 'and as one of the British nation I mean to have my share.'" It is well known that that is but a case in point.

When Captain Carter and Mr. Waynman Dixon wished to commence excavating round the Needle, they were much delayed and annoyed by the owner of the ground, who had made a claim against the Egyptian government for allowing the obelisk to encumber his property for so long. Great perseverance and tact were necessary to smooth matters with this person, but an amicable settlement was finally reached, and the work was begun early in June.

As soon as the obelisk was disclosed to view stout balks of timber were introduced under it, and, with the help of hydraulic jacks, the smaller end was moved round so as to bring it parallel to the sea. It had been carried along about thirty feet when the earth appeared to be yielding under the weight, and, on examination, the crown of a vault was discovered about six feet long by three wide and four high. Several small jars were found in there, and two human skulls in a perfect state of preservation, also several arm and leg bones. The skulls were eventually put on board the "Cleopatra," but as they were never seen after the gale in the Bay of Biscay, it is supposed that the superstitious Maltese crew threw them overboard to save the ship. Several larger vases were also found, hermetically sealed, which on being opened proved to contain only a little dust. Rich archæological treasures would undoubtedly be unearthed by excavations in this immediate vicinity; but unfortunately a large five-story dwelling now covers the exact spot, and future examinations will probably be delayed many years, at least until the gradual subsidence of the shore shall cause the abandonment and final destruction of that building.

The materials of the cylinder soon arrived, and the diaphragms were put in place round the obelisk, being packed so as to be water-tight, and separated from the stone by the elastic cushions previously mentioned. As soon as a few of the middle bulkheads were on, the plates of the iron shell were riveted to them and to each other, and bit by bit the entire casing was built up.

While this work was going on, under the superintendence of Mr. Waynman Dixon, the sea-wall was demolished and the land graded. Divers were also employed by Captain Carter to remove the numerous blocks of stone lying in the water near by; many of these were covered with hieroglyphics, and, could their early history be traced, might add to our knowledge of the glories of those ancient monarchs. Farther out the remains of an immense wall were encountered, composed of blocks weighing over twenty tons. Dynamite had to be used to blast them, as it was necessary to carry the grade out to a depth of nine or ten feet. A great number of stones were thus removed, but it was foreseen that there were probably others barely below the muddy surface which could not be seen, but which would assert themselves as the weight of the vessel came upon them. To

[1] See chap. vi, "London Obelisk."

Removal of the Fallen Obelisk of Alexandria to London. 103

guard against danger in this quarter, two rings of nine-inch timber were strapped round the cylinder, near the ends, constituting in effect two wheels sixteen and a half feet in diameter and twelve feet in the tread, on which the vessel would roll. Planking was also laid as far as the water's edge.

One other precaution had to be taken before the launch. The stone being four inches below the centre of the cylinder, the motion in rolling would be hard to control, for as soon as the heavy part got over the perpendicular, it would give a great lurch forward. This eccentricity was counterbalanced by packing a quantity of old iron rails in a recess that had been made for the purpose in the round skin where the cabin was afterward to be built.

The last stage of the preparations was reached when the ropes were arranged to start the cylinder. Wire hawsers were used. They were passed from seaward over the top and nine times round the vessel, so that on applying power to them they would cause her to roll down the incline; the hauling ends were taken to winches on board heavy lighters moored some distance out; other hawsers were also provided on the land side to check the movement when desired.

The 28th of August, 1877, was the day fixed for the launch. It began rather inauspiciously with a thick fog, something rather unusual at that time of year; but as the day wore on it cleared away. By six in the morning the slack of the wire hawsers had been taken in on board the lighters, and four powerful screw-jacks were placed against the cylinder. Two steam-tugs were also ready to lend assistance, one belonging to the Egyptian government, and one to Messrs. Greenfield & Co. Several thousands of the mixed population of Alexandria were on hand at an early hour, crowding every spot from which a view of the operations was obtainable; and during the day many locally distinguished personages came and watched the proceedings.

When all was ready the winches were hove round, and the screw-jacks plied, and in a few minutes the ponderous vessel began to roll toward the sea, but so slowly that the movement was barely perceptible. By noon the cylinder had only made one revolution, equal to about fifty feet. The work went on uninterruptedly in spite of the heat, 90° in the shade not being sufficient to dim the interest of even the spectators. Working the hawsers from the lighters had to be given up, however, because the *holding ground* was so poor that their anchors dragged under the strain. So the ropes were taken to the tugs, which, steaming ahead at full power, could just keep the cylinder moving. By half past five it had reached the water's edge, where the planking ended and a comparatively steep incline commenced, and there it made an attempt to run off to sea, but was checked at twelve feet. After this the progress was as gradual as before, and the screw-jacks had to be kept in constant operation. Just before seven she took another start, and made a sudden half-turn, bringing up in three feet of water, where she was left for the night.

It was not a bad day's work, on the whole, although, of course, some disappointment was felt that the obelisk had not been got afloat. It seems to be a peculiarity, however, of operations with obelisks, that unforeseen hitches will occur and cause delay.

Soon after daylight on the 29th the screw-jacks were manned again and the tugs began towing away. Not much was gained until about noon, when the cylinder took a fine roll and got out so far that it was thought to be afloat. This proved not to be the case, however, and all the rest of the day the tugs were kept at work with but little effect. The next morning the remarkable discovery was made that the vessel was apparently half full of water. What made this all the more awkward was, that what was properly the upper half was under water, and it was impossible to open the manhole doors to examine into the cause of the leak. Arab divers were employed but failed to discover what was the matter. A hole was then cut in the surface above water, and a fifteen-inch double-suction pump set to work; but that did not seem to affect the level of the water inside. A regular diver in proper diving-dress was then sent down, and he reported that a large stone, hidden in the sand, had penetrated the bottom forward of the end bulkhead.

104 *Removal of the Fallen Obelisk of Alexandria to London.*

When a large vessel founders after a collision, one of the first questions asked by the court of inquiry is: "Were the bulkhead-doors shut?" Mr. Dixon, in alluding to this phase of the operations, in a lecture delivered before the Royal United Service Institution, London, said: "Now I shall never be hard, and never be severe, on any naval captains, or any one else after what occurred. There were six or seven of us with every inducement to pay every attention to that vessel. There was Mr. Waynman Dixon in actual charge of the operations, the others looking on. We had provided bulkheads, we had provided water-tight doors through them, and we had so carefully managed that the man whose duty it was to close those doors had forgotten to do so, and all were left open!" The whole vessel had filled, therefore, as soon as the hole was made in that end compartment.

The first thing to be done was to remove the stone, which took days, for it proved to be a rock weighing over half a ton. The cylinder was then rolled over to seaward to bring the injured plate out of water. On the 5th of September the hole appeared above the water's edge and was found to measure eighteen inches across. A patch was riveted on, and the next day passed in pumping the vessel dry. On the 7th the tugs were recalled, and by eleven that morning the cylinder was observed to rise and fall with the swell, showing unmistakably that it was afloat. The wooden casing was immediately stripped off, the counterbalancing weight of rails removed from the top, and, amid cheers from the shore, the novel craft was towed out of the bay and round to the harbor. With child-like confidence a number of Arabs and Maltese had perched themselves upon her arched back, with nothing to save them in case of her rolling. Owing to her shape, however, the amphibious fabric moved along, as steady as a church, while the tugs ahead were rolling sponsons under.

After this not much remained to be done. The cylinder was put on the magnificent floating dock belonging to the Egyptian government, and bilge-keels riveted on, some forty feet in length. The cabin and bridge were also fitted, the mast stepped, the rudder hung, and all preparations made for sea, including the stowage of twenty tons of iron ballast. In doing the last the overseers were so negligent as not to have the rails properly secured, and this neglect nearly led to the loss of the vessel afterward. When all ready for sea the total displacement was 290 tons.

Christened on the 19th, by the daughter of Admiral MacKillop Pacha, the "Cleopatra" weighed anchor on the 21st of September, and moved out of the harbor in tow of the steamer "Olga." Stoppages were made at Algiers and Gibraltar, and early in the morning of October 10th, Cape St. Vincent was rounded under pleasant auspices. Indications of bad weather soon came on, though, and on the morning of the 14th a heavy gale broke on the vessels from south-southwest. The "Cleopatra," which did not steer very well at any time, yawed considerably, and occasionally tremendous seas would strike the cabin, threatening to wash it overboard bodily. Captain Carter decided to bring the vessel head to wind before dark, and ride to a sea anchor. A signal was made to the "Olga" to cast off, but before this could be done a tremendous sea broke on board, causing such a lurch that the ballast shifted to leeward and the vessel went over on her "beam ends." All attempts to secure the ballast proving unsuccessful, it was decided to abandon the vessel. The little life-boat was cleared away and lowered, but was immediately dashed to pieces under the yoke of the rudder. In the meantime, Captain Booth, of the "Olga," surmising what had happened, called for volunteers to go on board the "Cleopatra" and help secure the ballast. Six noble-hearted sailors responded, and manned their boat; they got safely away from their own ship, but on nearing the "Cleopatra," a sea swept over them and launched them into eternity.

The "Olga" finally managed to throw a line over the "Cleopatra," by which a boat was hauled alongside, and Captain Carter and his crew reached the steamer in safety. Captain Booth immediately cast off his tow, and went in search of the boat and crew that had been swamped, but found no trace of them. Neither could the "Cleopatra" be found again afterward. Concluding somewhat hastily that she had foundered, the "Olga's" head was laid northward, and they reached Falmouth

THE ENGLISH METHOD OF ERECTING THE LONDON OBELISK.

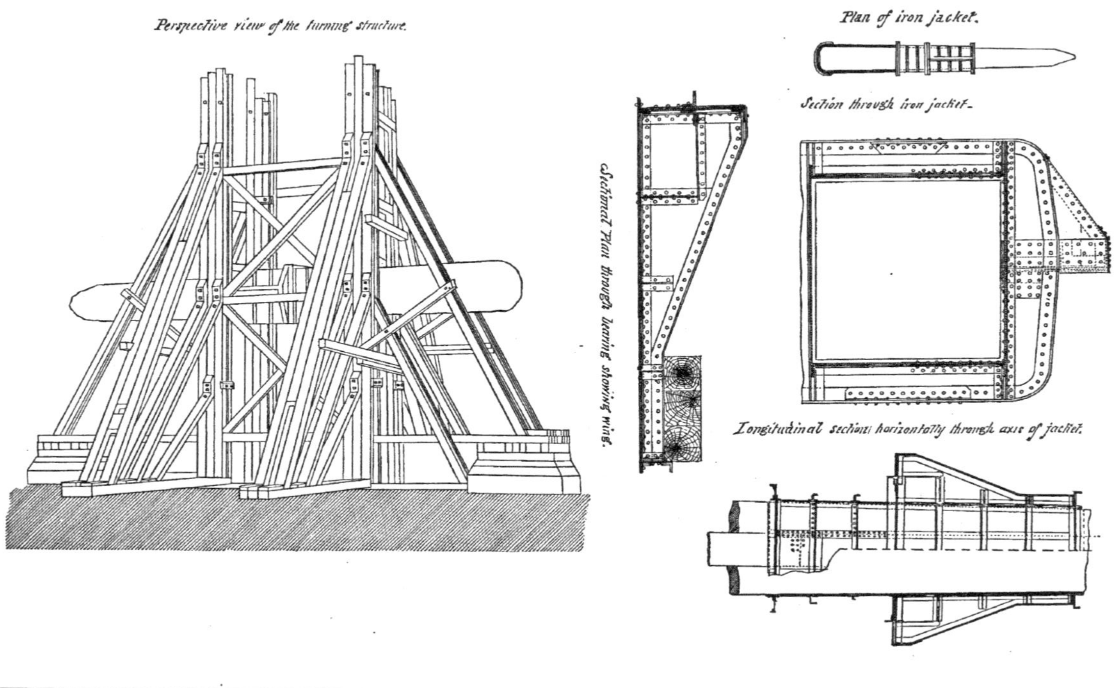

Plan of iron jacket.

Section through iron jacket.

Longitudinal section horizontally through axis of jacket.

Sectional Plan through bearing showing wing.

Perspective view of the turning structure.

Plate XXXV.

Removal of the Fallen Obelisk of Alexandria to London. 105

on the 17th. Had Captain Booth remained in the neighborhood, possibly a little to windward for safety during the night, he might have picked up his consort again. As it was, the "Fitzmaurice" espied the prize seventy miles from Ferrol, towed it into that port, and sent in a claim for salvage to the amount of £5,000. When the case was tried in the Admiralty Court, however, the sum of £2,000 was adjudged,—1,200 to the owners, 250 to the master, and the rest to the crew.[1]

The "Cleopatra" remained about three months in the harbor of Ferrol, finally reaching the Thames on January 20, 1878, in tow of the "Anglia" tug. Mr. James Lloyd Ashley, M. P., had made a generous offer of his steam-yacht, the "Eōthen," for the purpose, but this was declined.

By this time it had been decided where to erect the Needle, though the discussion had been warm, the "Battle of the Sites" having been obstinately fought in many papers. The centre of two acres of ornamental ground on the Thames embankment had been originally granted to General Alexander in 1872, but that was very generally objected to on the score that the monument would not be sufficiently detached from the rear of the houses in the Strand. Among the situations proposed may be mentioned the following: St. James' Park, near the marginal railing dividing it from the parade in rear of the Horse Guards; the esplanade of the Horse Guards, between the western façade of that gateway and the boundary of St. James' Park; the four poplars in the Green Park; the front of the British Museum; Regent's Circus at the top of Portland Place; Quadrangle Square, Greenwich Hospital. Mr. Dixon's favorite site was near Westminster Abbey, in the centre of the garden plot, where there are the statues of the Earl of Derby and Lord Palmerston; he even went to the length of trying the effect by putting up a wooden model there. This position would perhaps have been chosen but for the fact that it was over the Metropolitan Underground Railway, and the directors of that company said that if it were placed there, even though secured by iron girders, they would require a perpetual indemnity against the risk of its breaking through into the tunnel.

The obelisk, being national property, came at first under cognizance of Her Majesty's Office of Works, but before long was turned over to the Metropolitan Board of Works, which body finally decided upon the Adelphi steps, on the Victoria Embankment of the Thames, between Charing Cross and Waterloo bridges. Whatever the objections to this site in regard to the fitness of its surroundings, none can apparently be urged on engineering grounds. A very broad and thick concrete base was provided, resting on the stiff clay which underlies the mud of the river bank, and the arched vaults of the embankment were filled in solid with cement concrete. It is not thought probable that the weight of the monolith will affect the embankment.

The selection of this site naturally facilitated the remainder of Mr. Dixon's work, as the "Cleopatra," with her burden, could come right alongside, and the Needle had only to be lifted out and erected without any farther journeying. So the vessel was brought up from the East India docks, and grounded at high tide on a sunken timber cradle. After cutting the cabin away, the cylinder was turned one quarter round, to bring the best face of the obelisk toward the roadway. The iron ship was then taken to pieces, and the obelisk raised by hydraulic jacks, and slid on to the embankment by screw traversers, until its centre of gravity came exactly over the centre of the proposed site.

This done, work was commenced on the apparatus for erecting the Needle. (See Plate xxxv). First of all, four immense uprights were fashioned, each formed of six heavy balks of timber over sixty feet high and a foot square, strengthened and braced together by tie-beams, and supported in their vertical position by struts thrown out on all sides. These uprights were to do duty as guide-rods for the carriage, so to speak, on which the obelisk would be borne aloft and held while turning. This carriage consisted of two horizontal box-girders, one on either side of the stone, supported on wooden

---

[1] There is some uncertainty on this point. Some reports state that the claim was for £10,000, and that the award was £7,000.—H. H. G.

106   *Removal of the Fallen Obelisk of Alexandria to London.*

blocking fitted in between the balks composing the uprights. A wrought-iron jacket, twenty feet long, was riveted round the Needle, from which projected on opposite sides, at the centre of gravity, two knife-edge pivots, which should rest on the box-girders. The jacket was made twenty feet long, to guard against any possible danger of the Needle being fractured by the weight of its own ends. Wooden packing was driven in between it and the sides of the monolith to save the surface of the stone from injury. To prevent the middle from slipping through while being swung into a vertical position, a stirrup-strap was passed round the base from two sides of the jacket. The object in having the movable girders take the weight during the operation of turning was to afford the means of lowering the Needle on the pedestal after being swung into the vertical. Hydraulic jacks under the girders would effect this easily.

As soon as the scaffolding was ready the monolith was slowly raised in a horizontal position by hydraulic jacks, being followed up in the ascent by timber-blocking. The position of the computed centre of gravity was tested by actual trial before it reached a great height. The location, by figures, of the centre of gravity of a conglomerate mass, consisting of the obelisk with its lower corners irregularly broken, the iron jacket, and the heavy stirrup-strap under the heel, is naturally liable to error; the exact point was found to be at twenty-seven feet six inches from the larger end.

While the Needle was climbing upward, the three steps and pedestal were built up under it to a total height of eighteen feet eight inches. The lower course of steps, resting on the level of the embankment, is sixteen feet one and one-half inches square and four feet three inches high; the second or middle step is fourteen feet square and two feet four inches high; the top step is twelve feet square by one foot ten inches high, all being built of brick-work with a Cornish granite outercasing. Above these steps is the pedestal, unfortunately not a monolithic mass worthy of the shaft it supports, but built up of masonry in five courses. It is ten feet square at the base tapering to nine feet three inches at the top, in a height of ten feet five inches. The three lower courses are of brick and Portland cement within, surrounded by a casing of Cornish granite; the two upper are entirely of Cornish granite. In building up this pedestal the middle row of stones in an east and west direction were left out to allow room for the strap under the heel of the obelisk; on this being removed when the weight came on the pedestal, the missing blocks were put in place.

Within the pedestal were deposited two earthen jars containing the following objects :—Standard foot and pound; bronze model of the obelisk (scale, half inch to the foot); memorial printed on vellum, giving a brief account of the removal of the obelisk, with plans of the various arrangements; jars of Doulton ware; a piece of the obelisk stone, chipped in leveling the base; complete set of British coinage, including an Empress of India rupee; parchment copy of Dr. Birch's translation of the obelisk hieroglyphics; standard gauge to one thousandth part of an inch; portrait of the Queen; Bibles in several languages; the Hebrew Pentateuch; the Arabic Genesis, and a translation into two hundred and fifteen languages of the sixteenth verse of the third chapter of St. John's Gospel; Bradshaw's Railway Guide; Mappin's shilling razor; a case of cigars, pipes, box of hair-pins, and sundry articles of female adornment; Alexandra feeding-bottle and children's toys; a Tangye hydraulic jack, such as used in raising the obelisk; wire ropes and specimens of marine cables; map of London; copies of the daily and illustrated papers; photographs of a dozen pretty Englishwomen (presented by gallant Captain Carter); a two-foot rule; a London Directory, and Whitaker's Almanac.

When the obelisk reached such a height that on being turned the heel would be several inches above and clear of the pedestal, controlling tackles were secured to both heel and point, and, a preliminary trial on the 11th proving successful, September 12th was fixed upon for the erection. The time was three P.M. An inopportune shower coming on suddenly early in the afternoon somewhat thinned out the crowd that had begun to assemble; but the sun reappeared, and, under the pleasant auspices of a clearing sky, a vast concourse lined the river front. At the appointed hour

PLATE XXXVI.

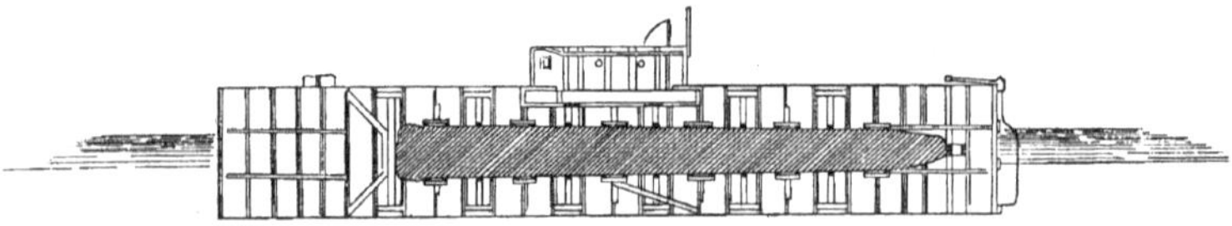

LONGITUDINAL SECTION.

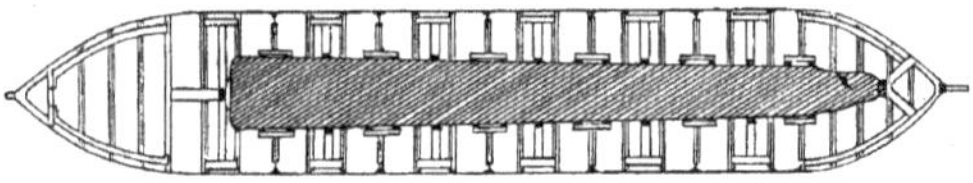

HORIZONTAL SECTION.

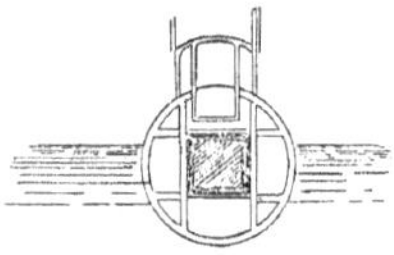

MIDSHIP SECTION. 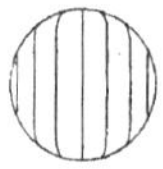   LINES AT BOW & STERN.

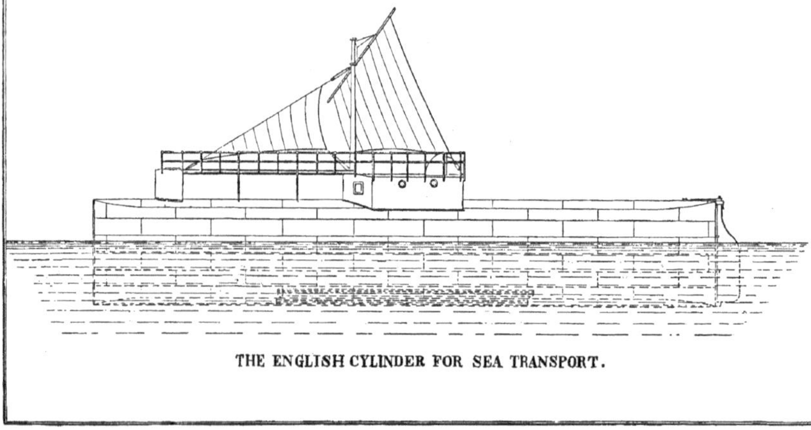

THE ENGLISH CYLINDER FOR SEA TRANSPORT.

Removal of the Fallen Obelisk of Alexandria to London.

the controlling tackles were handled, and in half an hour the obelisk was vertical. The Union Jack and Turkish flag were run up in token of success, and ringing cheers bespoke the congratulations of the multitude. The operation of lowering the monument to the pedestal was deferred until the following day, and was then performed with complete success.

Much circumspection was shown in deciding upon the embellishments for the Needle and its immediate vicinity. In August, 1880, a plaster-cast of a sphinx, colored to resemble bronze, was placed on one of the smaller pedestals on either side of it, to judge of the effect prior to having the castings made. In the same way, and for the same purpose, wings of ornamental design were placed under the broken corners of the Needle where it rests on the masonry base, with filling-pieces between them. This work was designed by Mr. Vulliamy, the architect of the Metropolitan Board of Works, and the effect proving satisfactory, the castings were ordered and commenced in March, 1881. They are not shown in the view of the obelisk contained on Plate xxxvii, which, although the most recent photograph taken up to the present time, antedates the placing of the bronzes. The two sphinxes are enlarged copies of one in stone in the collection of the Duke of Northumberland, at Alnwick Castle, which is supposed to be of the same period as the obelisk, as it bears on the breast the cartouch of Thothmes III. Each one is nineteen feet long, six feet wide, nine feet high over all, and weighs about seven tons; the alloy is ninety parts of copper and ten of tin. The filling-pieces between the wings at the base of the Needle were made to represent the cartouch of Thothmes III.

The casting of the sphinxes was completed in September, 1881, and it was expected that in the course of a month or so every thing would be completed, including the inscriptions on the pedestal. These read as follows: West face: "This obelisk, prostrate for centuries in the sands of Alexandria, was presented to the British nation A. D. 1819, by Mohammed Ali, Viceroy of Egypt,—a worthy memorial of our distinguished countrymen, Nelson and Abercromby."—North face: "This obelisk, through the patriotic zeal of Erasmus Wilson, F. R. S., was brought from Alexandria encased in an iron cylinder. It was abandoned during a storm in the Bay of Biscay, recovered and erected on this spot by John Dixon, C. E., in the 42d year of the reign of Queen Victoria, 1878."—River face: "William Askin, James Gardiner, Joseph Benbow, Michael Burns, William Donald, William Patan, perished in a bold attempt to succor the crew of the obelisk ship 'Cleopatra' during the storm, October 14, 1877."[1] This last inscription is said to have been added at the suggestion of the Queen.

The question of the durability of Egyptian red granite in the climate of London was also considered, and, in 1879, the obelisk was indurated with an invisible solution prepared by Mr. Henry Browning. Opinions differ as to its effect on the stone.

In connection with the removal of such magnificent relics of a great past as the obelisks of Egypt, the question of expense is properly the last to be considered. In this particular case the exact amount of money that changed hands is not easy to state positively, for the reason that the new element was introduced of litigation with insurance companies. Before leaving Egypt the "Cleopatra" was insured for £4,000, and Mr. Dixon, after a prolonged suit, recovered a portion of that for part payment of salvage to the owners of the "Fitzmaurice." That verdict, however, was appealed against later, and resulted adversely to Mr. Dixon, who, it appears, had also to bear the costs of both sides on that occasion, and therefore lost heavily as a contractor. The cost proper of the removal is believed to be in the vicinity of £13,500, or about £11,500 for the bare expenses of transporting and erecting the obelisk alone, and £2,000[2] for its recovery from the salvors. This does not include the building of the immense concrete foundation, nor the casting of the sphinxes and ornamental work round the base, all of which was done by the Metropolitan Board of Works. The timber and a large

---
[1] Baedeker's Guide Book for 1881. It is obviously not the intention to leave the east face of the pedestal bare, though the inscription was not in place at the date of preparing this work. At the time of a recent visit to the British capital none had been finally decided upon.
[2] £7,000 is the amount stated by some authorities to have been awarded.—H. H. G.

108 *Removal of the Fallen Obelisk of Alexandria to London.*

amount of other material used in erecting the obelisk were furnished Mr. Dixon free of cost by merchants.

Unlike Fontana and LeBas, his two modern predecessors in the field, Mr. Dixon received no public recognition of his services in beautifying the capital of his country. In the busy modern world the assumption of risks, in the hope of gain, is considered an every-day matter; and, this affair having assumed the aspect of a private transaction, royal favor could but ill have graced final success. The time-worn shaft will remain erect, however, for many years to come, and just so long will it be a monument to the liberality and enterprise of two of London's citizens.

RECORD OF THE LONDON OBELISK. (BY H. H. G.)

The record of the London obelisk is the same as that of its mate now standing in the Central Park, until the former was thrown from its pedestal in Alexandria. Thothmes III (1591 to 1565 B. C., Lepsius), erected them before the great temple at Heliopolis. They were removed to Alexandria and re-erected there before the temple of the Cæsars during the reign of Augustus, B. C. 22.

The London obelisk remained standing at Alexandria until the beginning of the thirteenth century. There is conclusive evidence of its having been mounted, in the same manner as its companion, on four bronze supports. The Arabian geographer, Edrizi, writing before 1154 A. D., refers to the obelisks at Alexandria as if both were still standing. The Arabian physician Abd-el-Lateef, writing in 1201 A. D., mentions two obelisks near the sea at Alexandria, and says nothing of one being prostrate, while he carefully notes, in his description of Heliopolis, that one of the obelisks there had fallen. The next mention of these obelisks, that I can find, is that of Petrus Bellonius, who visited Alexandria in the middle of the sixteenth century and saw one of them prostrate. From Mallet's "Earthquake Catalogue," of the British Association it appears that a severe earthquake occurred at Alexandria and Acre and throughout the Peloponnesus, Candia, and the Adriatic Sea, on August 8, 1303. This earthquake nearly demolished the walls of Alexandria. In Colonel Howard Vyse's explorations and discoveries it is recorded that during the reign of En Nasir, A. D. 1301, an earthquake occurred, so severe that it is said to have nearly ruined Cairo, giving it the appearance of a city demolished by a siege. Other chroniclers give the dates as 1302 and 1304.

The London obelisk was doubtless thrown down by this earthquake. Cooper and other authorities allege that it was overthrown by plunderers who coveted its bronze supports. This cannot be correct, for the crabs remained in some way connected with the obelisk, and were studied and written about by travellers during the seventeenth and eighteenth centuries.

According to Birch, the vignettes of the pyramidion represent Thothmes III, in the form of a sphinx, presenting offerings to Ra and Tum, the chief deities of Heliopolis.

Three columns of hieroglyphs appear on each of the four faces: the central column of each side being that of Thothmes III; the lateral columns were added by Ramses II. The south and east sides, as erected at Alexandria, are much worn.

The inscriptions of Thothmes III, according to Birch, indicate that the obelisk was erected late in this monarch's reign: their one theme is his devotion to the Temple of the Sun. He is the "ruler of An" (Heliopolis); he "supplies the altar of the spirits of An"; "his father Tum has set up to him his great name, placing it in the temple belonging to An"; mention is made of "his festivals in the midst of the place of the Phœnix"; "crowned in Uas (Thebes), he has made his monument to his father, Haremachu; he has set up to him his great obelisks, capped with gold."

The inscriptions of Ramses II, according to Birch, were added in that monarch's youth; they are chiefly devoted to the praise of his conquests. He is "the powerful victor," "making his frontiers wherever he wished"; "the guardian of Egypt, the chastiser of foreign countries, dragging the South to

THE LONDON OBELISK.

Plate XXXVII

the Mediterranean Sea,¹ the North to the poles of heaven"; "leading captive the Rutennu (Syrians) and Peti (Libyans) out of their countries to the seat of the house of his father"; "the eyes of mankind behold what he has done."²

---

¹ To the Indian Ocean.—*Chabas.*
² The translation of *all* of the hieroglyphs on the London obelisk cannot be found in any publication. Cooper, Wilson, and others, give partial translations which it is hardly worth while to republish here.

CHAPTER V.

RE-ERECTION OF THE VATICAN OBELISK.

BY LIEUTENANT SEATON SCHROEDER, UNITED STATES NAVY.

IN the Piazza di San Pietro stands the largest entire obelisk out of Egypt, and the second in size in the world. The one that surpasses it in height is that of Queen Hatasou at Karnak. The tallest ever quarried, that of St. John Lateran, is now in three pieces, having shared the general destruction that befell those monuments in Rome.

Brought from Heliopolis by the Emperor Caligula early in the first century of the Christian era, the Vatican obelisk was originally set up in the Circus of Caligula, afterward named the Circus of Nero, the scene of the Christians' martyrdom. There it remained undisturbed for fifteen centuries, the only one of all those now to be seen in the papal city that escaped being overthrown. It is probable that but for its timely transplantation it would soon have shared the fate of its companions in exile, for when examined by Fontana in 1585, it was found to be leaning toward the neighboring Basilica of St. Peter's, the summit being seventeen inches from the perpendicular.

Standing on a pedestal hidden in rubbish, in a muddy, unfrequented quarter of the city rarely visited by the travellers that flocked annually to Rome, it contributed little to the decoration of the modern capital, and several of the popes entertained the idea of setting it up in some more conspicuous place. Prominent among them was Nicholas V, who also first undertook to replace the Basilica of Constantine the Great by a new and more extensive building, which, in the course of three centuries and a half, became the present magnificent pile designated by Gibbon as "the most glorious structure that ever has been applied to the use of religion." The project was revived at various times, but the obstacles appeared so enormous, that it was as often abandoned. It was reserved for Sixtus V, to display the unconquerable zeal and tenacity of purpose necessary to smooth away all difficulties. Animated by great religious fervor, inspired by a wish to destroy all vestiges of idolatry, and purify the obelisks and all other monuments erected by the pagans in honor of their gods, he determined to begin with this superb shaft, and purge it of its stains by making it serve to support the holy cross. His purpose was to transform the column of Sesostris into a Christian monument, and make it a trophy of Christ.

A commission was convened of distinguished prelates and savants to deliberate upon the most appropriate site, and more particularly upon the best method of effecting its removal. This body met on the 24th of August, 1585, but the members fell to generalizing and discussing vague principles, and came to no conclusion. Nothing daunted by this failure, the pope issued an appeal to the lights and talent of the century, offering a prize for the best plan. Over 500 persons attended this second meeting, which took place on the 18th of September of the same year; Milan, Venice, Florence, Lucca, Sicily, even Rhodes and Greece were represented in the assembly, and every one present had a drawing, a

Re-erection of the Vatican Obelisk.

model, or a written description. Notwithstanding great divergence of opinion in matters of detail, most of the contestants argued that it would be safer, easier, and more prudent to transport it erect than to lower it and raise it again on a new pedestal; some even proposed to move it not only erect, but on its pedestal. Others advocated a middle course—to incline it at an angle of forty-five degrees, and haul it along in that position. There is no written description extant of the various methods proposed, but in Fontana's book[1] there are representations of several, giving early proof of the ingenious workings of the human mind when grappling with the subject of obelisks. In one diagram an immense timber half-wheel is shown, erected with the diameter vertical along a side of the monolith; on being made to roll it would bring the stone horizontal on top of it; the erection to be performed presumably in the same way. In another, wedges alone were to be used for raising it clear of the ground, a heavy scaffolding keeping it steady in an upright position during the removal. According to a third it was to be inclined by means of screws to an angle of forty-five degrees, when a stout cradle would hold it. Another provided an immense lever, rigged as the beam to a scales; the short arm was connected to the obelisk, and power applied to the long arm would raise or lower it at will. In another diagram was a large timber half-wheel, with the diameter horizontal and resting on the ground; the centre of the wheel was close to the foot of the obelisk, and on its circumference were a number of notches or cogs in which supports would rest, and the stone be lowered from one to another. In still another, four immense endless screws are represented in a vertical position, two on each opposite side of the Needle, parallel and nearly equal to it in height; two others, horizontal, were apparently to work in these, and thus raise or lower the shaft. Many of the plans were rather unpractical, but the collection speaks well for the mechanical ingenuity of the sixteenth century.

Among the contestants was Dominicus Fontana, an architect, native of Mili, a village on the border of Lake Como, who advised lowering the obelisk flat, hauling it on rollers to the new site, and raising it again by means of tackles and capstans. He had made a small model of the obelisk in lead, and one of the hoisting apparatus in wood, and illustrated his plan by actual operation on a small scale before his hearers. The assembly were soon won to declare it the best method of all proposed, and the prize was awarded him. At the same time it was decided that such an immense work should be done under the superintendence of two older architects, Ammanati and Jacques de la Porte, skilled in the art of moving heavy weights; Fontana was too young; he was only forty-two. Deeply grieved at such apparent lack of confidence in his ability, our young friend bided his time, and after the works had begun he joined a party of friends going to Monte Cavallo. The pope naturally questioned him about the obelisk, to which he replied that it was impossible for him to reason about that matter. "At present," said he, "but one idea fills my mind and absorbs my intellectual faculties. I am afraid modifications will be introduced into my system that may cause serious accidents, for which I would be held partly responsible. The more I think of it the more convinced I am that injustice has been done me, for no one can carry out a design as well as the designer." The justice of his complaint was evident, and he was directed forthwith to assume charge of all operations. Overjoyed at his success Fontana hastily collected fifty men and ran to the selected site to begin the trench for the foundation; this was on Wednesday, September 25, 1585.

Wishing to hasten and facilitate the work in every possible way, Pope Sixtus gave him authority to demolish all buildings that might interfere with the carrying out of his plans, and to take, in Rome or other cities of the Holy See, all materials, instruments, or provisions necessary, for which an indemnity would be paid the proprietors afterward. All papal employés were likewise enjoined to aid and second Fontana in every possible way, under penalty of incurring the extreme displeasure of the sovereign

---

[1] *Della Trasportatione dell' obelisco Vaticano, et delle fabriche di nostro Signore Papa Sisto V. Fatte dal cavallier Domenico Fontana. Roma, 1590.* This work is to be found in the Astor Library, New York. The drawings were reproduced in *Templum Vaticanum et ipsius origo etc. Editum ab equite Carolo Fontana, Romæ, 1694*; also in *Castelli a Ponti, di Mæstro Niccola Zabaglia, 1743.*

pontiff. Armed with these full powers, he sent trusted agents to various points to collect the materials necessary. The timber was drawn from the forests of Campo Morto, twenty miles from Rome, immense balks being hewn and drawn to the city in vehicles to which were harnessed seven pairs of oxen. While the materials were being thus collected he personally superintended the manufacture of the rope to be used in raising the monolith. He also tested by actual experiment the power of each capstan and the strength of the rope, and decided what power to apply to each to insure not surpassing the elastic limit of the hemp. Many critics said that it would be impossible to apply an equal power through all the capstans, and that some would therefore bear all the strain; to obviate this he proportioned the capstans so that the full power developed by each would not be great enough to part its tackle. Thus, when the men and horses on a capstan had hove to their utmost, they would simply be unable to heave any farther, and others which might not be bearing a proper strain would then catch up.

The first thing to be done was to ascertain the weight to be lifted. Careful measurements proved the dimensions of the obelisk to be as follows:

			FEET.	INCHES.				FEET.	INCHES.
Length of main shaft,	107¼ palmi[1]	=	78	8.92	Height of pyramidion,	6 palmi	=	4	4.74
Side of base,	12 1/12 "	=	8	10.21	Total height,	113¼ "	=	83	1.66
Side of top,	8¼ "	=	5	11.05					

The slight height of the pyramidion struck Fontana as being strange, and on studying it out he concluded that Pliny was right in saying that it had been broken during the erection in the first century. The rule generally adhered to in fixing the proportions of obelisks seems to have been that the height of the pyramidion should be once and a half a side of its base, and Fontana verified this rule at the time by measurements of other obelisks in the city. It is fair to suppose, therefore, that the original height of this pyramidion was eight feet, 10.45 inches, making the entire height eighty-seven feet, 6.30 inches. Mr. Joseph Bonomi gives the height of this obelisk as eighty-eight feet two inches.[2]

Accepting Fontana's figures, the dimensions of the obelisk give a volume of 4,403 cubic feet, and a weight of three hundred and twenty-six English tons, the specific gravity of the stone being 2.66. There being no hieroglyphics on it, this may be regarded as very nearly its exact actual weight. Fontana carefully weighed a cube of the stone measuring precisely one palm, and found it to be eighty-six *libbre* or 64.302 pounds avoirdupois, and deduced 973,537 11/16 *libbre* or 324.92 tons as the weight of the monolith. To this had to be added a certain allowance for the sheathing and the attachments necessary in handling it.

Having found the weight to be moved and the power capable of being transmitted by each apparatus, it was decided that forty tackles worked by as many capstans, moved by eight hundred men and seventy-five horses, together with five great levers worked by one hundred and six men, and wedges driven under the base, would furnish sufficient power to allow for lack of simultaneity in heaving. So we see that Fontana used all three of the fundamental mechanical applications of power, —the pulley, the lever, and the inclined plane. The capstans were made with four bars; to the first and third bars horses were harnessed, while the other two were worked by men.

The plan of lowering the obelisk involved first raising it bodily about two feet, in order to introduce underneath it a platform on rollers, on to which it would be lowered, and on which it would be rolled to its new site. As tackles were to be used in hoisting it, it was necessary to provide fixed points for the upper blocks of the pulleys, and for this purpose was built an immense scaffolding ninety feet high, which was universally dubbed Fontana's castle. On Plate xxxviii is a perspective view of this scaffolding, the details of construction being as follows: The principal feature consisted in eight timber

---

[1] Palmi d' architettura; one palmo = 0.7325 feet, = 8.79 inches.   [2] Erasmus Wilson.

Plate XXXVIII.

APPARATUS FOR TRANSPORTING AND ERECTING THE VATICAN OBELISK

Perspective view of Structure.

Perspective view of Structure.

Section through Structure.

Section through movable Strut.

Method of transporting.

Re-erection of the Vatican Obelisk.   113

uprights, three and a half feet apart, four on either side of the column. Each upright was forty inches square in section, built of oak and walnut, four beams in thickness; the butts of the pieces were carefully shifted, the various parts put together without tenons or mortises, but secured by key-bolts, iron bands at every nine feet, and rope lashings equally spaced. The latter were tightened by wedges driven between them and the wood. The uprights were sustained in their vertical position by struts, which had also to be fashioned by uniting several pieces of timber; the struts and uprights were secured to each other by cross and diagonal tie-beams, iron bands, and wooldings. The tops of the uprights were connected by trusses, as is shown in *section through structure*, Plate xxxviii, the string-pieces running along over these trusses being over two feet square; to these were lashed the upper blocks of the tackles. It was seen that when the pressure was thrown on the uprights, the struts branching out would prevent their buckling outward, but that they were liable to bend inward. To prevent this, horizontal tie-beams were thrown across from upright to upright, bolted to them, and butted against the struts; afterward they had to be removed one at a time as the obelisk was lowered. The entire "castle" rested upon a heavy timber platform, into which the uprights and struts were stepped with tenon and mortise; in the construction of the whole fabric, none but key-bolts, or such as could be easily drawn, were used, to facilitate dismantling it and setting it up again on the new site. Finally, for perfect security, eight heavy shrouds or stays were fitted to the top of the castle, and set up taut to ensure stability.

While this scaffolding was being put up, the ground was levelled off, houses that interfered with the efficient working of the capstans torn down, and the obelisk encased in a protective covering of matting and two-inch plank. Twelve iron bars, four inches wide and two inches thick, were passed beneath the heel and up, three along each face; they had shoulders against which butted nine horizontal iron bands, which did the double duty of securing the planking and affording means of attaching the lower blocks of the tackles. The obelisk resting on four bronze blocks made it possible to pass the bars under the base without injuring the pedestal. Not trusting entirely to iron, additional rope lashings were unsparingly provided, and Fontana, estimated the weight of the matting, wood, rope, and iron thus used to be about 23 tons, increasing the entire weight to be handled to about 350 tons. The brass globe surmounting the obelisk was taken down as soon as it could be reached; it had been thought possible that this contained the ashes of one of the Cæsars, but it was found to be a solid casting. There were a number of deep dents in it, which were conjectured to be the marks of arquebuse-shots inflicted possibly during the storming of the ancient Western capital; the dust collected in them certainly bespoke a moderate antiquity.

The excavations at the new site in St. Peter's Square were also continued in search of solid ground, and a number of commemorative medals were deposited in the pit, most of them being contained in two caskets of travertine stone, holding a dozen each. On one face they bore the image of our Saviour, and on the other various symbols among which were the following: a man asleep under a tree, with the motto *Perfecta Securitas;* three mountains of which the right-hand one was surmounted by a cornucopia, the left by a laurel branch, and the middle one by a sword the point of which, turned heavenward, supported a balance, the inscription below being *Fecit in monte convivium pinguium;* St. Francis kneeling before a church in ruins, with the exhortation *Vade Francisce et repara.* On some of the coins was struck the effigy of Pope Sixtus V, with the figures of Religion and Justice on the reverse side.

On the 28th of April, 1586, every thing was ready, and the 30th was appointed for the lowering. On the 29th Fontana received the papal benediction, and before daylight of the 30th he and his assistants took communion; two masses were also held to implore the light of the Holy Spirit. By daybreak the workmen were all at their posts, and every avenue leading to the ground was thronged by dense crowds, which comprised all the most distinguished literary and scientific men of the city;

a great many strangers had also flocked to Rome to witness the operation, and due precautions were taken against disorders liable to be caused by such a gathering. A large surrounding area was fenced off, and a proclamation pronounced a sentence of death on any one that should force his way through the barricade; absolute silence was also commanded under severe penalties.

Fontana first exhorted the workmen to do their duty loyally, and to pay strict attention to orders, and recalled to them the signals to be used. At the first sound of the trumpet the capstans were to heave round together; the signal to stop was a stroke of a bell at the scaffolding. He then visited every part of the enclosure to satisfy himself that all were in their proper places; men and horses were at the capstan-bars; the levers, forty-four feet long, were adjusted, three on the west side and two on the east, with ropes hanging from the ends, some of which were taken to small capstans; the twelve carpenters were in readiness to drive the wood and iron wedges under the obelisk, the object of these being partly to help raise the mass, and partly to form permanent supports for the monolith as it rose from the bronze crabs, so that the weight should at no time be borne wholly by the tackles. The men detailed for this duty were provided with iron helmets as a protection against fragments of wood or iron that might come tumbling from aloft.

The architect then assumed a conspicuous position whence he could be seen by all, and, speaking in a loud voice, recalled the religious motives that prompted the transplantation of the obelisk. "The work that we are about to undertake is in the cause of religion, and for the exaltation of the holy cross. Implore with me the help of God, the sovereign moving power; let us ask for His help, without which all our efforts must be in vain." And all within hearing—noblemen, citizens, priests, strangers—fell on their knees and recited a *pater* and an *ave*. A striking scene must it have been, and typical of that curious age.

A blast of the trumpet set the capstans revolving round their spindles; the tackles assumed the strain, the ends of the levers descended slowly, the hammers were heard ringing against the heads of the wedges, and the majestic shaft, heretofore leaning toward the cathedral, drew itself up to a vertical pose amid a portentous creaking of wood and tackles. A stroke of the bell brought every thing to a standstill. The vibration was only caused by the compression due to lifting bodily a dead weight of three hundred and fifty tons, and no material harm had been done. The topmost iron band was found broken and was immediately replaced by a rope lashing held down by frappings under the heel. Another heave was then ordered, and the obelisk left its metal supports; the signals were repeated a dozen times, and finally, at about four in the afternoon, it had been raised twenty-four inches. This was announced by the firing of a small cannon, and immediately the batteries of the city responded with a joyous salute.

An inspection of the apparatus the next day revealed the fact that most of the horizontal iron bands were broken, twisted, or displaced; disaster had probably been averted only by Fontana's careful foresight in rigging rope preventers. The obelisk now resting on the wedges under the corners, and steadied by the tackles, the blocks that had supported it for fifteen centuries were removed. Two of these gave no trouble, but the others were connected with the pedestal by long dovetailed spurs, solidly leaded in place, and it required four days and four nights to break them out; in the end it was only accomplished by chipping away the stone round the mortises. From a small drawing in one of Fontana's plates, it appears that these blocks were very similar to the crabs which were found under Cleopatra's Needle, and which are now to be seen in the Metropolitan Museum of Art in New York. The two with spurs weighed six hundred pounds each, or about the same as those used by Pontius.

The operations still to be performed required extensive alterations in the various apparatus. The end of the rolling cradle was introduced beneath the obelisk, between the wedges at the corners, from right to left as viewed in the left-hand figure of Plate xxxviii. It was necessary then to change the movable blocks of the tackles from what was to be the under side of the Needle to some other

Re-erection of the Vatican Obelisk. 115

$p_r^a t$. Four tackles were also rigged to pull the cradle along to the left as the monolith was lowered. As a precaution against a possible yielding of the ropes at any time, a heavy movable strut was devised and placed against the Needle, near the middle, the upper end being seized by an iron collar round the shaft, which formed the axis on which it could revolve, the lower end being free to move away to the right when desired. To afford means of checking this movement so as to make it support the weight, a roller was placed between two parts of the strut (see *section through movable strut*, Plate xxxviii); two ropes were wound several times round this roller, and the ends secured to the columns of the scaffolding; the roller revolving permitted the foot of the strut to recede as the obelisk was lowered, but by placing a lever in a mortise cut for the purpose, this rotation could be stopped, and the strut kept steady. As a prop of this kind could only act efficiently at certain favorable angles, several were prepared of different lengths, so that at no period of the descent need the obelisk be left without proper support.

All the preparations for the new work were completed by the 7th of May, and the operations were resumed on that day. The trumpet and the bell were used as before to regulate the capstans. As the lowering tackles were slacked, the cradle and the heel of the monolith were pulled away to the westward. It was Fontana's intention at first to keep the lowering tackles nearly vertical, but as the work progressed that had to be given up; toward the end also the thrust of the obelisk was such as not only to render the four tackles on the heel unnecessary, but to require one from the opposite direction to check it. To prevent all shock in landing it, five tackles were also taken from the point of the Needle to the arch of the sacristy of St. Peter's. The operation was entirely successful, though frequent interruptions were necessary to rig the new tackles, and to remove cross-beams of the scaffolding that were in the way of the descending shaft. By four o'clock the obelisk lay safe and sound on the cradle, and, amid shouts and universal greetings, Fontana was carried home in triumph escorted by drums and trumpets.

The monument had now to be dragged to its new site in St. Peter's Square, a distance of two hundred and seventy-five yards. The level of the ground here was a little more than twenty-nine feet lower than at the old site, but when the height of the pedestal, twenty-seven feet, was considered, it was found that the descent would be only about two feet in the two hundred and seventy-five yards. A roadway of earth was built on that grade, the sides being supported by a wood revetement propped up by struts; the revetement was further supported from within by transverse and diagonal braces. The height of this viaduct increased from zero at the old site to twenty-seven feet at the new, the breadth being seventy-three feet at the bottom and thirty-six and one half at the top. The obelisk was only hauled away clear of the pedestal at first, so as to admit of taking down the scaffolding, and of removing the underlying masonry, which was rebuilt in precisely the same shape at the new site. The foundations required a great deal of labor and expense, as the nature of the ground was not favorable for supporting a heavy weight. An excavation forty-three feet square had been made to a depth of twenty-four feet, and as the soil then reached was not firm enough, oak and chestnut piles eighteen feet long and nine inches in diameter, after being barked, were driven in a solid mass. Over this was laid an immense bed of concrete, reaching nearly to the ground level, made of basalt and a mortar composed of lime and puzzolana.

As Fontana dug down to unearth the old pedestal, he found the various courses laid as follows, beginning with the top. First was a plinth ninety-six and one half inches high, one hundred and seven and one half broad on the east side, one hundred and fourteen and one quarter on the west, and one hundred and sixteen and one half on the north and south; the weight was computed to be fifty-five and one half tons. Under this was found a block thirty-five inches high, one hundred and thirty-two inches broad at the top, and one hundred and fourteen and one quarter at the bottom, weighing twenty-two and one half tons. Then came another plinth one hundred and fourteen and one quarter inches high, but, strange to say, less broad than the top one, being only one hundred and three and one quarter inches on the east side, and one hundred and fourteen and one quarter on the others. The finish of this block was much less perfect than that of the topmost, and Fontana concluded that the latter might be of more ancient origin, not successfully reproduced by the architect of the other. For this reason he decided to replace them in the same relative positions. The weight of this third block is not given in his account, but, assuming the specific gravity of the material to be 2.75, which was evidently that adopted by him, it is about sixty-three tons.

Next beneath was found white marble, in blocks connected by iron clamps cased in lead; the iron was found to be in a perfect state of preservation although it had been under water apparently for centuries. Last of all were the courses of travertine stone forming three steps, which rested on decomposed concrete.

In rebuilding this substructure, two inches had to be chiselled off the top of the upper plinth to form an even surface, in consequence of its having been chipped away to remove the crabs. Some more medals, similar to those previously deposited in the concrete, were placed within the masonry. Two gold ones, on the upper tier of steps, bore the effigy of the pope on one side, and on the other the images of Religion and Justice. Between the two inferior strata of marble was placed a slab of the same stone, on which were carved in Latin the names of Pope Sixtus V, and of Fontana, and the name of the latter's native town, together with an account of the operations. Finally, eight square holes were made in the travertine slabs to receive the heels of the uprights of the scaffolding; these, in consequence, had to be made some twenty-seven feet longer than before. When all this was done, earth was compactly rammed all around, forming a continuation of the viaduct, which here widened out to ninety-one and one half feet at the bottom and sixty-nine and one half at the top. The scaffolding was then rebuilt, and the obelisk slowly dragged by means of tackles and capstans until the point was over the centre of the pedestal, a commemorative slab having been left to mark the spot where it had stood for so many centuries.

On the 10th of September, 1586, the erection took place, being preceded by the same religious ceremonies as the lowering. As the apex of the shaft rose under the action of forty capstans, worked by one hundred and forty horses and eight hundred men, horizontal tackles pulled the heel and cradle forward, for the purpose of keeping the hoisting gear acting as nearly vertically as possible. At about three o'clock, when an angle of forty-five degrees was reached, a respite was granted for dinner, all having been at work without intermission since daylight; the movable strut was again brought into play and proved itself an efficient auxiliary support. At nearly sunset, thirteen hours after beginning operations, the obelisk was vertical over the pedestal, but separated from it by the cradle. To free the latter, the monolith had to be raised bodily, and this was accomplished, on the following day, with the same combination of apparatus as on the old site,—forty capstans, five levers, and the wedges. Acted upon simultaneously by all these motors the obelisk was lifted a certain distance, and then rested on the wedges, while the cradle was removed and the bronze crabs replaced precisely as they had been found. All this took some time, and it was not until the eighth day after the erection that the tackles were slacked, the levers eased up, the wedges carefully and slowly withdrawn, and the obelisk landed firmly and permanently on its four supports.

There is a very pretty little anecdote related in connection with this operation, which naturally appeals to one's imagination, but which will scarcely stand the test of practical inquiry. It is said that the progress of the work was interrupted, and the process of erection on the eve of failing from the stretching of the ropes, when a sailor named Bresca, regardless of consequences, cried out, "Acqua alle funi!" (wet the ropes!), and that this practical advice being acted upon the weight was lifted. The legend goes on to the effect that not only was Bresca pardoned for violating the strict orders regarding silence, but that the pope conferred upon him and all his posterity the privilege of supplying

Re-erection of the Vatican Obelisk.

St. Peter's with palm leaves on Palm Sunday, as an acknowledgment of his services on that memorable occasion. It seems that there is now a family of that name in Bordighera, possessing that privilege, but, iconoclastic as it may appear, the story of the origin of the grant will not hold water. If the ropes were stretching it was because the elastic limit of the hemp had been exceeded by too severe a strain; wetting the rope would have had the effect of contracting the fibre and, therefore, of increasing the strain. Moreover, the whole weight of the monolith was never allowed to come entirely upon the tackles, except in lowering. Fontana, in speaking of the wedges used in lifting it, carefully explained that their object was mainly to prevent the Needle resting unsupported in air.[1] In describing the preparations for lowering he also weighed upon the similar use of the movable strut, which was again called into requisition in raising the obelisk.

If the anecdote has any foundation in fact, it could only be that the power applied was insufficient, and that the contraction of the ropes by moisture supplied the deficiency. But this theory is also open to serious objections. When a rope is subjected to a strain such as was sustained by these, the fibres are so compressed and the surface of the rope so hard, that it would be impossible for any moisture to penetrate into it for a long time, especially if new rope as this was. Also, if, unfortunately, the moisture had penetrated into any or all of the forty tackles used, an irregularity of contraction would have been produced that in all probability would have led to their successive rupture.

Honor to whom honor is due. There is no valid reason for imputing threatened failure to Fontana, averted only by the timely inspiration of a practical sailor. After computing the weight to be lifted, and supervising personally the making of the rope, he tested the power of every apparatus by actual trial, and, from that, in support of what theory had pointed out, decided upon the number of motors necessary. His subsequent account of it also seems to be so explicit and so frank, that we cannot believe he would have omitted mentioning any such incident. Rewards, pecuniary and honorary, were lavished upon him. The pope made him a Knight of the Golden Spur, and gave him a pension of 2,000 gold *scudi*, reversible to his heirs, besides an immediate present of 5,000 more; also all the wood and other material left from the operations, the value of which was estimated at 20,000 *scudi*. The cost of the removal and erection is stated by Carolo Fontana to have been 36,975 *scudi*, equivalent to about 44,000 dollars.[2]

On the apex of the obelisk was placed a bronze cross seven feet four inches high, which was removed in 1740, when some relics of our Saviour were deposited in a cavity made for the purpose. Bronze lions, gilded, were also placed under the corners and apparently sustain the weight, for they conceal the crabs which really do that duty.

Inscriptions on this obelisk and pedestal are numerous. On the east and west sides of the shaft itself, is still visible in duplicate the original dedication to Augustus and Tiberius, as follows: "DIVO. CAES. DIVI. IVLII. F. AVGVSTO. TI. CAES. DIVI. AVG. F. AVGVS. SACRVM." There are also brief modern inscriptions on all faces of the pedestal. On the south side is a simple record of the removal: "Sixtus V. Pont. Max. obeliscum Vaticanum diu gentium impio cultu dedicatum ad Apostolorum limina operoso labore transtulit. Anno MDLXXXVI." On the north side the consecration of the obelisk to the holy cross is commemorated: "Sixtus V. Pont. Max. cruci invictae obeliscum Vaticanum ab impia superstitione expiatum justius et felicius consecravit. Anno MDLXXXVI. Pont. II." On the east side is the pious apostrophe: "Christus vincit. Christus regnat. Christus imperat. Christus ab omni malo plebem suam defendat." On the west side is to be seen the somewhat vainglorious passage: "Ecce Crux Domini fugite partes adversae vicit Leo de Tribu Juda."

---

[1] "Acciò che mai non stesse la Guglia in aria sopra le corde."
[2] The papal gold *scudo* of the 16th century did not vary in weight materially from fifty grains. A silver *scudo* or more correctly *piastra* of Paul V, 1620, recently tested through the kind offices of a friend in the U. S. Mint, Philadelphia, weighed 482 grains, 913 fine; its original weight, according to Mr. J. Ross Snowden, was 491.89 grains, which would put its value at about $1.20 United States money.

Fontana also mentions an inscription on the side of the pyramidion facing St. Peter's, the illegibility of which now is easily laid to the charge of three centuries of rain and dust. It read: "Sanctissimæ cruci Sixtus V. Pont. Max. consecravit e priore sede avvlsvm et Caess. Aug. ac Tib. S. L. ablatum MDLXXXVI." Still one other remains to be mentioned, carved on the bottom course of the pedestal: "Dominicus Fontana ex pago Mili agri Novocomensis transtulit et erexit." This is shown, not very clearly, in one of the plates illustrating Fontana's book, and Quatrèmere de Quincy[1] mentions it being still discernible in 1830. Recent travellers and guide-books all fail to notice it however.

Three other obelisks were afterward erected by this same architect. One, in the Piazza del Popolo, is of about the same height as that in front of St. Peter's; while another in the Piazza di San Giovanni in Laterano is the largest known, being still one hundred and five feet and seven inches high after having three feet cut or broken off. Both of these, however, are in several pieces, and the chief care was to adapt the fragments so as not to mar the stability or the symmetry of the shafts. The third, now behind the Church of Santa Maria Maggiore, is still monolithic, but much injured and of smaller dimensions, being only forty-eight feet four inches in height; its pedestal, fortunately, being seventeen feet high, lends additional majesty to its presence.

During the remaining four years of the life of Pope Sixtus, Fontana was held in great esteem, and as pontifical architect added materially to the adornment of the city; but soon after the accession of Clement VIII he succumbed to the machinations of jealous enemies, and was degraded from his position. The Count of Miranda, Viceroy of Naples, sent for him, however, and made him architect and first engineer of the kingdom. There he passed the remainder of his life, loaded with riches and honors, and left a number of handsome edifices to bear witness to his skill and taste. Perhaps none of his works, though, will be more lasting than the graceful shaft that rears its tall form in the centre of the Piazza di San Pietro, an austere chronicle of silent ages. A fresco painting on one of the walls of the Vatican library recalls the great feat which lifted him into sudden prominence, and, which, more surely perhaps than any structure in Rome or Naples, will command a tribute of praise for the *young* architect of the sixteenth century.

The Vatican obelisk has no Egyptian hieroglyphs; it is, therefore, impossible to determine with certainty by whom it was originally erected. It is assumed to be identical with one which Pliny describes as having been erected by a certain King Nuncoreus in gratitude for the recovery of his sight. As Nuncoreus does not appear on the lists of Egyptian monarchs, Bunsen thinks that Pliny meant Meneptah I (xix dynasty, B. C. 1322–1302, Lepsius). The Emperor Caius Caligula removed it from Egypt to Rome about A. D. 40, and Claudius erected it on the Spina of the so-called Circus of Nero, where it is believed to have remained until removed by Fontana to its present site.

---

[1] "Vie des Architectes."

CHAPTER VI.

RECORD OF ALL EGYPTIAN OBELISKS.

THE REMAINING OBELISK AT LUXOR.[1]

THE temple at Luxor (Thebes, eastern bank of the Nile) was founded by Amenhotep III, xviii dynasty, who built its sanctuary, colonnade, and propylon. To this original structure Ramses II, xix dynasty, added a great court and a gigantic propylon; in front of which he erected two colossal statues of himself and the two most splendid obelisks of his reign. (See Plate xxxix.)

The present obelisk of Luxor was the eastern one of this pair. Its former companion has been removed, and is to-day the obelisk of Paris. They were quarried at Syene, exquisitely sculptured and highly polished. The dimensions of this pair are not the same.[2] They have one peculiarity that has been the cause of much speculation: the eastern and western faces of both are slightly curved.[3] Wilkinson believed that the object of this curvature was to obviate the shadow thrown by the sun. Donaldson observes that while in each obelisk one face is convex, the opposite face of the same obelisk is concave, and from this concludes that the peculiarity is a defect of quarrying, and not designed for effect.

The pyramidions of the remaining obelisk at Luxor and its mate in Paris are imperfect and unsculptured. The form is not that of a true pyramid, but rather that of a pyramid with curved faces, which is the earliest form. This has led to the conjecture that the Luxor obelisks were originally surmounted by metal caps. Certainly the dedicatory sculptures on them are on the sides of the shaft, instead of on the faces of the pyramidion, and this tends to confirm the conjecture. The artistic perfection of the sculptures on these obelisks is remarkable. The hieroglyphs are deeply cut. The surfaces within the characters of the central column are highly polished, while in the lateral columns they are rough. Champollion states that the name of Ramses II is found only in the central column on the western side. He translates the cartouch on the other sides as Ramses III, and conjectures that this monarch completed the sculptures on the obelisks that his predecessor had erected.

The question, very difficult of solution, is raised by Birch, whether these differing cartouches belong to two monarchs, or to but one (Ramses II). Rosellini, Champollion, and apparently, Birch maintain that two kings are intended; while Rawlinson, Lenormant, and Major Felix conclude, that only Ramses II is named. Lenormant's conclusion is based on the discovery of two cartouches on the bottom of the Paris obelisk when it was lowered, which Champollion had believed to be

---

[1] "Descrip. de l' Égypte, Antiq.," vol. iii., pl. 3, 6, 11. Lenormant, "Musée," pl. xv, No. 15. Champollion, "Mon.," t. iv., pl. cccxx, cccxxi. [View of the obelisk in Ebers (Philae), p. 311.]
[2] The obelisk now in Paris being shorter than its mate, was mounted at Luxor on a taller pedestal and placed farther from the pylon than the other, so that to the advancing spectator the difference in height would not be apparent.
[3] See Chapter III.

the name of Ramses III. He argued that if the name of Ramses II appeared on the obelisk at all it was erected by him, and the cartouches on the bottom could not have been cut since it was erected. No full translation of the inscriptions on the Luxor obelisk has been made.

A portion of the inscription, which has been translated by Birch, extols the monarch as a builder: he is "the constructor of memorials"; "he has arranged the temple of Amen, placing his name forever in Thebes"; "he has set up two obelisks of granite, placing them for millions of years at the divine residence of Rameses, whom Amen loves, at the house of Amen-Ra."

Plate xxxix conveys some idea of the grandeur of the ancient Egyptian edifices and the labor that was expended on them. The two massive walls that formed the pylons of the temple were covered with sculptures and hieroglyphs, which may still be traced and partly deciphered. Just without the gate, between them, are two colossal statues of the king, that are buried nearly up to the shoulders in the sands that have been accumulating in many centuries. Some idea may be formed of the size of these statues by comparison with the height of the obelisk near by, which rises about sixty feet above the ground, and is buried over twenty feet below.

It is inexplicable that the French archæologists residing in Egypt should have been so earnest and persistent in their efforts to prevent the removal of the New York obelisk from Alexandria, when their countrymen had set the example of modern times in the wanton destruction of the only remaining group of pylon, statues, and obelisks as they had been originally placed by their builders. Before opposing and condemning the removal of the New York obelisk from Alexandria, where it did not belong, and where it was doomed to speedy destruction had it remained, it would have been reasonable to expect from the French servants of the Khedive an effort to restore the Paris obelisk to its ancient home and surroundings. It was an open secret in Egypt that the French and German archæologists in charge of the Boulak Museum ceased their opposition to the Khedive's gift of the Alexandria obelisk to the United States, only in the expressed belief that the foreign residents of Alexandria would resist by force any attempt to remove it. They are in a measure responsible for the difficulties that attended the removal of the New York obelisk, that came so near culminating in bloodshed.

OBELISKS OF THOTHMES I. AT KARNAK.

The great temple of Karnak (Thebes, eastern bank) is pronounced by Fergusson[1] to be "the noblest effort of architectural magnificence ever produced by the hand of man." Within its walls are the most ancient obelisks now standing in Egypt, excepting only that at Heliopolis. They are the monuments of Thothmes I, and of his daughter, Queen Hatasou.

Entering at the portal of the first gigantic propylon (three hundred and seventy feet long; one side, or pylon, still standing, one hundred and thirty-five feet high) of Ramses II, xix dynasty, the visitor traverses the vast open court (two hundred and seventy-five by three hundred and twenty-nine feet) of the same monarch. Then passing the ruins of the second great propylon, even more massive than the first, of Seti I, the founder of the xix dynasty, he enters the grand hypostyle hall, or Hall of Columns,[2] also the work of Seti I, and, according to Fergusson, "the greatest of man's architectural works." Then, by the third propylon, that of Amenhotep III, xviii dynasty,—with each massive, portal going still farther back into antiquity,—he enters a long narrow corridor extending across the whole width of the temple. Here, in front of the fourth propylon, the work of Thothmes I [xviii, dynasty, B. C. 1646—1625, Lepsius], are the two obelisks of this monarch; one fallen and broken, the other still standing in its original position; it is the left one on Plate xl.[3] They originally stood in front of the entire temple.[4]

[1] Fergusson, "Hist. of Architecture," vol. i, p. 106.
[2] The central columns are sixty-six feet high, eleven and one half feet in diameter.
[3] "Descr. de l'. Égypte, Antiq.," vol. iii, pl. 24. Lepsius, "Denkmäler," vol. v, pl. 6. Rosellini, "Mon. Storici," pl. xxx.
[4] Savary, in Egypt, 1777 (letters, etc., published in 1785), says three obelisks *standing* at Karnak.

THE REMAINING OBELISK AND RUINS OF TEMPLE AT LUXOR

The pyramidion of the standing obelisk is apparently not sculptured. The absence of the dedicatory sculptures on the shaft indicates that it was sculptured originally. The authorities on Egypt contradict each other and themselves so frequently on this and other important matters that there is little satisfaction in quoting them.[1]

Three columns of hieroglyphs are cut upon each face of the shaft[2]; the central columns bearing the name and titles of Thothmes I; the lateral columns, according to Birch, bear the names of Ramses V or VI. Mariette ("Monuments," pp. 168, 169) states that the side columns show rather confused cartouches, among which are the names of Ramses VI engraved over those of Ramses IV, and adds that upon the many fragments of the fallen obelisk may be seen the name of Thothmes III. The inscriptions record that the king "has built his enduring edifice to his father, Amen-Ra," and "has erected two obelisks before the propylon" (Rosellini, vol. iii, p. 114).

OBELISKS OF HATASOU, KARNAK.

Still farther within the great temple of Karnak than are the obelisks of Thothmes I—that is, beyond the fourth propylon and within the narrow court of the Osiride figures—are the obelisks of Queen Hatasou.[3] In this court, erected by Thothmes I, his daughter, Hatasou [xviii dynasty, B. C. 1625–1591, Lepsius], set up the loftiest monoliths now remaining in Egypt, and, according to Mariette, the loftiest of all obelisks now existing. Of these, one is fallen; the other (the northern), still standing where it was placed by the queen, is the right one on Plate xl.

Ebers, Verninac St. Maur, and others bestow their highest praises upon this obelisk. Its fine proportions, its exquisite polish, the singularly delicate and perfect execution of its sculptures, the unique richness of its ornamentation, together with its gigantic size, make it, in the opinion of Rosellini, one of the most admirable examples of Egyptian work. A marked entasis, or convexity, of at least one of its faces was observed by Verninac St. Maur.

The pyramidion is unusually acute, and is sculptured with vignettes representing, according to Rosellini, Hatasou, in male attire, kneeling before Amen-Ra, with her face turned from the deity, who has his hand on her. The summit of the pyramidion above the vignettes, it appears from the inscriptions, was originally covered with "pure gold."

A single column of admirably cut hieroglyphs appears upon the centre of each face of the shaft, bearing the name of Hatasou. Thothmes III, her brother and successor, has attempted to erase her cartouch wherever it appeared, and to substitute for it his own, whether impelled, as some say, by hatred of his too domineering sister, or by the desire to appropriate these splendid shafts to himself; but the attempt was not successful, and the feminine grammatical forms still look through the names of Thothmes, to claim the obelisks for their original founder.

Upon either side of the hieroglyphic column of each face are eight vignettes, beginning just below the pyramidion, and descending more than half the distance from the summit to the base, thus enclosing the greater part of the inscription with a richly sculptured bordering, of which this is the only example. All the vignettes which border one side of the hieroglyphic column represent Amen-Ra; opposite the deity, on the other side of the column, stands a sovereign presenting offerings. The sovereign represented is, according to Rosellini, sometimes Hatasou herself, sometimes Thothmes I, her father, and sometimes her husband or her son. Upon the broken obelisk are exactly the same designs as those of the standing shaft. These sculptures have been cut and polished with the

---

[1] The plates of Lepsius and Rosellini show the pyramidion plain. So also do photographs of more recent dates. There is not even a line to be discovered on the pyramidion in the photographs.

[2] According to Cooper, p. 28, there is but one column on each face; and so, indeed, it is represented in the "Descr. de l' Égypte," pl. 24. But the plates of Lepsius and Rosellini show three columns; so do the photographs.

[3] "Descr. de l' Égypte Antiq.," vol. iii, pl. 21, 24, 27, 30. Lepsius, "Denkmäler," vol. v, pl. 22–24. Rosellini, "Mon. Storici," pl. xxxi–xxxiv. Lenormant, "Musée," pl. xvii, No. 10.

122   *Record of all Egyptian Obelisks.*

greatest care; those at the summit and farthest from the eye of the spectator just as carefully as those lowest on the shaft (" Descr. de l' Egypte ").

Our wonder at the elaborate decoration and perfect execution of these gigantic monuments is increased when we learn from their inscriptions that they were detached from the Assouan quarries, removed to Karnak, sculptured, polished, and erected in the short space of seven months. The engraven record shows that "the queen, the pure gold of monarchs, had dedicated to her father, Amen of Thebes, two obelisks of syenite taken from the quarries of the south. Their upper parts were ornamented with pure gold taken from the chiefs of all nations. Her Majesty gave two gilded obelisks to her father, Amen, that her name should remain permanent, always and forever in this temple. Each was made of a single piece of syenite (Machet stone), without joint or rivet. Her Majesty began the work in the fifteenth year of her reign, the first day of the month Mechir, of the sixteenth year, and finished it on the last day of the month Mesore, making seven months from its commencement in the quarry" (Birch, "Egypt," p. 85).[1]

The low, square pedestal of the standing obelisk is figured in Plate 24 of Lepsius, "Denkmäler"; its sides are covered with hieroglyphs.

SMALL OBELISKS, OR STELAE, OF THOTHMES III, KARNAK.[2]

Far within the great temple of Karnak, and in front of its ancient granite sanctuary, are two small shafts of syenite, called by Bonomi and Cooper decorative obelisks, but by Jollois and Rawlinson called stelae. Rawlinson compares them to the "Jachin and Boaz" of the Temple of Solomon. Strictly speaking, they are rather stelae than obelisks; they appear never to have had pyramidions; in their decorations they differ greatly from other monoliths. Jollois conjectures that statues were once placed upon them.

On their north and south sides are sculptured three lotus-flowers (the emblem of immortality, Heeren) in very high relief; the sculptures still show the traces of the brilliant colors with which they were formerly painted. Above the flowers is the royal cartouche. The east and west sides bear three bass-reliefs, representing the king received by the deity. Above these reliefs are a few hieroglyphs. According to Cooper, these inscriptions show the name of Thothmes III, though the shafts may have been erected by his sister Hatasou.

HELIOPOLIS OBELISK.

At the former site of the temple of Heliopolis stands the most ancient of all the great obelisks now existing, and the most ancient of all known obelisks (see Plate xli), if we except the small ones found by Lepsius at Memphis, and by Mariette and Villiers Stuart at Drah Abou'l Neggah. In front of the temple, as restored by Amenhat I, xii dynasty, and his son, Usortesen I,[3] and on either side of the great propylon, a pair of obelisks (the "Jachin and Boaz" of the Egyptian sanctuary, Rawlinson's "Egypt," ii, 148), was erected by Usortesen.[4] Of this pair, the present obelisk of Heliopolis alone

[1] "Descr. de l' Égypte Antiq.," vol. iii, pl. 170) : "The precision with which it is put on its base is remarkable; it is in the very axis of the temple, and this precision, considering its vast weight, shows the use of mechanical appliances the most exact and powerful. The inscriptions show that the summit of the obelisk was covered with 'pure gold.' Unless this means an apex overlaid with a casing of gilded copper (like the obelisk now at Heliopolis), this possibly refers to the sphere (of gold?) which is represented on certain bass-reliefs at Sakkarah. The obelisk itself was, no doubt, gilded from top to bottom: in examining closely, one may see that the hieroglyphs were carefully polished, and that the plain surface of the monument was left comparatively rugged, from which it may be inferred that the plain surface, having a coating of white stucco (the like of which may be seen in so many Egyptian monuments), alone received this costly embellishment of gilding, the hieroglyphics themselves retaining the original color and actual surface of the granite."

[2] "Descr. de l' Égypte Antiq.," vol. iii, pl. 30, Nos. 7, 8. Lenormant, "Musée," pl. xvii, No. 10. Rawlinson, "Egypt," vol. i, p. 229. Ebers, "Caire Philae," pp. 193, 272.

[3] *Various spellings:* Usortesen, *Baedeker ;* Usortasen, *Rawlinson* "Egypt"; Usirtasen, *Mariette ;* Sesortasen, *Rawlinson* ("Anc. Hist.") ; Asertisen, *Parker ;* Osirtasen, *Murray.*

[4] Usortesen I, B. C. 2371-25, Lepsius; 2433-2400, Brugsch. The xii dynasty, B. C. 2380, Lepsius; 2466, Brugsch; 2781, Bunsen; 3064, Mariette; 2080, Wilkinson.

THE OBELISKS AT KARNAK

Record of all Egyptian Obelisks. 123

remains, still occupying, after the lapse of thousands of years, the pedestal on which it was originally placed.

Both obelisks were originally adorned with copper caps. St. Ephrem Syrus (born about A. D. 308, died about 378), in his commentary on Isaiah, xxiii chapter, says: "The cap which is on the top of each of these columns is of copper, and of the weight of one hundred pounds, and even more."[1] The copper caps are also mentioned by Denys of Telmahre, Patriarch of Antioch, who wrote about A. D. 840.[2] Ebn-Khordadbeh, an Arabian writer of the third century of the Hegira, about the ninth century of our era, is quoted as follows: "At Ain-Schems (Heliopolis) are two columns, the remains of the greater number which were formerly here; at the top of each is a collar of copper. From one of the two the water descends to about midway of the column, which is discoloured."[3]

Mohammed ben-Abd-alrahin, who visited Egypt in A. D. 1118, writes as follows: "Upon its summit is a covering of copper, as beautiful as gold, on which is represented the figure of a man seated in a chair and looking to the east."[4] Abd-el-Lateef[5] describes the obelisk thus: "In this town are the two famous obelisks called Pharaoh's Needles; they have a square base, each side of which is ten cubits long, and about as much in height, fixed on a solid foundation in the earth. On this base stands a quadrangular column of pyramidal form, one hundred cubits high, which has a side of about five cubits at the base, and terminates in a point. The top is covered with a kind of copper cap of a funnel shape, which descends to the distance of three cubits from the summit; this copper through the rain and length of time has grown rusty and assumed a green color, part of which has run down along the shaft of the obelisk. I saw one of these obelisks that had fallen down and broken in two, owing to the enormity of the weight. The copper which had covered its head was taken away. Around these obelisks were many others too numerous to count, which are not more than a third, or a half as high as the large ones."[6]

The mate of the present obelisk of Heliopolis fell prostrate about A. D. 1160, and has now entirely disappeared.[7] Its fragments, says Ebers, perhaps lie deep buried in the vicinity of the standing shaft. The foundations of this missing obelisk have lately been discovered (Murray's "Egypt," 1875.)[8]

The obelisk still standing is of the red syenite of Assouan.[9] Its pyramidion is rough and was originally covered with a cap of metal.

The pedestal and bottom of the shaft cannot now be seen, being buried under successive deposits of the mud of the Nile. The pedestal is of sandstone, according to Lenormant, and consists of two broad steps or slabs, each about two feet high, and which seem to have formed part of the paved dromos.[10]

---

[1] Works of St. Ephrem, vol. ii, p. 144. Quoted in De Sacy's "Abd-el-Lateef," p. 226.   [2] De Sacy's "Abd-el-Lateef," p. 503.

[3] De Sacy's "Abd-el-Lateef," p. 225—. This story of water flowing down the obelisk is repeated by another Arabian writer, and has been re-told in our own times by M. de Hammer, who visited Heliopolis in 1801 (De Sacy).

[4] De Sacy's "Abd-el-Lateef," p. 225—. Kodhai, quoted by Donaldson, in Parker, p. 29, says the same. De Sacy adds a note that this figure of a man was engraven on the cap, and not—as had been said in an earlier and erroneous translation of the passage—a statue erected above the cap.

[5] "Abd-el-Lateef." Relation de l' Égypte. Traduit par Silvestre de Sacy. Paris, 1810.—Abd-el-Lateef, an Arabian physician from Bagdad, who visited Egypt about A. D. 1190 (Mariette), and wrote in 1201 (De Sacy).

[6] A highly exaggerated estimate of the amount of metal upon these obelisks is given by Mohammed ben-Ibrahim Djezi (or Djezeri) in his chronicle of the year 656 of the Hegira, corresponding to the year 1258 of our era (De Sacy): speaking of the obelisk then fallen, he says that "within it [dans son intérieur, De Sacy's translation] were found nearly twenty thousand pounds [two hundred quintaux] of copper, and from its top the same was taken to the value of ten thousand dinars." De Sacy's "Abd-el-Lateef," p. 225—.

[7] It fell in 1160, and not in 1260 as MaKrizi states (Ebers). For the error of Djezi (Djezeri) and MaKrizi as to this date, see De Sacy's Abd-el-Lateef, p. 225—. Abd-el-Lateef saw the obelisk lying prostrate. The notes of Langles upon this point in Norden should be corrected, says De Sacy.

[8] Lenormant says it was overthrown by the Arabs in their search for hidden treasure.

[9] For plates or descriptions of this obelisk see: Kircher, "Œdipus," vol. iii, p. 333. "Descr. de l' Égypte, Antiq.," vol. i, p. 229. Lepsius, "Denkmäler," pt. ii, pl. 118. "Thomas Shaw's Travels," Oxford, 1738, (plate,) p. 412. Lenormant, "Musée," pl. xxix No. 3.

[10] I cannot find the record of the excavation and measurement of this pedestal.

A single column of boldly and simply cut hieroglyphics, repeated on each of the four faces of the shaft, bears the name of Usortesen I, "the loved of the gods of Heliopolis." The inscription on two sides is rendered illegible by the cells of bees filling up the deeply engraved hieroglyphics.

Dean Stanley thus described his impressions at the sight of this venerable shaft : " In these gardens [gardens which partly cover the site of Heliopolis] are two vestiges of the great Temple of the Sun, the high-priest of which was the father-in-law of Joseph, and, in later times, the teacher of Moses.—One is a pool, overhung with willows and aquatic vegetation—the spring of the Sun.—The other, now rising wild amidst garden shrubs, the solitary obelisk, which stood in front of the temple, then in company with another, whose base alone now remains. It has stood for nearly 4,000 years. It was raised about a century before the coming of Joseph : it has looked down on his marriage with Asenath : it has seen the growth of Moses : it is mentioned by Herodotus : Plato sat under its shadow : of all the obelisks which sprang up around it, it alone has kept its first position. One by one it has seen its sons and brothers depart to great destinies elsewhere. This remarkable pillar (for so it looks from a distance) is now almost the only landmark of the great seat of the wisdom of Egypt."

LARGE OBELISK OF CONSTANTINOPLE.[1]

The obelisk now standing in the Atmeidan, the ancient hippodrome at Constantinople, bears the cartouch of Thothmes III, but where he erected it is in doubt; Brugsch states at Heliopolis, Birch at Karnak, and Cooper at Thebes, and between these three opinions the weight of authorities is about equally divided. There is some excuse for the belief that it was originally the companion of the one in Rome now known as the Lateran obelisk. Birch speaks of Bonomi's intention, apparently never carried out, to write a paper on its history. He attributes it to the earliest period of the reign of Thothmes III. It is imperfect, the lower end having been removed or broken off. Ancient Byzantine writers, quoted by Zoega, affirm that the lower part was standing in the Strategium in their time.

It is believed that this obelisk was removed during the reign of Constantine the Great (A. D. 306-337) from its original site to Alexandria. The Emperor Julian (A. D. 360-363), in a letter addressed to the citizens of Alexandria, makes mention of a monolith then lying at that city, and which Constantine had transported thither with the intention of removing it to Constantinople; he urges the citizens to forward the shaft to the place of its destination, and offers, in return for such a service, to present them with his own colossal statue. According to Zoega, the ship which conveyed the obelisk from Alexandria was driven ashore in a storm at some point near Athens, whence the shaft was at last brought to Constantinople in the reign of Theodosius (A..D. 379-395).

The inscriptions on the pedestal show that the obelisk was set up in its present position by Theodosius about A. D. 399, Cooper; A. D. 390, Zoega.

Birch conjectures that this obelisk at first stood in the fifth quarter of the city. Having been overthrown by an earthquake and broken, it was removed to and re-erected where it now stands. Balt's translation of Petrus Gyllius' "Antiquities of Constantinople" (first edition, published in 1562) describes the obelisk as "supported by four square, broad pieces of brass, each one and one half feet high. From the ground there rise two steps against the pedestal, the lowermost of which is one foot high and of the same breadth. The upper step is two feet high, and projects four feet and four fingers' breadth beyond the pedestal. The steps are not laid within the pedestal, but are joined to it outside, as appears by the cement. Upon the steps stands the pedestal, which is every way twelve feet broad, four feet eight digits in height, and projects beyond the base one and one half feet. Somewhat above one foot higher it is more contracted, and does not project beyond its base; for from the top of the

---

[1] P. Gyllius, "De Constantinopoleos Topographia," bk. i, c. 11. Kircher, "Œdipus," vol. iii, p. 305. C. Niebuhr, "Reisebeschreibung nach Arabien," vol. i, pl. iv. "Transac. Roy. Soc. Lit.," second series, vol. ii, p. 218. Lepsius, "Denkmäler," vol. v, pl. 60.

THE OBELISK AT HELIOPOLIS AND POMPEY'S PILLAR AT ALEXANDRIA

pedestal there is a flushing on the four sides of the obelisk, which is cut out of the same stone of which the pedestal is made, and is one foot thirteen digits high. The corners of the top of the pedestal are worn and defaced, but are repaired by four stones of Thebaic porphyry marble, each of them one and one half feet high; for all the fluted part of the pedestal that lies between these four angular stones, together with the upper part of it, supports the base, which is seven feet thirteen digits high, and projects one and one half feet beyond the bottom of the shaft of the obelisk, to the breadth of nine feet nine digits. It is also carved on all sides, as is also the pedestal, which is carved with curious statues cut in *basso-rilievo*." John Sanderson, who was at Constantinople in 1594, has the following: "In the midst of the Atmeidan is to be seen, raised upon four dice of fine metal, a very fair pyramid of mingled stone, all of one piece, fifty cubits high, carved with heroical letters; resembling the Agulia of Rome. Its foot is double; in the first foundation, which is two cubits high, is carved the manner and the way which they took to set up this pyramid or obelisk; in the second foundation, which is four cubits high, are carved the tyrants conquered by Theodosius, who bring presents and render obedience on every side to the said emperor, he also being carved in the midst."

The faces of the pyramidion are sculptured with square vignettes, in which is Thothmes III standing before the divinity Amen. On each face of the shaft, just below the pyramidion, is another square vignette, in which Thothmes is kneeling before the enthroned god and presenting offerings.

A single column of large and finely chiselled hieroglyphs appears on each face of the obelisk. The inscriptions have a certain historical importance, as they are among the earliest Egyptian records which mention Naharana, or Mesopotamia. This country is here termed the frontier of the Egyptian realm: the first attack upon it by Egypt had taken place in the reign of Thothmes I.

The following is Chabas' translation of the inscriptions in two vignettes and on the four sides.

OVER THE KING SITTING DOWN.

Amen Lord of the thrones of the two lands,
Dwelling (in Thebes), great god,
He gives all life, all happiness, all stability.

OVER THE KNEELING PHARAOH.

The good God, Lord of the earth,
Master of making things,
The king of upper and lower Egypt
Ra-men-kheper, son of the sun,
Thothmes, giving all life like the sun, for ever.

WEST SIDE.

The heaven, the kingly Horus,
Strong bull, swaying through truth,
The king of upper and lower Egypt,
Ra-men Kheper-iri-em-Ra,
Who has gone through the great circuit of Naharana,
In strength and victory, at the head of his troops,
Making a great slaughter. . . . .

SOUTH SIDE.

The heaven
The kingly Horus,
The strong bull swaying through
Truth,

The Lord of diadems
Enlarging royalty,
Like the sun on high,
The golden hawk,
Of hallowed diadems,
Warlike dominator,
King of upper and lower Egypt,
Ra-men-Kheper-Sotep-en-Ra,
He made (the obelisk) in
His monuments to his father,
Amen-Ra, Lord of the thrones of The two lands.
He erected . . . .

EAST SIDE.

The heaven
The kingly Horus,
Uplifting the white crown,
Beloved by the sun,
King of upper and lower Egypt,
Lord of diadems,
Swaying through truth
The love of the two lands:
Ra-men-Kheper, son of the sun,
Lord of victory,
Chastiser of the whole earth,
Who has set his boundary
At the horn of the earth,
At the extremities of Naharana[1]
. . . .

---

[1] Here the term, horn of the earth, refers to the southern mountains; and the extremities of Naharana, to the northern limit of Egypt at the time.

Record of all Egyptian Obelisks.

NORTH SIDE.

The heavens,	Foster child
The kingly Horus,	In the arms of Neith, the
Strong bull,	Divine mother;
Beloved by the sun,	As a king;
The king of upper and lower Egypt,	He has conquered all lands.
Ra-men-Kheper, whom Kheper-Ra has magnified,	Protracted (is) his life;
Nursling of Tum,	Lord of feasts of thirty years.

SMALL OBELISK AT CONSTANTINOPLE, OR PRIOLI OBELISK.

The syenite obelisk now standing, according to Long, in the gardens of the Sultan at Constantinople, is so little known—its inscriptions never having been published—that it is impossible to decide upon its history, or properly to describe it.[1] Long identifies it with the smaller obelisk of Constantinople, mentioned by Peter Gyllius, whose description of that city was published in 1632. The words of Gyllius are as follows: "When first I arrived in Constantinople I saw two obelisks: one in the Circus Maximus; another in the Imperial Precinct, standing on the north side of the first hill. It was of a square figure, and erected near the houses of the Grand Seignor's glaziers. A little time after, I saw it lying prostrate without the precinct, and found it to be thirty-five feet in length. Each of its sides, if I mistake not, was six feet broad, and the whole was eight yards in compass. It was purchased by Antonius Priolus, a nobleman of Venice, who sent it thither, and placed it in St. Stephen's Market." Long, however, states that it was never removed from Constantinople.

Cooper concludes from its dimensions that it is probably a monument of the Middle Empire; but Parker assigns it to Nectanebo I, B. C. 378-360, xxx dynasty,—one of the three independent dynasties given by Manetho as interrupting the rule of the Persian power in Egypt. Nectanebo, while bravely contending against these foreign foes, yet found opportunity for some additions to the buildings at Thebes, and built a small temple to the goddess Hathor at Philae.

OBELISKS IN ROME.

SANTA MARIA MAGGIORE AND MONTE CAVALLO.

The obelisks now standing in the piazza of the basilica of Santa Maria Maggiore and before the Quirinal Palace in Rome appear to have been formerly companions. Both are without hieroglyphical inscriptions, and, therefore, there is no means of determining where and by whom they were originally erected. Tradition ascribes them to a king of the vi dynasty, variously designated Pepi Merira, Papa Maire, Phiops, and Apappus, who reigned, according to Lepsius, B. C. 2714.[2] Zoega conjectures that they were erected at Heliopolis: one by a certain Smarres, B. C. 1050; the other by Phius or Phaseus, B. C. 1000. Kircher agrees with Zoega as to the former (Santa Maria Maggiore), but assigns the latter to Apries (Uhabra or Hophra), xxvi dynasty. Parker conjectures that the obelisk of Monte Cavallo was erected by Psammetik II,[3] xxvi dynasty. All of which goes to show that nothing definite is known of the origin of these two obelisks.

It is believed that they were removed from Egypt to Rome during the reign of the Emperor Claudius, A. D. 41-54.[4] They were subsequently erected before the mausoleum of Augustus, Zoega thinks by Vespasian or Titus about A. D. 79. When they were overthrown is not known. Some authorities assert by Robert Guiscard, who died A. D. 1085, who is supposed to have devastated this mausoleum. They were long afterward found in fragments. That of Santa Maria Maggiore

---

[1] Peter Gyllius, "Antiq. of Constantinople," Ball's translation, p. 104. Long, "Egyptian Antiquities," vol. i, p. 332.
[2] Kircher, "Œdipus," vol. iii, p. 368.
[3] Parker contradicts himself; on his p. 1 he says, "both perhaps by Popi"; on his pl. vi, "Cavallo by Psammetik II"; also, "brought by Augustus and set up as gnomon."
[4] Cooper and Murray state that Claudius removed these obelisks A. D. 57. Claudius died A. D. 54.

THE PARIS OBELISK.

THE CONSTANTINOPLE OBELISK.

Plate XLII

was unearthed during the pontificate of Sixtus V, in three pieces and without its pyramidion. Fontana restored and placed it on its present site in 1587. That of Monte Cavallo was not disinterred until 1789. It was found without a pyramidion and in two pieces, and re-erected where it now stands, by order of Pius VI, in the same year. The famous "Horse Tamers" discovered in the baths of Constantine in Rome are placed on either side of its pedestal.

THE LATERAN OBELISK.

The obelisk now standing in front of the basilica of S. Giovanni in Laterno was the largest of all known obelisks. The sculptures and hieroglyphs on it prove that it originally stood at Thebes.[1] Thothmes III ordered it to be made, but his successor, Thothmes IV, finished and placed it in position thirty-five years afterward. About A. D. 330 it was removed from Thebes to Alexandria during the reign of Constantine the Great, who designed transporting it to Byzantium. About 357 Constantius, his son, removed it to Rome and caused it to be erected in the Circus Maximus. There is no record of its fall. But during the pontificate of Sixtus V it was found buried among the ruins of the circus, broken into three pieces. Fontana restored and placed it in its present position in 1588.

The inscription[2] is engraved on the four sides. It bears the cartouches of Thothmes III, Thothmes IV of the xviii dynasty, and Ramses II of the xix, who restored and set it up again. It has a certain chronological interest from mention of thirty-five years between Thothmes III and Thothmes IV. The translation of those lines which relate to the kings of the xviii dynasty only is given. Next to the chronological data one of the most interesting notices found in the inscription is that of the barge of the god Amen-Ra, which was made of cedar, cut down in the land of Rutennu or Syria. These barges each had different names and that of Thothmes III is mentioned in the inscription of Amenhat. It will be observed that in the reign of Thothmes IV Egypt is mentioned as dominant over foreign nations and not undertaking further campaigns.

The text and a translation have been published by Ungarelli, "Interpretatio Obeliscorum," fo., Rom., 1842, tab. i ; the text only, by Zoega, "De Usu et Origine Obeliscorum," fo., Rom., 1797 ; and also by Kircher, "Œdipus," iii, 164. The latter part, owing to an incorrect joining of the fragments, is confused and unintelligible.

NORTH SIDE.

Scene on the pyramidion[3]: THOTHMES III adoring AMEN-RA, and the inscription,
"The good god RA-MEN-KHEPER like the Sun."
"AMEN, TUM."[4]
THOTHMES III kneeling to AMEN-RA seated on his throne.
"The King of the Upper and Lower country, RA-MEN-KHEPER, Son of the Sun, THOTHMES like the Sun, Immortal."
"AMEN-RA, Lord of the seats of Upper and Lower countries, gives all life, stability, and power."

ON THE OBELISK.

Central line of hieroglyphs: THOTHMES IV adoring the hawk of HAR-EM-AKHU.[5]
The good god, RA-MEN-KHEPERU Lord of the World, gives incense that he may be made a giver of life.
Central line: "The HARMACHIS, the living Sun, the strong Bull beloved of the Sun, Lord of Diadems very terrible in all lands, the Golden Hawk the very powerful, the Smiter of the Libyans, the King RA-MEN-KHEPER,

---

[1] Although the inscriptions repeatedly mention Thebes, yet Bonomi, Murray, Parker (p. 2), and Cooper (pp. 3 and 35) state that it was erected at Heliopolis. Kircher ("Œdipus," vol. iii. p. 162), Zoega (p. 591), Rawlinson (vol. ii, p. 241), Brugsch (vol. i, p. 404), and Birch (in "Records of the Past," vol. iv, p. 9) pronounce this to be a Theban obelisk. Ammianus Marcellinus (bk. xvii, ch. iv) speaks of the obelisk removed by Constantine, which has been identified as the Lateran obelisk, as "especially dedicated to the sun god and set up within the precincts of his magnificent temple," which would be as applicable to Thebes as to Heliopolis.

[2] "Records of the Past," vol. iv, p. 9.
[4] Titles of the god Amen-Ra.
[3] The apex of the obelisk.
[5] Harmachis, or sun in the horizon.

the son of AMEN-RA, of his loins, whom his mother MUT gave birth to in Asher, one flesh[1] with him who created him, the Son of the Sun, THOTHMES (III) the Uniter of Creation, beloved of AMEN-RA, Lord of the thrones of the Upper and Lower country, giver of life like the Sun for ever."

SOUTH SIDE.

Pyramidion, upper line: "The King RA-MEN-KHEPERU (THOTHMES IV), giver of life, beloved of AMEN-RA, Lord of the thrones of the two countries."
THOTHMES III adoring AMEN-RA.
"The Son of the Sun, THOTHMES (III), giver of life like the Sun for ever."
THOTHMES III kneeling, offering wine to AMEN-RA seated on a throne.
"The King RA-MEN-KHEPER, Son of the Sun, THOTHMES (III), giver of life like the Sun for ever."
The goddess UAT[4] gives a good life, AMEN-RA, Lord of the seats of the Upper and Lower country, gives life, power, and stability.
THOTHMES IV seated on a throne adoring the hawk of HARMACHIS.
"The good god RA-MEN-KHEPERU, giver of life like the Sun."
AMEN-RA, King of the gods, (says) "Thou has received life in thy nostril."
Central line: "The HAR-EM-AKHU, the living Sun, the strong Bull, crowned in Thebes, Lord of diadems, augmenting his kingdom like the Sun in heaven, the Hawk of Gold, the Arranger of diadems, very valiant, the King RA-MEN-KHEPER, approved of the Sun, Son of the Sun, THOTHMES (III), has made his memorial to his father, AMEN-RA, Lord of the seats of the Upper and Lower countries, has erected an obelisk to him at the gateway of the temple before Thebes, setting up at first an obelisk in Thebes to be made a giver of life."

EAST SIDE.

Pyramidion: THOTHMES III taken in hand by AMEN-RA.
"The good god, RA-MEN-KHEPER, giver of life like the Sun.'
THOTHMES III kneeling and offering wine to AMEN-RA seated on a throne.
"The King RA-MEN-KHEPER, Son of the Sun, THOTHMES (III), giver of life like the Sun, gives water."
"Amen-Ra, King of the gods, gives life, stability, and power."
THOTHMES III standing, offering a pyramidal cake to the hawk of HAR-EM-AKHU.[2]
"The good god, RA-MEN-KHEPER, giver of life, gives a pyramidal cake of white bread that he may become a giver of life."
Central line: The HAR-EM-AKHU, the living Sun, beloved of the Sun, having the tall crown of the Upper region, the Lord of diadems, celebrating the festivals in Truth, beloved on earth, the Golden Hawk prevailing by strength, the King of the Upper and Lower country, RA-MEN-KHEPER, beloved of the Sun, giving memorials to AMEN in Thebes, augmenting his memorials, making them as they were before so that each should be as at first; never was the like done in former times for AMEN in the house of his fathers, he made it the Son of the Sun, THOTHMES (III), Ruler of AN,[3] giver of life.

WEST SIDE.

Pyramidion: THOTHMES III received by AMEN-RA.
"AMEN, TUM."
"The good god, RA-MEN-KHEPER, giver of life like the Sun, immortal."
THOTHMES III kneeling to AMEN-RA seated on a throne.
"The King RA-MEN-KHEPER, Son of the Sun, THOTHMES (III), like the Sun, immortal, gives wine."
"UAT[4] gives life, duration, and health."
"AMEN-Ra, Lord of the seats of the Upper and Lower countries, King of the gods, Ruler of AN."
THOTHMES IV offering flowers to the hawk of HAR-EM-AKHU.
"The good god, the Lord of doing things, RA-MEN-KHEPERU, giver of life like the Sun, gives incense that he may be made giver of life."
Central line: "The HAR-EM-AKHU, the living Sun, the strong Bull, crowned by Truth, RA-MEN-KHEPER, who adores the splendor of AMEN in Thebes, AMEN welcomes him in . . . his heart dilates at the memorials of his Son, increasing his kingdom as he wishes, he gives stability and cycles to his Lord, making millions of festivals of thirty years, the Son of the Sun, THOTHMES (III), uniting existence (giver of life).

NORTH SIDE.

Right line: "The good god, the Image of diadems, establishing the kingdom like TUM, powerful in force,

---

[1] Or "substance."
[2] Harmachis, or the sun in the horizon, a title translated by Hermapion, "Apollo."
[3] Heliopolis.
[2] Buto, goddess of Northern Egypt.
[4] The goddess Buto.

OBELISKS IN ROME.

Record of all Egyptian Obelisks.

expeller of the Nine bow foreigners, the King of the Upper and Lower country, RA.MEN-KHEPER, taking by his strength like the Lord of Thebes, very glorious like MENTU[1] whom AMEN has given strength against all countries; the lands came in numbers, the fear of him was in their bellies, the Son of the Sun, Thothmes (IV) Diadem of Diadems, beloved of AMEN-RA, the Bull of his mother."

Left side: " The King of the Upper and Lower country, beloved of the gods, adorer of the circle of the gods, welcomed by the Sun in the barge, and by TUM in the ark, the Lord of the Upper and Lower countries, RA-MEN-KHEPERU, who has ornamented Thebes for ever, making memorials in Thebes, the circle of gods of the house of AMEN delight at what he has done, the Son of the god TUM, of his loins, produced on his throne, THOTHMES (IV), Diadem of Diadems."

SOUTH SIDE.

Right line: " The Son of the Sun, THOTHMES (IV), Diadem of Diadems, set it up in Thebes, he capped it with gold, its beauty illuminates Thebes; sculptured in the name of his father, the good god RA-MEN-KHEPER (Thothmes III), the King of the Upper and Lower country, Lord of the two countries, RA-MEN-KHEPERU (Thothmes IV), did it wishing that the name of his father should remain fixed in the house of AMEN. The Son of the Sun, THOTHMES (IV), giver of life, did it."

Left line: " The King of the Upper and Lower country, the Lord of doing things, RA-MEN-KHEPERU, made by the Sun, beloved of AMEN. His Majesty ordered that a very great obelisk should be completed which had been brought by his father RA-MEN-KHEPER (Thothmes III), after His Majesty died. This obelisk remained thirty-five years and upwards in its place in the hands of the workmen at the southern quarters of Thebes. My father ordered it should be set up. I his son seconded him."

EAST SIDE.

Right line: " RA-MEN-KHEPEU (Thothmes IV) multiplying memorials in Thebes of gold, lapis lazuli, and jewelry, and the great barge on the river (named) AMEN-USER-TA, hewn out of cedar wood which His Majesty cut down in the land of Ruten,[2] inlaid with gold throughout, and all the decorations renewed, to receive the beauty of his father AMEN-RA (when) he is conducted along the river. The Son of the Sun, THOTHMES (IV), Diadem of Diadems, did it."

Left line: " The good god, the powerful blade, the Prince taking captive by his power, who strikes terror into the Mena,[3] whose roarings are in the Anu.[4] His father AMEN brought him up, making his rule extended, the Chiefs of all countries are attentive to the spirits of His Majesty, to the words of his mouth, the acts of his hands, all that has been ordered has been done. The King of the Upper and Lower country RA-MEN-KHEPERU, whose name is established in Thebes, giver of life."

WEST SIDE.

Right line: " The King of the Upper and Lower country, the Lord of the upper and lower world, RA-MEN-KHEPERU son . . . . it making peaceful years, Lord of the gods, who knew how to frame his plans and bring them to a good end, who subdued the Nine bow foreigners under his sandals, the King of the Upper and Lower country . . . . watched to beautify the monuments, the King himself gave directions for the work, like him who is Southern Rampart,[3] he set it up, it remained for a while, his heart wished to create it, the Son of the Sun, Thothmes (IV), Diadem of Diadems."

Left line: " The King of the Upper and Lower countries, RA-MEN-KHEPERU (THOTHMES IV), approved of AMEN, dwelling amongst the Chiefs, born in . . . . him than every king, rejoicing at seeing the beauty of his greatness: his heart desired to place it. He gave him the North and South submissive to his spirits, he made his monuments to his father AMEN-RA, he set up a great obelisk to him at the upper gate of Thebes facing Western Thebes. The Son of the Sun whom he loves (THOTHMES IV), Diadem of Diadems, giver of life, did it."

At the base is a scene, RA seated.
" AMEN-RA, HOR; Lord of heaven."
" RA-USER-MA, approved of the Sun, RAMESES (II), Beloved of AMEN, giver of life like the Sun."
The winged disk HUT, RA again.
" AMEN.RA, lord of the seats of the Upper and Lower countries, HAR-EM-AKHU, great god, Lord of the heaven."
" The King of Upper and Lower Egypt, Lord of the two countries, RA-USER-MA, approved of the Sun, RAMESES (II), beloved of AMEN."

---

[1] A form of Ra or the Sun ; an Egyptian Mars. [2] Syria. [3] Asiatic shepherds.
[3] Title of the god Ptah or Vulcan, the eponymous deity of Memphis. [4] Libyans.

PIAZZA DEL POPOLO, OR FLAMINIAN OBELISK.

Bonomi considers this obelisk to be that which Pliny[1] mentions as the work of Sesostris; Kircher identifies it with that which Pliny ascribes to Semenpserteus; and Zoega calls it an obelisk of Ramses.[2] From the sculptures and inscriptions it appears to have been erected at Heliopolis by Seti I (xix dynasty, B. C. 1439–1388, Lepsius). Augustus caused it to be removed to Rome about B. C. 20 and re-erected in the Circus Maximus. The next record of this obelisk is that it was prostrate during the reign of Valentian, A. D. 364–375. In the pontificate of Sixtus V it was found in three pieces, removed to its present site, restored, and re-erected by Fontana A. D. 1589.

Deep holes in the upper part, similar to those in the Lateran obelisk, are supposed by Bonomi to have been the work of the Roman engineer to facilitate the work of erecting it.

The first attempt to decipher the ancient Egyptian hieroglyphics in "modern" times was made by an Egypto-Grecian priest, named Hermapion, in the fourth century after Christ. Ammianus Marcellinus[3] has preserved to us the professed translation of Hermapion, which is believed to have been of the characters engraved on this obelisk, although some authorities regard it as relating to obelisks generally, and others as relating to the Luxor, and others to the Lateran obelisks. Hermapion's translation has been sneered at by more modern Egyptologists as a shrewd effort on his part to please his masters and gain notoriety by professing a knowledge he was not possessed of. But an impartial judge may find it as satisfactory as the professed translations of his severest critics.

Hermapion's translation is as follows:

This says Helios to King Rhamestes;
We have given to thee all the world to reign over with joy,
Thee whom Helios loves and Apollo:
The strong, truth-loving son of Heron,
Born of the gods, the founder of the world
Whom Helios has chosen, strong in war, King Rhamestes,
To whom the whole earth is subdued
With strength and courage:
King Rhamestes of eternal life.

Apollo the strong, he who stands upon truth,
The Lord of the diadem, who possesses Egypt in glory,
Who has adorned the city of the sun,
And founded the rest of the world,
And has greatly honored the gods established in the city of Helios.
Whom Helios loves.

Apollo the mighty, the blazing son of Helios,
Whom Helios has chosen, and Ares the valiant has favored;
Whose good things last forever, whom Ammon loves;
Who fills the temple of the Phœnix with good things,
To whom the gods have given length of life;
Apollo the mighty, the son of Heron,
To Rhamestes the king of the world,
Who has protected Egypt by conquering foreigners;

Whom Helios loves, to whom the gods have given long life,
The Lord of the world, Rhamestes of eternal life.
Helios, the great god, the Lord of the heaven,
I have given to thee life free from sorrow,
Apollo the mighty, the Lord of the diadem, the incomparable,
To whom the Lord of Egypt has erected statues in this royal town,
And has adorned the city of Helios,
And Helios himself, the Lord of the heavens.
He has completed his noble work,
The son of Helios, the ever living king.

Helios, the Lord of the heavens:
To King Rhamestes have I given might and power;
Whom Apollo loves, the Lord of the times,
Whom Hephæstus the father of the gods has chosen through Ares,
The noble king; the son of Helios, by Helios beloved.

The great god of the city of Helios,
The heavenly, Apollo the mighty, the son of Heron,(?)
Whom Helios loves, whom the gods honor,
Who rules the whole earth, whom Helios chose,
The king mighty through Ares, whom Ammon loves;
And the bright burning king for ever.

---

[1] "Nat. His.," bk. xxxvi, ch. 14.
[2] "Œdipus," vol. iii, p. 213. Ungarelli, "Interp. Obelisc.," tab. ii. G. Tomlinson in "Trans. Roy. Soc. Lit.," second series, vol. i, p. 176. Parker, pl. v.
[3] Bk. xvii, ch. iv.

The Rev. G. Tomlinson's translation is as follows:

EAST SIDE.

Centre Column.

The Horus, the powerful, beloved of justice,
King Pharaoh, guardian of justice, approved of the sun,
Amen-Mai Rameses,
He erected edifices like the stars of heaven,
He has made his deeds to resound above the heaven,
Scattering the rays of the sun, rejoicing over them in his house of millions of years.
In the . . . . year of His Majesty,
He has made good this edifice of his father, whom he loved,
Giving stability to his name in the abode of the sun.
He who has done this is the son of the sun, Amen-Mai Rameses,
The beloved of Tum, the Lord of Heliopolis, giving life for ever.

Left-hand Column.

The Horus, the powerful, the beloved of justice,
The resplendent Horus,
The director of the years, the great one of victories,
The king, Pharaoh, guardian of justice,
Approved of the sun, son of the sun,
Amen-Mai Rameses, has adorned
Heliopolis with great edifices, honoring the gods
By (placing) their statues in the great temple.
He, the Lord of the world,
Pharaoh, guardian of justice,
Approved of the sun, son of the sun,
Amen-Mai Rameses, giving life for ever.

Right-hand Column.

The Horus, the powerful,
The beloved of the sun, the Ra,
The offspring of the gods, the subjugator of the world,
The king, the Pharaoh, guardian of justice,
Approved of the sun, son of the sun,
Amen-Mai Rameses,
Who gives joy to the region of Heliopolis,
When it beholds the radiance of the solar mountain.
He who does this is the Lord of the world,
The Pharaoh, guardian of justice,
Approved of the sun, son of the sun,
Amen-Mai Rameses, giving life like the sun.

NORTH SIDE.

Centre.

The Horus, the powerful,
Sanctified by truth,
Lord of diadems, Lord of upper and lower Egypt,
Mouth of the world, possessor (?) of Egypt,

The resplendent Horus, the Osiris (?), the divine priest of Totanen,
The king, Pharaoh, the establisher of justice,
Who renders illustrious the everlasting edifices of Heliopolis,
By foundations (fit) for the support of the heaven,
Who has established, honored, and adorned the temple of the sun,
And of the rest of the gods,
Which have been sanctified by him, the son of the sun,
Menephtha-Sethai the beloved of the spirits of Heliopolis,
Eternal like the sun.

Left.

The Horus, the powerful, the son of Set,
The resplendent Horus,
The director of the years, the great one of victories,
The king, Pharaoh, the guardian of justice,
Approved of the sun, son of the sun,
Amen-Mai Rameses,
Who fills the temple of the phœnix with splendid objects,
The Lord of the world, Pharaoh, the guardian of justice,
Approved of the sun, the son of the sun,
Amen-Mai Rameses, giving life forever.

Right.

The Horus, the powerful the beloved of the sun,
The Ra, begotten of the gods,
The subjugator of the world,
The king, Pharaoh, approved of the sun,
Son of the sun, Amen-Mai Rameses,
Who magnifies his name in every region
By the greatness of his victories,
The Lord of the world,
Pharaoh, guardian of justice,
Approved of the sun, son of the sun,
Amen-Mai Rameses, giving life like the sun.

SOUTH SIDE.

Centre.

The Horus, the powerful,
The piercer of foreign countries by his victories;
The Lord of diadems, Lord of upper and lower Egypt,
The establisher of everlasting edifices;
The resplendent Horus,
Making his sanctuary in the sun who loves him;
The king, Pharaoh, establisher of justice,
The adorner of Heliopolis,
Who makes libations to the sun,
And the rest of the Lords of the heavenly world,
Who gives delight by his rejoicings and by his eyes.

He does it, the son of the sun, Menephtha-Sethai,
Beloved of Horus, the Lord of the two worlds.

Left.

The Horus, the powerful, the beloved of justice,
Lord of the panegyries.
Like his father Ptah-Totanen; the king,
Pharaoh, guardian of justice, approved of the sun,
Son of the sun, Amen-Mai Rameses,
Begotten and educated by the gods,
Builder of their temples, Lord of the world;
Pharaoh, guardian of justice, approved of the sun,
son of the sun,
Amen-Mai Rameses, giving life like the sun.

Right.

The Horus, the powerful, the son of Ptah Totanen,
Lord of diadems, Lord of upper and lower Egypt,
Possessor of Egypt, chastiser of foreign countries,
The King, Pharaoh, guardian of justice,
Approved of the sun, son of the sun,
Amen-Mai Rameses, who causes rejoicing in Heliopolis
By displaying his royal attributes,
Lord of the world, Pharaoh, guardian of justice,
Approved of the sun, son of the sun,
Amen-Mai Rameses, giving life forever.

WEST SIDE.

Centre.

The Horus, the powerful,
The beloved of the sun and of justice,
Lord of diadems, Lord of upper and lower Egypt,
Source of foreign countries, piercer of the Shepherds,
The resplendent Horus,

Beloved of the sun, whose name is magnified;
The king, Pharaoh, establisher of justice,
Who fills Heliopolis with obelisks,
To illustrate with (their) rays the temple of the sun;
Who, like the phœnix,
Fills with good things the great temple of the gods,
Inundating (?) it with rejoicings.
He does it, who is the son of the sun,
Menephtha-Sethai, beloved of the rest of the gods
Who inhabit the great temple giving life.

Left.

The Horus, the powerful, the beloved of the sun,
Lord of panegyries like his father Ptah-Totanen,
The king, Pharaoh, guardian of justice,
Approved of the sun, son of the sun, Amen-Mai Rameses,
Lord of diadems, possessor of Egypt,
Chastiser of foreign countries, Lord of the world;
Pharaoh, guardian of justice, approved of the sun, son of the sun,
Amen-Mai Rameses, son of Totanen, giving life.

Right.

The Horus, the powerful, the son of Tum,
The Ra, offspring of the gods, subjugator of the world;
The king, Pharaoh, guardian of justice approved of the sun,
The son of the sun, Amen-Mai Rameses,
The resplendent Horus, the director of years,
The great one of victories, the Lord of the world,
Pharaoh, guardian of justice, approved of the sun, the son of the sun,
Amen-Mai Rameses, the son of Totanen, eternal.

The hieroglyphs on the central columns are deeper and better cut than those of the lateral columns, and the surfaces within them were carefully polished, while those of the lateral columns were apparently left rough.

The dedicatory sculptures on the north, south, and west faces of the pyramidion represent Seti I, those of the east face, Ramses II, both in the form of a sphinx presenting offerings to the gods. At the summit of the shaft, just below the pyramidion, and also at the bottom, are other dedicatory sculptures in which the kings are in human form. The central columns of hieroglyphs on the north, south, and west sides refer to Seti I, all others to Ramses II.

Bonomi has noticed that the figure of the god Set has been cut out by Ramses from the cartouch of his father, and the figure of Ra engraved in its place. The obliteration, however, could not be made perfect, and the long, erect ears of Set still appear above the hawk's head of Ra. This substitution by Ramses may indicate a change of religious opinion.[1]

[1] The fortunes of Set (Typhon) in Egyptian worship were extremely varied. Under the early monarchy, he appears to have had a party in his favor. The Hyksos made him the sole Egyptian deity. At their expulsion, he naturally fell back into an inferior position in the national esteem. But at the rise of the xix dynasty, he was again made prominent. Ramses I, in naming his son Seti, seems to have placed the prince under Set's protection. At a later period, though it is not known exactly when, the worship of this deity entirely ceased, and his name was erased from all monuments. Cf. Rawlinson's "Egypt," vol. i, p. 390; vol. ii, 347-350.

Record of all Egyptian Obelisks. 133

MONTE CITORIO OBELISK.

Zoega considered this obelisk to have been originally the most beautiful of all, and the best specimen of Egyptian workmanship. Evidences of these qualities still exist in spite of the grievous injuries it has sustained. Bonomi identifies it with the obelisk that Pliny ascribes to Semenpsterteus, although it is generally identified with the one he ascribes to Sesostris. Birch ascribes it to Psammetik II (xxvi dynasty, B. C. 596–591, Lepsius).[1] The inscription by Pius VI attributes it to Sesostris. There is no doubt that it originally stood at Heliopolis whence it was removed to Rome during the reign of Augustus, about B. C. 20, and re-erected in the Campus Martius. Zoega believed that it was overthrown during the invasion of Robert Guiscard, A. D. 1084, and discovered near the church of S. Lorenzo in Lucina during the pontificate of Julius II, A. D. 1503–1513. Cooper, however, states that it was not discovered until 1748. It was found in five pieces, the lower part so much damaged that it could not be used in the restoration. The pieces were removed to the present site by Antinori in 1792, by order of Pius VI. Fragments of a column of Antoninus Pius were used to repair the shaft, and for a pedestal.

The dedicatory sculptures on the pyramidion represent the king as a sphinx adoring Ra and Tum. One peculiarity of this obelisk is that it had two instead of one or three columns of hieroglyphs upon each face. All but three of the eight columns have been effaced, and those that remain are very much injured.

Pliny thus describes the use to which this obelisk was put by the Romans[2]:

> The one that has been erected in the Campus Martius has been applied to a singular purpose by the late Emperor Augustus: that of marking the shadows projected by the sun, and so measuring the length of the days and nights. With this object, a stone pavement was laid, the extreme length of which corresponded exactly with the length of the shadow thrown by the obelisk at the sixth hour [noon] on the day of the winter solstice. After this period, the shadow would go on, day by day, gradually decreasing, and then again would as gradually increase, correspondingly with certain lines of brass that were inserted in the stone; a device well deserving to be known, and due to the ingenuity of Facundus Novus,[3] the mathematician. Upon the apex of the obelisk he placed a gilded ball, in order that the shadow of the summit might be condensed and agglomerated, and so prevent the shadow of the apex itself from running to a fine point of enormous extent; the plan being first suggested to him, it is said, by the shadow that is projected by the human head. For nearly the last thirty years, however, the observations derived from this dial have been found not to agree: whether it is that the sun itself has changed its course in consequence of some derangement of the heavenly system; or whether that the whole earth has been in some degree displaced from its centre,—a thing that, I have heard say, has been remarked in other places as well; or whether that some earthquake, confined to this city only, has wrenched the dial from its original position; or whether it is that in consequence of the inundations of the Tiber, the foundations of the mass have subsided, in spite of the general assertion that they are sunk as deep into the earth as the obelisk erected upon them is high.

OBELISK IN THE PIAZZA DELLA MINERVA.

The small obelisk of the Piazza della Minerva[4] is, according to Rawlinson and Parker, the work of Uhabra (Apries, Hophra, xxvi dynasty, B. C. 591–570, Lepsius); Cooper, however, ascribes it to Psammetik II, also of the xxvi dynasty. It was probably originally erected at Saïs, the favored city of this dynasty; being dedicated to "Tum, who dwells in Saïs," and to Neith, the local deity.

The pyramidion is without sculptures. Each face bears a single column of hieroglyphs. The characters are more narrow and slender than is usual, and show imperfections of execution (Zoega). The sides are more inclined than those of other obelisks.

It is one of two obelisks (the other now stands before the Pantheon) which were removed from

---
[1] Cooper, p. 20, states that this obelisk was erected by Seti Menepthah I, and on p. 96 by Psammetik I. See Bandini, "Dell' obelisco di Cesaro Augusto," Roma, 1750. Ungarelli, "Interp. Ob.," tab. iii. Zoega (plates at end). Parker, pl. ii.
[2] Pliny, "Nat. Hist.," bk. xxxvi, ch. 15. Translation of Bostock and Riley.
[3] The name of Facundus Novus is omitted in Le Maire's edition.
[4] Kircher, "Ob. Minerveus," Ungarelli, "Interp. Ob.," tab. iii. Parker, pl. iii.

Egypt by the Romans, and used as a pair to adorn the temple of Isis and Serapis in the Campus Martius; perhaps in the time of Domitian, when the worship of the Egyptian deities became more prevalent at Rome.

It was found, together with that now before the Pantheon, in 1665, among the ruins of this temple, in a spot now occupied by the convent of the Minerva. At the direction of Alexander VII, it was erected on its present site by Bernini, in 1667. The architect placed it, most inappropriately, upon the back of a marble elephant.

PANTHEON, OR MAHUTEAN OBELISK.

The small obelisk now standing in front of the celebrated Pantheon is a monument of Ramses II,[1] xix dynasty, B. C. 1388-1322, Lepsius. It was originally erected, according to Birch, before one of the portals of the Temple of the Sun at Heliopolis.

Nothing but the cartouches of Ramses II appear on the pyramidion. Zoega says that the pyramidion was left obtuse, and is in form rather like a long cone than a pyramid. A single column of hieroglyphs is engraved upon each of the four sides of the shaft, bearing the titles of this monarch, and recording that he has "made many gifts to the house of the Sun." According to Cooper, the name of Psammetik II is also cut upon the shaft.

It is one of two obelisks (the other is that of the Piazza della Minerva) which, on their removal to Rome, were erected before the temple of Isis and Serapis in the Campus Martius; perhaps in the time of Domitian, A. D. 81-96.

It was found in 1665, together with that of the Piazza della Minerva, among the ruins of the above-named temple. The shaft had been broken[2]; the lower portion of unknown length, says Bonomi, is lacking. It was erected on its present site, by order of Clement XI, in 1711.[3]

OBELISK OF THE VILLA MATTEI, ROME.

Another small obelisk in the grounds of the Villa Mattei (now called Villa Celimontana), on the Cœlian Hill, belongs to the time of Ramses II (xix dynasty, B. C. 1388-1322, Lepsius). It is but the upper portion of the original shaft; the lower portion, as at present erected, being of modern workmanship. The place of its erection in Egypt is unknown, as is also the time of its removal to Rome; Parker (Descr. of pl. viii) says it was removed by Augustus.[4]

The inscriptions, according to Birch, are unimportant, giving only the titles of Ramses II. Cooper states that the cartouch of Psammetik II has been added.

It was found among the ruins of the ancient temple of Isis. According to Zoega, it was formerly erected in the gardens of the Convent of Ara Cœli; was presented by the Roman senate and people to Cyriacus Matthæius, and by him erected in his gardens on Monte Cœlio, in 1582. The ordinary statement, however, is that it was placed in its present position by Sixtus V, in 1590. The story is told that, at the time of its erection, the architect directing the work thoughtlessly laid his hand on the pedestal at the moment that the shaft was let fall into its place; there was no resource but to amputate the hand, leaving its crushed fingers beneath the obelisk,—where, to the eye of Roman imagination, they are still to be seen.

---

[1] See Kircher, "Œdipus," vol. iii, p. 327. Ungarelli, "Interp. Ob.," tab. iii. (No plate in Parker). Called Mahutean from the Church of St. Mahutaeus, near which it was formerly erected.—Zoega.

[2] Zoega says, "apparently broken in two pieces, of which the lower is lost." Birch says, "a truncated shaft, the lower part imperfect."

[3] According to Parker, p. 8, before its erection by Clement XI in 1711, it had been removed from the site of the Circus Maximus (Rawlinson, ii, 489, says both Minerva and Pantheon before the temple of Isis) and set up earlier in the Piazza di S. Martino, by Paul V (1605-1621). This is contradictory to the date 1665 given above. Zoega says nothing of this.

[4] Kircher, "Œdipus," vol. iii, p. 322. Ungarelli, "Interp. Ob.," tab. iii. Parker, pl. viii.

LA TRINITA DEI MONTI, OR SALUSTIAN OBELISK.

The obelisk standing opposite the church of La Trinita dei Monti is believed to have been cut from the quarry of Syene by one of the Roman emperors. Birch thinks that it stood originally in the circus of Sallust.[1]

The pyramidion is unsculptured. Three columns of hieroglyphs appear on each of the four faces; the central columns bearing the name of Seti I, and the lateral columns that of Ramses II. So little, however, does the cutting of its inscriptions resemble genuine Egyptian work, that it is the opinion of the best Egyptologists that these hieroglyphic columns are only an old Roman copy from the obelisk of the Piazza del Popolo, and are not worth the attempt to fully translate them. In the opinion of Zoega and of Birch, its rude and incomplete characters show that, though quarried in Egypt, it was brought to Rome uninscribed, and its hieroglyphs cut there Zoega says, about the time of Alexander Severus, A. D. 222–235.[2]

Clement XII (1730–1740) intended to erect it at the Lateran, but did not carry out this intention (Zoega). It was placed in its present position by the architect Antinori, in 1789, at the direction of Pius VI, whose inscription is seen on the base.

PIAZZA NAVONA, OR PAMPHILIAN OBELISK.

The obelisk standing in the Piazza Navona, although cut from the quarry of Syene, is not an Egyptian obelisk. It was executed by order of Domitian, A. D. 81–96. Rawlinson thinks that it was first erected in Egypt. According to Birch, Domitian built a Serapeum and Iseum in the Campus Martius, appointed a choir of priests with offerings of Nile water, and erected there this obelisk. He certainly revived in Rome the worship of Isis and Serapis, which had been introduced under the republic and continued under the empire but without meeting with popular favor.

In the pontificate of Innocent X this obelisk was found broken in six pieces, lying in the Circus of Romulus, sometimes called the Circus of Caracalla, but no record can be found, by the author, of how it came there. It was restored and erected in its present position by Bernini, in 1651, by order of Innocent X.

The dedicatory sculptures of the pyramidion represent Domitian adoring the gods. A single column of badly cut and shallow hieroglyphs appears on each side of the shaft, in which Domitian assumes the titles of the Egyptian monarchs and records his fame from his own standpoint.[3]

MONTE PINCIO, OR BARBERINI OBELISK.

The small obelisk of Monte Pincio was cut in Egypt by the order of the Emperor Hadrian (A. D. 118–138).[4] An oracle had foretold that the happiness of this emperor could be secured only by the sacrifice of whatever was dearest to him. His chief favorite, Antinoüs, who had accompanied Hadrian in a visit to Egypt, conceived that the sacrifice of his own life might avert the threatenings of fate, and drowned himself in the Nile. The emperor, in grief at this loss, and in memory of this self-sacrificing affection, built on the banks of the Nile, near the spot where Antinoüs had perished, a city which he called Antinoë, or Antinoöpolis. Here he raised a temple, where divine honors should be paid to the deceased favorite.

This obelisk was erected, according to Birch, about A. D. 122 by Hadrian in Rome, as he infers from the inscription, which shows that the ashes of Antinoüs were deposited in a sepulchre at Rome.

---

[1] Parker (p. 40) ascribes it to Seti I ; (p. 2) says it bears the name of Ramses II.
[2] See Ungarelli, "Int. Obelisc.," tab. vi. Zoega (plates at end). (No plate in Parker) Kircher, "Œdipus," vol. iii, p. 257.
[3] Ungarelli, "Interp. Ob.," tab. iv. Parker, pl. iv. Kircher, "Obeliscus Pamphilius."
[4] See Kircher, "Œdipus," vol. iii, p. 271. Zoega (plates at end). Ungarelli, "Interp. Ob.," tab. vi. Parker, pl. vii. Sometimes called the Veranian obelisk, from the Circus Varianus, in which it was once erected ; the Barberini obelisk, from Urban VIII (Barberini), in whose time it was discovered ; or the Ob. della Passeggiata, from the promenade on which it now stands.

On the other hand, Cooper thinks it probable that the shaft was one of a pair originally placed before the temple at Antinoë.

The sculptures on the north side of the summit of the shaft represent Hadrian standing before Ra; the other sides, Antinoüs presenting offerings to the deities.[1]

Two columns of hieroglyphs appear on each face; the engraving is shallow and not sharply cut at the edges. The inscriptions call Hadrian "the Pharaoh, the ever living, the beloved of the Nile," and mention the empress, Sabina. The most important inscription, says Birch, is this: "The divine Antinoüs, who is at rest in this city, which is in the midst of the fields [probably the Campus Martius] of the district of the powerful lord of Harama (Rome). He is recognized for a god in the divine city which is in Egypt: temples have been built to him."

At a later period, the obelisk was standing, it is said, in the Circus Varianus, having been removed thither, according to Birch, from some other position; Parker says it was erected there by Heliogabalus about A. D. 220.

Under the pontificate of Urban VIII (1623–1644) the obelisk was found near the Church of S. Croce in Gerusalemme, on the site of the Circus Varianus. It was broken into three pieces, and the apex was injured. In 1822 it was removed to its present position, by order of Pius VII, but by what architect or engineer does not appear from any record the author can find.

ESMEADE OBELISKS.

Besides the well-known twelve Egyptian obelisks in Rome, there is, according to Parker (Descrip. of pl. viii), yet another obelisk, in the garden of Mr. Esmeade, close to the Porta del Popolo, on the site of the Villa of the Domitii, the burial-place of Nero. Probably, adds Parker, this obelisk is a rude imitation of the eighteenth century.

FRAGMENTS IN ROME.

In the time of Kircher (born 1601, died 1680) there were to be seen, near the church of S. Ignazio, three fragments of obelisks, each fragment showing two columns of hieroglyphs. One of these fragments (length not given) was built into a wall; another, seven palms long, had been made the corner-stone of a building; a third, six palms long, was removed in Kircher's time to the museum which he founded, and which is now contained in the Collegio Romano. This third fragment, according to Birch, is a portion of an obelisk of Ramses II, containing his name and titles.

A fourth fragment was to be seen in front of the church of S. Bartolommeo, on the island of the Tiber. On this spot, according to Publius Victor, an obelisk was formerly erected; it is supposed, before a temple of Esculapius. The whole island was anciently faced with walls of travertine, giving it the form of a ship; the obelisk was so placed as to represent the mast. From the remains of the foundations of this shaft, discovered by Bellori in 1676, the monolith is supposed to have been of large size. The fragment described by Kircher, and afterward by Pococke, appears from the plates to be the sculptured summit of the shaft, immediately below the pyramidion. It was long preserved in the Villa Albani, but afterward removed to Urbino, and there erected.[2]

OTHER EGYPTIAN OBELISKS IN EUROPE.

OBELISK OF BENEVENTO, ITALY.

In the ancient city of Benevento is a small broken obelisk of syenite, now standing in the Cathedral Square. It was found in four fragments, the pyramidion and lower part gone. It was erected in its

---
[1] Zoega's plate shows the apex plain. Cooper (112) says the apex is *plain*. Birch says it is *sculptured*.
[2] Kircher, "Œdipus," vol. iii, pp. 379–383. Pococke, "Descrip. of the East," pl. xcl.

present position in 1698 (Zoega). A fragment of another obelisk is imbedded in the wall of the episcopal palace.[1]

The two, according to Birch, were a pair originally erected before the temple of Isis in Beneventum, by the Emperor Domitian (A. D. 81-96).

A single column of hieroglyphs was inscribed on each face of these shafts, bearing the cartouch of Domitian. The inscriptions also mention the name of Lucilius Lupus as the founder of the temple.

BORGIAN OR ALBANI OBELISK, NAPLES.

The small Borgian obelisk, once in the Borgian Museum at Velletri, is now preserved in the Museo Nazionale at Naples.[2] It was found in 1791, in four pieces, among the ruins of Præneste, now Palestrina. The upper portion of the shaft is lacking. A single column of hieroglyphs appears on each of the four faces. The characters are rather rudely and hastily done (Zoega). The much injured inscriptions afford little information; they bear the Roman names Tacitus, Sextus, and Africanus. According to Birch, this shaft was once, in all probability, the companion of the Albani[3] obelisk, and the two were erected about the time of Domitian. The Albani obelisk has disappeared. Cooper thinks it is at Munich.

OBELISKS IN THE MUSEUM AT FLORENCE.

Two very small syenite obelisks are mentioned by Cooper as now in the Egyptian Museum at Florence; the smallest examples existing, if we except that found by Lepsius. Their history, he adds, is unknown. Zoega speaks of but one obelisk, of which he says that it is uncertain at what time, or from what place, it was brought to Florence. Zoega states that the pyramidion is plain, and two columns of hieroglyphs are inscribed upon each face of the shaft.[4]

OBELISK IN THE BOBOLI GARDENS, FLORENCE.

The small obelisk now in the Boboli Gardens, Florence, is, according to Birch, a monument of Ramses II, and was formerly erected at Heliopolis. It was removed to Rome, and there set up by the Emperor Claudius, Kircher, in the Circus of Flora. In Kircher's time (early part seventeenth century) it had been transferred to the grounds of the Villa Medici, Rome. At what time it was removed to Florence and erected in its present position, the writer is unable to state.

On the pyramidion are sculptured the name and prenomen of Ramses II; above these is engraved a winged scarabæus. A single column of hieroglyphs is cut upon each face. The inscriptions speak of the king as "powerful in all countries, beloved of Tum and Ra."[5]

THE ALNWICK OBELISK, ENGLAND.

The small syenite obelisk which, according to Bonomi, is in the museum of Alnwick Castle, a seat of the Duke of Northumberland, is a monument of Amenhotep (Amenophis) II (xviii dynasty, B. C. 1565–1555, Lepsius).[6] It is the only obelisk of this dynasty after the time of Thothmes II. Its original site is not known. It was found in a village of the Thebaid in 1838; was presented by the Pacha of Egypt to Lord Prudhoe, afterward Duke of Northumberland, and was removed to England in 1840.

Its apex is broken. Immediately under the pyramidion is a vignette in which Amenhotep II is represented as kneeling and offering a conical cake to Num-Ra, the sun of the lower world; especially

---

[1] Ungarelli, "Interp. Ob.," tab. v. Champollion, "Précis," p. 95. Zoega, p. 644.
[2] Zoega, p. 192. Champollion, "Précis," p. 98. [3] Kircher, "Ob. Minervews," p. 176.
[4] Kircher, "Œdipus, vol. iii, p. 348." [5] Kircher, "Œdipus," vol. iii, pp. 317, 325.
[6] Bonomi, in "Trans. Roy. Soc. Lit.," Second Series, vol. i, p. 170. M. Prisse, in "Rev. Arch.," vol. iii, p. 731. Sharpe, "Egypt. Inscriptions," Second Series, pl. 69.

worshipped in Elephantine. Only one face of the shaft is inscribed, and that with a single column of hieroglyphs.

Bonomi remarks upon a peculiarity in the cutting of the hieroglyphs: viz., that the surface within their contour is nearly flat,—a style of cutting which, as he says, is elsewhere found only in tombs and on stelæ, generally of the age of Psammetik, xxvi dynasty. According to Birch, the name of Amenhotep has been at some time obliterated; perhaps under Amenhotep IV, who attempted to restore a ruder and more ancient worship of the sun. At a later period the monarch's name was again inserted; but, by error or by design, the name of Amenhotep III was substituted for that of the original erector.

The following is the full translation by Chabas, as given by Cooper:

VERTICAL COLUMN.
The heaven,
The Horus, King of the two lands, sun of life,
Strong bull,
Very valiant,
King of upper and lower Egypt,
Ra-aa-Kheperou (Sun, the greatest of existences),
Son of the sun,
Amen-hotep-hik-An (the peace of Amen, sovereign of Heliopolis),
He made (the obelisk)

In his monuments to his father Num-Ra;
Making to him two obelisks . . . . with the food of Ra.
He made it,
The vivifier, for ever.

AT THE APEX OF THE OBELISK.
The heaven,
Homage to Num,
He gives all life and bliss,
(To) Amen-hotep, the vivifier, for ever.

THE SION HOUSE OBELISK, ENGLAND.

According to Birch ("Egypt from the Earliest Times," p. 107), there is at Sion House, a seat of the Duke of Northumberland, a small obelisk which was originally erected in front of a temple of Khnum, built at Elephantine in the time of Thothmes III. No further particulars can be learned. It is not mentioned by Bonomi. Cooper mentions it only to say that it has not yet been published. Rawlinson ("Egypt," vol. i, p. 350) strangely says that it "was to be seen at Sion House until its demolition in 1875"; presumably referring to the demolition of Northumberland House.

This obelisk is probably identical with the preceding.

THE OBELISKS OF AMYRTÆUS, BRITISH MUSEUM.[1]

The last of the Pharaonic obelisks, according to Birch, unless the Prioli obelisk, at Constantinople, should be considered later, are the two small, broken examples now in the British Museum. Excepting the sandstone shafts of Philae, other obelisks are of the red syenite, which best typified the creating light and heat of the sun; but these shafts of Amyrtæus are, by exception, of dark green basalt. The upper portions of both obelisks are missing: one has been broken into two pieces; the other, into four pieces.

A single column of finely cut hieroglyphs appears on the four faces of each shaft, bearing the name of Amyrtæus (Cooper and Parker), a descendant of a princely Egyptian family, who, about B. C. 465, the period of Artaxerxes I, revolted against the Persian domination over his native land. Birch (in Parker, p. 54) ascribes the obelisks to Nectanebo I, B. C. 378-364, and adds that they were dedicated to Thoth (Trismegist Hermes), the god of measures, of numbers, and of the sciences and arts, and were originally erected before some small temple of that deity at or near Memphis. According to Birch, the inscriptions on both declare that the king is "beloved of Thoth, the lord of hieroglyphs"; he has "set up an obelisk in his house of basalt; it is capped with black metal (iron)." The portion of the

---

[1] Brit. Museum, Nos. 523, 524. "Descr. de l' Égypte, Antiq.," vol. v, pls. 21, 22. Lenormant, "Musée," pl. xxviii, Nos. 4, 6. Sharpe, "Egypt. Antiq.," p. 107. Bp. of Gibraltar, in "Transac. Roy. Soc. Lit.," vol. ii, p. 457. Long, "Egypt. Antiq.," vol. i, p. 50.

inscription given by Cooper is as follows: "Amyrtæus, the living, like Ra, beloved of Thoth, the great lord of Eshmunayn."

These obelisks were found at Cairo: one, noticed by Pococke, had been used as part of the framework of a window in the castle; the other was first remarked by Niebuhr, who found one of its fragments forming part of the portal of a mosque, and the other fragment used as a common doorstep. The shafts were removed by the French to Alexandria, but fell into the possession of the English in 1801, at the withdrawal of the French from Egypt.

FRAGMENT AT WANSTED, ESSEX, ENGLAND.

Zoega, whose work was published in 1797, records that the fragment of an obelisk existed at that time in Wansted, England.[1] It is not mentioned by Cooper, and no information respecting it, later than that of Zoega, can be found at present.

The fragment, as described by Zoega, was a pyramidion of pale syenite, broken from its shaft, and probably not quite complete. Its dimensions were two and one half feet in height, and nearly three feet in width. Upon each face was sculptured a vignette, representing an enthroned deity, before another figure, presumably a king, was kneeling. The deities represented were, according to Zoega, Osiris and Horus.

The fragment was brought from Alexandria to England in 1722, and placed in the grounds of Sir J. T. Long, at Wansted, Essex.

OBELISK OF CORFE CASTLE, ENGLAND.

In the sacred island of Philae, beyond the sandstone shafts at the landing-place (see obelisk of Philae), there were anciently in front of the temple of Isis two lions in stone, crouching as if to guard the approach to the shrine, and beyond them two obelisks of red syenite standing on either side of the portal. At Philae to-day the lions are broken in pieces, and of the two obelisks there remains but a fragment of one; the other has been removed to England and is now the obelisk of Corfe Castle.[2] It is a monument of a Macedonian ruler of Egypt, Ptolemy Euergetes II, B. C. 170–117.

In 1815 this monolith was found by Belzoni in front of the ancient temple of Isis. By his energy and perseverance against many obstacles it was removed from Philae in 1819 and transferred, together with its pedestal, to its purchaser, Mr. W. J. Bankes, who transported it to England and re-erected it in front of his residence, Kingston Hall, Dorset. It is now, according to Cooper, in the possession of Mr. J. W. Bankes, of Corfe Castle.

From the plate of Lepsius it appears that the pyramidion is broken and was unsculptured. A single column of carefully cut hieroglyphs is cut on each of its faces, bearing the cartouches of Ptolemy Euergetes II and his wife Cleopatra. According to Birch, the inscriptions, though filled with religious phrases, state hardly more than that the king has erected this obelisk to his mother Isis. By a singular exception to the usual rule, the hieroglyphs which relate to the monarch face in an opposite direction from that of the hieroglyphs which relate to the deity.

The pedestal is of sandstone, and is five feet nine inches high. Upon it are three Greek inscriptions of great interest: the lowest of these was cut in the stone, and is a petition to the king from the priests of the temple of Isis, to be relieved from certain taxes laid upon them by the different public officers. The two inscriptions above this are, according to Long, only painted in red letters; Cooper states that they were originally written in letters of gold. They consist of the king's reply to the petition, and of the royal order to Lochus, governor of the Thebaid; they appear from the plate of Lepsius to be much defaced, but have been restored by M. Letronne.

---

[1] Zoega, p. 108.
[2] "Descrip. de l' Égypte, Antiq.," vol. i, pl. 5. Lepsius, "Auswahl," tab. xvii. Letronne, "Éclaircissements sur une inscription grecque contenant une pétition des prêtres d'Isis dans l' Île de Philae." Belzoni, "Narrative," p. 105. W. J. Bankes, "Geometrical Plan of the Obelisk discovered at Philae."

Record of all Egyptian Obelisks.

These Greek inscriptions have played an important part in the interpretation of Egyptian hiero. glyphs. It was from their publication, together with the hieroglyphic columns of the shaft, that Champollion was enabled to decipher the cartouches of Ptolemy and Cleopatra, thus verifying the conclusions which had been previously drawn from a study of the celebrated Rosetta Stone.
The following is the original Greek inscription and its translation.

BAΣIΛEIΠTOΛEMAIΩIKAIBAΣIΛIΣΣHIKΛEOΠATPAI
THIAΔEΛΦHIKAIBAΣIΛIΣΣHIKΛEOΠATPAITHIΓΓYNAI
KIΘEOIΣEΥEPΓETAIΣXAIPEINOΠEPEIΣTHΣENTΩIABA
TΩIKAIENΦIΛAIΣIΣIΔOΣΘEAΣMEΓIΣTHΣEΠEIOIΠAPEΠI
ΔHMOΥNTEΣEIΣTAΣΦIΛAΣΣTPATHΓOIKAIEΠIΣTATAI
KAIΘHBAPXAIKAIBAΣIΛIKOIΓPAMMATEIΣKAIEΠIΣTATAIΦY
ΛAKITΩNKAIOIAΛΛOIΓPAMMATIKOIΠANTEΣKAIAIA
KOΛOΘOYΣAIΔYNAMEIΣKAIHΛOIΠHYΠEPEΣIAANAΓKA
TOΥΣIHMAΣΠAPOΥΣIAΣAΥTOIΣΠOIEIΣΘAIOΥKEKONTAΣ
KAIEKTOΥTOIOYTOΥΣTMBAINEIEΛATTOΥΣΘAITOIEPONKAI
KIΔΥNEΥEINHMAΣTOΥMHEXEINTANOMITOMENAΠPOΣTAΣ
ΓINOMENAΣΥΠEPTEΥMΩNKAITΩNTEKNΩNΘΥΣIAΣ
KAIΣΠONΔAΣΔEOMEΘΥMΩNΘEΩNMEΓIΣTΩNEAN
ΦAINHTAIΣΥNTAΞAINOΥMHNIΩITΩIΣΥΓΓENEKAIEΠIΣTO
ΛOΓPAΦΩIΓPAΨAIΛOXΩITΩIΣΥΓΓENEIKAIΣTPATHΓΩITHΣ
ΘHBAIΔOΣMHΠAPENOXΛEINHMAΣΠPOΣTAΥTAMHΔΛΛ
ΛΩIMHΔENIEΠITPEΠEINTOAΥTOΠOIEINKAIHMINΔIΔONAI
TOΥΣKAΘHKONTAΣΠEPITOΥTΩNXPHMATIΣMOΥΣENOIΣ
EΠIXΩPHΣAIHMINANAΘEINAIΣTHΔHNENHIANAΓPAΦOMEN
THNΓEΓONΥIANHMINΥΦΥMΩNΠEPITOΥTΩNΦIΛANΘPΩΠIAN
INAHΥMETEPAXAPIΣAEIMNHΣTOΣΥΠAPXEIΠAPAΥTHIEIΣTON
AΠANTAXPONONTOΥTOΥΔEΓENOMENOΥEΣOMEΘAKAIEN
TOΥTOIΣKAITOIEPONTOTHΣIΣIΔOΣEΥEPΓETHMENOIEΥTΥXEITE

TRANSLATION.

To King Ptolemy, and Queen Cleopatra his sister, and Queen Cleopatra his wife, gods Euergetæ, welfare: we, the priests of Isis, the very great goddess (worshipped) in Abaton and Philæ, seeing that those who visit Philæ—generals, chiefs, governors of districts in the Thebaid, royal scribes, chiefs of police, and all other functionaries, as well as their soldiers and other attendants—oblige us to provide for them during their stay, the consequence of which is that the temple is impoverished, and we run the risk of not having enough for the customary sacrifices and oblations offered for you and for your children, do therefore pray you, O great gods, if it seem right to you, to order Numenius, your cousin and secretary, to write to Lochus, your cousin and governor of the Thebaid, not to disturb us in this manner, and not to allow any other person to do so, and to give us authority to this effect, that we may put up a stele with an inscription commemmorating your beneficence toward us on this occasion, so that your gracious favor may be recorded for ever ; which being done, we and the temple of Isis shall be indebted to you for this, among other favors. Hail.

The following are translations of the king's reply to the petition, and of his order to Lochus (not here given in the original Greek text).

LETTER OF THE KING TO THE PRIESTS.

To the priests of Isis in Abaton and Philæ, Numenius, cousin and secretary, and priest of the god Alexander, and of the gods Soters, of the gods Adelphi, of the gods Euergetæ, of the gods Philopatores, of the gods Epiphanes, of the god Eupator, of the god Philometer, and the gods Euergetæ, greeting : Of the letter written to Lochus, the cousin and general, we place the copy here below, and we give you the permission you ask of erecting a stele. Fare ye well. In the year . . . . of Panemus . . . . and of Pachons 26.

ORDER OF THE KING.

King Ptolemy and Queen Cleopatra the sister, and Queen Cleopatra the wife, to Lochus our brother, greeting;

Record of all Egyptian Obelisks.

Of the petition addressed to us by the priests of Isis in Abaton and Philæ, we place a copy below, and you will do well to order that on no account they be molested in those matters which they have declared to us. Hail.

OBELISK OF CATANIA, SICILY.

The so-called obelisk of Catania is placed, like that of the Piazza della Minerva, Rome, upon an elephant cut in stone, and is erected in front of the cathedral.[1] It is not an Egyptian obelisk. According to Westropp, it is probably a Roman imitation. D' Orville, quoted by Zoega, states that the citizens of Catania claim that it was made there. It is probable that it formerly served as the meta of a circus. Four columns of hieroglyphs are cut upon it, each column occupying two of its faces.

In the museum of this city is preserved a fragment, a broken apex, with a part of the upper portion of the shaft. This, according to Westropp, is a fragment of a second obelisk. Zoega, however, concludes that it belonged originally to the standing obelisk: it has, he says, the same polygonal form, and the little of inscription that remains upon it would well join on upon the inscriptions of the standing shaft.

OBELISK OF ARLES, FRANCE.

In the Place de l' Hôtel de Ville of the city of Arles, Southern France, there stands an obelisk of gray granite.[2] As it is uninscribed, its ancient history is not known. Zoega conjectures that it was brought from Egypt to Arles about A. D. 315, in the reign of Constantine the Great. The gray granite from which it is hewn exactly resembles that of the not far remote quarries of Mt. Esterel, near Frejus, France. It is probable, therefore, that it is not of Egyptian, but of Roman origin, made and transported hither in the time of some one of the later Roman emperors. It is supposed to have been intended for the meta of an ancient circus at Arles; but it was never so employed; it was suffered to lie in neglect on the riverbank where it was landed.

According to Buchoz, it was found lying buried in a garden on the bank of the Rhone, 1389. The annals of the city record that Charles IX of France A. D. (1560–1574) gave orders that the shaft should be transported to some other city; but these orders were never carried out. In 1676 it was erected in its present position by the citizens of Arles, in honor of Louis XIV. Upon the apex was set a gilded sun, the emblem or device of that monarch,—such as is seen, for example, on the gates of Versailles,—and on the four faces of the pedestal were cut high-sounding inscriptions in his praise. Some restorations were made in 1829, at which time four bronze lions were placed at the angles of the base. Later, an inscription has been added in honor of Napoleon III.

LEPSIUS' OBELISK, BERLIN.

The most ancient of all obelisks now existing is that found by Lepsius, in the year 1843, in a tomb near the pyramids of Gizeh.[3] In his "Letters from Egypt," he speaks of this tomb as belonging to the beginning of the vii dynasty; but in his "Denkmäler," he classes the obelisk among the monuments of the iv-v dynasties. Its form is that of the earliest representations of an obelisk on scarabei. The following is his own account of the discovery of the shaft, in a letter written at Gizeh, Jan. 28, 1843:

"Some days ago we found, standing in its original place in a tomb of the beginning of the vii dynasty, an obelisk of only some feet in height, but well preserved, and bearing the name of the person to whom the tomb was erected. This form of monument, which plays so conspicuous a part in the New Empire, is thus thrown some dynasties farther back into the Old Empire than even the obelisk of Heliopolis."

---
[1] Zoega, pp. 87, 647.
[2] Zoega, p. 87. Buchoz, "Correspondence d' Histoire Naturelle." Murray's "France." (Wood-cut in English Encyclopædia.)
[3] Lepsius, "Briefe aus Ægypten, p. 40. "Denkmäler," vol. iv, pl. 88.

The obelisk is the smallest known, being only two feet, one and one-half inches high. It is preserved in the Royal Museum at Berlin.

OTHER OBELISKS IN EGYPT.

OBELISK OF BEGIG, OR CROCODILOPOLIS.

Near Begig (or Ebgig) in the Fayûm, and in the vicinity of the site of the ancient Crocodilopolis, and of the former position of Lake Moeris, there lies prostrate in the sands a shaft of syenite broken into two pieces.[1] It is a monument of Usortesen I (xii dynasty, B. C. 2371-2325, Lepsius,) who also erected the obelisk now standing at Heliopolis.

The broken shaft at Begig is so peculiar in form, showing two large and two small faces, that it is often called a stele rather than an obelisk. Instead of terminating in a pyramidion, it has a rounded summit, in the centre of which a deep groove is cut,—it is not known for what purpose.

As the shaft now lies, only one of its broad faces is visible. Its upper portion is occupied by five vignettes, representing the king as appearing before ten pairs of divinities, five on the right, five on the left (Chabas); the most honorable positions being assigned to the deities Amen and Phthah (Rawlinson, ii, 149). The inscriptions here give only the names of the king and the divinities. Below these vignettes are nineteen vertical columns of hieroglyphs, separated by grooved lines : the characters are very small, and, for the most part, illegible ; but the name of the monarch is recognizable. On the narrow faces of the shaft are inscriptions which speak of the king as "beloved by Phthah and by Month," Mentu, a local deity of Hermonthis, or Erment.

OBELISK IN CAIRO (?)

In Loftie's "Ride in Egypt," p. 84, is a wood-cut of a part of an obelisk, built into a gateway. No description of this fragment, however, is afforded in the text, and it may be identical with one of the Amyrtæus obelisks in the British Museum.

OBELISKS OF SÂN (TANIS).

The city of Sân in the Delta (Tanis; the Zoan of the Bible, the scene of the miracles of Moses, Psalm lxxviii, 43, and the starting-point of the Exodus, Brugsch) was made the capital of the Hyksos, or Semitic Shepherd Kings, xiii–xvii dynasties. After their expulsion, at the beginning of the xviii dynasty, it was for a time neglected; but, under the xix dynasty, it was made a royal residence, and adorned with new structures, replacing those of the hated Shepherds. Especially was it favored by Ramses II, who transferred his court to this place, and made it a new temple-city, filling it with sanctuaries, statues, and obelisks (Brugsch, "Egypt," ii, 94).

The fragments of ten or more (twelve obelisks, Ebers ; thirteen obelisks, Fergusson [2]) prostrate obelisks are found on this site [3]; the largest number ever discovered at one place. They seem to have formed a great avenue in front of a temple of Ra, and are assigned to the time of Ramses II. One, figured in the "Desc. de l' Egypte," is represented as nearly perfect ; its pyramidion is sculptured with vignettes in which a single sitting figure is shown. Some of the shafts bear one column, others two columns of hieroglyphs. Two of these obelisks, both by Ramses II, are especially mentioned by Birch : on one the scenes of the pyramidion depict the king adoring Ra and Tum : the inscriptions declare that he is "the smiter of the Shepherds," and that he "makes his frontiers wherever he wishes."

The shafts vary in size : some have a mean diameter of about five feet, and when entire may

---

[1] "Descr. de l' Égypte, Antiq.," vol. iv, pl. 71. Lepsius, "Denkmäler," vol. iv, pl. 119. Lenormant, "Musée," pl. xxvi. Lawrence Oliphant, in *Blackwood*.

[2] Ebers, "Alexandria," p. 110. Fergusson, i, 111.

[3] "Descr. de l' Égypte, Antiq.," vol. v, pl. 28, 29. Denon, "Voyage," pl. 17. Lenormant, "Musée," pl. xxix, No. 7. Burton, "Exc. Hier.," pl. xxxviii–xl.

have been from fifty to sixty feet high; those at the lower extremity of the avenue measured about thirty-three feet (Murray, Westropp, and Cooper).

OBELISK OF ASSOUAN (SYENE).

In the Syenite quarries of Assouan (Syene), from which so many splendid monuments were taken to adorn the cities of ancient Egypt, is still lying an unfinished obelisk. According to Wilkinson, the shaft was left in the quarry because of a fracture of its centre: Murray states that there is only the semblance of a fracture. It is finished on three sides, but it is still united to the quarry by its lower face. It is remarkable, says Ebers, as showing that the Egyptians often finished their works in the quarry.

OBELISK OF PHILÆ.

In the myth of Osiris, Typhon, the darkness and death, is represented as cutting the body of Osiris into fourteen fragments, and scattering them far and wide. Isis sought and gathered up the fragments, and, on each spot where one was found, raised a monument in its honor. Philæ was one of these burial-places.

In the sacred island of Philæ, especially consecrated to the worship of Osiris, the hall of reception, which visitors approached from the landing-place, was originally decorated with obelisks of sandstone (Ebers). At this point there still remains an uninscribed sandstone shaft, the apex of which is broken off and missing.[1] It is assigned to the times of the Ptolemies, by whom the principal buildings of Philæ were erected. (See obelisk of Corfe Castle.)

OBELISK OF SARBUT EL-KHADEM, SINAITIC PENINSULA.

In the Sinaitic Peninsula, on the way from Suez to Mount Sinai, are the hills called Sarbut el-Khadem, overlooking the Wadi Nasb (see obelisk of Wadi N_{as_b}). Here are ancient copper mines, once extensively worked by the Egyptians. Inscriptions here found show that mining was carried on at this point in the reign of Amenhem II, xii dynasty; centuries before the Israelites passed by in their weary march to Sinai. Inscriptions of Hatasou and Thothmes III show that mining went on under their rule. A colony of workmen was established here, bringing with them, though in their plain workmen fashion, the life and architecture of Egypt into the Peninsula. At Sarbut el-Khadem a temple was erected to the goddess Hathor, the ruins of which still remain. Here are found still standing seven or eight stelæ, from seven to ten feet high, from eighteen inches to two feet wide, and from fourteen inches in thickness, bearing the cartouches of different monarchs (Robinson's "Biblical Researches").

Here too, according to Baedeker, there stands, on a hill above the mines, an ancient Egyptian obelisk with partially obliterated hieroglyphics.[2]

OBELISK OF WADI NASB, OR NAHASB, SINAITIC PENINSULA.

The Wadi Nasb lies near the western shore of the Sinaitic Peninsula, about seventy miles S. S. E. from Suez. A little farther on to the S. E. is Sarbut el-Khadem, on the hills of that name.

At Wadi Nasb, on a hill which covers one of the old mines, the German traveller Rüppell discovered, in 1817, a small sandstone obelisk which had fallen from its pedestal.[3] The face which lay on the ground, and was thus protected from injury, proved on examination to be covered with finely cut hieroglyphs: the inscriptions on the other sides had been obliterated. Unfortunately, no

---
[1] "Descr. de l' Égypte, Antiq.," vol. i, pl. 1, 2, 4.
[2] Baedeker, "Lower Egypt," p. 512. Baedeker alone mentions this obelisk. I have quoted all that he says. I have examined all the books in Astor Library on the Sinaitic Peninsula, and find no mention of this shaft. It is not the same with the obelisk of "Nahasb" (Cooper, p. 102), for that was prostrate, while Baedeker's obelisk of Sarbut el-Khadem is standing.
[3] Rüppell, "Reisen in Nubien, Kordofan, und dem peträischen Arabien," p. 266.

copy of the hieroglyphs was preserved, and it is impossible to decide to which reign the shaft belonged. Cooper conjectures that it is to be referred to the Saïtic period,—the xxvi dynasty.

OBELISKS OF DRAH ABOU'L NEGGAH, THEBES.

In the necropolis of Drah Abou'l Neggah, on the western bank of the Nile at Thebes, were found the mummy-cases of two kings named Antef or Entef, of the xi dynasty (B. C. 2423-2380, Lepsius), which have been removed to Paris.

A small obelisk bearing the name of one of the Antefs of this dynasty was discovered here by Mariette. Its height was not more than 3.5 metres, that is, less than eleven feet (Rawlinson).[1]

Villiers Stuart reports that in 1878 he discovered in this necropolis, close to the spot where the mummy of Queen Ah-hotep had been found, two prostrate obelisks, each broken into several pieces.[2] On removing the sand in which they were buried he found them to be inscribed with well-preserved hieroglyphs, which prove, as he says, that the two shafts were erected by a king Antef of the xi dynasty. The plate which he gives shows one face of each. The inscriptions shown in this plate are translated by him as follows: on one obelisk, "The crowned Horus, sovereign of the mountain-lands, perfected of god, son of the Sun, granted life forevermore"; on the other obelisk, "Noub-Kafer-Ra, perfect of god, made for himself good and splendid temples." No dimensions are given for these shafts.

These obelisks of Drah Abou'l Neggah, if accepted as belonging to the xi dynasty, are the most ancient of all known obelisks, with the single exception of the small example found by Lepsius.

---
[1] Rawlinson, "Egypt," vol. ii, p. 148. Mariette, "Monuments Divers," pl. 50, a.
[2] Villiers Stuart, " Nile Gleanings," p. 273.

Record of all Egyptian Obelisks.

TABLE OF COMPARATIVE DIMENSIONS AND WEIGHT OF OBELISKS AS FAR AS CAN BE ASCERTAINED.

NAME OR DESIGNATION.	TOTAL HEIGHT.			THICKNESS AT BASE.			Proportion of H. to T.	Weight in pounds.
	Max. given.	Probably correct.	Min. given.	Max. given.	Probably correct.	Min. given.		
Lateran,	108'-7"	105'-6"	104'-11"	{9'-8".5 × 9'-10}	{9'-0" × 9'-10}	9'-6"	11.2	1,020,000
Hatasou, Karnak,	108–0	97–6	90–0	8–6	7–10	7–10	12.5	742,000
Assouan,[1]	95–0	95–0	95–0	11–1.5	11–1.5	11–1.5	8.5	1,540,000
Vatican,	83–1.5	83–1.5	82–4	9–4	8–10	8–10	9.4	721,000
Luxor,	82–0	82–0	77–0	8–2.5	8–2.5	7–8	10.0	568,000
Piazza del Popolo,	78–6	78–6	78–0	8–5	8–0	8–0	9.8	525,000
Paris,	82–0	74–11	74–4	8–0	7–11	7–6	9.4	498,000
Thothmes I, Karnak,	93–6	71–7	63–3	8–1.5	6–1	5–1	11.7	346,000
Monte Citorio,	72–0	71–5	69–0	7–11	7–11	7–4	9.0	460,000
New York,	71–0	69–6[2]	53–4	8–8	{7–9.25 × 7–8.25}[2]	7–5	9.0	448,000
London,	68–5.5	68–5.5	64–0	{7–8 × 7–10.3}	{7–8 × 7–10.3}	7–7	8.8	418,000
Heliopolis,	68–2	67–0	66–0	{6–0 × 6–4}	{6–1 × 6–3}	6–0	10.9	271,000
Constantinople,	59–7	55–4	50–0	7–2	7–0	6–10	8.1	299,000
Piazza Navona,	54–3	54–3	51–0	4–5	4–5	4–5	12.2	118,000
S. Maria Maggiore,	48–5	48–5	48–5	4–3	4–3	4–3	11.4	102,000
Monte Cavallo,	45–0	45–0	45–0	—	4–2	—	10.8	96,000
Trinita dei Monti,	48–0	43–6	43–6	4–3	4–3	4–3	10.8	90,000
Begig,	43–0	42–9	41–6	{6–8.5 × 4–8}	{6–8 × 4–0}	{6–8 × 4–0}	7.9	120,000
Prioli,	35–0	35–0	33–0	6–0	5–10	5–9	6.0	118,000
Philæ,	33–0	33–0	33–0	—	—	—	—	—
Monte Pincio,	30–0	30–0	30–0	3–11	3–11	3–11	7.6	42,000
Corfe Castle,	22–1.5	22–1.5	22–1	2–2	2–2	2–2	10.2	12,000
Pantheon,	20–2	20–0	17–0	2–7	2–7	2–7	8.0	13,500
Amyrtæus,	19–9	19–9	17–0	2–4	2–4	2–4	8.5	12,000
Thothmes III, Karnak,	20–0	19–0	18–10	3–6	3–6	3–6	5.2	34,000
Piazza Minerva,	17–7	17–7	16–2	2–6	2–6	2–6	7.0	11,000
Boboli Gardens,	16–1	16–1	16–1	2–5	2–5	2–5	6.6	10,000
Catania,	12–4	12–4	12–4	—	—	—	—	—
Thebes,	11–0	11–0	11–0	—	—	—	—	—
Benevento,	11–9	9–0	9–0	2–1	2–1	2–1	4.3	5,000
Villa Mattei,	8–3	8–3	7–4	2–7	2–7	2–7	3.2	4,000
Alnwick,	7–3	7–3	7–3	{0–9.7 × 0–9}	{0–9.7 × 0–9}	0–9	9.2	600
Wadi Nasb,	7–11	7–11	7–11	—	—	—	—	—
Florence,	7–0	7–0	7–0	—	—	—	—	—
Borgian,	6–7	6–7	6–7	1–8	1–8	1–8	—	—
Florence,	5–10	5–10	5–10	—	—	—	—	—
Frag. Rome,	—	5–1	—	—	—	—	—	—
Frag. Rome,[3]	—	4–5	—	—	—	—	—	—
Albani,	—	—	—	—	—	—	—	—
Sân (Tanis),[4]	—	—	—	—	—	—	—	—
Cairo,	—	—	—	—	—	—	—	—
Essex,[5]	—	2–6	—	—	—	—	—	—
Lepsius,	2–1.5	2–1.5	2–1.5	0–9	0–9	0–9	2.4	200

[1] Still in the quarry at Syene.
[2] Measurements exact.
[3] There are also other fragments at Rome.
[4] A number of fragments of obelisks exist here.
[5] A pyramidion only.

CHAPTER VII.

NOTES ON THE ANCIENT METHODS OF QUARRYING, TRANSPORTING, AND ERECTING OBELISKS.

QUARRYING.

WE can only admire, but not explain, the marvellous achievements of the Egyptian engineers. At a time when other ancient nations had hardly felt the first breath of civilization, Egypt had made a vast advance in all the arts and sciences. Gifted with great intellectual powers,—coming to even those works of theirs which are the oldest to us with the experience of many centuries, their monuments appear to us as marvels. We count some of their processes among the "lost arts." The daring modern world, so self-conscious as it is of its superiority in knowledge and in almost intelligent machinery over the world of any preceding age, would yet hesitate to compete with those long-dead Egyptians in many an architectural or mechanical *tour de force*. "It is doubtful," says Rawlinson ("Egypt," vol. i, p. 484), "whether the steam-sawing of the present day could be trusted to produce in ten years from the quarries of Aberdeen, a single obelisk such as those which the Pharaohs set up by dozens." To have built the pyramids; to have erected the great "Hall of Columns" at Karnak; to have sculptured and polished colossal statues of syenite with the care and delicacy of gem-cutting; to have severed from their native rock, transported, finished, and set up the giant obelisks of Queen Hatasou in the short space of seven months,—these are achievements which rank their authors among the foremost of the builders of the world, the foremost of the monumental nations.

We come now to speak of the quarrying, transportation, and elevation of obelisks. The data are few; the questions are difficult, and we cannot hope to give them full solution. It may be that papyri as yet unknown, tablets of inscriptions yet to be deciphered, paintings on the walls of some royal tomb which is yet inviolate, may hereafter throw light upon the mechanical methods which are at present obscure to us; but, as yet, the veil of oblivion which has fallen over the secrets of Egyptian engineering skill has never been wholly lifted.

All obelisks now existing are of red granite from Syene (Assouan), except the sandstone example at Philæ, and the basalt shafts of Amyrtæus in the British Museum. The situation of the quarries of Assouan was most favorable for the transportation of the enormous blocks of stone which were there extracted; the quarries are below the first cataract, and the great roadway of the Nile was open thence to the gates of the various cities of Egypt. The rock of these quarries, called from the name of the place syenite, is remarkably free from cracks and from veins of foreign matter, as hard as iron, of the fine ruddy color which symbolized to the Egyptian the rays of the sun god, and taking the most beautiful and brilliant polish. The quarries still show the traces of the workmen's labor; the marks of their tools are on many an unremoved block or column. There still lies a gigantic monolith, chiselled into form on three of its sides, but its fourth face not yet severed from the rock.

Quarrying, Transporting, and Erecting Obelisks.

(See the obelisk of Assouan.) How sure of their skill must have been those quarrymen, so carefully and with such labor to three fourths complete their work, while still the shaft made but one piece with the formless mass of stone beneath it!

It is from the examination of this shaft and of other blocks lying near by, together with the observations of Gau and De Rozière at the quarries of Gertaas and Silsileh, that the methods of the Egyptian quarrymen have been, to a certain extent, made known to us.

On a mass of quarried syenite, lying three hundred metres southeast of modern Syene, De Rozière found tool-marks of an unusual character. The whole surface of the rock is covered with marks of the chisel, but cut with such change of direction of the tool as to form to the eye parallel horizontal lines about seven inches apart. Thirty such parellel lines were observed, and in a single line three hundred and forty-seven chisel-strokes were counted. De Rozière can offer no full explanation of this, but it is his opinion that the strokes indicate more than the force of the human hand, and that they were probably produced by some sort of machine capable of striking a violent blow. ("Descr. de l' Egypte, Antiq.," vol. i, pl. 32.) No other example of this kind of quarry-work was found by the French engineer.

Belzoni, in his narrative, says of the Assouan quarries: "It appeared to me that the pieces of granite were procured by cutting a line with a chisel, about two inches deep, around the stone intended to be removed, and then giving a great blow by some machine, which separated the part like glass when cut by a diamond." Very curious figures of such machines had been given by Kircher—the construction of his own imagination—in his "Œdipus," vol. ii, long before Belzoni's day.

It is certain, however, that in by far the greater number of instances which have been observed, the quarry-marks indicate that the blocks were severed from their native bed by processes much more simple: either by the use of fire, or of wedges, whether of wood or iron.

It has been supposed by some that the cleavage of the rock was accomplished by fire. According to Sir J. F. Herschell, this method is employed to-day in India: "In the granite quarries near Seringapatam, the most enormous blocks are separated from the solid rock by the following neat and simple process. The workmen having found a portion of the rock sufficiently extensive, and situated near the edge of the part already quarried, lays bare the upper surface, and marks on it a line in the direction of the intended separation, along which a groove is cut with a chisel, about a couple of inches in depth. Above this groove a narrow line of fire is then kindled, and maintained till the rock below is thoroughly heated, immediately on which a line of men and women, each provided with a pot full of cold water, suddenly sweep off the ashes, and pour the water into the heated groove, when the rock at once splits with a clear fracture. Square blocks of six feet in the side, and upwards of eighty feet in length, are sometimes detached by this method." Long before, Agatharcides, in his account of the gold mines of Egypt, had mentioned that the rocks were split by burning wood, but had not described the process employed.

The grooves mentioned above by Herschell, cut to define the size and form of the block to be extracted, have been observed in the Egyptian quarries in repeated instances, cut two or three inches wide and deep. But within these grooves are cut holes which indicate the use of wedges. Often, according to De Rozière, the grooves are not found, but only the wedge-holes, about two inches long and deep, by one inch wide, arranged in one long straight line. From six to seven of these holes were found in the extent of one metre. The slow but ever-increasing pressure of the inserted wedges rent the rock asunder more surely and exactly than could the heavy blow of Belzoni's fancied machine.

In more modern quarrying two sorts of wedges are employed: wedges of iron, which are struck all at once with repeated blows along the whole line of the intended separation; and wedges of well-dried wood, first driven to their place, and then drenched with water. In the opinion of Wilkinson, the grooves so often found served not only to define the form of the block, but also to conduct water to the wedges. The use of wooden wedges, says De Rozière, would be much more convenient and effectual, because the pressure exerted by the expansion of the wetted wedges against the sides of the cleavage is exerted uniformly and simultaneously, so that the block is split off always in the direction of the line already traced. This he regards as the method, *par excellence*, for detaching large blocks when it is desired that they should preserve certain determined forms. He adds that it is probable that the Egyptians employed these wooden wedges in their quarrying, nor can he conceive of any other method for detaching the giant blocks required for the obelisks; percussion of iron wedges, he says, could never be instantaneous along the whole length of the block, and the risk would be incurred of breaking the shaft into at least two pieces.

An interesting account of the mode of cleavage by iron wedges, as practised by Hindoo workmen at the present day, is given in a paper on the Seringapatam obelisk, published in the "Edin. Philos. Transactions," vol. ix.[1] We have quoted above Sir J. F. Herschell's account of a mode of splitting large masses of rock by the use of fire, as practised in India: the following is Col. Wilks' description of another Hindoo method of accomplishing the same by the use of iron wedges or chisels :

The workman looks for a plain, naked surface of sufficient extent, and a stratum [Col. Wilks confesses that this term is ungeological, as applied to granite, but says that no other word will well describe the kind of mass from which these large blocks are taken] of proper thickness, sufficiently near the edge of the rock to facilitate the separation, or made so by previous trimming. The spot being determined, a line is marked along the direction of the intended separation, and a groove, about two inches wide and deep, is cut with chisels; or, if the stratum be thin, holes of the same dimensions, at one and one half feet or two feet distance, are cut along the line. In either case, all being now ready, a workman with a small chisel is placed at each hole or interval, and with small iron mallets the line of men keep beating on the chisels, but not with violence, from left to right or from right to left; this operation, as they say, is sometimes continued for two or three days before the separation is effected. Those who have seen the mode of cutting, as it is called, plate-glass, will not be surprised at their beating from one end, and the fissure also taking place from one end to the other. This is the mode by which the Seringapatam stone was separated.

Col. Wilks adds that the other method, by the use of fire, does not produce so clean fracture as this, by beating.

A saw, with which sand was employed, was sometimes (very rarely, according to De Rozière), used in the deep vertical cuttings. Saw-marks are found, for example, on the side of a basalt sarcophagus in the British Museum, and which indicate, according to Cooper, the last cutting which separated the block from the quarry. The marks of a saw were observed by De Roizère on blocks in the Assouan quarries; from their appearance, and from the traces of oxide of copper upon them, he concluded that the saw employed was of copper, and that its cutting edge was curvilinear.

It is the opinion of Cooper that, at the separation of a block from its native rock, the under horizontal surface having been cut free, the last cutting was a vertical one. He further states that, the props which supported the block from beneath having been removed, the stone, when nearly sawed through, was allowed to break off by its own weight, thus having a rough and disfiguring fracture at the lower edge: examples of this, he mentions, are to be seen in sarcophagi, now in

---

[1] The Seringapatam obelisk, to which we shall have occasion several times to refer, is thus described in a letter by Col. Wilks (" Ed. Philos. Transac.," vol. ix): The obelisk was erected at Seringapatam, in 1805, to the memory of Josiah Webbe. It was entirely the work of the Hindoos, except the design, which was furnished by a European. The plinth of the obelisk is one and one half feet thick, formed of three stones of equal dimensions, which rest on three similar stones, placed, as Col. Wilks believes, on the solid rock, which was levelled to receive them. The pedestal is a single stone, nine feet high and about seven feet wide. The base of the shaft was six feet in diameter, and a hole about three inches deep was cut in the top of the pedestal to receive it, leaving a ledge of about six inches on each side between the bottom of the shaft and the edge of the pedestal. In the judgment of Col. Wilks, the shaft is not more than sixty feet high, but he adds that others, speaking from their remembrance, make it to be at least seventy feet. The first block quarried was eighty-four feet long, but after it had been moved a few yards, it was broken by an explosion of gunpowder which was intended to break a detached stone which stood in the way.—From the plate given in the "Philos. Trans.," this obelisk tapers more rapidly as it ascends than is the case with any Egyptian obelisk.

the British Museum. Such instances as these we must believe to be the result of accident, and by no means indicate the usual mode of procedure. The unfinished obelisk now lying in the quarries of Assouan is evidence that, at least in the extraction of blocks intended as obelisks, the under horizontal surface was the last to be separated from its native rock, and we conclude, with Wilkinson (vol. ii, p. 310), that in cutting under this lower surface, supports of the native rock were at first left at regular intervals; the openings which had been excavated between these supports were then filled with beams of wood; last of all, the rock supports were cut away, leaving the block standing, without a jar or risk of fracture, upon the beams.

Both Gau and Ebers remark upon the great care shown by the Egyptian workmen that the valuable syenite should nowhere be cut to waste. Gau remarked that the blocks were taken from the quarry in the precise shape and size required. "The economy," says Ebers ("Caire à Philæ," p. 393), "with which they divided the smaller blocks excited our admiration. On the surface of a mass of stone, cut on three sides, you saw the tracing-line of the master-workman, who intended to cut from it two pillars and a slab for roofing."

On the mode of removing the blocks from the quarries, the following may be of interest. At the sandstone quarries of Hagar Silsileh, or Silsilis, there was found sculptured on the rock a representation of some implements employed by the workmen. Two of these appear to be wedges, somewhat differing in shape. The other exactly resembles in form the modern *lewis*, used by masons for raising stones: it has a circular top—which might be a kind of ring,—then a horizontal bar or bolt, while the lower part is a truncated triangle, the base of which forms the lowest part of the instrument. As these quarries, at a later date, were worked under the Macedonian and Roman rule, it is not certain that this implement is of Egyptian construction. (Long, "Egypt. Antiq.," vol. i, p. 360.)

When the blocks had been obtained from the quarry, they were then cut to exact form, reduced to a smooth surface by the chisel, and then polished by rubbing. The exactness of angle to which the huge stones employed in the Egyptian buildings were cut, the perfect jointing of contiguous blocks, and the exquisite finish given to the surface, show that in these branches of the mason's art, the workmen of Pharaonic times have never been surpassed. The immense blocks of syenite in the king's chamber in the Great Pyramid are so truly and so closely fitted together that a knife-blade could not be forced in between them. This sharp and accurate cutting of the hardest stones is especially illustrated in their sculpture of colossi and sarcophagi of syenite and basalt, and in the delicate and minute engraving seen in the best specimens of hieroglyphs, which are sometimes cut on the obelisk face to the depth of two inches, yet finished with the perfection of gem-cutting.

In Wilkinson's "Manners and Customs," vol. ii, pp. 310, 311, are representations, copied from the wall paintings of Theban tombs, of workmen engaged in levelling and squaring a block to be used in building, while others, raised on scaffoldings around a colossal statue, are cutting upon it hieroglyphs and giving it its final polish. They use both pointed and broad-edged chisels. The perfect polish of the faces of an obelisk contribute, according to De Rozière, to their preservation, since the glassy, smooth surface prevented the retention of moisture, which, acted on by heat, is the cause of the deterioration of the stone.[1]

In a paper read before the Royal Society in 1821, is mentioned the very great difficulty of repairing

[1] The process by which a fine polish is given to granite by the Hindoo workmen of to-day is described as follows by Dr. Kennedy in the *Edin. Philos. Journal*, vol. iv, p. 349: "A block of granite, of considerable size, is rudely fashioned into the shape of the end of a large pestle. The lower face of this is hollowed out into a cavity, and this is filled with a mass composed of pounded corundum stone mixed with melted beeswax. This block is moved by means of two pieces of bamboo, placed one on each side of its neck, and bound together by cords, twisted and tightened by sticks. The weight of the whole is such as two workmen can easily manage. They seat themselves upon, or close to, the stone they are to polish, and by moving the block backwards and forwards between them, the polish is given by the friction of the mass of wax and corundum. The beauty of the glossy blackness thus produced is equal to that of fine marble, and the polish is almost as durable as is the stone itself."

150 *Quarrying, Transporting, and Erecting Obelisks.*

one of the Theban statues preserved in the British Museum, and the great number of English-made tools which had been broken in replacing one of its arms. Precisely of what metal the Egyptian tools were made, and how they were tempered to the hardness requisite for their sharp and powerful cutting, has long been a theme for wonder and for much learned discussion.

The Egyptian tools were of bronze, of iron, and, in all probability, of steel.

The collections of Egyptian antiquities preserve to us swords, daggers, carpenters' tools (see chisel, saw, etc., etc., figured in Wilkinson's "Manners and Customs," vol. i, p. 401), and even chisels for cutting stone, all in bronze. The use of bronze for such implements continued, according to Wilkinson (vol. ii, p. 249), among the Greeks and Romans long after the period when iron was known.

A bronze dagger, preserved in the Berlin Museum (Wilkinson, vol. i, p. 212, and ii, 256; Rawlinson, vol. i, p. 458), is so finely tempered that even now, after the thousands of years since it came from the armorer's anvil (it was hammered and peculiarly alloyed, Wilkinson), it still springs with almost the elasticity of steel. A bronze chisel was found by Wilkinson (vol. ii, p. 255) as it had been dropped by the workman among the chippings of limestone rock in a tomb at Thebes. In general, its form is that of the chisel used by the stone-cutter of to-day: it is nine inches long; its diameter at the top is one inch; its point is seven tenths of an inch in its greatest width; it is alloyed with five and nine tenth parts of tin in one hundred. "It was very remarkable," says Wilkinson, "that its top was turned over by the blows which it had received from the mallet, while its point was intact, as if it had recently left the hands of the smith who made it." Yet he adds that the point is now easily turned by striking it against the very stone it was made to cut.

It has been queried by Donaldson and others whether the Egyptians, working with such tools, did not, by the use of some chemical agents, first soften the stone which they were to cut; or whether the stone was not first "stunned" by pounding, so that it might more easily yield to the chisel's edge; but, according to Wilkinson (vol. ii, p. 254), these suppositions are insufficient to account for the facility and efficiency of Egyptian work. He conjectures that the Egyptian workman must have dipped his chisel in moistened emery powder, and by its aid have enabled the soft tool to do its hard work. Yet even this supposition of his own does not appear to be quite satisfactory to himself, and he adds that unless the chisel's point was sheathed with steel, we must confess that the Egyptians appear to have possessed certain secrets for hardening or tempering bronze, with which we are totally unacquainted (Wilkinson, vol. ii, p. 255).

It is difficult to understand how stone-cutting under the Pharaohs could have been accomplished with tools of bronze. The use of bronze, no doubt, preceded the use of iron; but, on the other hand, it is certain that from a very early period, iron was known and employed by the Egyptians. Rawlinson ("Egypt," vol. i, p. 94) conjectures that iron may have been supplied to Lower Egypt from Phœnicia, and from the Upper Nile, where it abounds. According to Brugsch, meteoric iron was first wrought into tools; then came the working of the iron mines in the Sinaitic Peninsula and in the mountainous district between the Nile and the Red Sea. The ancient mine at Hammami, containing the metal in the form of specular and red iron ore, is especially mentioned by Wilkinson.

It is true that few examples of iron tools have been discovered in ancient Egypt. But it is to be remembered that implements of this metal, when buried in that nitrous soil, or exposed to the oxidizing air, would, in so many centuries become decomposed and disappear.

According to Herodotus (ii, 125), iron tools were used in building the pyramids. Among the earliest existing specimens of this metal in Egypt may be mentioned a thin piece of wrought plate-iron, found in one of the air-passages of the Great Pyramid; in the same pyramid have been discovered iron clamps which maintain a granite portcullis in its position. Later examples are the iron blade of a falchion found beneath a sphinx at Karnak, and the iron blade of an adze. Inscriptions of Thothmes III, according to Brugsch's translation, distinctly mention the use of iron.

Quarrying, Transporting, and Erecting Obelisks. 151

With all the knowledge and improvements of the nineteenth century, it is an arduous task to accomplish with our modern implements what the old Egyptians accomplished with theirs. The French engineers who removed the obelisk from Luxor found it a difficult labor to cut a space less than two feet deep along the face of its partially decomposed pedestal (Wilkinson, vol. ii, p. 253). A block of syenite soon turns the edge of our best steel tools. There is reason to believe that the Egyptians were as well acquainted with the use of steel as we are, and it is possible that they possessed some secret of tempering bronze which we have not as yet discovered. In the paintings on the walls of Theban tombs, the blue color given to the blades of butchers' knives, to some of the weapons of Ramses III, and to a chisel which a workman is represented as using in sculpturing a sphinx, leads Wilkinson and others to conclude that the implements so represented were made of steel.

In several instances we have occasion to compare the methods of Egyptian workmen with those of the Hindoos. From whatever source the Hindoo workman may have derived his arts, they have no doubt descended to him unchanged from the remotest antiquity. The following description, by Dr. Kennedy, of the tools employed by the Hindoo stone-cutter of to-day, may therefore be of interest: "The tools which the Hindoos use, are a small steel chisel and an iron mallet. The length of the chisel is not more than about twice the breadth of the hand of the Hindoo workman, which, as is well known, is very small; and it tapers to a round point, like a drawing-pencil. The iron mallet is a little longer than the chisel, but not weighing more than a few pounds. Its head is fixed at right angles to the handle, and has but one striking face, which is formed into a tolerably deep hollow and lined with lead to deaden the force of the blow. With such simple instruments they formed, fashioned, and scarped the granite rock which forms the tremendous fortress of Dowlutabad, and excavated the wonderful caverns of Ellora; for it seems by no means probable that the Hindoo stone-cutters ever worked with any other tools."

TRANSPORTATION.

It is remarkable that the Egyptian records throw so little light upon the transportation and erection of obelisks. Their inscriptions carefully record the warlike deeds of the kings, and the long lists of their pious gifts to the temples; they recount the monarch's building of propylæa, and even his setting up obelisks in front of them; but how the obelisks were removed, how they were erected, we are never told. The paintings in the tombs depict for us, with such wealth of illustration, the battles, the feastings, the industrial arts, the home life, the funeral rites of this ancient people, that it seems as though there could be nothing Egyptian which was left unrevealed to us; but when we look for information on the transportation and erection of obelisks, we find, as yet, almost nothing. The celebrated painting of the "Colossus on a Sledge," is almost the only guide and help that we have.

The removal of these enormous monoliths to great distances must have been, of course, by water.[1] This must be preceded by the difficult transportation of the shaft from the quarry to the river bank; on its arrival at the point to which it had been shipped, there was a second and a longer transportation by land to the temple before which it was to be erected.

The Nile was the great highway of Egypt, offering the easiest of all communication, following its current from the south to the north of the land. And hence it resulted, as is remarked by Lepsius, that although in Thebes and Lower Egypt, nothing but limestone is at hand, yet sandstone and syenite were employed there almost as freely as they were in the Upper Egypt where they were quarried.

Boats of large size were not wanting to convey these enormous weights. Some of the Egyptian war vessels had twenty-two oars on a side, which, according to Wilkinson (vol. i, p. 276), allowing for bow and stern, would make their length about one hundred and twenty feet. Diodorus

---
[1] Wilkinson (vol. ii, p. 304) states that although small blocks of stone were sent by water to their place of destination, yet blocks of very large dimensions were dragged overland.

mentions a sacred boat of cedar, dedicated by Sesostris to the god Amen of Thebes, measuring two hundred and eighty cubits, or four hundred and twenty feet in length (Wilkinson, vol. ii, p. 211). At a later period, Ptolemy Philopator is said to have built a galley of forty banks of oars, two hundred and eighty cubits long (Wilkinson, vol. ii, p. 212). It is probable, however, that these great weights were usually carried upon rafts.

The inscriptions, says Brugsch (vol. i, p. 75), record the merit of high officials to whom were intrusted the responsible task of superintending the removal of blocks from the quarries, and their conveyance, by way of the Nile, to the pyramids or temples where they were to be employed. In the inscription of Una, an Egyptian governor under the vi dynasty (translated by Birch, in "Records of the Past," vol. ii, p. 1), he recounts the transport of stones for the pyramid Shanefer, erected by the King Merenra, in six boats of burthen or rafts, three towing boats, three boats of eight lengths, and one war vessel. Again, for the transport of an immense stone, he says: "I made for it a boat of burthen (or raft, as Brugsch translates), sixty cubits long and thirty cubits broad"; that is, a raft one hundred and four feet long and fifty-two feet wide. In another inscription by a governor and chief architect under Amenhotep III, is recorded the transportation, by the Nile, of the colossal statues of that monarch: "I caused eight ships (probably rafts) to be built; the statues were carried on the river." Brugsch, "Hist. of Egypt," vol. i, p. 425.

Many conjectures have been made as to the manner of removing the shaft from the quarry to the raft. Goguet ("Origine des Lois") supposes that a canal was cut from the river to a point immediately below the quarried shaft. Zoega objects that it would be an infinite toil so to cut through the syenite river bank so far inland, and conjectures instead that the shaft, placed upon such a "chamulcus" or "cradle" as Ammianus Marcellinus reports, was used at the much later date of Constantius for the carriage of the obelisk (now the Lateran) from the Tiber into Rome, and resting on rollers, was drawn by capstans down an inclined bridge of strong beams, and so transferred to the raft.

If we turn from these conjectures to the only positive testimony that we have, that is, to the testimony of the inscriptions and to that of the painting of the "Colossus on a Sledge," it would appear that the shaft, placed upon a sledge, was drawn only so far as the inundation level, where it was left till the rising of the Nile should allow it to be drawn on board the raft. "As soon as the water rose," says the inscription of Una, as quoted by Brugsch, "I loaded the rafts with immense pieces of granite for the pyramid." (Brugsch, vol. i, p. 106.)

In two inscriptions quoted by Brugsch (vol. i, pp. 113, 124), great blocks cut for royal sarcophagi in the valley of Hammamat are described as being rolled down the valley to the riverside.

On the arrival of the shaft by river at the place of its destination, it was again drawn by sledge to the spot where it was to be erected.

The only representation we have of such transportation by land is the celebrated painting, before referred to, of the "Colossus on a Sledge." This painting, discovered in a tomb near El Bersheh, is of the time of Usortesen II, xii dynasty. A wood-cut representing this painting and a description of it will be found in Wilkinson's "Manners," etc., vol. ii, p. 305.

The weight and size of single blocks of stone transported by the Egyptians are remarkably great, as well as the distances to which they were conveyed. A monolithic chapel, weighing about three hundred and fifty tons, removed by Amasis from Elephantine to Saïs, is thus described by Herodotus (bk. ii, ch. 175):

What I admire still more is a monument of a single block of stone, which Amasis transported from the city of Elephantine. Two thousand men, of the class of boatmen, were employed to bring it, and were occupied three years in this arduous task. The exterior length is twenty-one cubits (thirty-one and a half feet), the breadth fourteen (twenty-one feet), and the height eight (twelve feet); within, it measured eighteen cubits,

Quarrying, Transporting, and Erecting Obelisks.

twenty digits (twenty-eight feet, three inches) in length, twelve cubits (eighteen feet) in breadth, and five (seven and a half feet) in height. It lies near the entrance of the temple, not having been admitted into the building, in consequence, as they say, of the engineer, while superintending the operation of dragging it forward, having sighed aloud, as if exhausted with fatigue, and impatient of the time it had occupied; which being looked upon by Amasis as a bad omen, he forbade it being taken any farther. Some, however, state that this was in consequence of a man having been crushed beneath it while moving it with levers.

A similar syenite chapel was that of Tel-et-Mai, the external dimensions of which are given as twenty-one feet, nine inches in height, thirteen feet in breadth, and eleven feet, seven inches in depth. The colossal syenite statue of Ramses II, at the Memnonium, Thebes, must have weighed when entire more than nine hundred tons. It was transported overland a distance of one hundred and thirty-eight miles. But largest of all was the monolithic chapel, "each wall forty cubits (sixty feet) square," which is recorded by Herodotus (bk. ii, ch. 155) to have been brought from Elephantine to Buto, in the Delta: the weight of this, supposing the walls to have been only six feet thick, has been estimated at over 5,000 tons.[1]

According to Ebers ("Caire à Philae," p. 272), sledges only were employed for the transportation of the heaviest weights, and these drawn by human strength alone. Criminals condemned to the quarries were compelled to assist in moving a certain number of stones; the man of greater guilt must tug the longer and the harder. An inscription mentioned by Ebers ("Caire à Philae," p. 374), cut in the breccia quarries of Hammamat (on the desert track leading from Keneh, near Thebes, to Kosseir, on the Red Sea), records that Ramses IV sent to these quarries a party of 8,665 men, to obtain stone for buildings of his at Thebes: of these, five thousand were soldiers; two thousand were men to draw the stones on sledges, with eight hundred Aperiou (either Hebrews, says Ebers, or prisoners of war condemned to hard labor). Three hundred yoke of oxen drew chariots or wagons, and apparently were not used in dragging the stone-laden sledges. The labor of drawing the heavily weighted sledges across the desert cost the lives of nine hundred men.

The Seringapatam obelisk, mentioned before, was placed upon a low frame of timber, which rested upon eight low wheels: to this ropes were attached, drawn by about six hundred men at a time. The distance from the quarry to the site of the obelisk's erection was about two miles. Timbers were laid along the road, to prevent the sinking of the low wheels in the earth.

Beasts of burthen were little used for the transportation of these great weights. Camels appear to have been used only for the transport of baggage and provisions. Horses, which in Solomon's time were exported from Egypt, were unknown in the early period of Egyptian history; although introduced by the Hyksos, they are not represented on monuments before the xviii dynasty, and then only as attached to chariots. Oxen were employed to draw stones of small size: in the limestone quarries of Masara (from these quarries and those of Turra, nearly opposite Memphis, was taken the ordinary stone for the pyramids of Gizeh) is a sculpture representing six oxen drawing a sledge, on which is a block of stone measuring eight feet by four feet (Sharpe, vol. i, p. 23; Wilkinson, vol. ii, p. 302).

In many instances, as shown by the "Colossus on a Sledge" and by the obelisk still in the Assouan quarries, the stone was cut to shape before transportation, thus lessening the weight; in other instances, e.g., huge blocks lying near Assouan, the blocks were removed in the rough.

Of the mechanical appliances which were known to the Egyptians we have little information; Rawlinson (vol. i, 308) is very certain that no levers or rollers were employed to facilitate the task of transportation. But Herodotus, in his account of the removal of the monolithic chapel to Saïs (previously quoted), expressly mentions the use of levers. Brugsch ("Hist. of Egypt," vol. i, p. 73) states that the stones for the pyramids of Gizeh were drawn upon rollers up a prepared causeway extending from the Nile to the plateau of the pyramids. A machine, imperfectly described by Herodotus (bk. ii, ch.

---
[1] Donaldson (in Parker, p. 35) mentions a colossus at Koorneh, Thebes, fifty-seven feet, five inches high, and which, according to Mariette, weighed 1,198 tons.

154   *Quarrying, Transporting, and Erecting Obelisks.*

125) as made of short pieces of wood, is recorded by him to have been used, in the building of the pyramids, for lifting blocks of stone from one step or tier of masonry to the step above; Wilkinson (vol. ii, p. 309) considers this to have been a sort of crane. The Egyptians, according to Wilkinson (vol. ii, p. 305), were not ignorant of the pulley, and, in his opinion, used it in hoisting sail. (This has been much doubted, *e. g.*, by Sharpe, " Hist. of Egypt," vol. i, p. 44.) A pulley has been found in Egypt, which is now in the Museum of Leyden, but its date is uncertain; it seems to have been used in drawing water from a well (Wilkinson, vol. ii, p. 225). The single mast of boats, replacing the double mast of the iv dynasty, had bars or rollers at top, which served as pulleys, and over which the halliards ran, though sometimes they ran through rings at the mast-head (Wilkinson, vol. i, p. 276).

ASSYRIAN TRANSPORTATION.

Of the transportation of heavy blocks of stone by the ancient Assyrians, some records are preserved. The first is that of the not very reliable Diodorus Siculus, who tells us of the somewhat mythical Queen Semiramis, that she had quarried, in the mountains of Armenia, an obelisk one hundred and thirty feet long and twenty-five feet square; this was drawn by many teams of mules and oxen to the Euphrates, placed on a raft, and floated down to Babylon, to which city the Assyrian queen is said to have transferred her court.

A very interesting series of sculptured slabs, discovered by Layard at Nineveh, and now in the British Museum, represents the removal and setting in place of colossal stone bulls, under the direction of Sennacherib (B. C. 704-676, Oppert.). A huge block of stone is seen placed on a low flat-bottomed boat, which is towed on the river by cables drawn by about three hundred men. Again, the stone, now carved into a colossal bull, is seen placed on a sledge drawn by men attached to four cables. Rollers are laid beneath the sledge, and its hinder part is lifted and eased by the use of huge levers. Lastly, the sledge is drawn up an inclined plane constructed of earth, and the colossus is set in its place (see Layard's " Discoveries," p. 104 and plates 10-17; Bonomi's " Nineveh," p. 378).

The great conqueror Assurbanipal (B. C. 660-647, Oppert: the Sardanapalus of the Greeks), in his second campaign in Egypt, captured Thebes and removed thence many treasures. In an inscription by this monarch, which recounts his triumph and the spoils of his victory, he makes special mention of two obelisks: " Two lofty obelisks, covered with beautiful carving, I removed and brought to Assyria" (George Smith's " Hist. of Assurbanipal," p. 54). The shafts were probably drawn along the desert track from Keneh to Kosseir, on the Red Sea, thence to be shipped to the mouth of the Euphrates; but no record informs us how this transport was effected.

TRANSPORTATION BY PTOLEMY PHILADELPHUS.

In the prosperous days of Alexandria under the successors of Alexander in Egypt, an obelisk was removed to that city, from what spot we are not told, by Ptolemy Philadelphus (B. C. 286-247: the patron of Manetho), and by him erected at the Arsinoëum, a monument which he had built to the memory of his favorite sister Arsinoë. The following account of this is from Pliny (" Nat. Hist.," bk. xxxvi, ch. 14):

> Ptolemæus Philadelphus had an obelisk erected at Alexandria, eighty cubits high, which had been prepared by order of King Necthebis; it was without any inscription, and cost far more trouble in its carriage and elevation than had been originally expended in quarrying it. Some writers inform us that it was conveyed on a raft under the inspection of the architect Satyrus, but Callixenus gives the name of Phœnix. For this purpose, a canal was dug from the river Nilus to the spot where the obelisk lay; and two broad vessels, laden with blocks of similar stone a foot square, the cargo of each amounting to double the size, and, consequently, double the weight of the obelisk, were brought beneath it; the extremities of the obelisk remaining supported by the opposite sides of the canal. The blocks of stone were then removed, and the vessels, being thus gradually

Quarrying, Transporting, and Erecting Obelisks.

lightened, received their burden. It was erected on a base of six square blocks, quarried from the same mountain, and the architect was rewarded with the sum of fifty talents. This obelisk was placed by the king above-mentioned in the Arsinoëum, in testimony of his affection for his wife and sister Arsinoë. At a later period, as it was found to be an inconvenience to the docks, Maximus, the then Prefect of Egypt, had it transferred to the Forum there, after removing the summit for the purpose of substituting a gilded point; an intention which was ultimately abandoned.

This Necthebis of Pliny, according to Wilkinson (vol. i, p. 139), is Nectanebo, B. C. 378-364, xxx dynasty. Birch (in Parker, p. 55), considers this obelisk to be that of Semenpserteus, afterward removed by Augustus to Rome.

ROMAN TRANSPORTATION.

Next to the Egyptians themselves as removers of obelisks, the Romans occupy the most important place. It was the glory of their emperors to bring the spoils of conquered foreign countries to the one centre of power and luxury—imperial Rome. Among these trophies they especially prized the monoliths brought from before the portals of Egyptian temples, and adorned their city with a large number of these captured shafts. The treatise on Roman topography by the so-called Publius Victor mentions six obelisks of large size, besides forty-two of smaller dimensions, as existing in Rome; but the authenticity of this book is, at present, seriously questioned.

The following extracts from Pliny and Ammianus Marcellinus are our only records of Roman transportation.

The most difficult enterprise of all was the carriage of these obelisks by sea to Rome, in vessels which excited the greatest admiration. Indeed, the late Emperor Augustus consecrated the one which brought over the first obelisk, as a lasting memorial of this marvellous undertaking, in the docks of Puteoli; but it was destroyed by fire.—Pliny, "Nat. Hist.," bk. xxxvi, ch. 14.

This first obelisk transported to Rome is usually identified with that which was erected by Augustus in the Circus Maximus,—the present obelisk of the Piazza del Popolo.

The other instance of Roman transportation mentioned by Pliny is the removal, by the Emperor Caius Caligula, of the shaft now known as the Obelisk of the Vatican.

The third obelisk at Rome is in the Vaticanian Circus, which was constructed by the emperors Caius and Nero; this being the only one of them all that has been broken in the carriage. Nuncoreus, the son of Sesoses, made it. As to the vessel in which, by order of the Emperor Caius, the other obelisk had been transported to Rome, after having been preserved for some years and looked upon as the most wonderful construction ever beheld upon the seas, it was brought to Ostia, by order of the late Emperor Claudius; and towers of Puteolan earth being first erected upon it, it was sunk for the construction of the harbor which he was making there. There was a fir, too, that was particularly admired, when it formed the mast of the ship which brought from Egypt, by order of the Emperor Caius, the obelisk that was erected in the Vaticanian Circus, with the four blocks of stone intended for its base. It is beyond all doubt that there has been seen nothing on the sea more wonderful than this ship; 120,000 modii of lentils formed its ballast; and the length of it took up the greater part of the left side of the harbor at Ostia. It was sunk at that spot by order of the Emperor Claudius,—three moles, each as high as a tower, being built upon it; they were constructed with cement which the same vessel had conveyed from Puteoli.—Pliny, "Nat. Hist.," bk. xxxvi, ch. 14, 15; bk. xvi, ch. 76.

This account of the sinking of the ship is confirmed by Suetonius, "Vita Claudii," ch. 20.

Ammianus Marcellinus (bk. xvii, ch. 4) records as follows the removal of the obelisk now known as the Lateran, first by Constantine the Great as far as Alexandria, and afterward by Constantius to Rome:

Because the flatterers, who were continually whispering into the ear of Constantius, kept always affirming that when Augustus had brought two obelisks from Heliopolis, a city of Egypt, one of which was placed in the Circus Maximus, and the other in the Campus Martius, he yet did not venture to touch or move this one which has just been brought to Rome, being alarmed at the greatness of such a task; I would have those, who do not know the truth, learn that the ancient emperor, though he moved several obelisks, left this one untouched, because it was especially dedicated to the Sun-god, and was set up within the precincts of his magnificent temple, which it was impious to profane; and of which it was the most conspicuous ornament. But Constantinus, deeming that a consideration of no importance, had it torn up from its place, and thinking rightly that he should not be offering any insult to religion if he removed a splendid work from some other temple to dedicate it to the gods at Rome, which is the temple of the whole world, let it lie on the ground for some time. while arrangements for its removal were being prepared. And when it had been carried down the Nile and landed at Alexandria, a ship of a burden hitherto unexampled, requiring three hundred rowers to propel it, was built to receive it. And when these preparations were made, and after the aforenamed emperor had died, the enterprise began to cool. However, after a time it was at last put on board ship, and conveyed over sea, and up the stream of the Tiber, which seemed as if it were frightened, lest its own winding waters should hardly be equal to conveying a present from the almost unknown Nile to the walls which itself cherished. At last the obelisk reached the village of Alexandria, three miles from the city; and then it was placed in a cradle (or sledge; *chamulcus*), and drawn slowly on, and brought through the Ostian, passing by the Piscina Publica, or great public swimming-bath, to the Circus Maximus.

ERECTION OF OBELISKS.

The testimony from Egyptian sources concerning Egyptian transportation is far from satisfactory; but from these sources we learn, as yet, absolutely nothing concerning the Egyptian erection of obelisks. These secrets of their engineering skill have remained, to this day, buried with them.

The Roman writer Pliny, whose entire information respecting Egypt appears to have been of the most vague and uncritical kind, mentions, but does not explain, the use of machinery in the elevation of an obelisk by King Rhamsesis (presumably Ramses), but the evident exaggeration as to the number of men employed and the idle fable of binding the monarch's son to the shaft, impair the value of his statement. His account ("Nat. Hist.," bk. xxxvi. ch. 14) is as follows:

Rhamsesis, who was reigning at the time of the capture of Troy, erected one [an obelisk] one hundred and forty cubits [two hundred and ten feet] high. Having quitted the spot where the palace of Mnevis [the sacred bull of Heliopolis] stood, this monarch erected another obelisk, one hundred and twenty cubits [one hundred and eighty feet] in height, but of prodigious thickness, the sides being no less than eleven cubits [sixteen feet, six inches] in breadth. It is said that 120,000 men were employed upon this work, and that the king, when it was on the point of being elevated, being apprehensive that the machinery employed might not prove strong enough for the weight, with the view of increasing the peril that might be entailed by the want of precaution on the part of the workmen, had his own son fastened to the summit, in order that the safety of the prince might at the same time insure the safety of the mass of stone. It was in his admiration of this work that, when King Cambyses took the city by storm, and the conflagration had already reached the very foot of the obelisk, he ordered the fire to be extinguished; entertaining a respect for this stupendous erection which he had not entertained for the city itself.

Pliny also records, but without the least explanation how the task was accomplished, the elevation of an obelisk at Alexandria by the Macedonian ruler of Egypt, Ptolemy Philadelphus. His entire account of this has been already given.

In the absence of any positive evidence in what manner the Egyptians erected their obelisks, we can only submit the conjectures, more or less ingenious, which have been formed upon this point.

Sharpe, in his "Hist. of Egypt" (vol. i, p. 44, with figures from Bonomi), explains this much more to his own satisfaction than to that of his readers: "If," he says, "an obelisk ninety feet long, or a statue fifty feet high, was to be placed upright, a groove or notch was first cut in the pedestal on which it was to stand, so that while it was being raised, one edge of its lower end might turn in that groove as on a hinge. The obelisk or statue was then brought by means of rollers till its lower end rested over this groove, *and then its head was lifted up, probably by means of a mound of earth*, which was raised higher and higher till the stone which leaned on it was set up on end." There is something mysterious in this conjecture, for it does not explain exactly how a mound of earth could lift up an obelisk. To get the mound under the obelisk it must first have been lifted either directly or indirectly. By indirectly is meant drawing it up an inclined plain.

Letronne, quoting Pliny's account (book xxxvi. ch. 21) of the raising of heavy masses forming the architraves of the temple of Ephesus, states that the architect effected it by means of bags of sand piled to form an inclined plane extending beyond the capitals of the columns. The architraves were hauled up the incline, and lowered into position by allowing the sand to run out of the bags. Letronne conjectures that the Egyptians used some such method for raising the architraves of the Hall of Columns at Karnak, and adapted it to raising obelisks. Wilkinson shows that the obelisks of Hatasou, could not have been erected by any form of inclined plane, as the narrow court in which they stood antedated their erection.

Cooper conjectures that the Egyptians erected their obelisks by driving under them rollers of gradually increasing diameter. He describes the method as graphically as if he had witnesssed it or discovered some sculpture or inscription that gave it. Diligent search by the author and by others employed expressly for the purpose, through all the sources of information available for examination, has been ineffectual in discovering any thing that would warrant such a conjecture.

Zoega, and indeed almost all modern writers on obelisks have speculated on the methods of the ancient Egyptians for erecting them, but no satisfactory system that does not involve the application of "brute force" has yet been suggested. Rawlinson says (vol. i, p. 309) : "The raising of obelisks can scarcely have been managed without machines. As we have no representations or descriptions of them, it is impossible to determine their character. But, at any rate, they were such that works, difficult of execution even at the present day, were accomplished by them." In this the author fully concurs. The development of the Egyptian mind was such as to warrant a belief in their knowledge of applied mathematics and mechanics. The genius ˙ that designed the pyramids and temples could readily have devised the means of constructing them without the waste of life and power involved in the crude methods some writers attribute to them. "Main strength and stupidity," as the sailors say, consume time. The record on Queen Hatasou's obelisks is proof enough that the time occupied in quarrying, transporting, and erecting them would not have been sufficient, unless the application of power involved in the execution of the work was at least equal to any modern application of mechanical force.

Cooper and Sharpe appear to have had in mind the manner of erecting the Seringapatam obelisk (before referred to), as described by Col. Wilks in the "Transactions of the Royal Society of Edinburgh," vol. ix.

"Conceive the shaft finished," says Col. Wilks, "and placed ready for erection in a horizontal position, raised to the proper height, and with its base accurately placed for insertion in the top of the pedestal, when it should attain a vertical position. Then imagine a strong wall, built at right angles with the line of the shaft, and a few feet beyond its smaller end ; with two lateral retaining walls, parallel to the shaft, and a fourth wall of smaller elevation, near the pedestal, to support the mass of earth and the workmen to be employed. On such a platform, raised ten and a half feet, you will first conceive the shaft to be horizontally arranged. Two lines of timber, plank or balk, were then ranged along the two sides of the shaft, to serve as fulcra, and two lines of men with handspikes, attended by others with chocks, or pieces of timber of different thickness, to be inserted under the shaft for the purpose of keeping the elevation of the smaller end, effected by the handspikes, and distributing the pressure so equally as not to risk the accidents which would otherwise be inevitable with this very fragile substance. In proportion as elevation was thus gradually obtained for the smaller end, the space below was filled with rammed earth, and the same process was repeated with the parallel balks of timber, handspikes, and chocks : the small end gradually rising at each successive step, the wall behind increasing in height, and an inclined plane of solid earth gradually increasing its angle with the horizon, until it equalled that at which solid earth could with safety be employed : when, the force required being proportionally diminished, timber alone was employed for its elevation. Finally, a scaffolding of timber was erected, embracing three sides of the pedestal, and nearly equal to the ultimate height of the obelisk : ropes were applied to the summit of the shaft, in such directions as to steady and check it ; handspikes gave the requisite impetus, until it felt the power of the ropes, and was ultimately and safely lodged in its shallow receptacle."

Of course it was necessary that the bottom of the sunken socket in which the shaft was to stand, should be perfectly level. Colonel Wilks offered to test this by a spirit-level, but the Hindoo engineer preferred his own method: first rubbing the surface clean and dry, he dropped on it a little water; the portions where the water would not run were shown to be too high, and were worked down with the chisel; the repetition of this process at last produced a perfect level.

Of the erection of obelisks by the ancient Assyrians, we have no information. The setting a colossal bull in its place, as shown in Layard's plates, is no help to us here. The inscription that tells us that Assurbanipal brought two great obelisks from Thebes has nothing to say of their elevation at Nineveh. Two obelisks of Assyrian workmanship, both found at Nineveh, are now preserved in the British Museum: the earlier one is a shaft of white stone bearing the name of King Assurnasipal, and, according to Philip Smith ("Hist. of the East," p. 283), is twelve or thirteen feet high, with a base of two feet by about fourteen inches; the later one is the celebrated "Black Obelisk," of black marble, by Shalmaneser II, B. C. 858–823: its dimensions, according to Layard, are six feet, 8⅝ inches high; base of shaft one foot, 11¾ inches by one foot, 3¾ inches. Of course, the erection of obelisks of such small dimensions presents no difficulty.

Of the erection of obelisks by the Romans, we have, at least, some information. Although Pliny here, is as usual, of little service, yet the fuller account of Ammianus Marcellinus and the bass-reliefs on the pedestal of the obelisk erected by Theodosius at Constantinople, show the use of mechanical helps corresponding, in good degree, with those employed to-day.

The following extract from Pliny (bk. xxxvi, ch. 14) simply recounts the erection of two obelisks at Rome by Augustus: "The obelisk that was erected by the late Emperor Augustus in the great circus [the present obelisk of the Piazza del Popolo] was originally quarried by order of King Semenpserteus, in whose reign it was that Pythagoras visited Egypt. It is 85¾ feet in height, exclusive of the base, which is a piece of the same stone. The one that he erected in the Campus Martius [the present obelisk of Monte Citorio] is nine feet less in height, and was originally made by order of Sesothis. They are both of them covered with inscriptions, which interpret the operations of nature according to the philosophy of the Egyptians."

The account by Ammianus Marcellinus of the removal of an obelisk [the present obelisk of the Lateran] from Alexandria to Rome, under the Emperor Constantius, has been already given. The same author's description (bk. xvii, ch. 4) of its erection at Rome is as follows: "The only work remaining to be done was to raise it, which was generally believed to be hardly, if at all, practicable. Vast beams having been raised on end in a most dangerous manner, so that they looked like a grove of machines, long ropes of huge size were fastened to them, darkening the very sky with their density, as they formed a web of innumerable threads; and into them the great stone itself, covered over as it was with elements of writing, was bound, and gradually raised into the empty air, and long suspended, many thousands of men turning it round and round like a millstone, till it was at last placed in the middle of the square; and on it was placed a brazen sphere, made brighter with plates of gold; and as that was immediately afterward struck by lightning and destroyed, a brazen figure like a torch was placed on it, also plated with gold, to look as if the torch were fully alight."

Peter Gyllius, referring to this description by Ammianus, is reminded by it of the taking down from its pedestal of a column almost as large as the Constantinople obelisk. This he saw accomplished at Constantinople in the following manner: " Round the pillar, though at some distance from it, they fixed in the ground, near to one another, large poles, much taller than the pillar, at an equal distance from each other. At the top of these poles they laid others across them, which were fastened to them in the strongest manner, and to which were fixed the pulleys through which the ropes slipped, which reached from the bottom of the shaft of the pillar to the top, and were fastened to it. The ropes were so thick, both lengthways and crossways, that at some distance the scaffolding looked like a square tower. There were many capstans on all sides, which were turned by infinite numbers of the strongest

Quarrying, Transporting, and Erecting Obelisks. 159

youth, till they had moved it from its basis and laid it prostrate upon the earth." ("Ball's Translation of P. Gyllius," p. 106.)

The most interesting contribution to the history of Roman erection of obelisks is furnished by the bass-reliefs sculptured on the pedestal of the Constantinople obelisk, which commemorate the erection of the shaft under the Emperor Theodosius. These reliefs were first described by Peter Gyllius, in his "De Constantinopoleos Topographia," the first edition of which was published in 1562. The reliefs were first drawn and published by Spon and Wheeler, in their "Voyage d' Italie," etc., en 1675 et 1676," printed at Lyons in 1678.

This is a faithful reproduction of the drawing in Spon and Wheeler, as copied in Montfaucon's "L' Antiquité Expliquée," vol. iii, pl. 187. After careful comparison of the original engraving with Montfaucon's copy, the latter was preferred for reproduction here because, while exact in every detail, it was clearer and sharper in outline.

The plate brings together the reliefs of the north and south sides of the pedestal. In its lower portion is seen the relief found on the south side; it represents the circus after the erection of the obelisk. Two shafts are seen standing in this circus: the one is probably the obelisk as erected by Theodosius; and the other a shaft, or pillar, formerly covered with plates of brass and called by Gyllius a "structile colossus." Near the centre stands the superintendent of the public games who reaches out a crown to the victor. At the ends are the two goals.

The two upper portions of the plate, taken from the north side of the pedestal, are intended to represent the erection of the obelisk. The following is Peter Gyllius' description of these reliefs: "The sculptures on the north side stand in two ranges, the lowermost of which contains eighteen figures and two capstans, which are turned round with iron crows by four men and wind the ropes, which are drawn through pulleys, round the capstan, and so draw the obelisk along the ground. In the same range is engraved the obelisk in an upright posture, as it now stands, with three figures, one of which,

160   *Quarrying, Transporting, and Erecting Obelisks.*

as the inhabitants tell you, represents the master, and the other the servant, whom he designs to correct (if a third person had not interposed) because he had erected the obelisk in his absence. In the upper range are also figures of two capstans, with the same number of men working them, and laboring with those below them to drag the obelisk. The wreaths of the ropes, in particular, are very nicely cut." (" Ball's Translation of Gyllius," p. 104.)

Gyllius has here failed to remark the fifth man at each capstan, who "holds back," or keeps tight, the rope as it is hove in. The prostrate obelisk, says Zoega, is laid upon a "chamulcus," or "cradle," —using, to describe the low frame, with its large wheel, on which the obelisk rests, the same word which Ammianus Marcellinus employs in his account of the transport of an obelisk from the Tiber bank into Rome (the present Lateran obelisk). He adds that, besides the spectators, are seen two persons standing on platforms, perhaps the Emperor Theodosius and the Prefect Proclus; also that the building seen behind the prostrate obelisk may be taken as the barrier of the circus.

Two inscriptions upon the pedestal record the erection of the shaft by Theodosius. They were first published by Gyllius. At Niebuhr's visit to Constantinople, in 1761, the Greek inscription was partly covered with earth. Hobhouse mentions that in 1810 the fourth and fifth lines of one inscription were no longer visible. It will be noticed that the two inscriptions differ as to the number of days required for the task. Gyllius' copy of the Latin verses says thirty-two days: but both the Latin and Greek verses are here printed as given by Zoega (p. 55), after his careful examination not only of Gyllius' copy, but also of the copies made by later, and, as he believed, more accurate observers.

The Greek inscription, which is on the west side of the pedestal, runs thus:

KIONA TETPAΠΛEYPON AEI XΘONI KEIMENON AXΘOC
MOYNOC ANACTHCAI ΘEYΔOCIOC BACIΛEYC
TOΛMHCAC ΠPOKΛΩ EΠEKEKΛETO KAI TOCOC ECTH
KIΩN HEΛIOIC EN TPIAKONTA ΔYO

"[This] quadrilateral column, a weight continually lying on the ground, King Theodosius alone having ventured to erect, gave command to Proclus, and so great a column stood erect in thirty-two days."

The Latin inscription is on the east side of the pedestal:

DIFFICILIS QVONDAM DOMINIS PARERE SERENIS
IVSSVS ET EXTINCTVS PALMAM PORTARE TYRANNIS
OMNIA THEVDOSIO CEDVNT SOBOLIQVE PERENNI
TER DENIS SIC VICTVS EGO DOMITVSQVE DIEBVS
IVDICE SVB PROCLO SVPERAS ELATVS AD AVRAS

"I was once unwilling to obey imperial masters; but was ordered to bear the palm after [to commemorate the victory over] the destruction of tyrants. All things yield to Theudosius and his ever-during offspring. Thus I was conquered and subdued in thirty days, and elevated towards the sky in the prætorship of Proclus." (Translation in Long's "Egypt. Antiquities," vol. i, p. 331.)

CHAPTER VIII.

ANALYSIS OF THE MATERIALS AND METALS FOUND WITH THE OBELISK AT ALEXANDRIA.

ARRANGED BY PROFESSOR PERSIFOR FRAZER.

THE RED SYENITE GRANITE OF THE SHAFT.

THIS rock is of a general pinkish hue when viewed from a distance, and on nearer approach reveals the irregular mottling of pink, black, and white, admirably rendered on Plate xliv, Fig. 4. It is almost impossible to render by a flat print the translucency, or that effect of vividness produced by both lustre and color, but the attempt here is a very close approach to nature.

The first thing that strikes one is the freshness and soundness of the rock. No *maladie de granite* is observable, and this fact will answer the first and natural question as to why this rock was so much preferred by the Egyptians for monumental purposes. I made a number of careful determinations of its specific gravity, first in lump, as more applicable to questions of transportation, and afterward in powder to determine by comparison the porosity of the rock. The specific gravity of the rock, as it is, *i. e.*, with all the cavities it contains, is 2.6618, but, broken up to the size of a pea, the quartz pulverizes except in the interior of the small masses, and the specific gravity becomes 2.7188. It would perhaps rise to 2.75 or 2.76 if completely pulverized, but this can have no bearing, unless it be to determine in this way approximately how much of the desert sand is composed of the old granite and how much of the newer and generally lighter rocks. A cubic foot of the rock weighs 166.1625 pounds.

An independent series of experiments, made in 1878 by Professor G. W. Wigner, and published in the *Analyst*, established the specific gravity of the syenite at 2.682. The absorbent power of the unchanged stone was at the rate of about 7.8 grains of water per square foot; the weathered surface showed an absorbent power six times as great. After powdering the stone and separating the constituent minerals by means of Sonstadt solution, there were found of

Mica	2.986
Quartz	2.747
Felspar	2.595

The proportion of mica varied considerably in different parts of the stone. The stone as a whole contained:

Silica	68.18	Magnesia		0.48
Iron peroxide	4.10	Soda		2.88
Alumina	16.20	Potash		6.48
Lime	1.75	Manganese oxide		trace

Analysis of Materials and Metals.

The felspar contained:

Silica	63.38	Magnesia		0.45
Iron peroxide	} 22.25	Soda		1.84
Alumina		Potash		10.66
Lime	1.09			

The mica yielded:

Silica	46.16	Magnesia	6.77
Iron peroxide	7.30	Soda	0.92
Alumina	41.18	Potash	5.24

Dr. F. A. Genth, Professor of Chemistry at the University of Pennsylvania, has, at my request, separated under the microscope, and analyzed the felspar of this granite with the results given below. He writes:

Plagioclase from the Granite of the Obelisk.—White, with delicate striation. It was impossible to obtain it entirely free from quartz and in sufficient quantity for a complete analysis. The pieces which I could pick out contained

	P. C.
Silicic oxide	66.70
Aluminium oxide	21.41
Calcium oxide	4.17

These percentages indicate the plagioclase to be orthoclase. Calculating from the calcium oxide the requisite amount of aluminium oxide and silicium oxide for a "calcium oligoclase," and from the remaining aluminium oxide the required sodium oxide and silicium oxide for "sodium oligoclase," there are in one hundred parts:—

	MIXTURE OF QUARTZ AND OLIGOCLASE.	PURE OLIGOCLASE.
Quartz	9.87	
Silicium oxide	56.26	62.42
Aluminium oxide	21.41	23.75
Calcium oxide	4.17	4.62
Sodium oxide	8.30	9.21
	100.	100.

A specimen of this granite was sent to Prof. A. J. Julien, who made three thin sections of it. Two of them were selected for representation, together with a thin section of a specimen of syenite from near Germantown of different texture for comparison. These three thin sections were drawn and painted under my inspection by Mr. Faber from their images in the polarizing microscope, and afterward submitted to Dr. Alfred Steltzner, Professor of Geology in the Royal Saxon Mining School of Saxony. The following is his report. I may add that I have used the German word "petrographer," though little used in English, because no equivalent for it exists.

ON THE BIOTITE-HOLDING AMPHIBOLE-GRANITE FROM ASSOUAN (SYENE).

The handsome stone of which the ancient Egyptians, and after their time the Romans, made such splendid use for monumental and architectural purposes, is known to day in commerce as "red oriental granite." We have valuable information concerning its occurrence, among others from Joseph Russegger.[1] According to him, the "oriental granite" forms the principal mass of several parallel chains which stretch from the East Egyptian coast-range (that is from the Red Sea) westward, through Egypt and India, and only on the other side of the Nile in the Libyan desert, are lost under

---
[1] "Travels in Egypt, Nubia, and the East Soudan, with especial reference to the natural history relations of the respective countries; undertaken in the years 1836, 1837, and 1838," vol. ii, part i, Stuttgart, 1843. The work of Rozière, Descr. Mineral de la Vallée de Kosseir, in the "Mémoire sur l' Égypte," iii, p. 227, was unfortunately inaccessible to me.

Fig. 1

Thin section, in polarized light, of a portion of the Shaft of the Egyptian Obelisk erected in Central Park, New York.
Magnified 35 diameters.

Fig. 2

Thin section, in polarized light, of a portion of the Shaft of the Egyptian Obelisk erected in Central Park, New York.
Magnified 35 diameters.

Fig. 3

Thin section, in polarized light, of a Rock near Germantown, Phila.

Fig. 4

Fragment of the Shaft of the Egyptian

Analysis of Materials and Metals.

a covering of more recent sedimentary rocks. Numerous dykes and pockets of diorite and porphyry[1] intersect these granitoid chains, which, in consequence of more or less deep-seated weathering, are covered on their bald and knotty surfaces to a great extent with rock-labyrinths and gigantic blocks.

Another very remarkable phenomenon in which Russegger likewise sees a kind of decomposition, the result of a long exposure to the combined influence of the water and the atmosphere, is this, that the outside of the granite blocks, and of the granite rock itself generally, is often covered with a very thin, dark black, highly lustrous coating, which gives it the appearance of having been painted over with pitch. Russegger reports this coating as so thin, and so intimately mixed with the mass of the rock, that it cannot be separated from the latter, and he takes this material to be ferrous oxide.

According to the description at hand the structure and composition of the "oriental granites" are very variable. Coarsely granular varieties, made porphyritic by orthoclase crystals which are distributed without regularity in the main mass, seem to be the most usual. They occur immediately in the neighborhood of Assouan (Syene). Out of these are developed locally (for instance on the road along the cataracts of Assouan) such coarsely granular masses that the individual felspar and quartz constituents reach the size of a cubic foot; in other places the size of the grains diminishes, and then there results, by a parallel arrangement of the scales of mica, a gneissoid rock. Among the varieties of composition, three are especially given. That which seems to be most widely distributed is an amphibole-granite containing biotite, in the composition of which orthoclase, oligoclase, quartz, amphibole and biotite take part. Some of the principal localities for this are the old quarries near Assouan and, besides this, Djebel Gareb and Djebel Ezzeit. This principal rock, by the gradual diminution of its amphibole, either merges into normal biotite-granite, which may be either rich in mica (east side of the hill on which the town of Assouan is built), or poor in mica (Debu); or it passes, by disappearance of its quartz and the predominance of its amphibole, into normal syenite. Russegger satisfied himself, in various localities, that one of these rock varieties developed itself very gradually out of the other, and in such a way that, in the mountain chain of the cataracts of Assouan, he was not able to separate one from another. Also, on the east edge of the "Waddi el Hammer" he observed that the granite became fine-grained, and by visible diminution of the quartz passed into syenite; the latter seems generally to become more frequent toward the east.

In the above lines I have used for the varieties of rocks those names which at present are more common among German petrographers; nevertheless, as these names until recently, and perhaps even now, have not won universal acceptance, and as the different appellations of the rocks under consideration are derived from just the above-indicated variations which are to be observed in Egypt, it may be worth while to introduce a few historical remarks.

A. G. Werner, the founder of the present geology, defined with precision, for the first time, the nearly arbitrarily employed names of rocks. In his "Short Classification and Description of the Different Kinds of Rocks" Dresden, 1787, he defines granite as a "mixed rock, which consists of felspar, quartz, and mica, which are so united together in a granular network, that every part of the mixture penetrates and is attached to the rest."[2] In the following paragraph he describes, in conformity with the above definition, "a kind of granite which appears to be a particular species of rock," because it contains hornblende in its mass, partly together with mica, partly in place of mica. "If a more general occurrence of this species of rock (which at first was only known near Dresden and in the eastern part of Saxony—Oberlanditz) should be proved, a special name must be given to it, and it might be called greenstone." Shortly afterward, it appeared that these rocks, rich in hornblende, had quite a wide distri-

---

[1] Among the porphyries, the most interesting is that of "Dochbel Dohan," or the "Mons Porphyrites" of the ancients, which produces the beautiful red porphyry (porfido rosso antico) which was widely spread over the entire old classic world. Russegger, *l. c.* 351–356.

[2] "Welche in einem Körnigen Gewebe so mit einander verbunden sind dass ein jeder Theil des Gemenges in und mit dem Anderen verwachen ist." Werner, "Klassification und Berschreibung der verschieden Gebirgsarten," Dresden, 1787.

Analysis of Materials and Metals.

bution, and Werner himself even became acquainted with them, for example, from Upper Egypt. This latter circumstance evidently caused him to deviate again from his original proposition, and to give to this hornblende-carrying granite the name of syenite, which already was employed by Pliny (xxxvi. 13).[1] Werner, therefore, understood by syenite mixtures of felspar and hornblende both with *and* without quartz. As, however, in the further development of petrography, a sharper division between the acidic and basic rocks proved to be desirable, the German geologists designated the quartzose varieties of Werner's "syenite" as syenitic-granite or amphibole-granite, and used the name syenite exclusively for the mixture of orthoclase and hornblende free from quartz. This to-day is, in Germany, the usual terminology. Rozière followed a different course. He believed that the name of syenite must be given to that rock which is found near the cataracts of the old Syene (Assouan), and in which the old Egyptians had located their great quarries. But this stone, as was mentioned above, contains quartz. For its corresponding modification which was free from quartz, Rozière proposed the name *sinaite*, because in the meantime it had transpired that, along with others, this variety occurs on Mount Sinai. The French, English, and North American geologists for a long time followed at least the first suggestion of Rozière, and have generally called the "amphibole-granite" of the Germans syenite; on the other hand, the second proposition of Rozière has nowhere received any continuous acceptance[2]; the felspar, hornblende mixtures free from quartz have been called sometimes diorites and sometimes greenstones, by the French, English, and North American petrographers, without particular regard to the monoclinic or triclinic character of their felspar.[3] Thus a very unfortunate confusion arose, which until recently, has shown no signs of abatement, and now, it must be said, by a tendency in favor of the German terminology. I follow here this latter, and need fear no misunderstanding if I again mention that in Upper Egypt amphibole-granite is the predominating rock, but that both biotite-granite and syenite are found there. The amphibole-granite was employed with especial preference by the Egyptians for ornamental and architectural purposes; according to Delesse, the inside and outside linings[4] of the great pyramids of Cheops consist of it, as well as the numerous sphinxes and sarcophagi, Pompey's Pillar, the sacred monolith of Saïs, and the obelisks.

We have an extremely careful description of this Egyptian amphibole-granite (syenite of Rozière) from the distinguished French geologist, A. Delesse.

As the New York obelisk is cut from this rock, I consider it desirable to give the more important observations of Delesse concerning it.

According to him, the rock consists of quartz, orthoclase, oligoclase, mica, and often also of hornblende.[5]

The quartz is translucent and gray; it has occasionally a somewhat violet or smoky gray tint, which, as in the case of the quartz of protogine, is derived from a small quantity of organic matter. The orthoclase has a beautiful bright red, red, or yellowish-red color, which reminds one of the coloration of the orthoclase in the syenite of the Vosges, but is much brighter; it forms crystals of several centimetres in length,—twins, as in the case of granite rocks; it generally is the most prominent constituent of the mixture, is very often the mineral most largely represented, and generally gives the rock its reddish color. (See Plate xliv, Fig. 4.)

Delesse found the specific gravity to be 2.568.

At a red heat it loses only 0.35 p. c. This loss is very little, as is generally the case with orthoclase. When the felspar decomposes, it sometimes assumes a brown color, which is due to a little manganese oxide contained in it and which is set free. The triclinic felspar has not a greasy lustre as in the syenite of the Vosges, and

---
[1] Köhler, *Bergmannishes Journal* 1788, ii, 824.
[2] As little has the name hyposyenite, proposed by Dana for a mixture of orthoclase and hornblende free from quartz, been able to graft itself on the terminology.
[3] D. Forbes, "The Study of Chemical Geology," London, 1868, 10.
[4] In Delesse's original Mémoire," cited elsewhere, only the inside of the pyramid is mentioned.—P. F.
[5] Delesse on the light red syenite from Egypt, in Karsten's and Deehen's *Archiv für Mineralogy, Geology, Mining, and Metallurgy*, Berlin, 1851, xxiv, 63, 70.

Analysis of Materials and Metals.

appears to be oligoclase; it is commonly white, sometimes it is yellowish, or even greenish, as, for instance, in some specimens from Syene, in which it occurs very largely and even exceeds the orthoclase in quantity. The mica, rich in magnesia and iron, forms brilliant scales of mostly black color, but, according to Rozière, is also sometimes brown and green. When its color is black, it is not distinguishable from that of the hornblendes which is often united with the mica.[1] Also some pyrite and, as in all hornblende-granites, some magnetite occur in it. Garnet is found in it (but very infrequently) of a dark brown color and crystallized in the usual form of the rhombic dodecahedron.

According to his method, described in the *Annales des Mines* (4me série, t. xiii, p. 379), Delesse determined the relative volumes of the different minerals which appeared on the surface of a polished fragment, and found red orthoclase forty-three per cent.; gray quartz forty-four per cent.; white oligoclase nine per cent.; black mica four per cent. "This piece, which was very rich in quartz, seemed to contain no hornblende; it contained, notwithstanding, less orthoclase and especially less mica than from its appearance would have been supposed; furthermore, this optical deception is general and is to be ascribed to the fact that the minerals which possess bright and lustrous colors, like the bright red felspar and especially the mica, attract the attention much more than the quartz of gray or dull color." Delesse undertook an analysis of an Egyptian granite, by grinding up a large piece from the Egyptian Museum of the Louvre, which M. Dubois, one of the Conservators, had placed at his disposal; it exhibited the same characteristics as those mentioned above, but some hornblende was observable in it. Delesse found the following constituents:

	B. C.
Silicon oxide (SiO_2)	70.25
Aluminium oxide (Al_2O_3)	16.00
Oxide of iron, containing manganese	2.50
Lime (CaO)	1.60
Alkalies and magnesia (by loss)	9.00
Loss by incineration	.65
Total	100.00

Delesse thus summarizes the result of his investigations: "It appears that the chemical constitution of the Egyptian syenite does not vary in important respects from that which I have found for several granites; as it contains a great deal of quartz, it can be regarded as a hornblende-granite, or as a rock species which forms a transition from the granite family to the syenite family."

This result therefore corresponds perfectly with the nomenclature usual in Germany, and also with that which I set forth at the commencement of this paper.

At the time that M. Delesse wrote the above remarks, the microscope had not yet established its home on the work-table of the petrographer. I have carefully examined the thin sections which were made from the rock of the New York obelisk which Professor Frazer handed me. The results which have been obtained by the employment of this new method of research, and which I give in the following lines, may be regarded as a continuation of the remarks of the French savant.

At the first glance under the microscope it is apparent that the biotite-holding amphibole-granite of Syene has a thoroughly crystalline granular structure. Its principal components, however, are crystals imperfectly developed on every side, generally in the form of fragments; even for these, Werner's description holds perfectly good, that "every part of the mixture penetrates and is attached to the rest."

As an exception, two small and isolated parts of one of the sections show somewhat a granitophyre structure,—an extremely fine permeation of felspar and quartz-like graphic-granite.

---

[1] Russegger, whose communications on the rock of the quarries of Syene (Assouan) agree well with those of Delesse, says: "Hornblende forms an accessory constituent, with the increase of which the mica decreases and the familiar transition into syenite is established." Hornblende and biotite can thus replace each other.

The essential elements of the rock are microcline, oligoclase, quartz, and amphibole, with which some biotite is associated.

The microcline is the constituent mentioned by Delesse as red orthoclase. It is very fresh and free from interpositions; between the crossed Nicols it shows in an exceptionally beautiful manner, in the sections parallel to the basal plane, the "grating" structure dependent upon its peculiar lamellar construction. On those sections which are parallel to the brachypinacoid a simpler flame structure is observable.

Plate xliv, Figs. 1 and 2 give a good idea of the splendid bright picture which the observer of these thin sections obtains in the polarizing microscope. The OLIGOCLASE shows on its basal sections, in contrast to the microcline, only one fine, but very apparent twin striation parallel to the edge PM (see Fig. 2, right hand lower part). It is also free from interpositions, but less fresh than the microcline, and in the vicinity of clefts which intersect it, has a "mealy" opacity. That this is really oligoclase, Delesse had already made probable, and the analyses of Professor F. A. Genth add additional confirmation to this hypothesis.

Some isolated grains of felspar have become, in consequence of advancing decomposition, perfectly opaque. Whether these also are to be reckoned as plagioclase, or whether they are to be considered as orthoclase, I am not able to decide from the two sections before me.

The QUARTZ occurs partly in large individual grains, partly in fine-grained aggregates. These latter have the form of veins, and cross between the fragmentary, shattered, larger felspar and quartz constituents. There is therefore here the *mortar* structure described by Toernebom as occurring in the Swedish granites, and which, according to his view, is characteristic of the oldest, but is wanting in the later granites.[1] The larger quartz grains belonging to the first separation are irregularly shaped, as has been already remarked. They contain a considerable number of fluid cavities, which to a certain extent are arranged in the well-known cloud-like zones. The bubbles of the larger liquid inclusions are immovable; those of the smaller, on the other hand, show invariably a greater or less movement. Besides this, the quartz contains a few small reddish translucent scales of hematite (either hexagonal or distorted to rhombs); also in one of its grains numerous hair-like black needles lying confusedly over each other are to be seen. In ordinary light the sections of the quartz grains are clear as water, but between crossed Nicols, they shine in monochromatic bright colors (Fig. 2, below).

In one of the two thin sections under consideration, there is accidentally a quartz grain which has been cut parallel to its base. This remains in all horizontal positions dark, and shows a very perceptible interference cross when the eye-piece is pulled out.

The HORNBLENDE occurs in prismatic, but otherwise irregularly defined individuals. It is quite fresh and, in ordinary light, green and translucent. Tested with one Nicol, it shows in the direction of the axis of elasticity c a very powerful absorption.

The slight obliquity of the position of extinction to the prismatic edges (the axis c) and the very apparent, obtuse angles of the cleavage lines characterize this mineral in an exceptionally perfect manner.

BIOTITE occurs in single large brown translucent scales. The transverse sections show the usual lamellar structure and, by the employment of one Nicol prism, the strong absorption of the ordinary ray, of which the vibrations are perpendicular to c.

Besides the above-considered essential constituents in the composition of the rock, the following accessory minerals also associate themselves in it, though, it must be confessed, in a very subordinate manner. Of *primary* origin: titanite, apatite, magnetite, and zircon. Garnet and pyrite, mentioned by Delesse, are not contained in the sections before me.

---

[1] Naagra or dom granit och gneiss in Geol. Fœren i Stockholm. *Færh.*, Bd. V, 233. An excerpt from this in the *Neues Jahrbuch für Mineralogie*, 1881, ii, 50.

TITANITE is found in both sections in numerous small yellowish-red translucent grains, which, together with a very pure constitution, show an irregular outline.

The APATITE occurs in excessively fine water-clear acicular crystals.

The MAGNETITE appears in the form of opaque, partly irregularly bounded, and partly octahedrally crystallized grains.

Finally, there are four small crystals of ZIRCON in one section and six in the other. When they lie parallel to the plane of their section, one can convince one's self that they are of prismatic habit, and that both poles are terminated by pyramidal planes; in other positions, one sees small square transverse sections. The little prisms are 0.13 to 0.16 mm. long, and have diameters of from 0.03 to 0.05 mm.

Secondary formations are almost entirely wanting in the sections before me; in only two places appear a little viridite and yellowish-green translucent needles of pislazite. The rock of the Needle can therefore be regarded as unusually fresh and *healthy* in spite of the honorable age which it possesses.

Amphibole-granites which have a like, or at least a similar constitution to that of Syene, are rocks of frequent occurrence; thus, amongst others, Ferdinand Zirkel has made known numerous American localities: as, for example, from the north end of the Truckee Range; from the Pah-tson Mountains; from Agate Pass; Cortez Range; Egan Cañon, Nevada; Cottonwood Cañon in the Wahsatch Range, etc.; and, moreover, according to the determination which Clarence King and his associated geologists have set up, they appear at all these points to be later eruptive rocks.[1]

In Europe, rocks of the kind under discussion are known, for instance, from Odenwald, from the Vosges, and from Scandinavia.

Since F. Zirkel[2] with reference to the North American, and H. Rosenbusch[3] with regard to the European amphibole-granites, have called attention to the fact that all these amphibole-granites contain titanite so constantly that this latter should be reckoned as one of their characteristic accessory constituents, it is not without interest to observe that the Egyptian rock conforms to the experience gained elsewhere.

Professor Frazer has added to the plates of thin sections from the monolith, a third, prepared from a rock in the vicinity of Germantown, in the city of Philadelphia. I have also examined this section, and must confess that, as regards the nature of its constituents, the Germantown rock is very similar to that from Syene, but, on the other hand, differs from it by a somewhat different relation to each other of the constituents, and also in its more finely granular structure.

In conclusion, the following is a short diagnosis of the Germantown amphibole-granite (or amphibole-gneiss), of which a colored representation in polarized light is given in Plate x, Fig. 3. Its essential constituents are microcline, plagioclase, orthoclase (?), quartz, hornblende, biotite, and some muscovite.

The MICROCLINE and PLAGIOCLASE are both still very fresh, the separate felspar grains which show no twin striation may possibly be orthoclase. QUARTZ occurs only in rounded grains, and much more sparsely than in the Egyptian rock. It is almost free from interpositions; even fluid bubbles are only to be observed in certain places, and exhibit very small dimensions. The green translucent hornblende is in greater quantity than the brown biotite; in addition to which, also, large isolated scales of muscovite and very fine scales of a green micaceous mineral are observable. Among the accessory constituents of the rock from Germantown must be mentioned also, here again in the front rank, TITANITE, though in this case it occurs in numerous small rounded crystals. Finally, there are in the section before me a couple of very small prismatic crystals, which in consequence of their high refractive

---
[1] F. Zirkel, "Microscopical Petrography in the U. S. Geological Exploration of the Fortieth Parallel," Washington, 1876, 39.
[2] *L. c.*, 58.   [3] H. Rosenbusch, "Microscopical Physiography of the Massive Rocks," Stuttgart, 1877, 22.

power for light, I should again take for zircons. Magnetite or particles of other ore are entirely absent from the Germantown rock, so far as I can judge.

Mit der Uebersetzung ganz einverstanden.

FREIBERG, *December* 14, 1881.   A. STELZNER.

According to the geologists Rozière, Newbold, Russegger, d' Hericourt, and Frass, the limestone which forms the bluffs near Cairo and lines the Nile is "above the chalk." Its true position in the series is more definitely defined by the last-named traveller, who pronounces it of eocene age. Dr. Genth called my attention to a fossil taken from a part of "Specimen 2" of Lieut.-Commander Gorringe's series, and which was kindly identified by Dr. Joseph Leidy as a mummulite, in which view geheimrath Dr. Geinitz, of the Royal Saxon Natural History Museum in the Dresden Zwinger, concurred. Its geological age is thus well known, but it would be impossible to state the particular quarry whence it was taken; but as there are so many, the source of this one was probably one of the nearest quarries to Heliopolis. Professor Robert H. Richards, of the Massachusetts Institute of Technology, to whom a specimen was referred, says: "The specimen" (No. 2 of Lieut.-Commander Gorringe's numbers), weighing about fifty grains, proved to be a very compact limestone containing occasional crystals of transparent calcite, varying from one mm. square downward. The compact portion appeared to be almost flint-like in texture. No fossils were detected, although there were some markings and variations of color which seemed to suggest the possibility of organic remains that would be distinguished in other parts of the rock. The color of this sample varies somewhat from pure white, and may be described as slightly buff-colored. Examination with the microscope revealed nothing especially noteworthy in regard to the structure. The specific gravity of this sample is 2.6208. A fragment yielded to analysis:

	P. C.
Calcium carbonate	99.62
Magnesium carbonate	.27
Ferric oxide	trace
Residue (insoluble in acid)	.18
	100.07

If this remarkable purity of composition characterized the rock of the entire quarry, the Egyptians had a treasure of which they doubtless knew the value.

Mortars and Cements.—There are two kinds of mortar or cement in which the steps of the obelisk were laid, and which are represented by the numbers in the series of Lieut.-Commander Gorringe as Nos. 3 and 4. Besides these, there is another cement, of which only an extremely small portion was obtained, but with which an important archæological question was connected,—the cement of the pyramidion.

The first of these, "No. 3—Samples of mortar in which all the steps and the pieces enclosed were laid, except the one piece in the east angle." This sample was sent to Prof. R. H. Richards for examination. He says: "The sample weighed about fifty grains, and proved to be a very soft, white, friable, chalk-like substance, quite porous, and pitted with little depressions. It contained some splinters of wood which did not seem to be an essential ingredient of the mass. Under the microscope the powder and fragments gave the usual indications of gypsum. Chemical analysis showed the powder to be composed of:—

	P. C.
"Calcium carbonate	12.91
Calcium sulphate	69.36
Silicious residue	2.69
Ferric oxide	.63
Water (loss just below redness)	13.42
	99.01

"This material seems therefore to be an impure plaster of Paris. The calcium carbonate may perhaps have been purposely added with the intention of hardening the plaster, and in this way making it more durable."

The same chemist thus reports the result of his investigation of "No. 4, the yellow cement in which the corner-, or *standard of measure* stone was laid," and alongside of his analysis is placed one of the same material by Leonard P. Kinnicutt. Prof. Richards says: Of this sample, about twenty grams were received for examination. It was very friable, crumbling to sand in the hands, and was of a dark yellowish color. An analysis of this cement was made with the following results —

	PER CENT.		
	RICHARDS.	KINNICUTT.[1]	
Silica as quartz sand	86.16	87.25	Silica as SiO_2
Calcium carbonate	9.89	5.02	Carbonic acid as CO_2
Ferric oxide	2.05	1.52	Iron as Fe_2O_3 / Aluminium as Al_2O_3
Calcium sulphate	1.83	5.90	Calcium as CaO
Water	trace	0.36	Magnesium as MgO
	99.93	100.05	

Prof. Richards adds: "It seems therefore to have been a lime mortar containing a very high rate of sand, the lime being present in such small quantity as scarcely to cement the grains of sand together.

"Lieut.-Commander Gorringe will unquestionably explain the reason for desiring to know whether in the cement which remained attached to the pyramidion, or small pyramid, surmounting the shaft of the obelisk there were to be found any traces of gold or of copper.[2] A qualitative examination made in my own laboratory with this question above in view gave negative results, but for greater certainty, in view of the importance which Lieut.-Com. Gorringe attached to it, a specimen was sent to Dr. F. A. Genth, whose report on it here follows.

"'Fragments of a grayish-white color, consisting of a mechanical mixture of a grayish-white earthy material, and more compact scale-like particles attached to quartz with little felspar and hornblende. A qualitative examination showed that the earthy matter was mostly calcium carbonate; there were also present in the cement considerable quantities of calcium phosphate, hydrous calcium sulphate, and hydrous silicates of aluminium, iron, magnesium, calcium, sodium, and potassium, together with a small quantity of a brownish tarry or resinous matter soluble in alcohol. Only a little over one gram of the mixture served for the analysis, which gave:—

	P. C.
"Quartz, felspar, and hornblende	13.98
Silicic acid	4.79
Phosphoric acid	4.70
Sulphuric acid	1.98
Carbonic acid	12.58
Cupric oxide	0.04
Ferric oxide	2.01
Manganic oxide	0.16
Alumina	3.81
Magnesia	2.02
Lime	32.95
Soda	0.44
Potash	0.36
Organic matter, water, etc.	20.18
	100.00 "

---

[1] Mr. Kinnicutt's analysis was furnished me by Lieut.-Commander Gorringe without further explanation than the above table affords.

[2] To determine whether or not the pyramidion had been gilded or covered with bronze, traces of which would certainly have been detected if it had been.—H. H. G.

Analysis of Materials and Metals.

"It is remarkable that bone ash as well as gypsum have been used by the old Egyptians in the preparation of this cement. Calculating from this analysis, as far as it can be done, the principal components of this cement, we find it to contain:—

	P. C.
"Quartz, etc.	13.98
Calcium carbonate ($CaCO_3$)	28.59
Calcium phosphate ($Ca_3P_2O_8$)	10.26
Hydrous calcium sulphate ($CaSO_4 + 2 H_2O$)	4.25
Water, organic matter, etc.	19.29, etc."

It is hardly necessary to add that these results render it very clear that so far as the material furnished for examination was concerned, there was no evidence of either gold or copper having been attached to it at a previous period. The very slight trace of the latter metal—four hundredths of one per cent.—is an amount of impurity which is too insignificant to lend support to the opposite hypothesis. Parts of one of the iron clamp dogs (No. 5 in Lieutenant-Commander Gorringe's list) were submitted by him to officers of the U. S. Ordnance for physical and chemical tests, and the results given to me for embodiment in this chapter. No comment is necessary on this fine piece of work, and I have simply taken the liberty of introducing, in italics, into the list of substances determined by Captain Butler's analysis, others found by the analysis of Dr. Wendel for Mr. A. L. Holley, in order that the two may be compared. It will be noticed that the constituent to which Captain Butler in a foot-note attributes the high temperature necessary to forge this iron is entirely wanting in the analysis of Dr. Wendel (arsenic).

It would be very interesting to know more of the history of the production of that iron, and especially to have authentic information as to its age,[1] for while we have abundant testimony as to the existence of mines and furnaces in the times of the Egyptians, one of the most distinguished of Egyptologists has doubted their possession of iron. Mr. Holley, in a letter to the editor of the *New York World*, says of this iron:

Our friend, Mr. Fred. E. Church, lately handed me a piece of iron found under our Egyptian obelisk, and asked me to report to you about its quality and the probable method of its manufacture. The specimen was too small for any physical test whatever. A clean fracture revealed to the expert eye a rather highly carbonized and granular but tough-looking metal, not unlike what is called puddled steel. I sent the specimen to Dr. Wendel, the able chemist of the Albany and Rensselaer Iron and Steel Works, who took such an interest in the matter that he made the following very complete analysis.[2] If we had not known from the general history of the iron manufacture that the specimen must have been made by the Catalan process, the analysis would have so indicated. The notable facts are: about a half per cent. of carbon, giving the hardness of ordinary rail steel; very low silicon and phosphorus, due to the method of manufacture; and a remarkably large amount of calcium, indicating the plentiful use of lime as a flux in the process. The small amount of slag (for a Catalan product) as well as the fine fracture indicate frequent reworking, etc., etc.

This fragment was a part of one of the iron dogs used for clamping the stones of the steps together. The following is the report of Captain J. G. Butler, U. S. A., on the same material:

WATERTOWN ARSENAL, May, 20, 1881.

Submitted for mechanical test by Major Clifton Comly per Captain J. G. Butler on the Emery Testing Machine, one iron clamp dog used in foundation of obelisk in Egypt.

Clamp Dog (see Plate xi): About 10 inches long, 1 inch wide, $\frac{1}{2}$ inch thick, partly encased in lead, and flaked with rust.

Cut off one end, forged it to a point; tried to harden it by plunging it red-hot into water. Would not harden. Cut off other end and forged into a ring at third attempt, at a much higher heat than necessary or proper for wrought iron[3] (probably the effect of copper, which is apparently incorporated mechanically, judging by appearance only of copperish streaks and spots, which appeared more distinctly when the specimen was large than when reduced.)

[1] The information on this point is authentic. The age of the iron in 1882 is 1904 years. The doubting Egyptologist may profit by reading Chapter I "Steel," by J. S. Jeans. 1880. (H. H. G.)
[2] See analysis at the end of Captain Butler's paper.
[3] Appended analysis shows this effect to have been due probably to arsenic.

Analysis of Materials and Metals.

In order to adapt the specimen to the machine it was necessary to apply the ends to "holders" by means of screw threads, hence two specimens were cut out of the dog as shown below.

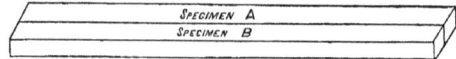

The above figures represent one of the two specimens A and B, cut from the dog, as below.

SPECIMEN A—DIAMETER, $0''.273$.

ELONGATION, SET, AND BREAKING WEIGHT OF FOREGOING SPECIMEN OF OBELISK IRON OR ALLOY.

Strain applied.	Load per □ in.	Gauge reading.	Elongation per inch.	Set per inch.	
292	5,000	.0426	.000000		
468	8,000	.043	.000078		
585	10,000	.0432	.000117		
—	5,000	.0425	—	.000019	
702	12,000	.0436	.000194		
877	15,000	.0442	.000311		
—	5,000	.0425	—	.000019	
1,053	18,000	.0450	.000467		
1,170	20,000	.0455	.000565		
—	5,000	.0425	—	.000019	
1,228	21,000	.0456	.000584		
1,287	22,000	.0460	.000662		
1,345	23,000	.0461	.000681		
1,404	24,000	.0462	.000701		
1,462	25,000	.0465	.000760		
1,521	26,000	.0466	.000778		
1,579	27,000	.0468	.000818		
1,638	28,000	.0470	.000856		
1,696	29,000	.0473	.000914		
1,755	30,000	.0475	.000954		
—	5,000	.0430	—	.000078	Fracture granular.
1,813	31,000	.0480	.001051		
1,872	32,000	.0485	.001149		
1,930	33,000	.0488	.001206		
1,989	34,000	.0490	.001245		
2,047	35,000	.0492	.001284		
2,106	36,000	.0496	.001362		
2,164	37,000	.0525	.001933		
2,223	38,000	.0596	.003304		
2,340	40,000	.0980	.010698		
3,190	54,530	—	.014199		Broke.

Diameter at fracture, $0''.18$; area, $0.0254\ □''$; contraction of area, 56.6 %.

SPECIMEN B—DIAMETER, $0''.274$.

ELONGATION, SET, AND BREAKING WEIGHT OF FOREGOING SPECIMEN OF OBELISK.

Strain applied.	Load per □ in.	Gauge reading.	Elongation per inch.	Set per inch.	
295	5,000	.0700	.000000		
590	10,000	.0710	.000194		Deep seams extended almost through specimen longitudinally at point of fracture. Fracture slightly fibrous.
885	15,000	.0722	.000428		
1,180	20,000	.0730	.000584		
1,475	25,000	.0740	.000778		
1,770	30,000	.0755	.001070		
—	5,000	.0712	—	.000233	
1,829	31,000	.0762	.001206		
1,888	32,000	.0775	.001459		
1,947	33,000	.0786	.001673		
2,006	34,000	.0960	.005057		
2,065	35,000	.1100	.007780		
2,780	47,120	—	—	.010503	Broke.

Diameter at fracture about $0''.20$; area, $0.0314\ □''$; contraction of area, 46.8 %.

Analysis of Materials and Metals.

In the foregoing specimens wherever there appeared a flaw or seam there was oxidation.

A proper grip could not be obtained upon specimens otherwise than by threading the ends and reducing the diameter concentrically. This gave two specimens of almost the same size of area of cross section as one would have been. Machine operated by J. E. Howard, M. E.

(Signed)   J. G. BUTLER, *Captain of Ord.*

WATERTOWN, MASS., *July* 29, 1881.

Analysis of the iron clamp dog from obelisk as received from and made by Captain John Pitman, Ordnance Department, U. S. A.:

	CAPT. BUTLER.		DR. WENDEL.
Iron	98.756		98.738
Slag, etc.	1.917		0.150
Silicon	——		0.017
Arsenic	1.059		
Copper	0.102		0.102
Phosphorus	0.076		0.048
Manganese	0.005		0.116
Cobalt	None	}	0.079
Nickel	0.039	}	
Sulphur	Trace		0.009
Comb'd carbon	{ 0.033 0.032	} 0.138	0.521
Graphite	{ 0.036 0.037		
Calcium	——		0.218
Silica	0.060		
Aluminum	——		0.070
Lead	0.013		
Magnesium	——		0.028
Oxygen	0.056		
	100.235		100.096

Slag consists of ferric oxide 1.870 and silica 0.060.

(Signed)   J. G BUTLER,
Captain of Ordnance.

Density of ring	7.8218 }	Taken by Capt. Smith,
" " cylinder	7.7680 }	Ord. Dept., U. S. A.

Lead is another of the metals common in modern commerce and of which the production by the Egyptians was more likely on general grounds from the greater simplicity of the process; and better attested by the remains of their old explorations, the occurrence of galena in various igneous rocks. Specimen No. 6 of Lieutenant-Commander Gorringe's list is "part of the lead around the iron clamps just considered."

The date at which this work was accomplished (22 B. C.), as in the case of the mortars, leaves it to conjecture as to whether the same or a similar material was employed in the original erection of the obelisk. The following results were obtained by Prof. R. H. Richards to whom a specimen was given.

The piece received weighed 15 grams. This lead proved to be very soft and pure. It could be flattened to an exceedingly thin edge without cracking. Its specific gravity is 11.35 and it yielded to analysis:—

	P. C.
Lead	98.90
Copper	0.06
Iron	0.01
Silver	0.052
	99.022

Analysis of Materials and Metals.

No gold, antimony, or arsenic was detected. The sample was too small for a more complete analysis. This lead appears to have been quite well refined, and must have come from an ore in which the silver contents were very low, unless, as may possibly be the case, the silver was separated by the capellation process. Comparing this with other leads it is found that the specific gravity of the best Patinson lead is 11.395, Streng; 11.38, Kaisten. A sample of soft lead obtained by refining blast furnace lead in a reverberatory furnace was reported as of specific gravity 11.34.[1]
It yielded to analysis:

	P. C.
Lead	98.68
Copper	.54
Iron	.03
Nickel	.04
Antimony	.06
Arsenic	.05
	99.40

This seems to resemble the lead from the obelisk in some respects. It should, however, be borne in mind, when making the comparison, that the quantity of the latter was too small to obtain the low percentages of metallic impurities which were probably present.

Bronze.—Of all the objects submitted to examination none is more interesting than the bronze of which the crabs supporting the four angles of the shaft were made. Their date is placed by Lieut.-Com. Gorringe as B. C. 22, and the number in his list is seven. Small square prisms of about one cm. on the side were cut from the dowels holding in place these crabs, and one of these was submitted to Prof. F. A. Genth whose results here follow. "A fresh fracture shows a crystalline structure; it is somewhat brittle and not very dense, the specific gravity being 8.415; its color is reddish bronze-yellow; its composition was found to be:—

	P. C.
"Copper	90.700
Lead	0.312
Tin	8.127
Iron	0.201
Nickel	Trace
Cobalt	0.108
Sulphur	0.070
	99.518 "

Dr. Genth adds: "I do not know of any other Egyptian bronzes which have ever been analyzed (though there may be many) except that of an arrow-head from an Egyptian grave, in which was found (by Goebel-Scheigger 60.207):—

	P. C.
"Copper	77.62
Tin	22.02
	99.64 "

The methods of separating copper formation at that time were very imperfect, and it is very probable therefore that the tin determination is altogether *too high.*

Examination of paints on images about 4,000 *years old.*—Along with the objects immediately connected with the obelisk, Lieut.-Commander Gorringe handed to me some scales of pigment which had fallen from the surfaces of certain images which he had collected whilst in Egypt, and to which he assigns the above age. These were also submitted to Dr. Genth, whose description and analysis here follow. He says:

---
[1] Reich in *Berg und Hütten Zeitung,* 1860.

Analysis of Materials and Metals.

"There were three samples, one representing the gold and yellow, the others the black and red colors. They consisted of scaly materials, of about 0.5 mm. in thickness. Many were composed of a very thin yellowish-white bottom layer of a dull earthy appearance, and upon this a white layer of about equal thickness; finally, the paint. In many of the scales the bottom layer was wanting. When treated with dilute hydrochloric acid, most of the scales dissolved rapidly with effervescence, some more slowly, leaving the paint upon a thin film of a resinous substance. The yellow and gilt contain the largest quantity of this resinous film, which, on heating, gives off a pleasant odor, resembling that of the resin of balsam fir. It seems that the portions which were to be gilded were first coated with a varnish prepared from this resin, and that the gold, thinner than the thinnest gold-leaf, was laid upon it.

The yellow paint, of a brownish-yellow color, turning reddish on ignition, appears to have been a variety of ferric hydrate, the ordinary "yellow ochre"; the red paint, ferric oxide, or "red ochre"; and the black, "lamp-black."

The latter colors contain only a very small quantity of resinous admixture, the red the least, the black a larger portion.

I first thought when I observed the black particles swimming in the liquid, after dissolving the colored scales in hydrochloric acid, that the black was produced by a varnish prepared from asphaltum, but on dissolving the resinous matter by alcohol, the black was left as a fine powder, which on ignition burnt off like lamp-black.

The mineral constituents which formed the basis of the paints were principally variable mixtures of calcium carbonate and hydrous calcium sulphate, or gypsum.

The following results were obtained by the analyses of the three different specimens of paint.

GILT AND YELLOW PAINT.

The whole quantity for analysis was only 0.1902 grams, which gave:—

	P. C.
Silicic acid	3.79
Sulphuric acid	2.07
Carbonic acid	31.44
Ferric oxide	0.53
Alumina	2.05
Magnesia	0.57
Lime	48.24
Soda	0.57
Potash	0.22
Gold	0.31
Resin, water, etc.	10.21
	100.00

The principal constituents of this paint are, therefore,

	P. C.
Calcium carbonate	71.45
Hydrous calcium sulphate	4.45
Resin, water, etc.	9.28, etc.

BLACK PAINT.

The quantity for analysis was 0.4244 grams. The carbonic acid determination was unfortunately lost, by upsetting the apparatus. The following substances were found.

Silicic acid	2.76
Sulphuric acid	24.28
Ferric oxide	0.33
Alumina	0.75
Magnesia	0.23
Lime	38.87
Soda	0.31
Potash	0.13
Carbon and resin	4.50
Gold	trace
Carbonic acid, water, etc.	27.84
	100.00

Tewfik

Ismail

THE KHEDIVES

Analysis of Materials and Metals.

The principal constituents of this paint are, therefore, present in the following proportions:—

Calcium carbonate (about)	33.40
Hydrous calcium sulphate	52.21
Carbon and resin	4.50
Water, etc.	2.21, etc.

RED PAINT.

Only 0.1074 grams could be obtained for analysis, and the scales had only a very thin coat of paint (ferric oxide). I found:—

Silicic acid	1.96
Sulphuric acid	39.05
Carbonic acid	1.02
Ferric oxide	2.80
Alumina	1.13
Magnesia	0.27
Lime	35.53
Soda	0.30
Potash	0.06
Water and resin	17.88
	100.00

This paint contains, therefore, as follows:—

Calcium carbonate	2.32
Hydrous calcium sulphate	83.96
Resin, water, etc.	0.31, etc.

The quantities of material furnished for examination were unfortunately too small for a fuller investigation, but it is hoped that even these imperfect analyses may be of some value."

F. A. GENTH,
University of Pennsylvania.

INDEX.

Abandonment of the "Cleopatra" . . . 104–105
Abd-el-Lateef, cited, 108 ; quoted . 70, 72, 74, 123
Abercromby, *Sir* R. 97
Absorbent power of syenite 161
Address at laying corner-stone N. Y. obelisk, 34–35 ; at presentation ceremonies 50–54
Adelphi steps, site for London obelisk . . . 105
Age of obelisks : Albani, 137 ; Alnwick, 137 ; Amyrtæus, 138 ; Assyrian, 158 ; Begig, 142 ; Boboli, 137 ; Borgian, 137 ; Corfe Castle, 139 ; Drah Abou 'l Neggah, 144 ; Flaminian, 130 ; Heliopolis, 122 ; Lateran, 127 ; Lepsius', 141 ; London, 68, 96 ; Luxor, 119 ; Monte Cavallo, 126 ; Monte Citorio, 133 ; Monte Pincio, 135 ; New York, 4, 68 ; Pantheon, 134 ; Paris, 119 ; Piazza della Minerva, 133 ; Piazza Navona, 135 ; Prioli, 126 ; Santa Maria Maggiore, 126 ; Vatican, 118 ; Villa Mattei, 134 ; Wadi Nasb, 144. *See also* Oldest.
Agreement for removing London obelisk, 100 ; New York obelisk 5
Albani obelisk 137
Alexander VII re-erects Piazza della Minerva obelisk . 134
Alexander, *Sir* J. E., removal of London obelisk, 98 ; plan for its removal 98–99
Alexandria, surroundings of obelisk in, 1 ; relics of interest in, 3 ; removing N. Y. obelisk to, 4, 36, 52, 72 ; plans for moving N. Y. obelisk through, 15, 16 ; dock at, 24, 104 ; obelisks removed to, 108, 154, 155 ; removing Constantinople obelisk to 124
Alexandria, Gov. of, directed to transfer obelisk to Lieut.-Comdr. Gorringe, 10 ; letter from Lieut.-Comdr. Gorringe to, 10 ; application to, for permission to move obelisk through the city 15
All the Year Round, extract from 102
Alnwick obelisk 137–138
Alumina in syenite, 161–162 ; in cements . . 169
Aluminium oxide in felspar of the syenite . . . 162
Amenemha II, copper mining in reign of . . . 143
Amenhat I 122
Amenhotep II erected Alnwick obelisk . . . 137
Amenhotep III founds temple at Luxor, 119 ; erects propylon at Karnak 120
America, obelisks found in, 60 ; amphibole-granite found in 167
American Bible Society declines to contribute New Testament to deposit in the foundation, 33 ; names of officers not deposited 33

American Numismatic and Archæological Society presents medals of N. Y. obelisk 53–56
Amphibole in syenite 166
Amphibole-gneiss 167
Amphibole-granite 163, 164, 167
Amyrtæus, obelisks of 138–139
Analysis of materials and metals found with N. Y. obelisk at Alexandria 161–175
"Anglia" (The) tows the "Cleopatra" . . . 105
Anglo-Saxon Lodge, No. 137, contributes Masonic emblems for deposit in foundation of N. Y. obelisk . 33
Animals, Egyptian veneration of, 69 ; use of, . . 153
Antef, name on obelisk at Drah Abou 'l Neggah . 144
Anthony, J. B., lays corner-stone of N. Y. obelisk . 34–38
Antinori re-erects La Trinita obelisk . . . 135
Antinoüs, Monte Pincio obelisk erected in honor of, 135 ; name on, ... 136
Antiquity. *See* Age ; Archæology.
Apartment-house near N. Y. obelisk at Alexandria . 1, 2
Apatite in the syenite 166, 167
Apollo-Phœbus identified with the sun . . . 75
Apparatus. *See* Machinery ; Tools.
Ara Cœli, Convent of, former site of Villa Mattei obelisk 134
Arabs employed in removal of N. Y. obelisk . . 12
Archæological treasures on site of N. Y. obelisk, 12, 14 ; London obelisk 102
Archæology of N. Y. obelisk 59–76
Architecture, Egyptian, 35, 60 ; and Freemasonry . 37
Arles obelisk 141
Arnold, A., plan for removal of London obelisk . . 100
Arsenic used by Egyptians in forging iron . . . 170
Ashley, J. L., offers the "Eothen" for towing the "Cleopatra" 105
Aslambekoff, *Rear-Adm.*, ... 15
Assouan obelisk, 143, 146 ; quarries, 119, 122, 135, 146–147, 163. *See also* Syenite.
Assurbanipal, obelisks removed by 154
Assyrian obelisks, 60, 158 ; transportation, . . 154
Augustus, *Emp.*, obelisks removed to Rome by, 130, 133, 134
Babylon, removal of obelisk to, ... 154
Backsheesh 1, 56
Bædeker, quoted, 71 ; cited 143
Baker, B., plan of the "Cleopatra" 101
Bandini cited 133
Bankes, W. J., Corfe Castle obelisk 139
Barbarus, Prefect of Egypt 72, 76

178   Index.

	PAGE
Barberini obelisk	135–136
Basalt, obelisks of	138, 146
Base of obelisk. *See* Foundation.	
Bass-reliefs. *See* Inscriptions.	
Baur, T.,	46
Bayard, T. F.,	57
Begig obelisk	142
Bellonius, P., cited	74, 108
Bellori, discovery of fragment of obelisk	136
Belzoni, 97 ; cited, 139 ; quoted	147
Benevento obelisk	136–137
Bergh, H., contributes documents for deposit in foundation of N. Y. obelisk	33
Berlin, obelisk in,	141–142
Bernini, re-erects Piazza della Minerva obelisk, 134 ; re-erects Piazza Navona obelisk	135
Besson, plan for removing Paris obelisk	77
Bible deposited in pedestal of London obelisk, 106. *See also* American Bible Society.	
Bierstadt, E., photographs N. Y. obelisk	47
Biotite-granite	163, 164, 166
Birch, S., quoted, 62, 68, 122 ; cited, 108, 121, 124, 127, 134, 135, 136, 137, 138, 139, 152, 155	
Bishop, *Capt.*, in charge of guard of honor at re-erection of N. Y. obelisk	47
Bloomfield, *Sir* B., letter from Mr. Briggs to,	97–98
Boats of ancient Egypt, 151–152 ; use in moving obelisks, 154 ; Roman use, 155, 156. *See also* Rafts ; Vessels.	
Boboli Gardens, obelisk in,	137
Bombay Courier, extract from,	97
Bone ash in cements	170
Bonomi, J., cited	112, 127, 130, 132, 133, 134, 137, 138
Bonwick, J., cited, 59 ; quoted	62
Booth, *Capt.*,	104, 105
Borgian obelisk	137
Boswell, *Capt.*, plan for removing London obelisk	98
Boys, presentation to, of medals commemorative of N. Y. obelisk	54–56
Breakage: danger of, in moving N. Y. obelisk, 15, 21 ; of strands in embarking pedestal of N. Y. obelisk, 25 ; how prevented in voyage of "Dessoug," 27 ; of bottom of N. Y. obelisk, 75 ; of tackles in lowering Luxor obelisk, 86, 87 ; of heel of London obelisk, 102 ; in "Cleopatra," 103 ; how prevented in raising London obelisk, 106 ; of pyramidion of Vatican obelisk, 112. *See also* Crack ; Defacement ; Defects ; Fall ; Fragments ; Shaft	
Bresca	116
Briet	78
Briggs, S., letter to Sir B. Bloomfield	97–98
Bristow, G. F.,	49
British Museum, obelisks in	138–139
Bronze tools used by Egyptians, 150 ; analysis of that in crabs of N. Y. obelisk	173
Browning, H., solution for preservation of London obelisk	107
Brugsch Bey, translation of inscriptions on N. Y. obelisk, 65–68 ; cited, 62, 69, 70, 71, 72, 124, 127, 142, 150, 152, 153	
Bryce, *Sir* A.,	96
Buchoz, cited	141
Butler, *Capt.* J. G., analysis of iron clamp found under N. Y. obelisk	170–172
Byzantine emperors, removal of obelisks to Constantinople	51

	PAGE
Cæsareum in Alexandria	1, 72–73
Caillard, *Director-Gen. of Posts*,	24
Cairo obelisks	139, 142
Caissons, for N. Y. obelisk, 12, 15, 16, 20, 41 ; for London obelisk, 51. *See also* Launching.	
Calcium carbonate, in the limestone found near the Nile, 168 ; in the mortar and cement	168, 169
Calcium oxide in felspar of the syenite	162
Calcium sulphate in the mortar and cement	168, 169
Caligula, *Emp.*, removes Vatican obelisk from Heliopolis	110, 118
Cambyses, injuries to temples	72
Camels, to lighten draught of the "Luxor"	88
Camels, ancient use of,	153
Canal for moving obelisks from quarries to the Nile,	152, 154
Cangiahs	80
Cannon-balls, substitution of, for wheels	9, 15, 26, 27, 42, 44
Caoutchouc on Paris obelisk to protect it from climate,	92
Carbonic acid in cements	169
Carburi, *Count*, method of moving pedestal of statue of Peter the Great	8, 9
Carlisle, J. G.,	57
Carter, *Capt.* H., given command of the "Cleopatra," 101 ; compelled to abandon her	104
Cartouch. *See* Inscriptions.	
Carvings. *See* Inscriptions.	
Catania obelisk	141
Cavan, *Lord*,	96
Cements, analysis	168–170
Central Park selected as the site	31
Centre of gravity of London obelisk in its cylinder,	101, 106
Ceremonies. *See* Corner-stone ; Presentation.	
Cerisi, de,	77, 78
Chabas, cited, 62 ; translation of inscriptions on N. Y. obelisk, 63–64 ; on Paris obelisk, 94–95 ; on Constantinople obelisk, 125–126 ; on Alnwick obelisk	138
Champollion, J. J., cited, 77, 80, 119, 137 ; how enabled to translate inscriptions	140
Chamulcus for moving obelisks	152, 156
Channel iron tracks	9, 26, 40, 42, 44
Charles X	52, 78
Chérif Pacha, letter to, from Mr. Farman, 3 ; letter from, to Mr. Farman	3
Chisels used by Egyptians in quarrying obelisks, 147, 148, 149, 150 ; by Hindoos	151
Cholera, attack of, at Luxor	85
Christians, method of spending Sunday in Alexandria	14
Church, F. E.,	30, 170
Church steeples represent same idea as obelisks	60
Civilization. *See* Egyptian.	
Clamp dug found under N. Y. obelisk, analysis,	170–172
Clamps for attaching N. Y. obelisk to pedestal, 46 ; weight of	46
Claudius, *Emp.*, erects Vatican obelisk in Rome, 118 ; Boboli obelisk	137
Cleavage of obelisks from their quarries	147, 148
Cleaver, *Rev.* J. B., benediction at laying of corner-stone of N. Y. obelisk	38
Clement VI re-erects Pantheon obelisk	134
"Cleopatra" (The), 6 ; plan of, 101 ; enclosing obelisk in, 102 ; fitting for the voyage, 104 ; abandoned, 104–105 ; picked up, 105 ; insurance on,	107
Cleopatra, *Queen*, her connection with the obelisks	73

Index.

	PAGE
Cleopatra's Needle, N. Y. obelisk properly known by that name, 3; why so called unknown, 4; when the name was given, 36; its propriety	73
Climate, protection of Paris obelisk from, 92; of London obelisk	107
Coins, found in excavating, 12, 73; deposited in foundation of N. Y. obelisk, 33; of Paris obelisk, 91; of London obelisk, 106; of Vatican obelisk	113, 116
Comanos, N. D., letters from Mr. Evarts to,	6
Comparative dimensions and weight of obelisks, table,	145
Congress. See United States.	
Conly, Maj. C.,	170
Constantine, Emp., Constantinople obelisk removed to Alexandria in reign of,	124
Constantinople obelisks, 51, 68, 70, 124-126; inscriptions on	159, 160
Constantius, Emp., removes Lateran obelisk to Rome	127
Conté excavated obelisk	74
Contract. See Agreement.	
Cook, F. C., quoted	70, 71
Cooper, cited, 68, 69, 108, 121, 124, 126, 127, 133, 134, 136, 137, 138, 139, 143, 144, 148, 157	
Cooper, Com. G. H.,	46, 56
Cooper, M. W.,	57
Copper, Egyptian mines of, 143; no trace found on N. Y. obelisk	169, 170
Corfe Castle obelisk	139-141
Corner-stone, ceremonies in laying it in N. Y.	34-38
Correspondence relating, to N. Y. obelisk, 2, 3, 4, 5, 6, 10, 50; to registry of "Dessoug," 57; to Paris obelisk, 79; to London obelisk	97-98
Cost. See Expense.	
Crabs of N. Y. obelisk, 12; difficulty in removing them, 14; their weight, 46; securing them in position, 48; inscriptions on, 55; translation, 76; why that form of support was adopted	75-76
Crabs, of London obelisk, 102, 108; of Vatican obelisks,	114, 116
Crack, in base of N. Y. obelisk, 12; in Paris obelisk, 80, 86; in Assouan obelisk	143
Cradle, for moving N. Y. obelisk, 9, 15, 16, 44-45; for moving Paris obelisk, 89; for landing London obelisk, 105; for moving Vatican obelisk, 114; for moving Constantinople obelisk, 160; ancient use of, 152. See also Chamulcus.	
Crane, use of, by ancient Egyptians	154
Criminals anciently used in moving large stones	153
Crocodilopolis obelisk	142
Crosby, Dr. H., prayer at presentation ceremonies, N. Y. obelisk	49
Cross placed on Vatican obelisk	117
Cupric oxide in cements	169
Curvature of obelisks	83, 119
Daily Graphic	40
Dates. See Age; Time.	
Death symbolized by pyramids	59-60
Decorations. See Embellishments.	
Defacement of N. Y. obelisk at Alexandria	1
Defect, in Paris obelisk, 80, 86; in London obelisk, 102. See also Breakage; Crack.	
Delays in removing, N. Y. obelisk, 16, 17, 24, 29; Paris obelisk, 79, 80, 88, 89, 90, 93; London obelisk, 102,	103, 104

	PAGE
Delesse, A., quoted	164-165
Denon, cited	75, 142
Department of Parks, N. Y., approves site, 31; fails to prepare site for foundation	32
Depew, C. M.,	2
Deposit of articles in foundation, of N. Y. obelisk, 32-34; of Paris obelisk, 91; of London obelisk, 106; of Vatican obelisk	113, 116, 117
Derby, Lord,	98
"Dessoug," purchase of, 22-24, 56-57; voyage, 29-30; granted an American registry, 56-57; sale of,	57
Detaching obelisks from their quarries. See Cleavage.	
Dial found near base of obelisk	73
Dietrich, W. G.,	49
Digging. See Excavations.	
Dimensions of obelisks, table, 145. See also Size.	
Diodorus Siculus cited	151, 152, 154
Diorite found with syenite	163
Disembarking, pedestal of N. Y. obelisk, 31-32; N. Y. obelisk, 39-42; Paris obelisk, 89; London obelisk	105
Distance, N. Y. obelisk was moved, 42, 44, 45, 47, 48; Vatican obelisk was moved, 115; Egyptians moved blocks	152, 153
Diving operations in removing, N. Y. obelisk, 16, 21; London obelisk	102
Dixon, J., negotiations relating to removing N. Y. obelisk, 2; declines at proposed cost, 4; his plan of moving London obelisk unsuited to N. Y. obelisk, 5; his agreement to remove London obelisk, 100; tribute to him, 100, 108; cause of first failure of "Cleopatra," 104; site desired by him for London obelisk, 105; expense of its removal	107
Dixon, W.,	101, 104
Dock, at Alexandria, 24, 104; charges at N. Y., Phila., and Baltimore, 39; for disembarking obelisk at London	99, 105
Dock Department, N. Y., loans derrick	31
Docking the caisson and "Dessoug"	24
Domitian, Emp., quarries Piazza Navona obelisk, 135; erects Benevento, Borgian, and Albani obelisks	137
Donaldson quoted	119, 150, 153
Drah Abou 'l Neggah, obelisks of,	144
Drovetti	78
Dudgeon, R., makes hydraulic pumps used in removing N. Y. obelisk, 8; contributes one for deposit in foundation	34
Durability of obelisks, 61; how Paris obelisk was protected, 92; London obelisk	107
Dynamite used in clearing harbor of Alexandria	102
Earthquake, probable cause of fall of London obelisk, 108; overthrows Constantinople obelisk	124
East River landing, N. Y., why undesirable	31
Ebers, quoted, 69, 149; cited, 70, 72, 121, 122, 123, 142,	143, 153
Ebn-Khordadbeh quoted	123
Edrisi, quoted, 73-74; cited	108
Educational influences of obelisks	54, 61, 96
Effendi, K.,	80
Egmont, van, quoted	74
Egypt, postal service, 22; her associations with Freemasonry, 35; obelisks still in, 142-144 See also Aexandria; Khedive; Pharaohs.	
Egyptian civilization	35-36, 52, 62

Index.

Egyptian government, claims against, 11. *See also* Khedive.
Egyptian mythology, 59, 60, 69, 132, 143. *See also* Inscriptions.
Egyptologists, imperfect knowledge of, ... 62
Ehlers, E. M. L., Grand Marshal in laying the cornerstone of New York obelisk 34
Embarking, New York obelisk. 24-27 ; Paris obelisk, 87-88. *See also* Disembarking.
Embellishments, on London obelisk, 107 ; on Vatican obelisk, 117 ; on Arles obelisk 141
Emblems. *See* Inscriptions ; Symbolic.
Emery powder used in cutting stone 150
Encasing. *See* Sheathing.
Engine. *See* Steam.
Engineering skill of Egyptians 146
England, obelisks in. *See* Alnwick ; British Museum ; Corfe Castle ; London ; Sion House ; Wansted.
Entef 144
"Eothen" (The) offers to tow the "Cleopatra" . . 105
Ephrem Syrus, St., quoted 123
Erection of obelisks, ancient methods, 45, 156-160. *See also* Re-erection.
Esmeade obelisk 136
Europe, amphibole-granites found in, ... 167
Evarts, W. M., his aid in securing New York obelisk, v, 2 ; letters to Mr. Farman, 2, 4 ; letter from Mr. Farman, 3-4 ; letters to Mr. Comanos, 6 ; present at re-erection, 47 ; address at presentation ceremonies, 50-53 ; letters relating to American registry of "Dessoug" 57
Excavations around, New York obelisk, 12, 74 ; Paris obelisk, 81, 84 ; London obelisk, 102 ; Vatican obelisk 113, 115
Expense, in removing New York obelisk, 4, 5, 16, 17, 21, 23, 56 ; Paris obelisk, 52, 78, 79, 93 ; London obelisk, 100, 105, 107 ; in re-erecting Vatican obelisk . 117

Fall of obelisks : Begig, 142 ; Benevento, 136 ; Constantinople, 124 ; Drah Abou 'l Neggah, 144 ; Flaminian, 130 ; Heliopolis, 123 ; Karnak, 121 ; Lateran, 127 ; London, 73, 108 ; Monte Cavallo, 126 ; Monte Citorio, 133 ; Monte Pincio, 136 ; Pantheon, 134 ; Piazza della Minerva, 134 ; Piazza Navona, 135 ; Sân, 142 ; Santa Maria Maggiore, 126 ; Wadi Nasb 143
Farman, E. E., his efforts in obtaining N. Y. obelisk, 2 ; letters to M. Evarts, 2, 3-4 ; letter to Chérif Pacha, 3 ; from Chérif Pacha, 3 ; from Evarts, 4 ; his tact in negotiations 50
Feddam 82
Felspar, in syenite, 161, 162, 163, 164, 166 ; in cements, 169
Fergusson, J., quoted, 120 ; cited 142
Ferric oxide, in the limestone, 168 ; in the mortars and cements 168, 169
Feuardent, G. L., meaning of Masonic emblems on foundation of N. Y. obelisk, 19-20 ; why crabs were adopted for supports 75-76
Figures on obelisks. *See* Inscriptions.
Fire used in cleavage of obelisks 147
Fissure. *See* Crack.
"Fitzmaurice" (The) picks up the "Cleopatra" . . 105
Flaminian obelisk. *See* Piazza del Popolo.
Florence, obelisks in, ... 70, 137
Fontana, D., re-erects Vatican obelisk, 111-117 ; rewards and honors received by him, 117 ; other architectural work, 118 ; re-erects, Santa Maria Maggiore obelisk, 127 ; Lateran obelisk, 127 ; Flaminian obelisk . 130
Fontana's castle 112
Forbes, D., cited 164
Force exerted, in turning N. Y. obelisk, 14 ; in lowering it, 17 ; in moving caisson, 22 ; in raising its pedestal, 25 ; in embarking the obelisk, 26 ; in turning it in "Dessoug," 27 ; in transport through N. Y., 43 ; in raising it at Central Park, 45 ; in lowering Paris obelisk, 82, 83, 84 ; in disembarking it, 89 ; in moving it through Paris, 89, 90 ; in raising it, 91 ; in launching London obelisk, 103 ; in re-erecting Vatican obelisk, 112, 116 ; that used by ancients in moving heavy blocks 153, 154
Form of obelisks 60, 61, 83, 112, 119
Foundation of N. Y. obelisk affected by surf at Alexandria, 1, 12 ; its removal, 17 ; embarking it, 27 ; its weight, 27 ; its discharge from the "Dessoug," 31 ; preparation of site for, 32 ; replacing it, 32 ; date of, 34 ; objects deposited in, 32-34. *See also* Pedestal.
Foundation of Vatican obelisk, 115 ; objects deposited in, 113, 116 ; size and arrangement . . 115-116
Foundation-stone. *See* Corner-stone.
Fracture. *See* Crack.
Fragments of obelisks, in Rome, 136 ; in British Museum, 138 ; at Wansted 139
France, obelisks in. *See* Arles ; Paris.
Fraser, *Prof.* P., analysis of materials and metals found with the N. Y. obelisk at Alexandria . . 161-175
Frass cited 168
Freemasonry. *See* Masonic.
Friction, reduction of, in moving obelisk . . 42, 43

Garnet found in amphibole-granite 165
Gasparin, letter to M. Le Bas 93
Gau, ancient method of quarrying . . . 147, 149
Geinitz, *Dr.*, cited 168
Generation, obelisks symbolic of, ... 1, 59
Genth, *Dr.* F. A., analysis of felspar in syenite, 162 ; of cement, 169 ; of bronze of crabs, 173 ; of paints from images 173-175
Germantown amphibole-granite, analysis, . . . 167
Germany, obelisks in. *See* Berlin.
Gibbon, E., quoted 110
Gilder, R. W., hymn at presentation ceremonies, N. Y. obelisk 49
Gizeh, Lepsius' obelisk found near, 141 ; where its pyramids were quarried 153
Goff, N., present at re-erection of N. Y. obelisk . . 47
Goguet cited 152
Gold not attached to pyramidion of N. Y. obelisk 169, 170
Gorringe, *Lt.-Com.* H. H., tribute from Mr. Hurlbert, v ; letter from Mr. Vanderbilt and reply, 5 ; undertakes removal of N. Y. obelisk, 5 ; letters accrediting him to Egyptian government, 6 ; arrival at Alexandria, 9 ; interview with the Khedive, 10 ; letter to governor of Alexandria, 10 ; purchase of "Dessoug," 22-24 ; takes leave of Khedive, 28 ; selecting site for obelisk in N. Y., 31 ; tribute from Secretary of the Navy, 50 ; from Mr. Evarts, 51 ; from Mr. Sullivan, 54 ; commemorative medal, 54 ; expense of removing obelisk, 56 ; foot-notes, 105, 107, 169 ; record of London obelisk . . 108-109

Index.

Governor of Alexandria. *See* Alexandria.
Grace, W. R., present at re-erection of N. Y. obelisk, 47; receives the obelisk in behalf of N. Y. . . . 53
Grade of route of obelisk, in N. Y., 42, 44; in Paris . 89
Grading land, in Alexandria for moving obelisk, 15, 102; in N. Y., 43; in Rome 113
Grand Lodge of Freemasons, Egypt, emblems on foundation of N. Y. obelisk 19
Granite, obelisks made of, 141, 146. *See also* Amphibole; Syenite
Graphic 40
Graywacke Knoll selected as the site, 31; preparing it for the foundation 32
Greek inscriptions, on ruins at Alexandria, 1; on Corfe Castle obelisk, 140; on Constantinople obelisk . 160
Greek mythology 75
Green, *Judge* A., ... 2
Greenstone 163
Guiscard, R., said to have overthrown, Santa Maria Maggiore and Monte Cavallo obelisks, 126; Monte Citorio obelisk 133
Gyllius, P., quoted . . 124–125, 126, 158–159, 160
Gypsum in the mortar 168

Haddan, J. L., plan for removal of London obelisk . 99
Hadrian, *Emp.*, quarried Monte Pincio obelisk . . 135
Hagar Silsileh, quarries of, ... 149
Hall, *Rev.* C. H., prayer at laying of corner-stone of N. Y. obelisk 35
Hammamat, quarries of 152, 153
Hatasou, *Queen*, obelisks of, at Karnak, 121–122; not erected by use of inclined plane, 157; mining in reign of, ... 143
Haussez, *Baron* d', ... 77, 78
Height of obelisks. *See* Size.
Heliogabalus, *Emp.*, re-erects Monte Pincio obelisk . 136
Heliopolis, its ancient importance, 4; sketch of, 68-72; obelisks, removed from, 1, 4, 70, 110, 126, 127, 130, 133, 134
Heliopolis obelisk 122–124
Hematite in the quartz of the syenite 166
Herald 65
Hericourt, d', cited 168
Hermapion, translation of inscriptions on Flaminian obelisk 140
Herodotus, cited, 150; quoted 152, 153
Herschell, *Sir* J. F., quoted 147
Hewitt, A. S., ... 57
Hewitt, R., *Jr.*, ... 48
Heyman quoted 74
Hieroglyphs. *See* Inscriptions.
Hindoo. *See* India.
Historical sketch, of New York obelisk, 52, 68–76; of London obelisk, 108–109; of Paris obelisk . 119–120
Hittorf, J. J., ... 82
Hobhouse cited 160
Hoisting. *See* Raising.
Holley, A. L., iron of the Egyptians 170
Hornblende in syenite, 12, 164, 166; in amphibole-granite, 165; in cements 169
Horses, ancient use of, ... 153
Hospital at Luxor, ... 82
Howard, J. E., ... 172
Hudson River R. R., moving N. Y. obelisk across, . 41–42
Hume, J., ... 98

Hurlbert, W. H., preface, v; negotiations for securing N. Y. obelisk, 2, 4, 5; selecting its site in N. Y. 31; contributes, box for deposit in foundation, 33; gold plate with inscription describing removal, 33; present at re-erection 47
Hydraulic jacks, use in moving London obelisk, 102, 103, 106; one deposited in pedestal . . 106
Hydraulic pumps, use in removing N. Y. obelisk, 16, 17, 20, 21, 26, 40, 43, 44, 45; deposit of one in foundation 34
Hymn at presentation ceremonies, N. Y. obelisk . . 49
Hyposyenite, proposed name 164

Ibrahim 81
Imitation of Egyptian obelisks 141
Implements. *See* Tools.
Inclined plane, use of, in moving Vatican obelisk, 112; probable use of, by ancients 156, 157
Inclination, of N. Y. obelisk at Alexandria, 1, 73; of Vatican obelisk 110
India, obelisks found in, 60; methods of cleavage in, 147, 148; tools used in, 151. *See also* Seringapatam obelisk.
Innocent X re-erects Piazza Navona obelisk . . 135
Inscriptions, on ruins at Alexandria, 1; on medals commemorative of N. Y. obelisk, 54–55; on crabs of N. Y. obelisk, 75; on obelisks, 51, 59, 61, 151, 152; Alnwick, 138; Amyrtæus, 138–139; Arles, 141; Begig, 142; Benevento, 137; Boboli, 137; Borgian, 137; Catania, 141; Corfe Castle, 139–141; Constantinople, 125, 126, 159, 160; Drah Abou 'l Neggah, 144; Flaminian, 130–132; Florence, 137; Heliopolis, 124; Karnak, 121; La Trinita, 135; Lateran, 127–129; London, 97, 107, 108; Luxor, 119; Monte Citorio, 133; Monte Pincio, 135–136; New York, 4, 13, 17–20, 61–68; Pantheon, 134; Paris, 92, 93, 94, 95; Piazza della Minerva, 133; Piazza Navona, 135; Sân, 142; Sarbut el-Khadem. 143, 144; Vatican, 117–118; Villa Mattei, 134; Wadi Nasb, 143, 144; Wansted, 139; value of, 61; how translated, 62, 140; fineness of, 149; that of Prioli obelisk never published, 126; absence of hieroglyphs from Vatican, 112, 118; from Santa Maria Maggiore and Monte Cavallo, 126. *See also* Embellishments; Symbolic; Translation.
Insurance on "Desssoug," 27–28; on "Cleopatra" . 107
Interpretation. *See* Translation.
Iron, Egyptian production of, 170; analysis of clamp found under N. Y. obelisk . . . 170–172
Iron peroxide in mica and felspar of syenite . . 161–162
Iron tools used by Egyptians 150
Iron tracks 9, 26, 40, 42, 44
Isis, Temple of, ... 134, 137, 139
Ismail, gift of N. Y. obelisk 2, 3
Italian Consul at Alexandria interferes with removal of N. Y. obelisk 10, 11
Italy, obelisks in. *See* Albani; Benevento; Borgian; Florence; Rome.

Jauna, D., ... 74
Johnston, J. T., ... 48
Joining of blocks by ancients 149
Journal des Débats 90
Joussouf, B., letter to Count Sebastiani . . . 79

Index.

Julian, *Emp.*, cited 124
Julien, *Prof.* A. J., ... 162

Karnak, obelisks of, 78, 110, 120–122 ; temples of . 80
Kavasses 80
Kennedy, *Dr.*, quoted 149, 151
Khedive. *See* Egyptian government ; Ismail ; Mohammed Ali ; Tewfik Pacha.
Kiernan, F., ... 57
King, plan for transporting London obelisk . . 100
King, C., cited 167
Kings. *See* Pharaohs.
Kingston Hall, obelisk at, ... 139
Kinnicutt, L. P., analysis of the cement 169
Kircher, A., cited, 74, 124, 126, 127, 130, 133, 134, 135, 136, 137, 147

La Borde, de, ... 77, 78
Land transport, in Alexandria, 8, 9, 15 ; in N. Y., 31, 42–45 ; in Paris, 89, 90 ; ancient methods . . 152, 153
Landing. *See* Disembarking.
Largest known obelisk 127
Lateran obelisk . . . 110, 118, 127–129, 155–156, 158
Latin inscription on Constantinople obelisk . . . 160
Launching, N. Y. obelisk, 16, 20, 21, 22 ; London obelisk, 103, 104
Lawler's Marine Railway used in disembarking N. Y. obelisk 40
Lawsuit relating to salvage on the "Cleopatra" . 105, 107
Layard, A. H., cited 154, 158
Lead found with Iron clamp under N. Y. obelisk, analysis, ... 172–173
Leakage during voyage of "Dessoug," how prevented . 26
LeBas, A., removal of Paris obelisk, 5, 79 ; tribute to, 93 ; receives riband of Legion of Honor . . 93
Leidy, *Dr.* J., cited 168
Le Maire excavated N. Y. obelisk to base . . . 74
Lenormant, quoted, 75 ; cited . 119, 122, 123, 138, 142
Lepage receives cross of Legion of Honor . . 93
Lepsius cited . . 121, 122, 124, 134, 139, 142, 144, 151
Lepsius' obelisk 141–142
Letronne, restores inscriptions on pedestal of Corfe Castle obelisk, 139 ; cited 156–157
Letters. *See* Correspondence.
Levelling, Hindoo method 157–158
Lever, use of, in moving Vatican obelisk, 112 ; ancient use of, ... 153, 154
Library of Alexandria, situation, ... 1
Lifting. *See* Raising.
Lime, in mica and felspar of syenite, 161–162 ; in cements. 169
Limestone, in foundation and steps of N. Y. obelisk, 18 ; Egyptian quarries of, 153 ; analysis of that found near the Nile 168
Livron, de, ... 78
Loading. *See* Embarking.
Loftie cited 142
London obelisk, circumstances of gift, 3 ; plan of removal, 5, 6 ; delay in, 9 ; its removal, 51, 96–108 ; its age, 68 ; inscription on, 70 ; fall of, 73 ; record of, 108–109
Long, quoted, 74 ; cited . . 69, 126, 138, 149, 160
Long, *Sir* J. T., fragment of obelisk at Wansted . . 139
Loring, C. H., ... 46
Lotus-flowers on obelisks. 122
Louis XVIII negotiated gift of obelisk to Paris . . 77

Louis Philippe present at raising of Paris obelisk . . 91
Louvre, Museum of, ... 60
Lowering, N. Y. obelisk, 7, 8, 16, 17, 20 ; Paris obelisk, 81, 83–85, 86 ; Vatican obelisk . . . 112–115
Lucas, P. 74
Lupus, L., name on Benevento obelisk 137
Luxor, 80 ; obelisks at, 3, 61, 119–120. *See also* Paris obelisk.
"Luxor" (The), construction of, 78 ; behavior at sea, 6, 79 ; arrival at Luxor, 82 ; opening bow to admit obelisk, 87 ; voyage, 88 ; disembarking obelisk . 89
Lyman, D., ... 56

McCook, A. G., ... 57
Machinery, for removing N. Y. obelisk, 8, 13, 42, 45 ; Paris obelisk, 82, 83, 84, 90, 92 ; London obelisk, 105, 106 ; Vatican obelisk, 112, 113, 114 ; used by ancient Egyptians 153, 154, 156
Mackau, de, ... 78
Magnesia, in syenite, 162 ; in cements 169
Magnesium carbonate in the limestone found near the Nile 168
Magnetite, in amphibole-granite, 165 ; in syenite . 166, 167
Mahutean obelisk 134
Mallet cited 108
Mallets used by Hindoos 151
Manganese oxide in syenite 162
Manganic oxide in cements 169
Marcellinus, A., cited, 127, 130, 152 ; quoted, 155–156, 158
Mariette, cited, 68, 71, 72, 121, 153 ; discovers obelisk at Drah Abou 'l Neggah, 144 ; quoted . . 122
Marine railway, for disembarking N. Y. obelisk, 39–40 ; for transport in N. Y. 42–43
Masara, quarries of, ... 153
Masonic emblems on N. Y. obelisk, 18–20 ; emblems deposited in foundation, 33 ; ceremonies in laying corner-stone, 34–38. *See also* Grand Lodge.
Masonic skill of ancients 149
Mathematics, Egyptian knowledge of, ... 157
Mazacqui 80
Mechanical appliances known to Egyptians . 153–154, 157
Medals, deposited in foundation of N. Y. obelisk, 33 ; Paris obelisk, 91 ; Vatican obelisk, 113, 116 ; commemorative of N. Y. obelisk . . . 53–56
Mehemet. *See* Mohammed.
Men anciently employed in moving large stones . 153, 154
Meneptah I, Vatican obelisk erected in reign of, . . 118
Metals found with N. Y. obelisk at Alexandria, analysis of, ... 161–175
Methven, *Capt.*, plan for removing London obelisk . 100
Metropolitan Museum, N. Y., desirability of selecting a site near it, 31 ; use for presentation ceremonies . 48
Mica in syenite, 161, 163 ; in amphibole-granite . . 165
Microline, in syenite, 166 ; in Germantown amphibole-granite 167
Mimaut 78
Mimerel, appointed to remove Paris obelisk, 78 ; resigns position 79
Mining, copper, ... 143
Models of machinery for removal, of Paris obelisk, 92 ; of London obelisk deposited in its pedestal, 106 ; of Vatican obelisk 111
Mohammed Ali, gift of Paris and London obelisks, 3, 52, 79, 96, 97–98

Index.

Mohammed ben-Abd-alrahin, quoted . . . 123
Mohammedans, method of spending their Sabbath . 14
Monte Cavallo obelisk 126–127
Monte Citorio obelisk 133, 158
Monte Cœlio, former site of Villa Mattei obelisk . . 134
Monte Pincio obelisk 135–136
Monuments, obelisks the most common form of, . . 61
Morgan, H. de, translation of inscriptions on N. Y. obelisk 62
Mortars, analysis, ... 168–170
Mosaic pavement found around steps of N. Y. obelisk . 12
Mules, ancient use of, in moving obelisks . . . 154
Mummulite 168
Mummy-cases of Antef 144
Murray cited 126, 127, 141, 143
Muscovite in amphibole-granite 167
Mythology. *See* Egyptian.

Nahasb obelisk 143–144
Napier, *Lord*, visits the " Dessoug " 29
Naples. *See* Borgian obelisk
Napoleon I planned removal of obelisk to Paris . 52, 77
Nationality of the " Dessoug " 23, 24
Necropolis of Drah Abou 'l Neggah 144
Nectanebo I, Prioli obelisk erected in reign of, 126;
 Amyrtæus obeliskss ascribed to, ... 138
Negotiations, leading to gift and removal of N. Y. obelisk, 2–5 ; for removal of London obelisk . 97–78
Nelson, *Lord*, ... 97
" Nettuno," The 29
New Testament deposited in the foundation of N. Y. obelisk 33
New York obelisk, its removal, 1–58 ; its archæology, 59–76 ; inscriptions, 61–68 ; historical sketch, 68–76 ; first given to France, 77 ; relinquished by France, 79 ; analysis of metals, etc., found with it, 161–175
New York Herald 65
New York World, account of presentation ceremonies, 48–56
Newbold cited 168
Nicholas V planned re-erection of Vatican obelisk . 110
Niebuhr, C., cited, 74, 124 ; discovered obelisks at Cairo, 136
Nile, use of, for floating " Luxor," 82, 88 ; ancient use of, for transporting obelisks 151
Nineveh, removal of obelisk to, ... 51
Norden 74
North River landing, N. Y., why selected . . . 31
Northumberland, *Duke of*, obelisks at houses of, . 137, 138
Notes on ancient methods of quarrying, transporting, and erecting obelisks 146–160
Number of obelisks removed from Egypt . . 51, 61

Obelisks removed from Egypt, 51 ; record, 119–145 ; table of dimensions and weight, 145. *See also* Albani ; Alnwick ; Arles ; Assouan ; Begig ; Benevento ; Borgian ; British Museum ; Cairo ; Catania ; Constantinople ; Corfe Castle ; Drah Abou 'l Neggah ; Egypt ; Esmeade ; Florence ; Fragments ; Heliopolis ; India ; Karnak ; Lateran ; Lepsius ; London ; Luxor ; Monte Cavallo ; Monte Citorio ; Monte Pincio ; New York ; Pantheon ; Paris ; Philæ ; Piazza della Minerva ; Piazza del Popolo ; Piazza Navona ; Rome ; Sân ; Santa Maria Maggiore ; Sarbut el-Khadem ; Seringapatam ; Sion House ; Trinita ; Vatican ; Villa Mattei ; Wadi Nasb ; Wansted.

Obstruction. *See* Opposition.
Oldest known obelisks 122, 141, 144
" Olga " (The) deserts the " Cleopatra " . . . 104–105
Oligoclase, from the syenite, analysis, 162, 166 ; in amphibole-granite 165
Oliphant, L., cited 142
On, Temple of. *See* Heliopolis.
Opening, the " Dessoug " to admit the obelisk, 7, 26 ; for disembarking, 40 ; the " Luxor " to admit the Paris obelisk, 87 ; for disembarking 89
Opposition to removing N. Y. obelisk, 2, 9–13, 16, 17, 21, 23, 120
Ornamentations. *See* Embellishments.
Orthoclase, in syenite, 164 ; in amphibole-granite . . 165
Orville, d', cited 141
Osborn quoted 68
Overthrow. *See* Fall.
Oxen, ancient use of, ... 153, 154

Paints on Egyptian images, analysis, . . . 173–175
Pamphilian obelisk 135
Pantheon obelisk 134
Paris obelisk, circumstances of the gift, 3 ; plan of removal, 5, 6 ; delay in, 9 ; how turned, 44 ; its removal 52, 77–95
Parker cited, 62, 68, 126, 127, 133, 134, 135, 136, 138, 153, 155
Parker, T. H., ... 57
Paton, W. H., ... 57
Pedestal, of Karnak obelisk, 122 ; of Heliopolis obelisk, 123 ; of Constantinople obelisk, 124–125 ; of Corfe Castle obelisk 139
Pedestal of London obelisk, inscription placed on, by English, in 1802, 97 ; its location now unknown, 97 ; size of new one, 106 ; deposit of objects in, 106 ; inscription on, ... 107
Pedestal of N. Y. obelisk, 12 ; its removal, 17 ; transportation and embarking, 24–25 ; weight, 25, 32 ; disembarking and transportation, 31–32 ; placing in position 39
Pedestal of Paris obelisk, 89 ; weight, 90 ; deposit of objects in, 91 ; inscription on, . . . 92, 93, 94
Persia, obelisks found in, ... 60
Pharaoh's Needles 123
Pharaohs, connection with obelisks . . . 59–60
Philæ, original site of Corfe Castle obelisk . . 139
Philæ obelisk 143
Phœbus identified with the sun 75
Phosphoric acid in cements 169
Photographs, of N. Y. obelisk taken before removal, 12 ; taken during re-erection, 47 ; of the inscriptions and figures on, 61 ; deposited in foundation, 33 ; deposited in pedestal of London obelisk . . 106
Piankhi, *King*, visit to Heliopolis 71–72
Piazza del Popolo obelisk . . . 118, 130–132, 158
Piazza della Minerva obelisk 133–134
Piazza di San Pietro, site of Vatican obelisk, . . 110, 113
Piazza Navona obelisk 135
Pigments. *See* Paints.
Pislazite in the syenite 167
Pitching. *See* Fall.
Pitman, *Capt.* J., analysis of iron clamp found under N. Y. obelisk 172
Pius VI, inscription on La Trinita obelisk . . . 135

Index.

Pius VII re-erects Monte Pincio obelisk . . . 136
Place de la Concorde chosen as site for Paris obelisk . 89
Plagioclase, from the syenite, analysis, 162; in Germantown amphibole-granite 167
Plaster of Paris in the mortar 169
Pliny, quoted, 68, 133, 154, 155, 156, 158; cited, 70, 112, 118, 130, 133
Pocoke, quoted, 74; cited 136, 139
Polishing obelisks 149
Pontius re-erects N. Y. obelisk at Alexandria . . 72
Pontoons used in lifting and transporting N. Y. obelisk, 40–41
Porphyry found with syenite 163
Postal service of Egypt 22
Potash, in syenite, 162; in cements 169
Power. *See* Force; Hydraulic.
Prayers, at laying corner-stone N. Y. obelisk, 35; at presentation ceremonies, 49; at lowering Vatican obelisk, 114
Presentation ceremonies, N. Y. obelisk . . . 48–56
Price, F., tribute to, ... v, 9
Prioli obelisk 126
Priolus, A., erects Prioli obelisk 126
Prisse cited 137
Proportions in form of obelisks . . . 60–61, 112
Psametik II, cartouch on obelisks 134
Ptolemy Euergetes II erects Corfe Castle obelisk . . 139
Ptolemy Philadelphus, transportation by, . . 154–155
Pulley, use of, by ancient Egyptians, 154. *See also* Tackles.
Pumps. *See* Hydraulic pumps.
Pyramidion, of N. Y. obelisk, 61, 62; analysis of its cement, 169; Paris obelisk, 82; London obelisk, 101; Vatican obelisk, 112; Luxor obelisks, 119; Karnak obelisks, 121; Heliopolis obelisk, 123; Constantinople obelisk, 125; Piazza della Minerva obelisk, 133; Pantheon obelisk, 134; Corfe Castle obelisk, 139; Wansted fragment 139
Pyramids, their symbolic character, 35, 36, 59, 60; when quarried, 153; ancient method of lifting stones for, 154
Pyrite in amphibole-granite 165

Quarries of Masara and Hammamat 153
Quarrying obelisks, ancient methods, . . . 146–151
Quartz, in syenite, 161, 163, 164, 166; in amphibole-granite, 165, 167; in cements 169
Quincy, Q. de, cited 118

Raft, for removing Paris obelisk, proposed, 77–78; its ancient use in moving obelisks . . . 152, 154
Railway. *See* Marine.
Raising, N. Y. obelisk, 8, 13, 14, 25, 40, 45, 46; Paris obelisk, 90–92; London obelisk, 105–107; Vatican obelisk, 111, 112, 113, 114, 116; large blocks, ancient method, ... 154
Rameseion 80, 81
Ramses II, inscription of, on N. Y. obelisk, 62–68; on Paris obelisk, 86; on London obelisk, 108; on Flaminian obelisk, 132; on La Trinita obelisk, 135; erects Luxor obelisks, 119; restores Lateran obelisk, 127; erects, Villa Mattei and Pantheon obelisks, 134; Boboli obelisk, 137; Sân obelisks, 142; weight of statue of, ... 153
Ramses III, name on Luxor obelisks 119
Ramses IV 121
Ramses V 121
Ramses VI 121

Ransom, M. W., letter from Mr. Evarts to, . . . 57
Rawlinson, G., quoted, 62, 146, 157; cited, 71, 122, 127, 133, 134, 135, 138, 144, 150, 153
Reagan, J. H., letter from Mr. Evarts to, . . . 57
Record of all Egyptian obelisks, ... 119–145
Re-creation, obelisks symbolic of, ... 1, 59
Re-erecting, N. Y. obelisk, 46–48; Paris obelisk, 89–92; London obelisk, 105–107; Vatican obelisk, 110–118; Lateran, Santa Maria Maggiore, and Monte Cavallo obelisks, 126, 127; Pantheon obelisk, 134; Benevento obelisk, 136, 137; Arles obelisk, 141; obelisks at Alexandria 108
Refitting the "Dessoug" 23
Reft. *See* Crack.
Registry granted to the "Dessoug" . . . 56–57
Relics, broken from N. Y. obelisk at Alexandria, 1; from London obelisk, 102; found in excavating, 12; placed in cross on Vatican obelisk 117
Religion. *See* Egyptian mythology.
Removal, of the New York obelisk, 1–58; its removal from Heliopolis to Alexandria, 36, 52, 72; Paris obelisk, 77–95; London obelisk, 96–108; Vatican obelisk, 110–116; Constantinople obelisk, 124; Santa Maria Maggiore and Monte Cavallo obelisks, 126; Lateran obelisk, 127; Flaminian obelisk, 130; Monte Citorio obelisk, 133; Piazza della Minerva and Pantheon obelisks, 133, 134; La Trinita obelisk, 135; Monte Pincio obelisk, 136; Boboli obelisk, 137; Alnwick obelisk, 137; Amyrtæus obelisks, 139; Corfe Castle obelisk, 139; of obelisks from Egypt, 51, 61; to Alexandria, 108; from quarries, 149; ancient methods of, 151–156. *See also* Transportation.
Reproduction, obelisks symbolic of, ... 1, 59
Resistance of rollers increased by iron channels and cannon-balls 42
Resistance to interference with removal of N. Y. obelisk, 12, 15
Resurrection, Egyptian belief in, ... 59
Riaz Pacha, letter to governor of Alexandria . . 10
Richards, Prof. R. H., analysis, of mortars and cements, 168–170; of lead found with iron under N. Y. obelisk 172–173
Robinson cited 143
Roebling's Sons, J. A., ... 9
Rolland, *Baron*, plan for removing Paris obelisk . . 78
Rollers, for transport of obelisk in N. Y., 42, 43; use by ancient Egyptians 153, 154, 157
Rolling of "Cleopatra" 101, 103
Roman, inscriptions on ruins at Alexandria, 1; re-erection of obelisks at Alexandria, 1; mode of erecting obelisks, 45, 158–160; mythology, 75; use of Monte Citorio obelisk, 133; origin of Catania and Arles obelisks, 141; transportation of obelisk . . 155–156
Rome, removal of obelisks to, 51; obelisks in, 70, 126–136, 155. *See also* Esmeade; Fragments; Lateran; Monte Cavallo; Monte Citorio; Monte Pincio; Pantheon; Piazza della Minerva; Piazza Navona; Piazza del Popolo; Santa Maria Maggiore; Trinita (La); Vatican; Villa Mattei.
Rosellini, plate of, ... 121
Rosenbusch, H., cited 167
Rosetta stone, a key in translating hieroglyphs . 62, 140
Rotation. *See* Turning.
Rozière, de, ancient method of quarrying . 147, 148, 149

Index.

Rozière cited 162, 164, 165, 168
Rüppell cited 143
Ruins, in Alexandria, 1 ; in Egypt, 80 ; at Karnak . 120
Russegger, J., cited, 162, 163, 168 ; quoted . . . 165
Russian aid in resisting interference with removal of N. Y. obelisk 15

Sacy, S. de, cited 74, 123
St. Maur, V. de, removing Paris obelisk, 78 ; cited . 121
St. Peter's Square, Rome, site of Vatican obelisk . 109, 113
Saïs, probable original site of Piazza della Minerva obelisk 133
Salustian obelisk 135
Salvage on the "Cleopatra" 105, 107
Sân obelisks 142-143
Sand, bags of, use of, by ancients to raise heavy weights, 157 ; in the mortars 169
Sanderson, J., quoted 125
Sandstone, in foundation of N. Y. obelisk, 12 ; pedestals of, 123, 139 ; obelisks of, 143, 146 ; quarries of, 149
Santa Maria Maggiore obelisk . . . 118, 126-127
Sarbut el-Khadem, obelisk of, ... 143
Sardanapalus, removal of obelisk to Nineveh . . 51
Saw used in cleavage of obelisks 148
Scarabee found in excavating 12, 59, 60
School-boys, presentation to, of medals commemorative of N. Y. obelisk 54-56
Schroeder, Lieut. S., tribute to, v ; accepts position of assistant, 9 ; refits the "Dessoug," 23 ; removal of Paris obelisk, 77-95 ; removal of London obelisk, 96-108 ; re-erection of Vatican obelisk . . 110-118
Sculptures. See Inscriptions.
Sebastiani, Count, letter from Boghoz Joussouf to, . 79
Seizure of the "Dessoug," how avoided . . . 23
Semiramis, Queen 154
Separation of obelisks from their quarries. See Cleavage.
Sepulchral monuments, obelisks as, ... 61
Seringapatam obelisk 148, 153, 157
Sesostris, Monte Citorio obelisk attributed to, . . 133
Seti I, obelisks erected by, . . . 70, 130, 135
Shadrach, idol of, identified as an obelisk . . 60
Shaft of "Dessoug," breakage, ... 29
Shape of obelisks. See Form.
Sharpe, cited, 73, 74, 137, 138, 154 ; quoted . . 156
Shaw, W. J., translation of inscription on model of Temple of the Sun 70-71
Sheathing, N. Y. obelisk, 13 ; Paris obelisk, 82 ; London obelisk, 99 ; Vatican obelisk 113
Shipping. See Embarking.
Ship's papers of the "Dessoug" 24
Sicily. See Catania obelisk.
Silica, in the syenite, 161, 162 ; in the cements . . 169
Silicic acid in cements 169
Silicic oxide in the syenite 162
Silicious residue in the mortar 168
Sinaitic Peninsula, obelisks in. See Sarbut el-Khadem ; Wadi Nasb.
Sion House obelisk 138
Site of, N. Y. obelisk, 30, 31 ; Paris obelisk, 89 ; London obelisk, 105 ; Vatican obelisk 110
Sixtus V re-erects, Vatican obelisk, 110 ; Villa Mattei obelisk 134
Size, of obelisks, 60, 61, 110 ; table, 145 ; Assyrian, 158 ; Corfe Castle, 139 ; Drah Abou 'l Neggah, 144 ; Heliopolis, 123 ; Lepsius', 142 ; London, 101, 106 ; Monte Citorio, 158 ; New York, 20 ; Paris, 82, 83 ; Piazza del Popolo, 158 ; Sân, 142, 143 ; Sarbut el-Khadem, 143 ; Vatican, 112, 115, 116 ; Wansted, 139 ; of ancient boats of Egypt, 151, 152 ; of blocks moved by ancient Egyptians, 152, 153 ; of vessels used by Romans to transport obelisks . . . 155, 156
Sledges for moving obelisks . . 152, 153, 154, 156
Smallest obelisk 142
Smith, Capt., ... 172
Smith, G., cited 154
Smith, P., cited 158
Smith, W., quoted 68, 69
Smith & Sons, W. B., ... 32
Smyth, Adm., plan for removing London obelisk . . 98
Snowden, J. R., cited 117
Society for Prevention of Cruelty to Animals deposits documents in foundation of N. Y. obelisk . . 33
Soda, in syenite, 162 ; in cements 169
Sodium oxide, proportion in felspar of the syenite . 162
Softening stone before cutting 150
Specific gravity, of Paris obelisk, 83 ; of London obelisk, 102 ; of N. Y. obelisk, 161, 164 ; of limestone found near the Nile, 168 ; of lead found with iron clamps under N. Y. obelisk, 172 ; of bronze in crabs . . 173
Spectators. See Visitors.
Sphinxes, symbolic character, 60 ; in Egyptian temples, 72 ; on London obelisk 107
Spon and Wheler, copy of plate from, ... 159
Squalls during voyage of "Dessoug " . . . 29, 30
Squeezes made from the N. Y. obelisk 61
Stability, of N. Y. obelisk, 45, 48 ; of London obelisk in the "Cleopatra" 101
Stanley, A. P., quoted 96, 124
Stanton, Gen., ... 98
Staten Island, obelisk disembarked at, . . . 39-40
Steam-engine used, in transport of obelisk in N. Y., 43 ; in moving Paris obelisk, 90. See also Marine railway.
Stebbins, H. G., negotiations for securing N. Y. obelisk, 2-5 ; site for, 31 ; presentation ceremonies, 48 ; letter to Mr. Sullivan 50
Steel tools used by Egyptians 150, 151
Steeples represent same idea as obelisks . . . 60
Stelæ 122, 142, 143
Steltzner, Dr. A., analysis of syenite . . 162-168
Steps, of N. Y. obelisk, 12 ; removing, 17 ; embarking, 24 ; weight, 27 ; disembarking, 31 ; laying in, N. Y., 34 ; of London obelisk, 106 ; of Constantinople obelisk 124
Sterne, L., negotiations relating to gift of N. Y. obelisk . 2
Stone-cutting, of the Egyptians, 150 ; in India . . 151
Storm in voyage of the "Cleopatra" 104
Strabo quoted 72
Struts for supporting Vatican obelisk in lowering . . 115
Stuart, V., discovered fallen obelisks at Drah Abou 'l Neggah 144
Submarine work 16
Subsidence of land around the obelisk . . . 1, 12
Suetonius cited 155
Sullivan, A. S., 48 ; letter from Mr. Stebbins, 50 ; presents medals commemorative of N. Y. obelisk . 53-56
Sulphuric acid in cements 169
Sun-dial, use of Monte Citorio obelisk as, . . . 133

Index.

Sun, Temple of, . . . 4, 68, 69, 70, 71, 72, 122, 134
Sun-worship of Egyptians 59, 69, 75
Sunday-work in removal of N. Y. obelisk . . . 13
Supports, for N. Y. obelisk, 8, 12, 75; of London obelisk, 108; of obelisks in quarrying, 149. *See also* Crabs.
Syene. *See* Assouan.
Syenite, in foundation of N. Y. obelisk, 17, 18; obelisks of, 122, 123, 136, 137, 139; characteristics of, 146; economy in use of, 149; where found, 162, 163; choice of, for obelisks, 60, 161; analysis of, 161-168. *See also* Amphibole.
Symbolic character, of obelisks, 1, 4, 36, 59, 60; of pyramids, 59, 60; of sphinxes 60

Table of dimensions and weight of obelisks . . . 145
Tackles, for moving N.Y. obelisk, 14; breakage of one, 15; for moving Paris obelisk, 82, 83, 84, 86, 87, 89, 90; for moving Vatican obelisk, 112, 115. *See also* Pulleys.
Tanis. *See* Sân.
Taylor, *Baron*, removal of Paris obelisk . . . 77, 78
Tel-et-Mai, chapel of, size, ... 153
Telephone system, failure of attempt to secure it for deposit in the foundation 33
Temper of Egyptian tools 150
Temple, at Luxor, 118; of Isis, 134, 137, 139; of the Sun . . . 4, 68, 69, 70, 71, 72, 122, 134
Temples, associated with obelisks, 68, 72; at Karnak . 80
Testing apparatus by Fontana 117
Tewfik Pacha, confirms gift of N. Y. obelisk, 10; Mr. Gorringe's interviews with, 10, 28; thanks of Congress to, 57, 58; tributes to, . . 49, 52, 80
Thames Embankment selected as site for London obelisk 105
Thebaid, Alnwick obelisk found in the, ... 137
Thebes, obelisks at, 2; site of Lateran obelisk, 127. *See also* Drah Abou 'l Neggah; Karnak; Luxor.
Theodosius, *Emp.*, re-erects Constantinople obelisk . 124, 159
Thothmes I, obelisks at Karnak 120, 121
Thothmes III, erects N. Y. obelisk, 4; name on, 62-68; his character, 52, 62; cartouch on obelisks, 59; obelisks erected by, 68, 108; restores Temple of the Sun, 70; cartouch on London obelisk, 108; Karnak obelisks of, 122; erects Constantinople obelisk, 124; name on, 125; ordered Lateran obelisk, 127; name on, 127; mining in his reign 143
Thothmes IV erects Lateran obelisk 127
Thomas, T., ... 49
Tiberius, *Emp.*, removal of N. Y. obelisk to Alexandria in reign of, ... 4
Tide, use of, in disembarking N. Y. obelisk . . 39
Timber for use in moving, N. Y. obelisk, 9, 17, 26; Paris obelisk, 85, 88; London obelisk, 107, 108; Vatican obelisk 112
Time, allowed for removal of N. Y. obelisk, 5; of beginning active operations, 9; occupied in obtaining possession of obelisk, 10; in turning it, 14, 15; in diving operations, 16; in lowering obelisk, 21; in launching caisson, 21, 22; in waiting for use of dock at Alexandria, 24, 25; in embarking obelisk, 26; of setting sail, 28; of arrival at N. Y., 30; of laying foundation and corner-stone, 34; occupied in disembarking obelisk, 40; in transport through N. Y., 44, 45; in re-erection, 46; in entire removal, 47; of presentation ceremonies 48

Time, occupied in removing Paris obelisk, 78, 88, 91, 92; of first attempt to remove London obelisk, 96; occupied in its removal, 102, 103, 105, 106, 107, 108; of re-erecting Vatican obelisk, 110, 113, 116, 118; occupied in quarrying and erecting Karnak obelisks, 122; when Heliopolis obelisk, 123; of removing Constantinople obelisk, 124; Santa Maria Maggiore and Monte Cavallo obelisks, 126, 127; Lateran obelisk, 127; Flaminian obelisk, 130; Monte Citorio obelisk, 133; Piazza della Minerva obelisk, 134; of re-erecting Pantheon obelisk, 134; Villa Mattei obelisk, 134; of removing La Trinita obelisk, 135; Monte Pincio obelisk, 136; Benevento and Alnwick obelisks, 137; Amyrtæus, Corfe Castle, and Wansted obelisks, 139; Arles obelisk, 141; re-erecting Constantinople obelisk, 160. *See also* Age; Delays.
Titanite, in the syenite, 166, 167; in Germantown amphibole-granite 167
Toernebom cited 166
Tomlinson, G., translation of inscriptions on Flaminian obelisk 131-132
Tools used, by Egyptians, 149, 150, 151; by Hindoos . 151
Tott, *Baron* de, ... 74
Track, for embarking N. Y. obelisk, 25-26; for moving it in N. Y. 32
Tracks (channel) 9, 26, 40, 42, 44
Translation of inscriptions, on N. Y. obelisk, 62-68; on model of Sun Temple, 70-71; on N. Y. and London obelisks, 73, 74; on crabs, 76; on Paris obelisk, 94, 95; on London obelisk, 108; on Luxor obelisk, 120; on Karnak obelisks, 121, 122; on Constantinople obelisk, 125, 126, 160; on Lateran obelisk, 127-129; on Flaminian obelisk, 130-132; on Alnwick obelisk, 138; on pedestal of Corfe Castle obelisk, 140, 141; on Drah Abou 'l Neggah obelisk, 144; how done, 62, 140
Transportation of obelisks, ancient methods, 151-156. *See also* Land transport; Removal.
Trestle for transport of obelisk through Central Park 44-45
Trinita (La) dei Monti obelisk 135
Truss-cradle 15, 16
Tupinier, *Baron*, ... 78
Turn-table 27
Turning, N. Y. obelisk, 13, 14-16, 26, 27; Paris obelisk, 81, 83-86, 90, 91; London obelisk, 102; Vatican obelisk 114, 115
Turning apparatus in transport of obelisk in N. Y. . 45
Turning structure . . . 7, 8, 9, 13, 14, 25, 39, 45
Turnings in route, in N. Y., 42, 43, 44; in Paris . . 89

Una, inscriptions of, ... 152
Unfinished obelisk at Syene 143
Ungarelli cited . . . 127, 130, 133, 134, 135, 137
United States Coast and Geodetic Survey declined to contribute articles for deposit in the foundation . 33
United States Congress, grants American registry to "Dessoug," 56-57; thanks Khedive for gift . . 57-58
United States flag raised on the "Dessoug" . . 23
United States government accepts N. Y. obelisk, 4; deposits articles in foundation of N. Y. obelisk . . 33
Unloading. *See* Disembarking.
Urbino, document for Paris obelisk erected at, . . . 136
Usorken (Usortesen) I, name on N. Y. obelisk, 68; erects Heliopolis obelisk, 122, 124; erects Begig obelisk . 142

Index.   187

Vanderbilt, W. H., tribute to, from Mr. Hurlbert, v; guarantees expense of moving N. Y. obelisk, 2; letter to Mr. Gorringe and reply, 5; selecting site in N. Y., 31; tribute from Mr. Evarts, 51; from Mr. Sullivan, 54; receives commemorative medal, 54; cost of removal 56
Vases found on site of London obelisk 102
Vatican obelisk, re-erection of, . . . 110–118, 155
Vessels. *See* Boats; Rafts; *also* "Cleopatra"; "Dessoug"; "Luxor"; "Olga."
Victor, P., cited 155
Victoria Embankment. *See* Thames Embankment.
Villa Celimontana. *See* Villa Mattei.
Villa Mattei obelisk 134
Viridite in the syenite 167
Visitors, to N. Y. obelisk at Alexandria, 1; at turning of the obelisk, 15; to the "Dessoug" at Gibraltar, 29; in N. Y., 30; at laying corner-stone, 34; at disembarking obelisk, 40; at re-erection, 46; at presentation ceremonies, 48; at raising Paris obelisk, 91; at launching London obelisk, 103; at its re-erection, 106; at lowering Vatican obelisk 113
Voyage, of "Dessoug," 29–30; of "Luxor," 88; of "Cleopatra" 104–105
Vulliamy, designs for castings for London obelisk . . 107
Vyse, *Col.* H., cited 100

Wadi Nasb obelisk 143–144
Walker, J., plan for removing London obelisk . . 100
Walker, S. A., ... 48
Wansted, fragment of obelisk at, ... 139
Water, proportion in the mortar, 168; in the cements . 169
Water, used in cleavage of obelisks, 147; transportation on, by ancients 151
Water-spouts 30
Water-tight compartments in the "Cleopatra" . 101, 104
Ways beams for transport of obelisk in N. Y. . . 43

Ways for moving obelisk to the "Luxor" . . . 86
Wedges used in cleavage of obelisks . . . 147, 148
Weight, of N. Y. obelisk, 25, 26, 42; and caisson, 20; of its pedestal, 25, 32; of its base and steps, 27; of its clamps, 46; of its new crabs, 46; of Paris obelisk, 83; of its pedestal, 90; of London obelisk, 99, 102; of Vatican obelisk, 112; of obelisks, table, 145; of blocks moved by ancient Egyptians, 152, 153; of syenite 161
Wendel, *Dr.*, analysis of iron clamp found under N. Y. obelisk 170, 172
Werner, A. G., quoted 163, 165
Westropp cited 141, 143
Wharton, W. A., plan for removing London obelisk . 99
Whitin, L. F., advances money for removal of N. Y. obelisk 5
Whiting, *Lieut.-Comdr.* W. H., in charge of guard of honor at re-erection of N. Y. obelisk 47
Whitthorne, W. C., ... 57
Wigner, G. W., specific gravity of syenite . . . 161
Wilkinson cited, 62, 68, 69, 70, 119, 143, 147, 149, 150, 151, 152, 153, 154, 155, 157
Wilks, *Col.*, quoted 148, 157
Wilson, E., 97, 98, 101, 112; agreement with Mr. Dixon for removing London obelisk 100
Wood. *See* Timber.
Worship of obelisks an error 59

Young, translation of hieroglyphs 140

Zircon, in the syenite, 166, 167; in Germantown amphibole-granite 167–168
Zirkel, F., cited 167
Zoega cited, 74, 124, 126, 127, 130, 133, 134, 135, 136, 137, 139, 141, 152, 157, 160
Zucovich, E., ... 29
Zulficar Pacha present at the turning of the N. Y. obelisk, 15

www.ingramcontent.com/pod-product-compliance
Lightning Source LLC
Chambersburg PA
CBHW061255230426
43664CB00032B/2913